United States Department of State

Foreign Consular Offices in the United States

Spring/Summer 2007

PREFACE

This publication contains a complete and official listing of the foreign consular offices in the United States, and recognized consular officers. Compiled by the U.S. Department of State, with the full cooperation of the foreign missions in Washington, it is offered as a convenience to organizations and persons who must deal with consular representatives of foreign governments. It has been designed with particular attention to the requirements of government agencies, state tax officials, international trade organizations, chambers of commerce, and judicial authorities who have a continuing need for handy access to this type of information. Trade with other regions of the world has become an increasingly vital element in the economy of the United States. The machinery of this essential commerce is complicated by numerous restrictions, license requirements, quotas, and other measures adopted by the individual countries. Since the regulations affecting both trade and travel are the particular province of the consular service of the nations involved, reliable information as to entrance requirements, consignment of goods, details of transshipment, and, in many instances, suggestions as to consumer needs and preferences may be obtained at the foreign consular offices throughout the United States. **Note: Changes occur daily. Status of persons listed in this publication should be verified with the Office of Protocol.**

IMMUNITIES ACCORDED TO CONSULAR OFFICERS

Consular officers should be accorded their respective privileges, rights, and immunities as directed by international and domestic law. These foreign officials should be treated with the courtesy and respect befitting their positions. At the same time, it is a well established principle of international law that, without prejudice to their privileges and immunities, it is the duty of all persons enjoying such privileges and immunities to respect local laws and regulations. Unless otherwise provided under specific bilateral agreements, they are entitled to the limited immunities described in the Vienna Convention on Consular Relations (VCCR), which contains the current expression of international law on the subject of the rights, privileges, and immunities of consular personnel. Furthermore, recognized consular officers who also are accredited as diplomatic agents at certain diplomatic missions enjoy full immunity under the provisions of the Vienna Convention on Diplomatic Relations (VCDR).

Career Consular Officers

Article 43 of the VCCR states that the immunity to which consular officers are entitled relates only to acts arising in the exercise of consular functions. This limited form of immunity, generally referred to as "official acts immunity" or "functional immunity," must be asserted in court as an affirmative defense and is subject to court determination. It should be noted that civil actions relating to private contracts and damage arising from accidents caused by automobiles, vessels, or aircraft are specifically excepted from a claim of "official acts immunity" as are those based on private contracts. Although career consular officers enjoy only limited immunity from jurisdiction, Article 41 of the VCCR does grant them personal inviolability. Therefore, such individuals may not be arrested or detained pending trial, except in the case of a grave crime and pursuant to a decision of a competent judicial authority. Career consular officers can be identified by credentials issued by the U.S. Department of State, which bear its seal, the name of the officer, and title.

Families of Consular Officers

Family members of consular officers do not enjoy the same privileges and immunities with respect to the civil and criminal jurisdiction of the receiving state as do consular officers. However, they should be accorded appropriate courtesy and respect.

Consular Employees

Although foreign career consular employees are not listed in this publication, these individuals also are entitled to immunity from the civil and criminal jurisdiction of the receiving state as to official acts performed in the exercise of their consular functions, subject to court determination. They do not, however, enjoy personal inviolability and, thus, are not immune from arrest or detention.

Countries with Special Bilateral Agreements

The United States and the following countries have entered into bilateral agreements which, in certain cases, may provide greater privileges and immunities to consular officers, family members, and employees.

The Republic of Armenia	The Republic of Moldova
The Republic of Azerbaijan	The Philippines
The Republic of Belarus	The Republic of Poland
The Republic of Bulgaria	Romania
The People's Republic of China	Russia
The Czech Republic	Slovak Republic
The Republic of Georgia	The Republic of Tajikistan
The Republic of Hungary	Turkmenistan
The Republic of Kazakhstan	Ukraine
The Kyrgyz Republic	The Republic of Uzbekistan

For details in particular cases, please contact the Office of Protocol

CONSULAR PREMISES

Consular premises used exclusively for the work of the consular post cannot be entered without explicit permission of the head of the consular post or his designee or by the head of the diplomatic mission. This permission may be assumed in the case of fire or other disaster requiring prompt protective action.

CONSULAR ARCHIVES, DOCUMENTS, RECORDS, AND CORRESPONDENCE

The consular archives and documents are inviolable at all times and wherever they may be. The official correspondence of the consular post, which means all correspondence relating to the consular post and its functions, is likewise inviolable.

HONORARY CONSULAR OFFICERS

As a matter of U.S. policy, honorary consular officers recognized by the U.S. Government are American citizens or permanent resident aliens who perform consular services on a part-time basis. The limited immunity afforded honorary consular officers is specified in Article 71 of the VCCR. Such individuals do not enjoy personal inviolability and may be arrested pending trial if circumstances should otherwise warrant. However, appropriate steps must be provided to accord to such officers the protection required by virtue of their official position. In addition, the consular archives and documents of a consular post headed by an honorary consular officer are inviolable at all times and wherever they may be, provided they are kept separate from other papers and documents of a private or commercial nature relating to other activities of an honorary consular officer or persons working with that consular officer.

The **Foreign Consular Offices in the United States** list is available to the public for a fee through the Superintendent of Documents, U.S. Government Printing Office, Washington, D.C. 20402 (Telephone Number {202} 512-1800) and on the Department of State Internet web site under:

http://www.state.gov/s/cpr/rls

NOTE: The information contained herein was compiled as of August 1, 2007.

TABLE OF CONTENTS

TABLE OF CONTENTS (Continued)

CHANCERIES
Washington, D.C.

(Area Code 202)

AFGHANISTAN, 2341 Wyoming Ave., N.W., 20008 483-6410
ALBANIA, REPUBLIC OF, 2100 S Street, N.W., 20008 223-4942
ALGERIA, PEOPLE'S DEMOCRATIC REP. OF, 2118 Kalorama Rd., N.W., 20008 265-2800
ANDORRA, 2 United Nations Plaza, 27th Floor, New York, NY, 10017 .... (212)750-8064
ANGOLA, REPUBLIC OF, 2100-2108 16th Street, N.W, 20009 785-1156
ANTIGUA AND BARBUDA, 3216 New Mexico Ave., N.W., 20016 362-5122
ARGENTINE REPUBLIC, 1600 New Hampshire Ave., N.W., 20009 238-6400
ARMENIA, REPUBLIC OF, 2225 R St., N.W., 20008 319-1976
AUSTRALIA, 1601 Massachusetts Ave., N.W., 20036 797-3000
AUSTRIA, 3524 International Court, N.W., 20008 895-6700
AZERBAIJAN, REPUBLIC OF, 2741 34th St., N.W., 20008 337-3500
BAHAMAS, COMMONWEALTH OF THE, 2220 Massachusetts Ave., N.W., 20008 319-2660
BAHRAIN, KINGDOM OF, 3502 International Dr., N.W., 20008 342-0741
BANGLADESH, PEOPLE'S REPUBLIC OF, 3510 International Dr., N.W., 20008 244-0183
BARBADOS, 2144 Wyoming Ave., N.W., 20008 939-9200
BELARUS, REPUBLIC OF, 1619 New Hampshire Ave., N.W., 20009 986-1604
BELGIUM, 3330 Garfield St., N.W., 20008 333-6900
BELIZE, 2535 Massachusetts Ave., N.W., 20008 332-9636
BENIN, REPUBLIC OF, 2124 Kalorama Rd., N.W., 20008 232-6656
BOLIVIA, REPUBLIC OF, 3014 Massachusetts Ave., N.W., 20008 483-4410
BOSNIA & HERZEGOVINA, 2109 E St., N.W.20037 337-1500
BOTSWANA, REPUBLIC OF, 1531-1533 New Hampshire Ave., N.W. 20036 244-4990
BRAZIL, 3006 Massachusetts Ave., N.W., 20008 238-2700
BRUNEI DARUSSALAM, 3520 International Court, N.W., 20008 237-1838
BULGARIA, REPUBLIC OF, 1621 22nd St., N.W., 20008 387-0174
BURKINA FASO, 2340 Massachusetts Ave., N.W., 20008 332-5577
BURMA, UNION OF, 2300 S St., N.W., 20008 332-3344
BURUNDI, REPUBLIC OF, 2233 Wisconsin Ave., N.W., Suite 212, 20007 342-2574
CAMBODIA, ROYAL (EMB) OF, 4530 16th St., N.W., 20011 726-7742
CAMEROON, REPUBLIC OF, 2349 Massachusetts Ave., N.W., 20008 265-8790
CANADA, 501 Pennsylvania Ave., N.W., 20001 682-1740
CAPE VERDE, REPUBLIC OF, 3415 Massachusetts Ave., N.W., 20007 965-6820
CENTRAL AFRICAN REPUBLIC, 1618 22nd St., N.W., 20008 483-7800
CHAD, REPUBLIC OF, 2002 R St., N.W., 20009 462-4009
CHILE, REPUBLIC OF, 1732 Massachusetts Ave., N.W., 20036 785-1746
CHINA, PEOPLE'S REPUBLIC OF, 2300 Connecticut Ave., N.W., 20008 328-2500
COLOMBIA, 2118 Leroy Pl., N.W., 20008 387-8338
COMOROS, UNION OF, 420 E. 50th St., New York, N.Y. 10022 .... (212) 972-8010
CONGO, DEMOCRATIC REPUBLIC OF, 1726 M St., N.W., Suite 601, 20036 234-7690
CONGO, REPUBLIC OF, 4891 Colorado Ave., N.W., 20011 726-5500
COSTA RICA, 2114 S St., N.W., 20008 234-2945
COTE D'IVOIRE, REPUBLIC OF, 2424 Massachusetts Ave., N.W., 20008 797-0300
CROATIA, REPUBLIC OF, 2343 Massachusetts Ave., N.W., 20008 588-5899
CUBA (See Switzerland)
CYPRUS, REPUBLIC OF, 2211 R St., N.W., 20008 462-5772
CZECH REPUBLIC, 3900 Spring of Freedom St.,N.W., 20008 274-9100
DENMARK, 3200 Whitehaven St., N.W., 20008 234-4300
DJIBOUTI, REPUBLIC OF, 1156 15th St., N.W., Suite 515, 20005 331-0270
DOMINICA, COMMONWEALTH OF, 3216 New Mexico Ave., N.W., 20016 364-6781
DOMINICAN REPUBLIC, 1715 22nd St., N.W., 20008 332-6280
EAST TIMOR, DEMOCRATIC REPUBLIC OF, 4201 Connecticut Ave., N.W., Suite 504, 20008 966-3202
ECUADOR, 2535 15th St., N.W., 20009 234-7200
EGYPT, ARAB REPUBLIC OF, 3521 International Ct., N.W., 20008 895-5400
EL SALVADOR, 2308 California St., N.W., 20008 265-9671
EQUATORIAL GUINEA, REPUBLIC OF, 2020 16th St., N.W., 20009 518-5700

CHANCERIES (Continued)
Washington, D.C.

ERITREA, STATE OF, 1708 New Hampshire Ave., N.W., 20009..319-1991
ESTONIA, 2131 Massachusetts Ave., N.W. 20008...588-0101
ETHIOPIA, 3506 International Dr., N.W., 20008 364-1200
EUROPEAN UNION, 2300 M St., N.W., 20037 862-9500
FIJI, REPUBLIC OF, 2233 Wisconsin Ave., N.W., Suite 240, 20007 337-8320
FINLAND, 3301 Massachusetts Ave., N.W., 20008 298-5800
FRANCE, 4101 Reservoir Rd., N.W., 20007 944-6000
GABON, 2034 20th St., N.W., Suite 200, 20009...797-1000
GAMBIA, THE, 1156 15th St., N.W., Suite 905, 20005 785-1379
GEORGIA, REPUBLIC OF, 1101 15th St., N.W., Suite 602, 20005...387-2390
GERMANY, FEDERAL REPUBLIC OF, 4645 Reservoir Rd., N.W., 20007 298-8140
GHANA, 3512 International Dr., N.W., 20008 686-4520
GREECE, 2221 Massachusetts Ave., N.W., 20008 939-1300
GRENADA, 1701 New Hampshire Ave., N.W., 20009 265-2561
GUATEMALA, 2220 R St., N.W. 20008..745-4952
GUINEA, REPUBLIC OF, 2112 Leroy Pl., N.W., 20008 986-4300
GUINEA-BISSAU, REPUBLIC OF, P.O. Box 33813, 20033 ....(301)947-3958
GUYANA, 2490 Tracy Pl., N.W., 20008 265-6900
HAITI, REPUBLIC OF, 2311 Massachusetts Ave., N.W., 20008...332-4090
HOLY SEE, 3339 Massachusetts Ave., N.W., 20008...333-7121
HONDURAS, 3007 Tilden St., N.W., Suite 4-M, 20008 966-2604
HUNGARY, REPUBLIC OF, 3910 Shoemaker St., N.W., 20008..362-6730
ICELAND, 1156 15th St., N.W., Suite 1200, 20005 265-6653
INDIA, 2107 Massachusetts Ave., N.W., 20008 939-7000
INDONESIA, REPUBLIC OF, 2020 Massachusetts Ave., N.W., 20036...775-5200
IRAN (See Pakistan)
IRAQ, REPUBLIC OF, 1801 P St., N.W., 20036..483-7500
IRELAND, 2234 Massachusetts Ave., N.W., 20008 462-3939
ISRAEL, 3514 International Dr., N.W., 20008...364-5500
ITALY, 3000 Whitehaven St., N.W., 20008..612-4400
JAMAICA, 1520 New Hampshire Ave., N.W., 20036 452-0660
JAPAN, 2520 Massachusetts Ave., N.W., 20008 238-6700
JORDAN, HASHEMITE KINGDOM OF, 3504 International Dr., N.W., 20008 966-2664
KAZAKHSTAN, REPUBLIC OF, 1401 16th St., N.W., 20036 232-5488
KENYA, REPUBLIC OF, 2249 R St., N.W., 20008 387-6101
KOREA, REPUBLIC OF, 2450 Massachusetts Ave., N.W., 20008...939-5600
KUWAIT, STATE OF, 2940 Tilden St.,N.W., 20008 966-0702
KYRGYZSTAN, (KYRGYZ REPUBLIC), 1001 Pennsylvania Ave., N.W., Suite 600, 20004 338-5141
LAOS, (LAO PEOPLE'S DEMOCRATIC REP.) 2222 S St., N.W., 20008..332-6416
LATVIA, 2306 Massachusetts Ave., N.W., 20008..328-2840
LEBANON, 2560 28th St., N.W., 20008..939-6300
LESOTHO, KINGDOM OF, 2511 Massachusetts Ave., N.W., 20008 797-5533
LIBERIA, REPUBLIC OF, 5201 16th St., N.W., 20011 723-0437
LIBYA, LIAISON OFFICE, 2600 Virginia Ave., N.W., Suite 705, 20037..944-9601
LIECHTENSTEIN, 888 17th St., N.W., Suite 1250, 20006 331-0590
LITHUANIA, REPUBLIC OF, 2622 16th St., N.W., 20009..234-5860
LUXEMBOURG, GRAND DUCHY OF, 2200 Massachusetts Ave., N.W., 20008....................................265-4171
MACEDONIA, 1101 30th St., N.W., Suite 302, 20007 667-0501
MADAGASCAR, REPUBLIC OF, 2374 Massachusetts Ave., N.W., 20008 265-5525
MALAWI, 1156 15th St., N.W., Suite 320, 20005..721-0270
MALAYSIA, 3516 International Court, N.W., 20008..572-9700
MALDIVES, REPUBLIC OF, 800 2nd Ave., Suite 400E, New York, NY, 10017 ....(212)599-6195
MALI, REPUBLIC OF, 2130 R St., N.W., 20008..332-2249
MALTA, 2017 Connecticut Ave., N.W., 20008 462-3611
MARSHALL ISLANDS, REPUBLIC OF, 2433 Massachusetts Ave., N.W., 20008 234-5414
MAURITANIA, ISLAMIC REPUBLIC OF, 2129 Leroy Pl., N.W., 20008 232-5700
MAURITIUS, REPUBLIC OF, 4301 Connecticut Ave., N.W., Suite 441, 20008 244-1491

CHANCERIES (Continued)
Washington, D.C.

MEXICO, 1911 Pennsylvania Ave., N.W., 20006......728-1600
MICRONESIA, FEDERATED STATES OF, 1725 N St., N.W., 20036......223-4383
MOLDOVA, REPUBLIC OF, 2101 S St., N.W., 20008 667-1130
MONGOLIA, 2833 M St., N.W., 20007......333-7117
MOROCCO, KINGDOM OF, 1601 21st St., N.W., 20009 462-7980
MOZAMBIQUE, REPUBLIC OF, 1990 M St., N.W., Suite 570, 20036......293-7146
NAMIBIA, REPUBLIC OF, 1605 New Hampshire Ave., N.W., 20009......986-0540
NAURU, REPUBLIC OF, 800 2nd Ave., New York, NY., 10017......(212)937-0074
NEPAL, 2131 Leroy Pl., N.W., 20008 667-4550
NETHERLANDS, 4200 Linnean Ave., N.W., 20008......244-5300
NEW ZEALAND, 37 Observatory Circle, N.W., 20008 328-4800
NICARAGUA, REPUBLIC OF, 1627 New Hampshire Ave., N.W., 20009......939-6570
NIGER, REPUBLIC OF, 2204 R St., N.W., 20008......483-4224
NIGERIA, FEDERAL REP. OF, 3519 International Ct., N.W., 20008......986-8400
NORWAY, 2720 34th St., N.W., 20008......333-6000
OMAN, SULTANATE OF, 2535 Belmont Road, N.W., 20008......387-1980
PAKISTAN, 3517 International Ct. N.W., 20008 243-6500
  IRANIAN INTERESTS SECTION, 2209 Wisconsin Ave., N.W., 20007......965-4990
PALAU, REPUBLIC OF, 1700 Pennsylvania Ave., N.W, Suite 400, 20006 452-6814
PANAMA, REPUBLIC OF, 2862 McGill Terrace N.W., 20008 483-1407
PAPUA NEW GUINEA, 1779 Massachusetts Ave., N.W., Suite 805, 20036 745-3680
PARAGUAY, 2400 Massachusetts Ave., N.W., 20008......483-6960
PERU, 1700 Massachusetts Ave., N.W., 20036 833-9860
PHILIPPINES, 1600 Massachusetts Ave., N.W., 20036 467-9300
POLAND, REPUBLIC OF, 2640 16th St., N.W., 20009 234-3800
PORTUGAL, 2012 Massachusetts Ave., N.W., 20036 328-8610
QATAR, STATE OF, 2555 M St., N.W., 20037 274-1600
ROMANIA, 1607 23rd St., N.W., 20008 332-4846
RUSSIAN FEDERATION, 2650 Wisconsin Ave., N.W.. 20007......298-5700
RWANDA, REPUBLIC OF, 1714 New Hampshire Ave., N.W., 20009......232-2882
SAMOA, INDEPENDENT STATE OF, 800 2nd Ave., 4th Floor, New York, NY 10017 ......(212)599-6196
SAUDI ARABIA, 601 New Hampshire Ave., N.W., 20037 342-3800
SENEGAL, REPUBLIC OF, 2112 Wyoming Ave., N.W., 20008 234-0540
SERBIA, 2134 Kalorama Rd., N.W., 20008......332-0333
SEYCHELLES, REPUBLIC OF, 800 2nd Ave., Suite 400C, New York, NY 10017 ......(212) 972-1785
SIERRA LEONE, 1701 19th St., N.W., 20009......939-9261
SINGAPORE, REPUBLIC OF, 3501 International Pl., N.W., 20008 537-3100
SLOVAK REPUBLIC, 3523 International Court, N.W., 20008......237-1054
SLOVENIA, REP. OF, 1525 New Hampshire Ave., N.W., 20036......332-9332
SOLOMON ISLANDS, 800 2nd Ave., Suite 400L, New York, NY 10017........(212)599-6192
SOUTH AFRICA, 3051 Massachusetts Ave., N.W., 20008......232-4400
SPAIN, 2375 Pennsylvania Ave., N.W., 20037......452-0100
SRI LANKA, DEMOCRATIC SOCIALIST REP. OF, 2148 Wyoming Ave., N.W., 20008 483-4025
ST. KITTS AND NEVIS, 3216 New Mexico Ave., N.W., 20016......686-2636
ST. LUCIA, 3216 New Mexico Ave., N.W., 20016 364-6792
ST. VINCENT AND THE GRENADINES, 3216 New Mexico Ave., N.W., 20016 364-6730
SUDAN, REPUBLIC OF THE, 2210 Massachusetts Ave., N.W., 20008 338-8565
SURINAME, REPUBLIC OF, 4301 Connecticut Ave., N.W., Suite 460, 20008......244-7488
SWAZILAND, KINGDOM OF, 1712 New Hampshire Ave., N.W., 20009 234-5002
SWEDEN, 1501 M St. N.W., Suite 900, 20005......467-2600
SWITZERLAND, 2900 Cathedral Ave., N.W., 20008......745-7900
  CUBAN INTERESTS SECTION, 2630 16th St., N.W., 20009 797-8518
SYRIAN ARAB REPUBLIC, 2215 Wyoming Ave., N.W., 20008......232-6313
TAJIKISTAN, REPUBLIC OF, 1005 New Hampshire Ave., N.W. 20037......223-6090
TANZANIA, UNITED REPUBLIC OF, 2139 R St., N.W., 20008......939-6125
THAILAND, 1024 Wisconsin Ave., N.W., 20007 944-3600
TOGO, REPUBLIC OF, 2208 Massachusetts Ave., N.W., 20008 234-4212

CHANCERIES (Continued)
Washington, D.C.

TONGA, KINGDOM OF, 250 E. 51st St., New York, NY 10022 ....(917)369-1025

TRINIDAD AND TOBAGO, 1708 Massachusetts Ave., N.W., 20036 467-6490

TUNISIA, 1515 Massachusetts Ave., N.W., 20005... 862-1850

TURKEY, REPUBLIC OF, 2525 Massachusetts Ave., N.W., 20008 612-6700

TURKMENISTAN, 2207 Massachusetts Ave., N.W., 20008 588-1500

UGANDA, REPUBLIC OF, 5911 16th St., N.W., 20011 726-0416

UKRAINE, 3350 M St., N.W., 20007 349-2920

UNITED ARAB EMIRATES, 3522 International Court, N.W., 20008 243-2400

UNITED KINGDOM OF GREAT BRITAIN, 3100 Massachusetts Ave., N.W., 20008.. 588-6500

URUGUAY, 1913 I St., N.W., 20006... 331-1313

UZBEKISTAN, REPUBLIC OF, 1746 Massachusetts Ave., N.W., 20036... 293-6803

VENEZUELA, BOLIVARIAN REPUBLIC OF, 1099 30th St., N.W., 20007 342-2214

VIETNAM, 1233 20th St., N.W., Suite 400, 20036 861-0737

YEMEN, REPUBLIC OF, 2319 Wyoming Ave., N.W., 20008 965-4760

ZAMBIA, REPUBLIC OF, 2419 Massachusetts Ave., N.W., 20008... 265-9717

ZIMBABWE, REPUBLIC OF, 1608 New Hampshire Ave., N.W., 20009 332-7100

NATIONAL HOLIDAYS

JANUARY
January 1Haiti, Sudan, Slovakia
January 4........................Burma
January 26........ Australia, India

FEBRUARY
February 4.................Sri Lanka
February 6.......... .New Zealand
February 7....................Grenada
February 16............... Lithuania
February 18...........The Gambia
February 22........... .Saint Lucia
February 23..... Brunei, Guyana
February 24.................Estonia
February 25....................Kuwait
February 27.............Dominican
    Republic

MARCH
March 3.......................Bulgaria
March 6...........................Ghana
March 12...................Mauritius
March 17.......................Ireland
March 20.......................Tunisia
March 21.....................Namibia
March 23.....................Pakistan
March 25...................... Greece
March 26................ Bangladesh

APRIL
April 4 ....Senegal
April 16......................Denmark
April 17............................ Syria
April 18....................Zimbabwe
April 26.......................Tanzania
April 27...... Sierre Leone, Togo
April 27................ South Africa
April 30................ .Netherlands

MAY
May 1............. Marshall Islands
May 3 ....Poland
May 8   . ... Czech Republic
May 9   ....European Union
May 12 ....Israel
May 14 ....Paraguay
May 17 ....Norway
May 20 ....Cameroon
May 22 .... Yemen
May 24 ....Eritrea
May 25 .... Argentina, Jordan
May 26 ..Guyana, Great Britain
May 28 ....Azerbaijan, Ethiopia
May 30 ....Croatia

JUNE
June 1 ....Samoa
June 2 .... Italy

June 4 ....Tonga
June 6 .... Sweden
June 10 ....Portugal
June 12 ......Philippines, Russia
June 17 .... Iceland
June 18 ....Seychelles
June 23 ....Luxembourg
June 25 Mozambique, Slovenia
June 26 ....Madagascar
June 27 ....Djibouti
June 30 .... D. R. of Congo

JULY
July 1 .... Burundi, Canada
    Rwanda
July 3 ....Belarus
July 5 ...Cape Verde, Venezuela
July 6 .... Comoros, Malawi
July 7 .. Nepal, Solomon Islands
July 10 .... Bahamas
July 11 ....Mongolia
July 14 .... France
July 20 .... Colombia
July 21 .... Belgium
July 23 .... Egypt
July 26 ....Liberia
July 28 ....Peru
July 30 ....Morocco

AUGUST
August 1 .....Benin, Switzerland
August 2 .... Macedonia
August 5 .... Jamaica
August 6 .... Bolivia
August 7 ....Cote D'Ivoire
August 9 ....Singapore
August 10 ....Ecuador
August 11 ....Chad
August 15   Korea, R. of Congo,
    Liechtenstein
August 17 .... Indonesia, Gabon
August 19 ....Afghanistan
August 20 .... Hungary
August 24 .... Ukraine
August 25 .... Uruguay
August 29...................Slovakia
August 31 ....Kyrgyzstan,
    Malaysia, Trinidad and
    Tobago

SEPTEMBER
September 1 .... Uzbekistan,
    Slovakia
September 3 .... Qatar
September 6............. Swaziland
September 7.................... Brazil
September 15.........Costa Rica,
    El Salvador, Guatemala,
    Honduras, Nicaragua

September 16 .... Mexico,
    Papua New Guinea
September 18 ....Chile
September 19 .... St. Kitts
    and Nevis
September 21 ...... Belize, Malta
September 22 ....Mali
September 23 ....Saudi Arabia
September 24 .... Guinea-Bissau
September 30 ....Botswana

OCTOBER
October 1........ Cyprus, Nigeria,
    People's Republic of China,
    Palau
October 2.......................Guinea
October 3....................Germany
October 4......................Lesotho
October 9.....................Uganda
October 11...........................Fiji
October 12...Equatorial Guinea,
    Spain
October 18................Azerbaijan
October 22...................Holy See
October 24.................... Zambia
October 26....................Austria
October 27.......... Saint Vincent
    and the Grenadines,
    Turkmenistan
October 28...... Czech Republic,
    Turkmenistan
October 29.................... Turkey

NOVEMBER
November 1...................Algeria,
    Antigua & Barbuda
November 3..............Dominica,
    Panama
November 11.................Angola
November 17...............Slovakia
November 18.......Latvia, Oman
November 19............... Monaco
November 22...............Lebanon
November 25............. Suriname
November 28...........Mauritania
November 30............. Barbados

DECEMBER
December 1 ....Central
    African Republic, Romania
December 2..........Laos, United
    Arab Emirates
December 5 .... Thailand
December 6 .... Finland
December 11 .... Burkina Faso
December 12 ....Kenya
December 16 ....Bahrain,
    Kazakhstan
December 18 .... Niger
December 23 .... Japan

STATE* RESIDENCE	NAME AND RANK	DATE OF RECOGNITION	STATE* RESIDENCE	NAME AND RANK	DATE OF RECOGNITION

AFGHANISTAN

CALIFORNIA

LOS ANGELES (CG) 11040 SANTA MONICA BL., SUITE 300, 90025.
(310) 473-6583, FAX (310) 473-6775

MR. ATIQULLAH ATIFMAL, CONSUL GENERAL	Jul. 29, 2004
MR. SAYED MUJTABA AHMADI, CONSUL	May. 23, 2006
MR. SAFAR MOHAMMAD AMIRI, DEPUTY CONSUL	Mar. 29, 2007

NEW YORK

NEW YORK (CG) 360 LEXINGTON AV., FLOOR 11, 10017.
(212) 972-2277, FAX (212) 972-9046

MR. MOHAMMAD SADIQ DAUDZAI, CONSUL GENERAL	Jan. 06, 2006
MR. SAYED SARDAR AHMAD AHMADI, CONSUL	Dec. 03, 2002
MR. ABDUL BASHIR BASHARAT, CONSUL	Mar. 27, 2007
MS. SHAKILLA BEHZAD, VICE CONSUL	Jun. 26, 2006

ALBANIA

CONNECTICUT

GREENWICH (HC) 1 LANDMARK SQ., SUITE 315, STAMFORD 06901.
(203) 252-2800, FAX (203) 252-2810

MR. RICHARD STEELE LUKAJ, HONORARY CONSUL	May. 14, 2002

FLORIDA

FT. LAUDERDALE (HCG) 4077 N.E. 5TH TE., FORT LAUDERDALE 33334.
(954) 537-3571

MR. NASI LESKU, HONORARY CONSUL GENERAL	Sep. 23, 2003

GEORGIA

AVONDALE ESTATES (HCG) 310 SOMERLANE PL., 30002.
(404) 299-6803

MR. THEODORE ROOSEVELT , JR BRITTON, HONORARY CONSUL GENERAL	Mar. 16, 2006

LOUISIANA

NEW ORLEANS (HCG) 201 ST. CHARLES AV., SUITE 2401, 70170.
(504) 598-0106

MR. BRET ALDEN CLESI, HONORARY CONSUL GENERAL	Apr. 17, 2007

MICHIGAN

WEST BLOOMFIELD (HCG) 3300 LONE PINE RD., 48323.
(248) 851-7310

MR. EKREM BARDHA, HONORARY CONSUL GENERAL	Sep. 23, 2003

NEW YORK

NEW YORK (CG) 156 FIFTH AV., SUITE 1210, 10010.
(212) 255-7381, FAX (212) 255-7380

MR. ALBERT JERASI, CONSUL	Jul. 17, 2007

NORTH CAROLINA

PINEHURST (HCG) 130 SANDHURST PL., SOUTHERN PINES 28387.
(910) 690-8471, FAX (910) 295-4741

DR. DAVID FUNDERBURK, HONORARY CONSUL GENERAL	Jun. 23, 2004

OHIO

CLEVELAND (HCG) 1200 W. 58TH ST., 44102.
(216) 631-1755

DR. PETER KOLE, HONORARY CONSUL GENERAL	Nov. 10, 2003

TEXAS

HOUSTON (HC) 10 WATERWAY CT., THE WOODLANDS 77380.
(281) 548-4740, FAX (281) 354-7255

DR. PEDRO A. RUBIO, HONORARY CONSUL	Dec. 03, 1993

ANGOLA

NEW YORK

NEW YORK (CG) 866 UNITED NATIONS PL., SUITE 552, 10017.
(212) 861-5656

MS. JULIA MACHADO, CONSUL GENERAL	Nov. 24, 1999
MR. JERONIMO GASPAR DE ALMEIDA, VICE CONSUL	Jul. 11, 2000
MR. FRANCISCO LEANDRO DE ALMEIDA, VICE CONSUL	Jun. 02, 2004
MR. FRANSCISCO FLAMINIO DOS SANTOS, VICE CONSUL	Apr. 18, 2007
MR. AMORIM ANTONIO SEBASTIAO, VICE CONSUL	Apr. 30, 2007
MR. CRISTOVAO DA PAZ JULIO, CONSULAR AGENT	Jul. 31, 2000
MR. JOAO JOSE DA ROCHA, CONSULAR AGENT	Feb. 27, 2004

TEXAS

HOUSTON (CG) 3040 POST OAK BL., SUITE 780, 77056.
(713) 212-3840, FAX (713) 212-3841

MR. SIMAO MANUEL PEDRO, CONSUL GENERAL	Mar. 14, 2006
MR. FRANCISCO BENTO, VICE CONSUL	Apr. 08, 2004
MRS. STELA SANTIAGO, VICE CONSUL	May. 17, 2007
MRS. FRANCISCA PEDRO AUGUSTO DA COSTA, CONSULAR AGENT	Jan. 09, 2002
MR. ANTONIO BARBOSA MASCARENHA, CONSULAR AGENT	Mar. 10, 2006
MR. JOAQUIM G. CHAGAS, CONSULAR AGENT	Apr. 27, 2007

ANTIGUA AND BARBUDA

DISTRICT OF COLUMBIA

WASHINGTON (CHN) 3216 NEW MEXICO AV., NW, 20016.
(202) 362-5211, FAX (202) 362-5225

STATE* RESIDENCE	NAME AND RANK	DATE OF RECOGNITION	STATE* RESIDENCE	NAME AND RANK	DATE OF RECOGNITION
	HER EXCELLENCY DEBORAH MAE LOVELL, CONSUL GENERAL	Mar. 22, 2005		MR. POMPEYO CARLOS LAYUS, CONSUL GENERAL	Jun. 03, 2004
	MS. GRACELYN G. HENRY, CONSUL	Jan. 30, 1996			

FLORIDA

MIAMI (CG) 25 S. E. 2ND AV., SUITE 300, 33131.

	MR. IAN EARL ANDERSON SWEENEY, CONSUL GENERAL	Jan. 09, 2006

NEW YORK

NEW YORK (CG) 3 DAG HAMMARSKJOLD PZ., FLOOR 6TH #1, 10017.
(718) 882-7948

	MISS OMYMA ELSPETH IVY JEAN DAVID, DEPUTY CONSUL GENERAL	Oct. 21, 2005
	MR. MCCHESNEY GEORGE EMANUEL, HONORARY CONSUL GENERAL	Oct. 21, 2005

ARGENTINA

CALIFORNIA

LOS ANGELES (CG) 5055 WILSHIRE BL., SUITE 210, 90036.
(213) 739-5959

	MR. JORGE TEODORO LAPSENSON, CONSUL GENERAL	Oct. 17, 2005
	MRS. ALCIRA ANDREA CELORIA, DEPUTY CONSUL GENERAL	Oct. 17, 2005
	MR. JUAN CARLOS GARAGUSO, DEPUTY CONSUL GENERAL	Jan. 27, 2006
	MR. FERNANDO BRUN, DEPUTY CONSUL	Nov. 24, 2004
	MS. ADRIANA NORA PRIETO, CONSULAR AGENT	Apr. 22, 2005

FLORIDA

MIAMI (CG) 800 BRICKELL AV., PENTHOUSE 1, 33131.
(305) 373-7794

	MR. GREGORIO JORGE DUPONT, CONSUL GENERAL	Oct. 22, 2004
	MR. ALEJANDRO HECTOR NIETO, DEPUTY CONSUL GENERAL	Apr. 06, 1998
	MR. PABLO ANIBAL CHELIA, DEPUTY CONSUL GENERAL	Mar. 16, 2007
	MR. GUILLERMO RODRIGUEZ, DEPUTY CONSUL	Jul. 22, 1999
	MR. DIEGO ALVAREZ RIVERA, DEPUTY CONSUL	Apr. 16, 2004
	MR. HORACIO HUGO RAVERA, CONSULAR AGENT	Feb. 08, 2000
	MRS. ELSA CATALINA BARONE DE LAMELA, CONSULAR AGENT	Jan. 29, 2004
	MRS. ESTELA BEATRIZ CIRELLI, CONSULAR AGENT	Mar. 14, 2006

TOURISM OFFICE
MIAMI (CONA) 1101 BRICKELL AV., SUITE 901 S, 33131.
(305) 371-5559

GEORGIA

ATLANTA (CG) 245 PEACHTREE CENTER AV., SUITE 2101, 30303.
(404) 880-0805

ILLINOIS

CHICAGO (CG) 205 N. MICHIGAN AV., SUITE 4208/4209, 60601.
(301) 819-2620, FAX (312) 819-2626

	MR. ERNESTO MANUEL PAZ, CONSUL GENERAL	Oct. 07, 2003
	MRS. JULIA ADRIANA GABRIELA PAN, DEPUTY CONSUL GENERAL	Apr. 27, 2007

ARGENTINE TRADE OFFICE
CHICAGO (CONA) 205 N. MICHIGAN AV., SUITE 4208, 60601.
(312) 819-2610, FAX (312) 819-2612

NEW YORK

NEW YORK (CG) 12 W. 56TH ST., 10019.
(212) 603-0400

	MR. HECTOR MARCOS TIMERMAN, CONSUL GENERAL	Jul. 29, 2004
	MR. LUIS PABLO MARIA BELTRAMINO, DEPUTY CONSUL GENERAL	Aug. 13, 2002
	MR. ALEJANDRO ANTONIO BERTOLO, DEPUTY CONSUL GENERAL	May. 29, 2003
	MR. MARIO J. A. OYARZABAL, DEPUTY CONSUL	Aug. 31, 1998
	MR. CARLOS ALEJANDRO POFFO, DEPUTY CONSUL	Jul. 01, 1999
	MS. DEBORA ADRIANA BANDURA, DEPUTY CONSUL	Apr. 06, 2007
	MR. OSCAR ARTURO MADINA, CONSULAR AGENT	Jun. 23, 2005

ARGENTINE TRADE OFFICE
NEW YORK (CONA) 900 3RD AV., FLOOR 4TH, 10022.
(212) 759-6477

TEXAS

HOUSTON (CG) 3050 POST OAK BL., SUITE 1625, 77056.
(713) 871-8935

	MR. RICARDO AUGUSTO GAUTHIER, CONSUL GENERAL	Jun. 04, 2004
	MS. VALERIA MARIA GONZALEZ POSSE, DEPUTY CONSUL	Feb. 27, 2006
	MR. ARMANDO DAVID ALVAREZ, CONSULAR AGENT	Apr. 01, 2004

ARMENIA

CALIFORNIA

LOS ANGELES (CG) 50 N. LA CIENEGA BL., SUITE 210, BEVERLY HILLS 90211.
(310) 657-6102

	MR. ARMEN LILOYAN, CONSUL GENERAL	Jan. 03, 2007
	MR. HARUTYUN KOJOYAN, DEPUTY CONSUL GENERAL	Mar. 03, 2004
	MR. ARTUR MADOYAN, CONSUL	Mar. 14, 2006
	MR. SAHAK SARGSYAN, VICE CONSUL	May. 07, 2007

STATE* RESIDENCE	NAME AND RANK	DATE OF RECOGNITION	STATE* RESIDENCE	NAME AND RANK	DATE OF RECOGNITION

DISTRICT OF COLUMBIA

WASHINGTON (CHN) 2225 R ST., NW, 20008.
(202) 319-1976, FAX (202) 319-2982
   MS. ARMELLA SHAKARYAN,   Dec. 27, 2006
      CONSUL

AUSTRALIA

CALIFORNIA

LOS ANGELES (CG) 2029 CENTURY PARK UN., E, SUITE 3150, 90067.
(310) 229-4800, FAX (310) 377-5746
   MR. INNES ALEXANDER WILLOX,   Oct. 12, 2006
      CONSUL GENERAL
   MRS. KYLIE HARGREAVES,   Jul. 26, 2002
      DEPUTY CONSUL GENERAL
   MR. IAN GEOFFREY WING,   Aug. 07, 2003
      DEPUTY CONSUL GENERAL
   MR. PHILLIP JOHN MINOS,   Aug. 10, 2006
      DEPUTY CONSUL GENERAL
   MS. FIONA AILEEN MORRIS,   Jun. 08, 2004
      CONSUL
   MR. ANTHONY CHARLES WEYMOUTH,   Nov. 29, 2005
      CONSUL

SENIOR TRADE COMMISSION
LOS ANGELES (CG) 2049 CENTURY PARK UN., E, FLOOR 19TH, 90067.

SAN FRANCISCO (CG) 575 MARKET ST., SUITE 1800, 94105.
(415) 536-1970, FAX (415) 536-1982
   MR. DAVID ALAN LAWSON,   Jan. 06, 2006
      CONSUL GENERAL

COLORADO

DENVER (HC) 9200 W. CROSS DR., SUITE 100, LITTLETON 80123.
(303) 321-2234, FAX (303) 973-9938
   MR. MARK V. O'REGAN,   Sep. 12, 1994
      HONORARY CONSUL

DISTRICT OF COLUMBIA

WASHINGTON (CHN) 1601 MASSACHUSETTS AV., NW, 20036.
(202) 797-3000, FAX (202) 797-3168
   MR. JOHN JAMES MCANULTY,   Mar. 22, 2005
      CONSUL GENERAL
   MS. MARILYN ANNE PERRING,   Jun. 21, 2006
      CONSUL
   MRS. JENNA KATHLEEN YOUNG,   Feb. 12, 2007
      VICE CONSUL

FLORIDA

MIAMI (HC) 2223 CORAL WA., 33145.
(305) 519-8814, FAX (305) 361-7021
   MR. THOMAS E. FLYNN,   Dec. 07, 1999
      HONORARY CONSUL

GEORGIA

ATLANTA (CG) 3353 PEACHTREE RD., NE, SUITE 1140, 30326.
(404) 760-3400, FAX (404) 760-3401
   MS. AMANDA MICHELLE HODGES,   Jan. 07, 2005
      CONSUL GENERAL

HAWAII

HONOLULU (CG) 1000 BISHOP ST., SUITE PHOUSE, 96813.
(808) 529-8100, FAX (808) 529-8142
   MR. JOHN PATON QUINN,   Dec. 03, 2004
      CONSUL GENERAL
   WING COMMANDER STEPHEN JOHN KENNEDY,   Jul. 05, 2006
      CONSUL
   MR. PETER RAYMOND GRANT,   Apr. 30, 2007
      CONSUL

ILLINOIS

CHICAGO (CG) 123 N. WACKER DR., SUITE 1330, 60606.
(312) 419-1480, FAX (312) 419-1499
   MR. ROBERT EDWIN CHARLES,   Apr. 22, 2005
      CONSUL GENERAL
   MRS. KERRY ANTOINETTE HARRIS,   Jul. 26, 2005
      CONSUL
   MR. IAN CLIVE MITCHELL SMITH,   Aug. 18, 2006
      CONSUL

MASSACHUSETTS

BOSTON (HC) 22 THOMSON PL., SUITE SST3, 02210.
(617) 856-2513
   MR. ADAM JOHN BRYAN,   Nov. 08, 2004
      HONORARY CONSUL

NEW YORK

NEW YORK (CG) 150 E. 42ND ST., FLOOR 34TH, 10017.
(212) 421-6910
   MR. JOHN WAYNE OLSEN,   Apr. 12, 2006
      CONSUL GENERAL
   MR. DAVID STAUNTON HOWARD,   Apr. 14, 2003
      DEPUTY CONSUL GENERAL
   MR. CHARLES FARRUGIA,   Jun. 28, 2005
      DEPUTY CONSUL GENERAL
   MR. KEVIN BRUCE FILIPPI,   Mar. 14, 2006
      CONSUL

SENIOR TRADE COMMISSION (INFORMATION SERVICE)
NEW YORK (CONA) 630/636 5TH AV., 10111.

TEXAS

HOUSTON (HC) 4623 FEAGAN ST., 77007.
(713) 782-6009, FAX (713) 862-8364
   MS. NANA L. BOOKER,   Dec. 07, 1999
      HONORARY CONSUL

TRUST TERRITORIES OF THE PACIFIC ISLANDS

KOLONIA, MICRONESIA (CG) P.O. BOX S ., KOLONIA 96941.
(691) 320-5448
   MR. BRENDAN FRANCIS DORAN,   Feb. 21, 2002
      CONSUL GENERAL
   MR. MICHAEL GORDON CREAGH,   Aug. 27, 2001
      CONSUL
   MRS. INGER JENSEN ROWE,   Aug. 27, 2001
      VICE CONSUL

STATE* RESIDENCE	NAME AND RANK	DATE OF RECOGNITION	STATE* RESIDENCE	NAME AND RANK	DATE OF RECOGNITION

PAGO PAGO (CG) BEACH RD., APIA, WESTERN SAMOA 00000.
   MR. PETER HOOTON,　　　　　Apr. 26, 2001
      CONSUL GENERAL

WASHINGTON

SEATTLE (HC) 401 ANDOVER PARK UN., E, 98188.
(206) 575-7446, FAX (206) 708-2526
   MR. LEONARD FREDERICK REID,　　　　　Apr. 23, 2002
      HONORARY CONSUL

AUSTRIA

ALASKA

ANCHORAGE (HC) 939 W. 5TH ST., 99501.
(907) 276-6000
   MR. WALTER J., JR HICKEL,　　　　　Jun. 15, 1999
      HONORARY CONSUL

ARIZONA

SCOTTSDALE (HC) 23002 N. LAS LAVATAS RD., 85255.
(480) 502-8510
   MR. WOLFGANG JOSEF KLIEN,　　　　　Aug. 31, 2004
      HONORARY CONSUL

CALIFORNIA

LOS ANGELES (CG) 11859 WILSHIRE BL., SUITE 501, 90025.
(310) 444-9310, FAX (310) 477-9897
   MR. MARTIN WEISS,　　　　　Dec. 23, 2004
      CONSUL GENERAL
   MR. STEFAN HOCHMUTH,　　　　　Sep. 03, 2002
      CONSUL
   MR. BERNHARD FAUSTENHAMMER,　　　　　Oct. 01, 2004
      CONSUL

AUSTRIAN TRADE COMMISSION
LOS ANGELES (CONA) 11601 WILSHIRE BL., SUITE 2420, 90025.
(310) 477-9988, FAX (310) 477-1643
   MR. HANS CHRISTIAN KUEGERL,　　　　　Oct. 25, 2002
      CONSUL

SAN FRANCISCO (HCG) 220 MONTGOMERY ST., SUITE 931, 94104.
(415) 951-8911, FAX (916) 444-7835
   MR. DONALD C. BURNS,　　　　　Oct. 25, 1995
      HONORARY CONSUL GENERAL
   DR. STEPHEN J. ZUBER,　　　　　Feb. 16, 1989
      HONORARY CONSUL

COLORADO

DENVER (HCG) 621 17TH ST., SUITE 2455, 80293-2450.
(303) 292-9000, FAX (303) 292-5445
   MR. ARNOLD C. WEGHER,　　　　　Nov. 29, 1989
      HONORARY CONSUL GENERAL

DISTRICT OF COLUMBIA

WASHINGTON (CHN) 3524 INTERNATIONAL CT., NW, 20008-3035.
(202) 895-6700, FAX (202) 895-6750
   MR. MARTIN KRAEMER,　　　　　Jun. 14, 2001
      CONSUL GENERAL

FLORIDA

MIAMI (HCG) 1454 N. W. 17TH AV., SUITE 200, 33125.
(305) 325-1561, FAX (305) 325-1563
   MR. ARTHUR W. KARLICK,　　　　　Jul. 10, 1987
      HONORARY CONSUL GENERAL

ORLANDO (HC) 8044 FIRENZE BL., 32836.
(407) 926-3877
   MR. TOBY WILLIAM UNWIN,　　　　　Apr. 25, 2006
      HONORARY CONSUL

GEORGIA

ATLANTA (HCG) 4200 NORTHSIDE PW., NW, SUITE 300, 30327.
(404) 264-9858, FAX (404) 266-3864
   MR. FERDINAND C. SEEFRIED,　　　　　Apr. 04, 1995
      HONORARY CONSUL GENERAL

HAWAII

HONOLULU (HCG) 1314 S. KING ST., SUITE 1260, 96814.
(808) 923-8585, FAX (808) 597-1233
   MR. HANS J. STRASSER,　　　　　Jan. 18, 1983
      HONORARY CONSUL GENERAL

ILLINOIS

CHICAGO (CG) 400 N. MICHIGAN AV., SUITE 707, 60611.
(312) 222-1515, FAX (312) 222-4113
   MR. ROBERT ZISCHG,　　　　　Jun. 07, 2005
      CONSUL GENERAL
   MR. GERNOT WIEDNER,　　　　　Jan. 17, 2002
      CONSUL

AUSTRIAN TRADE COMMISSION
CHICAGO (CONA) 500 N. MICHIGAN AV., SUITE 1950, 60611.
(312) 644-5556, FAX (312) 644-6526
   MR. FRANZ ROESSLER,　　　　　Sep. 21, 2006
      CONSUL
   MS. DANIELA KOLL,　　　　　Dec. 13, 2006
      VICE CONSUL

LOUISIANA

NEW ORLEANS (HCG) 755 MAGAZINE ST., 70130.
(504) 581-5141, FAX (504) 566-1201
   MR. PHILIP D., III LORIO,　　　　　Sep. 05, 2002
      HONORARY CONSUL GENERAL

MASSACHUSETTS

BOSTON (HC) 15 SCHOOL ST., FLOOR 3, 02108.
(617) 227-3131, FAX (617) 277-8420
   MR. IRA A. KORFF,　　　　　Oct. 05, 1987
      HONORARY CONSUL
   DR. HEINZ KONRAD GROHS,　　　　　Feb. 27, 1996
      HONORARY VICE CONSUL

MICHIGAN

DETROIT (HCG) 300 E. LONG LAKE RD., SUITE 365, BLOOMFIELD HILLS 48304.
(248) 645-1444, FAX (248) 645-1482
   MR. ALOYS K. SCHWARZ,　　　　　Mar. 08, 1994
      HONORARY CONSUL GENERAL

---

* DEPENDENCIES SUCH AS GUAM, PUERTO RICO, AND THE VIRGIN ISLANDS ARE LISTED HERE.
CG-CONSULATE GENERAL　　C-CONSULATE　　VC-VICE CONSULATE　　CA-CONSULAR AGENCY　　H-HONORARY CONSULAR STATUS

STATE* RESIDENCE	NAME AND RANK	DATE OF RECOGNITION	STATE* RESIDENCE	NAME AND RANK	DATE OF RECOGNITION

MINNESOTA

ST. PAUL (HCG) 10700 HIGHWAY 55 ., PLYMOUTH 55441.
(763) 543-0114, FAX (612) 223-8383

MR. RONALD M. BOSROCK, HONORARY CONSUL GENERAL	Jun. 12, 1984	
MR. HERBERT FREDERICK KAHLER, HONORARY CONSUL	Feb. 02, 1998	

MISSOURI

KANSAS CITY (HCG) 1111 MAIN STREET ST., FLOOR 7TH, 64105.
(816) 474-3000

MR. DENNIS JAMES OWENS,   Aug. 09, 1993
HONORARY CONSUL GENERAL

SAINT LOUIS (HC) 1350 ELBRIDGE PAYNE RD., CHESTERFIELD 63017-8531.
(314) 537-0305, FAX (314) 537-3720

MR. DIETER K. UNGERBOECK,   Nov. 29, 1995
HONORARY CONSUL

NEVADA

LAS VEGAS (HC) 3959 SPRING MOUNTAIN RD., 89102.
(702) 258-0032

MR. M. EDWIN PRUD'HOMME,   Apr. 05, 2004
HONORARY CONSUL

NEW YORK

BUFFALO (HC) 74 MAIN ST., AKRON 14001.
(716) 542-5444

DR. FRED FRIEDMAN,   Apr. 23, 2002
HONORARY CONSUL

NEW YORK (CG) 31 E. 69TH ST., 10021.
(212) 737-6400, FAX (212) 772-8926

DR. BRIGITTA M. BLAHA, CONSUL GENERAL	Oct. 05, 2005
MR. GERALD FIALA, CONSUL	Oct. 23, 2001
MR. ANDREAS LAUNER, CONSUL	Oct. 01, 2004
MS. SUSANNE BARTON, VICE CONSUL	Jan. 13, 2005
MR. MATHIAS GRAZER, VICE CONSUL	Sep. 21, 2006
MR. DANIEL NAGELER, VICE CONSUL	May. 08, 2007
MRS. IRITH F. JAWETZ, CONSULAR AGENT	Dec. 31, 1997
MR. JOSEPH E. SHEEHAN, HONORARY DEPUTY CONSUL GENERAL	Oct. 12, 1993

CULTURAL AFFAIRS SECTION
NEW YORK (CONA) 11 E. 52ND ST., 10022.
(212) 759-5165

DR. CHRISTOPH THUN HOHENSTEIN, CONSUL	Sep. 30, 1999
MR. ERNST AICHINGER, CONSUL	Dec. 22, 1999
MR. MARTIN RAUCHBAUER, CONSUL	Feb. 20, 2007

MR. DENIS MICHAEL KARNING, CONSUL	Apr. 25, 2007
MS. ASTRID ADAM, VICE CONSUL	Sep. 15, 2004
MR. MANFRED KAPPER, CONSULAR AGENT	Feb. 06, 2002
MS. EDELTRUD J. DESMOND, CONSULAR AGENT	Nov. 03, 2005

AUSTRIAN TRADE COMMISSION
NEW YORK (CONA) 120 W. 45TH ST., FLOOR 9TH, 10021.
(212) 421-5250, FAX (212) 751-4675

DR. CHRISTIAN KESBERG, CONSUL	Oct. 10, 2006
MR. PETER A. GATSCHA, VICE CONSUL	Mar. 08, 1993
MR. MICHAEL OTTER, VICE CONSUL	Oct. 11, 2005

NORTH CAROLINA

CHARLOTTE (HC) 250 N. MAIN ST., MT. HOLLY 28120.
(704) 827-7246, FAX (704) 827-7248

MR. ROBERT FRIEDL,   Apr. 09, 1999
HONORARY CONSUL

OHIO

COLUMBUS (HC) 1555 LAKE SHORE DR., 43204.
(614) 224-5464, FAX (614) 224-6603

MR. FRIEDRICH K. M. BOEHM,   May. 29, 1992
HONORARY CONSUL

OREGON

PORTLAND (HC) 900 S.W. 5TH AV., SUITE 2600, 97204-1268.
(503) 294-9236

MR. CHRISTOPHER R. HERMANN,   Oct. 15, 1999
HONORARY CONSUL

PENNSYLVANIA

PITTSBURGH (HC) 125 TECHNOLOGY DR., CANONSBURG 15317-9566.
(724) 745-7599, FAX (724) 745-9570

MR. EDGAR BRAUN,   Feb. 04, 1998
HONORARY CONSUL

PUERTO RICO

SAN JUAN (HC) 525 F.D. ROOSEVELT AV., SUITE 1112, 00918.
(787) 767-1381, FAX (787) 999-5029

MS. MARIE HELENE MORROW,   Feb. 11, 1982
HONORARY CONSUL

TEXAS

HOUSTON (HCG) 1717 BISONNET ST., SUITE 306, 77005.
(713) 526-0127, FAX (713) 526-4592

MR. OTMAR KOLBER, HONORARY CONSUL GENERAL	Nov. 05, 1992
MRS. CHRISTA M. COOPER, HONORARY VICE CONSUL	Aug. 25, 1992

STATE* RESIDENCE	NAME AND RANK	DATE OF RECOGNITION	STATE* RESIDENCE	NAME AND RANK	DATE OF RECOGNITION

UTAH

SALT LAKE CITY (HC) 240 EDISON ST., 84111.
(801) 364-1045

    MR. FRANZ KOLB,   Jun. 14, 2002
        HONORARY CONSUL

VIRGIN ISLANDS

ST. THOMAS (HC) PARCEL 7 ESTATE TAARNEBJERG ., 00802.
(340) 774-1100, FAX (340) 776-0342

    MR. JAMES HENRY HINDELS,   Mar. 01, 1999
        HONORARY CONSUL

VIRGINIA

RICHMOND (HC) 11904 BROOKMEADE CT., GLEN ALLEN 23060.
(804) 364-8614

    MR. BERNHARD BARTA,   Oct. 28, 1999
        HONORARY CONSUL

WASHINGTON

SEATTLE (HC) 416-A E. MORRIS ST., LACONNER 98257.
(360) 466-1100, FAX (360) 466-1101

    MS. ELISABETH C. CHAPMAN,   Jan. 30, 1998
        HONORARY CONSUL

WISCONSIN

MILWAUKEE (HC) 411 E. WISCONSIN AV., SUITE 3000, 53202.
(414) 277-5000

    MR. ROBERT J. KALUPA,   Dec. 17, 1998
        HONORARY CONSUL

AZERBAIJAN

CALIFORNIA

LOS ANGELES (CG) 11766 WILSHIRE BL., SUITE 1410, 90025.
(310) 444-9101, FAX (310) 477-4860

    MR. ELIN EMIN SULEYMANOV,   Mar. 14, 2006
        CONSUL GENERAL
    MR. ELMAN TELMAN OGLU ABDULLAYEV,   Jul. 17, 2006
        CONSUL
    MR. ELSHAN ASHRAF OGLU BALOGHLANOV,   Mar. 14, 2006
        VICE CONSUL

DISTRICT OF COLUMBIA

WASHINGTON (CHN) 2741 34TH ST., NW, 20008.
(202) 337-3500, FAX (202) 337-5911

    MR. ALI GAMBAR OGLU GARAYEV,   Mar. 22, 2006
        CONSUL

BAHAMAS

DISTRICT OF COLUMBIA

WASHINGTON (CHN) 2220 MASSACHUSETTS AV., NW, 20008.
(202) 319-2660, FAX (202) 319-2668

    MR. EUGENE TORCHON NEWRY,   Oct. 21, 2003
        CONSUL
    MISS RHODA MAE JACKSON,   Apr. 10, 2007
        CONSUL
    MRS. MONIQUE DENEAN VANDERPOOL,   Nov. 15, 2000
        VICE CONSUL

    MS. BETTY LEONA GREENSLADE,   Mar. 07, 2001
        VICE CONSUL
    MS. CHARICE ABIGAIL ROLLE,   Aug. 26, 2006
        VICE CONSUL

FLORIDA

MIAMI (CG) 25 S.E. 2ND AV., SUITE 818, 33131.
(305) 373-6295, FAX (305) 373-6312

    MS. ALMA AUGUSTA ADAMS,   Oct. 15, 2003
        CONSUL GENERAL
    MS. SANDRA PATRICIA CAREY,   Nov. 10, 2003
        CONSUL
    MR. ARNOLD PATRICK WHYLLY,   Mar. 07, 2005
        VICE CONSUL

GEORGIA

FAIRBURN (HC) 195 MOSS CREEK WALK RD., 30213.
(687) 817-6862

    MR. MICHAEL MUNROE YOUNG,   May. 23, 2006
        HONORARY CONSUL

NEW YORK

NEW YORK (CG) 231 E. 46TH ST., 10017.
(212) 421-6420, FAX (212) 759-2135

    MR. ELDRED EDISON BETHEL,   Mar. 18, 2003
        CONSUL GENERAL
    MR. PETER J. GOULANDRIS,   Mar. 01, 1994
        CONSUL
    MS. RENEE MONIQUE PINDER,   Oct. 28, 2002
        VICE CONSUL
    MRS. SANDRA NAOMI POITIER,   Jul. 11, 2006
        VICE CONSUL

BAHAMAS MARITIME AUTHORITY
NEW YORK (CONA) 231 E. 46TH ST., 10017.
    MS. CHRISTINE ALICE SCAVELLA,   Nov. 17, 2004
        CONSUL

BAHRAIN

CALIFORNIA

SAN DIEGO (HCG) 1101 FIRST ST., SUITE 302, CORONADO 92118.
(619) 437-0044, FAX (619) 437-0066

    MR. CHARLES W. HOSTLER,   Dec. 13, 1993
        HONORARY CONSUL GENERAL

NEW YORK

NEW YORK (CG) 44TH ST., E, FLOOR 25TH, 10017.
(212) 223-6200, FAX (212) 319-0687

BANGLADESH

CALIFORNIA

LOS ANGELES (CG) 4201 WILSHIRE BL., SUITE 605, 90010.
(323) 932-0100, FAX (323) 932-9703

    MR. MD ABU ZAFAR,   May. 07, 2007
        CONSUL GENERAL
    MR. MD ZAHIDUL HAQUE,   Jan. 06, 2005
        CONSUL

STATE* RESIDENCE	NAME AND RANK	DATE OF RECOGNITION

MR. SHAH AHMED SHAFI,
   CONSUL — Jul. 07, 2005

HAWAII

HONOLULU (HCG) 3785 OLD PALI RD., 96817.
(808) 521-5353

   MR. RAYMOND Y. HO,
     HONORARY CONSUL GENERAL — Jan. 28, 1988

LOUISIANA

NEW ORLEANS (HCG) 321 ST. CHARLES AV., 70130.
(504) 586-8300

   MR. THOMAS BLAISE COLEMAN,
     HONORARY CONSUL GENERAL — Oct. 26, 1988

NEW YORK

NEW YORK (CG) 211 E. 43RD ST., SUITE 502, 10017.
(212) 599-6767, FAX (212) 682-9211

   MR. SALAHUDDIN NOMAN CHOWDHURY,
     CONSUL — Nov. 04, 2005

   MR. A.F.M. ZAHID UL ISLAM,
     VICE CONSUL — Sep. 26, 2006

TEXAS

HOUSTON (HCG) 35 N. WYNDEN DR., 77056.
(713) 621-8462

   MR. EDWARD J., JR HUDSON,
     HONORARY CONSUL GENERAL — Oct. 16, 1996

BARBADOS

CALIFORNIA

LOS ANGELES (CON) 3440 WILSHIRE BL., SUITE 1207, 90010.
(213) 380-2198

SAN FRANCISCO (HC) 442 POST ST., SUITE 800, 94102.
(415) 421-8789

   MR. GERALD B. LEVINE,
     HONORARY CONSUL — Jan. 13, 1983

COLORADO

DENVER (HC) 150 FAIRPLAY AV., BLOOMFIELD 80020.
(303) 466-0531

   MR. PETER KELLEY,
     HONORARY CONSUL — Jan. 10, 1997

DISTRICT OF COLUMBIA

WASHINGTON (CHN) 2144 WYOMING AV., NW, 20008.
(202) 939-9200, FAX (202) 332-7467

   MS. DONNA MICHELLE FORDE,
     CONSUL — May. 07, 2003

FLORIDA

MIAMI (CG) 150 ALHAMBRA CI., SUITE 1000, 33134.
(305) 442-1994

   MR. EDWARD STANLEY BUSHELL,
     CONSUL GENERAL — Mar. 24, 2004

MR. PHILIP H. ST. HILL,
   DEPUTY CONSUL GENERAL — Sep. 28, 2006

MR. URBAN GARFIELD CUMBERBATCH,
   CONSUL — Jul. 28, 2003

MR. FERDINAND STEPHEN GILL,
   CONSUL — Mar. 10, 2004

MRS. JACQUELINE MARIE MARTINEZ,
   CONSUL — Mar. 12, 2004

MISS SYLVIA ONETA WILKINSON,
   VICE CONSUL — Mar. 02, 1995

MR. BRIAN A. M. GREEN,
   VICE CONSUL — Aug. 06, 1998

MS. MARCIA PATRICIA DRAKES,
   VICE CONSUL — Nov. 29, 1999

MS. SANDRA ROSEMARY PAYNE,
   VICE CONSUL — Jul. 07, 2005

GEORGIA

ATLANTA (HC) 4160 GLEN DEVON DR., NW, 30327.
(404) 365-8353, FAX (404) 365-8354

   DR. EDWARD A. LAYNE,
     HONORARY CONSUL — Aug. 02, 1993

ILLINOIS

CHICAGO (HC) 6700 S. OGLESBY AV., SUITE 1603, 60649.
(773) 667-5963, FAX (773) 667-5964

   MR. ANDRE RICHARDSON KING,
     HONORARY CONSUL — Oct. 01, 1974

KENTUCKY

LOUISVILLE (HC) 3518 SORRENTO AV., 40241.
(502) 852-0574

   MR. BERNARD JAMES STRENECKY,
     HONORARY CONSUL — Mar. 28, 1997

LOUISIANA

NEW ORLEANS (HC) 321 ST. CHARLES AV., FLOOR 10TH, 70130.
(504) 586-1979

   MR. PETER DEE COLEMAN,
     HONORARY CONSUL — Jan. 29, 1985

MASSACHUSETTS

BOSTON (HC) 794 CUMMINS HW., 02126.
(617) 296-3360

   MR. JOHN W. LICORISH,
     HONORARY CONSUL — May. 19, 1992

MICHIGAN

DETROIT (HC) 28111 HOOVER RD., SUITE 1A, WARREN 48093.
(586) 751-8840, FAX (586) 751-8849

   DR. LACEY WALKE,
     HONORARY CONSUL — Aug. 13, 1976

NEW YORK

NEW YORK (CG) 800 2ND AV., FLOOR 2ND, 10017.
(212) 867-8435

   MRS. JESSICA CECELIA ODLE,
     CONSUL GENERAL — Nov. 19, 2003

STATE* RESIDENCE	NAME AND RANK	DATE OF RECOGNITION

STATE* RESIDENCE	NAME AND RANK	DATE OF RECOGNITION

	MR. HUGHLAND ST. CLAIR ALLMAN, CONSUL	Jun. 06, 1997
	MR. DAVID O. GIBBS, CONSUL	Feb. 21, 2003
	MR. PEARLIE AJASPAR DRAKES, CONSUL	Jul. 07, 2005
	MR. RICHARD ROBERT WILLIAMS, CONSUL	Jun. 19, 2007
	MR. COLTON S. CUMBERBATCH, VICE CONSUL	Mar. 29, 1994
	MR. JEAN PAUL DAVID CUMBERBATCH, VICE CONSUL	Jul. 26, 2001
	MS. CLAUDETTE VERONICA WALCOTT, VICE CONSUL	Sep. 04, 2002
	MR. RYAN G. BLACKETT, VICE CONSUL	Nov. 14, 2002
	MR. PETER MAYERS, VICE CONSUL	May. 04, 2007
	MS. NICOLE ELAINE GEORGE, VICE CONSUL	May. 08, 2007

OHIO

TOLEDO (HC) P.O. BOX 12177 UN., 43612.
(419) 476-5411, FAX (419) 476-5461

	DR. IAN D. MURPHY, HONORARY CONSUL	Sep. 29, 1983

OREGON

PORTLAND (HC) 10202 S.E. 32ND AV., SUITE 601, MILWAUKIE 97222.
(503) 659-0283

	MR. HAROLD DESMOND JOHNSON, HONORARY CONSUL	Feb. 10, 1982

TEXAS

SUGAR LAND (HC) 3027 SLEEPY HOLLOW DR., 77479.
(832) 725-5566

	DR. LOUIS A. BROWNE, HONORARY CONSUL	Aug. 05, 2004

BELARUS

DISTRICT OF COLUMBIA

WASHINGTON (CHN) 1619 NEW HAMPSHIRE AV., NW, 20009.
(202) 986-1604, FAX (202) 986-1805

	MR. ANDREI KOZHAN, CONSUL	Mar. 01, 2005
	MR. OLEG POPOV, VICE CONSUL	Feb. 21, 2006

NEW YORK

NEW YORK (CG) 708 3RD AV., SUITE 2101, 10017.
(212) 682-5392, FAX (212) 682-5491

	MR. NIKOLAI LEPESHKO, CONSUL GENERAL	May. 27, 2005
	MR. VIKTOR CHEREKHOVICH, VICE CONSUL	Jul. 28, 2005

BELGIUM

ALASKA

ANCHORAGE (HC) 1031 W. 4TH AV., SUITE 400, 99510-7502.
(907) 276-5617, FAX (907) 257-6394

	MR. CARL F. BRADY, HONORARY CONSUL	Feb. 05, 1991

ARIZONA

PHOENIX (HC) 2944 N. 44TH ST., SUITE 200, 85018.
(602) 852-3870, FAX (602) 852-3878

	MR. REGINALD WINSSINGER, HONORARY CONSUL	Dec. 09, 1991

CALIFORNIA

LOS ANGELES (CG) 6100 WILSHIRE BL., W, FLOOR 12TH, 90048.
(213) 857-1244

	MR. RONALD F. A. M. DE LANGHE, CONSUL GENERAL	Sep. 29, 2004
	MS. VERONIQUE C. R. MAROUNEK, CONSUL	Aug. 05, 2003
	MR. DIRK VERLEE, CONSULAR AGENT	Sep. 21, 2006

SAN DIEGO (HC) P.O. BOX 130051 ., CARLSBAD 92013-0051.
(619) 943-9121

	MR. PATRICK JOHN SEBRECHTS, HONORARY CONSUL	Aug. 02, 1990

SAN FRANCISCO (HC) 1663 MISSION ST., SUITE 400, 94103.
(415) 861-9910, FAX (415) 861-9801

	MRS. RITA M. BRAL, HONORARY CONSUL	Jan. 26, 1993

COLORADO

DENVER (HC) 1900 WAZEE ST., SUITE 202, 80202.
(303) 295-9703, FAX (303) 295-9701

	MR. FRANK J. SCHUCHAT, HONORARY CONSUL	Dec. 03, 1998
	MR. MICHEL ALBERT REYNDERS, HONORARY VICE CONSUL	Dec. 29, 1986

DISTRICT OF COLUMBIA

WASHINGTON (CHN) 3330 GARFIELD ST., NW, 20008.
(202) 333-6900, FAX (202) 333-3079

	AMBASSADOR DOMINICUS STRUYE DE SWIELANDE, CONSUL GENERAL	Mar. 23, 2007
	MR. LEO M. CORTENS, CONSUL	Jun. 30, 2003

FLORIDA

MIAMI (HC) 100 N. BISCAYNE BL., SUITE 500, 33132.
(305) 935-3762

	MR. MANUEL MOLINA, HONORARY CONSUL	Sep. 17, 2004

GEORGIA

ATLANTA (CG) 230 PEACHTREE ST., NE, SUITE 2710, 30303.
(404) 659-2150, FAX (404) 659-8474

	MR. JAN R. E. VERBEECK, CONSUL	Sep. 24, 2004

STATE* RESIDENCE	NAME AND RANK	DATE OF RECOGNITION

MR. LUDWIG S. M. VAN DEN BOSSCHE,   Nov. 16, 2006
  CONSULAR AGENT

HAWAII

HONOLULU (HC) 707 RICHARDS ST., SUITE 600, 96813.
(808) 535-1420
  MR. JEFFREY DANIEL LAU,   Nov. 16, 2000
    HONORARY CONSUL

ILLINOIS

CHICAGO (HC) 1713 W. BEACH AV., 60622.
(773) 342-6884
  MR. PAUL MICHEL VAN HALTEREN,   Oct. 21, 2004
    HONORARY CONSUL

MOLINE (HC) 4101 60TH ST., 61265.
(309) 743-1856, FAX (309) 736-9460
  MR. PATRICK A. VAN NEVEL,   May. 23, 2003
    HONORARY CONSUL

KANSAS

KANSAS CITY (HC) 2301 ARNO RD., PRAIRIE VILLAGE 66208.
(913) 362-5039
  MR. DAVID L. BARBER,   May. 23, 2003
    HONORARY CONSUL

KENTUCKY

LOUISVILLE (HC) 1009 S. 4TH ST., 40203.
(502) 584-8583, FAX (502) 584-1826
  MR. ALFRED JOHN WELSH,   Jun. 20, 1983
    HONORARY CONSUL

LOUISIANA

NEW ORLEANS (HC) 701 POYDRAS ST., SUITE 4500, 70139.
(504) 581-3234
  MR. ROLAND MANIL , JR VANDENWEGHE,   Apr. 10, 2002
    HONORARY CONSUL

MARYLAND

BALTIMORE (HC) 799 CROMWELL PARK DR., SUITE A, GLEN BURNIE
  21061.
(410) 863-0255, FAX (410) 863-1377
  MR. LOUIS G. CONNOR,   Mar. 23, 1994
    HONORARY CONSUL

MASSACHUSETTS

BOSTON (HC) 11 FOSTER ST., 02135.
(617) 779-8700, FAX (617) 770-7923
  MR. ALAN MARCELO MARCUSE,   Dec. 19, 2001
    HONORARY CONSUL

MICHIGAN

BLOOMFIELD HILLS (HC) 30 EDGEMERE RD., GROSSE POINTE
  FARMS 48236.
(313) 530-4436
  MR. DAVID PAUL CORNILLIE,   May. 27, 2003
    HONORARY CONSUL

MINNESOTA

ST. PAUL (HC) 238 S. MISSISSIPPI BL., SAINT PAUL 55105.
(651) 699-2528
  MRS. LYDIE JUSTINE STASSART,   May. 19, 2003
    HONORARY CONSUL

MISSOURI

SAINT LOUIS (HC) 3466 BRIDGELAND DR., BRIDGETON 63044.
(314) 770-2200
  MRS. MARIA LENA CANDRIES,   May. 27, 2003
    HONORARY CONSUL

NEW YORK

NEW YORK (CG) 1065 AVENUE OF THE AMERICAS ., FLOOR 22ND,
10018.
(212) 586-5110, FAX (212) 582-9657
  MRS. RENILDIS LOECKX,   Sep. 29, 2004
    CONSUL GENERAL
  MRS. GENEVIEVE M. VERBEEK,   Nov. 10, 2003
    CONSUL
  MRS. VERONIQUE EVAN PIERETTE SIKLOSI,   Oct. 01, 2004
    CONSUL
  MR. LUC M. LIPPENS,   Jan. 18, 1983
    CONSULAR AGENT
  MR. JURGEN MAERSCHAND,   Oct. 12, 2004
    CONSULAR AGENT
  MRS. EDITH MAYEUX,   Sep. 26, 2006
    CONSULAR AGENT

NEW YORK (HC) 41 CAUSEWAY UN., LAWRENCE 11559.
(516) 371-2323
  MR. ISRAEL SINGER,   Oct. 26, 2004
    HONORARY CONSUL

WALLONIA TRADE OFFICE
NEW YORK (U) 12 EAST 41ST ST., FLOOR 15TH, 10017.
(212) 684-0187

OHIO

CINCINNATI (HC) 312 WALNUT ST., SUITE 1400, 45202.
(513) 352-6627
  MR. PAUL ALLAER,   Jun. 19, 1997
    HONORARY CONSUL

OREGON

PORTLAND (HC) 1024 S.W. MYRTLE DR., 97201.
(503) 226-2121, FAX (503) 226-9636
  MR. JOHN H. HERMAN,   Jun. 16, 1994
    HONORARY CONSUL

PENNSYLVANIA

PHILADELPHIA (HC) 1701 MARKET ST., 19103.
(215) 963-5092
  MR. STEPHEN ANTHONY JANNETTA,   Apr. 19, 2007
    HONORARY CONSUL

PITTSBURGH (HC) 700 N. BELL AV., SUITE 290, 15106.
(412) 279-2121, FAX (412) 279-6429

STATE* RESIDENCE	NAME AND RANK	DATE OF RECOGNITION	STATE* RESIDENCE	NAME AND RANK	DATE OF RECOGNITION

MS. ANNE B. LACKNER, HONORARY CONSUL — Apr. 04, 1988

PUERTO RICO

SAN JUAN (HC) 14 CALLE SAN SEBASTIAN ., VIEJO SAN JUAN 00901.
(787) 883-2570, FAX (787) 883-3244

MR. MICHAEL SPECTOR, HONORARY CONSUL — Aug. 29, 2000

TEXAS

FORT WORTH (HC) 6201 SOUTH FW., 76134.
(817) 551-8389

DR. G. ANDRE BENS, HONORARY CONSUL — May. 27, 2003

HOUSTON (HC) 2009 LUBBOCK ST., 77007.
(713) 426-3933, FAX (713) 224-1120

MR. JACQUES E. BOUCHEZ, HONORARY CONSUL — May. 27, 2003

MS. CARINE L. LION, HONORARY VICE CONSUL — Apr. 18, 2005

SAN ANTONIO (HC) 106 S. ST. MARY ST., SUITE 200, 78205.
(210) 271-8820, FAX (210) 225-1951

MR. ROBERT P. BRAUBACH, HONORARY CONSUL — Jun. 12, 1991

UTAH

SALT LAKE CITY (HC) 1378 PERRYS HOLLOW DR., 84103.
(801) 240-6642, FAX (801) 240-3698

MR. CHARLES AMAN ANDRE DIDIER, HONORARY CONSUL — May. 16, 1986

VIRGINIA

NORFOLK (HC) 1023-K LASKIN RD., VIRGINIA BEACH 23451.
(757) 422-5571, FAX (757) 491-1845

MRS. MIA S. LANESE, HONORARY CONSUL — Jul. 16, 1987

WASHINGTON

SEATTLE (HC) 2200 ALASKAN WA., SUITE 470, 98121.
(206) 728-5145, FAX (206) 282-9544

MR. HERBERT RONALD MASNIK, HONORARY CONSUL — Dec. 21, 1981

WISCONSIN

MILWAUKEE (HC) 411 E. WISCONSIN AV., SUITE 1111, 53202.
(414) 272-8633, FAX (414) 223-5000

MR. CHARLES C. MULCAHY, HONORARY CONSUL — Feb. 06, 1986

BELIZE

CALIFORNIA

LOS ANGELES (CG) 4801 WILSHIRE BL., SUITE 250, 90010.
(323) 469-7343

MR. ROY G. YOUNG, CONSUL GENERAL — Mar. 16, 1999

MRS. IRENE WU, VICE CONSUL — Jul. 03, 2003

MR. PHILIP ANTHONY, JR BUCKNOR, HONORARY VICE CONSUL — Oct. 25, 2001

SAN FRANCISCO (HC) 916 KEARNY ST., 94133.
(415) 788-7500

MR. FRANCIS F. COPPOLA, HONORARY CONSUL — Mar. 09, 1993

DISTRICT OF COLUMBIA

WASHINGTON (CHN) 2535 MASSACHUSETTS AV., NW, 20008.
(202) 332-9636, FAX (202) 332-6888

MS. LAUREN LAVERNE QUIROS, CONSUL — Nov. 10, 1993

FLORIDA

MIAMI (HC) 4173 S. LE JEUNE RD., 33146.
(305) 666-1121

MS. STEPHANIE ABIGAIL SYLVESTRE, HONORARY CONSUL — Feb. 11, 1999

ILLINOIS

BELLEVILLE (HC) 1849 SPRUCE HILL DR., 62221.
(618) 235-7143, FAX (618) 235-7143

MR. EUGENE MICHAEL VERDU, HONORARY CONSUL — Oct. 02, 1995

CHICAGO (HC) 1200 HOWARD DR., WEST CHICAGO 60185.
(630) 293-0010, FAX (630) 293-0463

MR. EDWIN T. SMILING, HONORARY CONSUL — Feb. 04, 1992

LOUISIANA

NEW ORLEANS (HC) 39 BURLEIGH CT., N, MARRERO 70072.
(504) 347-6230

MRS. JEAN SMITH BENARD, HONORARY CONSUL — Dec. 08, 1998

MICHIGAN

DETROIT (HC) 24984 GLEN ORCHARD DR., FARMINGTON HILLS 48336-1732.
(810) 477-8768

DR. LENNOX A. PIKE, HONORARY CONSUL — May. 10, 1991

NEVADA

LAS VEGAS (HC) 4300 RIDGECREST DR., 89121.
(702) 451-8444

SIR LONNIE LEE , MD HAMMARGREN, HONORARY CONSUL — Aug. 27, 2002

NORTH CAROLINA

WILMINGTON (HC) 1213 CULBRETH DR., 28405.
(910) 509-7161

STATE* RESIDENCE	NAME AND RANK	DATE OF RECOGNITION

DR. EDWARD LEE , JR PAUL,
HONORARY CONSUL — Jun. 16, 2005

OHIO

DAYTON (HC) 130 W. SECOND ST., SUITE 1818, 45402.
(937) 226-1212, FAX (937) 226-1224
MS. KAREN DENISE BRADLEY,
HONORARY CONSUL — Mar. 28, 2001

PUERTO RICO

SAN JUAN (HCG) 567 RAMON GANDIA ST., HATO REY 00918.
(809) 766-7709, FAX (809) 764-2087
MR. WILLIAM VINCENT BURN,
HONORARY CONSUL GENERAL — Jul. 31, 2000

TEXAS

DALLAS (HC) 1315 19TH ST., SUITE 2A, PLANO 75074.
(214) 579-0070
MR. ARTHUR C., JR. ELLIS,
HONORARY CONSUL — Oct. 04, 1994

HOUSTON (HCG) 7101 BREEN ., 77086.
(713) 999-4484
MR. HUGH D. MCCAIN,
HONORARY CONSUL GENERAL — Sep. 17, 1997

BENIN

CALIFORNIA

LOS ANGELES (HC) 9111 S. LA CIENEGA BL., SUITE 204,
INGLEWOOD 90301.
(310) 641-3688
MR. MERVYN M. DYMALLY,
HONORARY CONSUL — Nov. 23, 1993

BHUTAN

DISTRICT OF COLUMBIA

WASHINGTON (HC) 4426 VOLTA PL., NW, 20007.
(202) 841-8656
DR. BRUCE WALTER BUNTING,
HONORARY CONSUL — Jan. 11, 2006

NEW YORK

NEW YORK (CG) 2 UN PZ., FLOOR 27TH, 10017.
(212) 826-1919
MR. SANGYE RINCHHEN,
CONSUL GENERAL — Jul. 18, 2006

BOLIVIA

ALABAMA

MOBILE (HC) 3413 CANACEE DR., 36693.
(334) 666-6969, FAX (334) 661-2873
MR. THOMAS PURVIS,
HONORARY CONSUL — Mar. 25, 1998

CALIFORNIA

CONSULATE GENERAL
LOS ANGELES (CG) 3701 WILSHIRE BL., SUITE 1065, 90010.
(213) 388-0475, FAX (213) 384-6272
MS. ROXANA W. OLLER CATOIRA,
CONSUL — Jun. 21, 2005
MS. ROCIO JOSEFA ZEBALLOS SALMON,
CONSULAR AGENT — Feb. 21, 2007

SAN FRANCISCO (CG) 870 MARKET ST., SUITE 575, 94102.
(415) 495-5173, FAX (415) 399-8958

DISTRICT OF COLUMBIA

WASHINGTON (CHN) 3014 MASSACHUSETTS AV., NW, 20008.
(202) 483-4410, FAX (202) 328-3712
MR. OSWALDO CUEVAS GAETE,
CONSUL GENERAL — Jun. 28, 2004

WASHINGTON (HCG) 4339 GARFIELD ST., NW, 20008.
(202) 244-7648
MR. WILLIAM R. JOYCE,
HONORARY CONSUL GENERAL — Jul. 10, 1973

CHANCERY ANNEX
WASHINGTON (CHA) 4420 CONNECTICUT AV., SUITE 250, 20037.
(202) 232-4828
MR. RENE EFRAIN VERDUGUEZ LINARES,
VICE CONSUL — Aug. 06, 2007

CONSULATE OF BOLIVIA
WASHINGTON (CHA) 1819 H ST., NW, SUITE 240, 20006.
(202) 232-4828, FAX (202) 232-8017
MRS. KELLY ARDAYA DE LOPEZ,
VICE CONSUL — Apr. 29, 2005

FLORIDA

MIAMI (CG) 1101 BRICKELL AV., SUITE 1103, 33131.
(305) 670-0710, FAX (305) 358-6305
MR. JAVIER RAMIRO CUSICANQUI FORTUN,
CONSUL GENERAL — Jun. 13, 2007
MISS MARIA ISABEL CARRASCO DE MAUBRAS,
CONSUL — Mar. 08, 2004

GEORGIA

ATLANTA (HCG) 1401 PEACHTREE ST., NE, SUITE 240, 30309.
(404) 522-0777, FAX (404) 873-3335
MR. S. GEORGE HANDELSMAN,
HONORARY CONSUL GENERAL — Jul. 09, 1996

ILLINOIS

CHICAGO (HC) 1111 W. SUPERIOR ST., SUITE 309, MELROSE PARK
60160.
(708) 343-1234, FAX (708) 343-4290
MR. JAIME ESCOBAR,
HONORARY CONSUL — Jul. 15, 1986
MR. JUAN CARLOS , III BOSACOMA,
HONORARY VICE CONSUL — May. 30, 2006

STATE* RESIDENCE	NAME AND RANK	DATE OF RECOGNITION	STATE* RESIDENCE	NAME AND RANK	DATE OF RECOGNITION

BOSNIA AND HERZEGOVINA

MASSACHUSETTS

BOSTON (HCG) 85 DEVONSHIRE ST., SUITE 1000, 02109.
(617) 742-1500, FAX (617) 742-9130
    MR. RUSSELL D. LEBLANG,   Aug. 07, 1996
        HONORARY CONSUL GENERAL

MINNESOTA

MAPLE GROVE (HC) 18036 65TH AV., N, 55311.
(763) 478-9495, FAX (763) 478-6631
    MRS. GLORIA STEINE,   May. 06, 1997
        HONORARY CONSUL

NEW YORK

NEW YORK (CG) 211 E. 43RD ST., SUITE 702, 10017.
(212) 687-0530, FAX (212) 687-0532
    MR. JORGE EDMUNDO HEREDIA CAVERO,   Apr. 16, 2004
        CONSUL GENERAL
    MRS. TERESA PINTO ROMAN VDA DE CASAP,   Nov. 19, 2003
        CONSUL
    MS. ANA DEL ROSARIO DURAN RUIZ,   Aug. 15, 2005
        CONSUL
    MRS. GEOVANNIA MELGAR DE ROMAN,   Oct. 27, 2003
        CONSULAR AGENT
    MS. DEISY QUISBERT FLORES,   Mar. 06, 2007
        CONSULAR AGENT

OKLAHOMA

OKLAHOMA CITY (HC) 210 PARK AV., 73102.
(405) 239-7900, FAX (405) 235-5852
    MR. JOE RAY SIMON,   Sep. 08, 2000
        HONORARY CONSUL

PUERTO RICO

SAN JUAN (HC) 1409 CALLE LUNCHETTI UN., 00907.
(787) 722-5449, FAX (787) 722-8457
    MR. HUGH ALANSON ANDREWS,   Jun. 15, 1999
        HONORARY CONSUL

TEXAS

DALLAS (HC) 1881 SYLVAN AV., SUITE 110, 75208.
(214) 571-6131
    MS. MARIA URIOSTE,   Jun. 30, 1997
        HONORARY CONSUL

HOUSTON (HCG) 800 WILCREST UN., SUITE 100, 77042.
(713) 977-2344, FAX (713) 977-2362
    MRS. DIANA GALINDO DE WALKER,   Feb. 29, 2000
        HONORARY CONSUL GENERAL
    MR. JUAN JOSE FRIAS,   Aug. 14, 2003
        HONORARY CONSUL
    MS. MARILYN HARRIS BAUTISTA,   Aug. 14, 2003
        HONORARY VICE CONSUL

WASHINGTON

SEATTLE (HC) 15215 52ND AV., SUITE 100, 98188.
(206) 244-6696, FAX (206) 243-3795
    MR. RENE RICARDO ANTEZANA MONTANO,   Dec. 21, 1970
        HONORARY CONSUL

DISTRICT OF COLUMBIA

WASHINGTON (CHN) 2109 E ST., NW, 20037.
(202) 337-1500, FAX (202) 337-1502
    MR. SVETOZAR MILETIC,   Jan. 17, 2007
        CONSUL GENERAL

ILLINOIS

CHICAGO (CG) 737 N. MICHIGAN AV., SUITE 820, 60611.
(312) 951-1245, FAX (312) 951-1043
    MS. FILOMENA NIKOLIC,   Jan. 21, 2005
        CONSUL GENERAL
    MRS. ALMIJANA RUDIC,   Mar. 03, 2006
        CONSUL
    MR. MARINKO AVRAMOVIC,   Jan. 21, 2005
        VICE CONSUL

NEW YORK

NEW YORK (CG) 866 UN PLAZA ., SUITE 580, 10017.
(212) 751-9018, FAX (212) 751-9135

BOTSWANA

CALIFORNIA

LOS ANGELES (HC) 355 S. GRAND AV., SUITE 4000, 90071.
(213) 626-8484
    MR. WILLIAM BARNUM RUDELL,   Oct. 30, 1970
        HONORARY CONSUL

SAN FRANCISCO (HC) 2333 OCTAVIA ST., 94109.
(415) 885-2733
    MR. CHARLES L. FRANKEL,   Apr. 02, 2003
        HONORARY CONSUL

GEORGIA

ATLANTA (HCG) 5580 QUEENSBOROUGH DR., NE, 30338.
(770) 394-3303
    MS. JENNIFER CECILIA JENKINS,   Nov. 23, 2005
        HONORARY CONSUL

TEXAS

HOUSTON (HC) 10000 MEMORIAL DR., SUITE 400, 77024.
(713) 680-1155, FAX (713) 680-8055
    MR. STEPHEN V. VALLONE,   Jan. 18, 1983
        HONORARY CONSUL

BRAZIL

ALABAMA

BIRMINGHAM (HC) 1901 6TH AV., N, SUITE 2900, 35203.
(205) 214-7321
    MR. MICHAEL HUGH JOHNSON,   Jul. 08, 1996
        HONORARY CONSUL

ARIZONA

SCOTTSDALE (HC) 9721 E. DESERT COVE AV., 85260.
(480) 767-7639
    MR. BRAD BRADOS,   Nov. 10, 2003
        HONORARY CONSUL

STATE* RESIDENCE	NAME AND RANK	DATE OF RECOGNITION

CALIFORNIA

LOS ANGELES (CG) 8484 WILSHIRE BL., SUITE 730,711,74, BEVERLY HILLS 90211.
(323) 651-2664, FAX (323) 651-1274

MRS. THEREZA MARIA MACHADO QUINTELLA, CONSUL GENERAL	Apr. 08, 2005
MR. HENRIQUE LUIZ JENNE, DEPUTY CONSUL GENERAL	Mar. 03, 2006
MR. AFFONSO JOSE SANTOS, DEPUTY CONSUL GENERAL	Apr. 30, 2007
MR. JULIO VICTOR DO ESPIRITO SANTO, DEPUTY CONSUL	Apr. 30, 2007
MR. ANTONIO PEREIRA, VICE CONSUL	Feb. 07, 2007

SAN DIEGO (HC) 2380 CAMINITO AGRADO ., 92107.
(619) 224-1145

MR. NELSON PEREIRA, HONORARY CONSUL	Dec. 11, 1997

SAN FRANCISCO (CG) 300 MONTGOMERY ST., SUITE 900, 94104.
(415) 981-8170, FAX (415) 981-4931

MR. MAURICIO EDUARDO CORTES COSTA, CONSUL GENERAL	Apr. 06, 2007
MRS. MARCIA LOUREIRO, DEPUTY CONSUL GENERAL	Apr. 06, 2007
MR. MIGUEL MAGALHAES, DEPUTY CONSUL GENERAL	May. 04, 2007
MRS. SUZANNE REGINA SILVA, VICE CONSUL	Jun. 16, 2005
MRS. ELIZABETE GONCALVES DO AMARAL, VICE CONSUL	May. 31, 2007

DISTRICT OF COLUMBIA

WASHINGTON (CHN) 3006 MASSACHUSETTS AV., NW, 20008.
(202) 238-2700, FAX (202) 238-2827

MRS. MARIA LUIZA RIBEIRO LOPES SILVA, CONSUL	Jun. 14, 2007
MR. FRANCISCO CAVALCANTI, VICE CONSUL	Jan. 08, 2003
MS. MARCIA MOREIRA, VICE CONSUL	Sep. 07, 2005
MRS. URSULA REY GONZALEZ ZALUAR, VICE CONSUL	Oct. 10, 2006
MR. LUIZ ALBERTO DE MIRANDA MENDES, VICE CONSUL	Jun. 14, 2007

FLORIDA

MIAMI (CG) 80 S.W. 8TH ST., FLOOR 26TH, 33133.
(305) 285-6200, FAX (305) 285-6229

MR. JOAO ALMINO DE SOUZA FILHO, CONSUL GENERAL	Sep. 09, 2004
MR. LUIZ FELIPE MENDONCA FILHO, DEPUTY CONSUL GENERAL	Mar. 09, 2005
MR. JOAO ZICCARDI NAVAJAS, DEPUTY CONSUL GENERAL	May. 24, 2005
MR. RAFAEL DE MELLO VIDAL, DEPUTY CONSUL GENERAL	Jul. 07, 2005
MRS. LEONILDA BEATRIZ CAMPOS G CORREA, DEPUTY CONSUL GENERAL	Mar. 15, 2006
MR. ADALNIO SENNA GANEM, DEPUTY CONSUL GENERAL	May. 04, 2007
MR. HERVELTER DE MATTOS, DEPUTY CONSUL	Nov. 07, 2003

MR. ARTUR JOSE SARAIVA DE OLIVEIRA, DEPUTY CONSUL	Mar. 07, 2005
MR. ROBERTO PARENTE, DEPUTY CONSUL	Apr. 30, 2007
MRS. IEDA MARIA AFFONSO SANTIAGO DIAS, VICE CONSUL	Jun. 17, 2005
MR. CESAR SGUARIO AREVALO, VICE CONSUL	May. 19, 2006
MRS. ANAMARIA NOBREGA FERNANDES, VICE CONSUL	Apr. 04, 2007
MRS. LOURDES D. GUIMARAES, CONSULAR AGENT	Dec. 30, 2005
MRS. MARIA A. BENVENUTO DA SILVA, CONSULAR AGENT	May. 18, 2006
MR. ALBERTO DE LIMA, CONSULAR AGENT	Apr. 03, 2007
MRS. HERCY T. MARTINS DOS SANTOS, CONSULAR AGENT	Apr. 04, 2007

GEORGIA

ATLANTA (HC) 1201 W. PEACHTREE ST., 30309.
(404) 881-7987

MR. TIMOTHY SEWELL PERRY, HONORARY CONSUL	Jul. 14, 2000

SAVANNAH (HC) 107 PROSPERITY DR., 31408.
(912) 964-0711, FAX (912) 964-0771

MR. JAMES MYRICK, HONORARY CONSUL	Dec. 03, 1998

HAWAII

HONOLULU (HC) 345 QUEEN ST., SUITE 400, 96813.
(808) 235-0571

MR. ERIC GUIMARAES CRISPIN, HONORARY CONSUL	Jan. 08, 2001

ILLINOIS

CHICAGO (CG) 401 N. MICHIGAN AV., SUITE 1850, 60611.
(312) 464-0244, FAX (312) 464-0299

MR. RICARDO LUIZ VIANA DE CARVALHO, CONSUL GENERAL	Oct. 06, 2005
MR. JOSE MARIA DE CARVALHO COELHO, DEPUTY CONSUL	Nov. 04, 2005
MR. PEDRO HENRIQUE EDUARDO MAGALHAES, DEPUTY CONSUL	May. 04, 2007
MR. JR., NELSON DA COSTA ESTEVES, VICE CONSUL	Oct. 26, 2004

KENTUCKY

COVINGTON (HC) 100 E. RIVERCENTER BL., SUITE 1100, 41011.
(859) 292-5505

MR. JAMES WILLIAM , III BLACKHAM, HONORARY CONSUL	Mar. 25, 2004

LOUISIANA

NEW ORLEANS (HC) 365 CANAL ST., SUITE 1600, 70130.
(504) 561-6206

MR. DAVID PAUL SCHULINGKAMP, HONORARY CONSUL	Nov. 10, 2003

STATE* RESIDENCE	NAME AND RANK	DATE OF RECOGNITION	STATE* RESIDENCE	NAME AND RANK	DATE OF RECOGNITION

MASSACHUSETTS

BOSTON (CG) 20 PARK PZ., SUITE 1420, 02116.
(617) 542-4000, FAX (617) 542-4318

MR. MARIO ERNANI SAADE, CONSUL GENERAL	Jan. 16, 2007	
MR. PAULO FERNANDO TELLES RIBEIRO, DEPUTY CONSUL GENERAL	Jun. 24, 2004	
MR. ANDRE BAKER MEIO, DEPUTY CONSUL	Jul. 23, 0004	
MR. RODOLFO BRAGA, DEPUTY CONSUL	Sep. 26, 2006	
MR. FRANCISCO DACIO BALBINO, VICE CONSUL	May. 07, 2004	
MS. PAULA DE VASCONCELLOS ROCHA, VICE CONSUL	Jul. 07, 2005	
MS. LUCILA MARIA RODRIGUES ESTEVES, VICE CONSUL	Jan. 26, 2006	
MS. CARLA MANZO, VICE CONSUL	Mar. 15, 2006	
MRS. MARCIA MARIA MENEZES SAADE, VICE CONSUL	Apr. 23, 2007	

BRAZILIAN AIR FORCE OFFICE
BOSTON (CONA) 20 PARK PLAZA ., SUITE 1420, 02116.
(617) 542-4000

NEW YORK

NEW YORK (CG) 1185 AVENUE OF AMERICAS UN., FLOOR 21ST, 10036.
(917) 777-7777, FAX (212) 827-0225

MR. JOSE ALFREDO GRACA LIMA, CONSUL GENERAL	Jan. 06, 2006
MR. CLAUDIO FREDERICO ARRUDA, DEPUTY CONSUL GENERAL	Apr. 05, 2004
MR. LUIS ANTONIO SILOS, DEPUTY CONSUL GENERAL	Jul. 31, 2006
MR. MARCELO RAMOS ARAUJO, DEPUTY CONSUL	Jul. 24, 2006
MR. DAVINO RIBEIRO DE SENA, DEPUTY CONSUL	Aug. 09, 2006
MR. DARIO V. CAMPOS, VICE CONSUL	Oct. 08, 1997
MS. FLAVIA XAVIER RIBEIRO, VICE CONSUL	May. 21, 2004
MS. ANDRESSA AGOSTINI CARVALHO, VICE CONSUL	Mar. 18, 2005
MR. FRANCISCO CARLOS LEAL, VICE CONSUL	Jul. 29, 2005
MR. EWERTON OLIVEIRA, VICE CONSUL	Jan. 31, 2006

OFFICE OF FINANCIAL COUNSELOR
NEW YORK (CONA) 565 5TH AV., FLOOR 17TH, 10017.
(212) 489-7930

MRS. MARIANA MOSCARDO, DEPUTY CONSUL	Jun. 01, 2000
MR. GILBERTO C. PARANHOS VELLOSO, DEPUTY CONSUL	Jun. 27, 2002
MR. CLAUDIO JOSE DE CAMPOS, DEPUTY CONSUL	Oct. 12, 2006
MR. JOSE BORGES DOS SANTOS JUNIOR, DEPUTY CONSUL	Apr. 30, 2007

TENNESSEE

MEMPHIS (HC) 1256 N. MCLEAN BL., 38108.
(901) 272-6505

MR. EDSON P. PEREDO, HONORARY CONSUL	Aug. 12, 1998

TEXAS

HOUSTON (CG) 1233 WEST LOOP ., S, SUITE 1150, 77027.
(713) 961-3063, FAX (713) 961-3070

MR. CARLOS ALBERTO AZEVEDO PIMENTEL, CONSUL GENERAL	Sep. 24, 2003
MR. MILTON TORRES SILVA, DEPUTY CONSUL GENERAL	Apr. 25, 2003
MRS. MARIA A. DE GOIS FERNANDES WEISS, DEPUTY CONSUL GENERAL	May. 18, 2006
MR. PAULO VASSILY CHUC, DEPUTY CONSUL	Aug. 14, 2006
MS. CARMEN CASTILHO ALONSO, VICE CONSUL	May. 12, 2003
MR. LUCIANO NASCIMENTO DE OLIVEIRA, VICE CONSUL	Nov. 10, 2003
MS. SELMA TELES DE MORAES, VICE CONSUL	Apr. 07, 2004
MR. CLAUDIO TEIXEIRA, VICE CONSUL	Dec. 13, 2006
MR. CYRO ESPIRITO SANTO CARDOSO NETO, VICE CONSUL	Feb. 07, 2007

TRUST TERRITORIES OF THE PACIFIC ISLANDS

HONG KONG (CG) 11 DUDDELL ST., 00000.
(852) 525-7002

UTAH

SALT LAKE CITY (HC) 30 E. 100TH UN., S, SUITE 950, 84111.
(801) 363-4936

MR. GARY JOHN NEELEMAN, HONORARY CONSUL	Sep. 10, 2003

VIRGINIA

NORFOLK (HC) 500 PLUME ST., E, SUITE 600, 23510.
(757) 627-6286

MR. THOMAS PARKER, III HOST, HONORARY CONSUL	Jul. 23, 2007

BULGARIA

CALIFORNIA

LOS ANGELES (CG) 11766 WILSHIRE BL., SUITE 440, 90025.

MR. IVO GUEORGUIEV MOUSKOUROV, CONSUL GENERAL	Oct. 17, 2005
MRS. ALEXANDRINA EVUGUENIEVA GUIGOVA, CONSUL	Mar. 15, 2006

SACRAMENTO (HCG) 917 7TH ST., FLOOR 2ND, 95814.
(916) 447-9827

MR. BROOKS D. OHLSON, HONORARY CONSUL GENERAL	Aug. 11, 2004

DISTRICT OF COLUMBIA

WASHINGTON (CHN) 1621 22ND ST., NW, 20008.
(202) 387-0174, FAX (202) 234-7973

---

* DEPENDENCIES SUCH AS GUAM, PUERTO RICO, AND THE VIRGIN ISLANDS ARE LISTED HERE.
CG-CONSULATE GENERAL   C-CONSULATE   VC-VICE CONSULATE   CA-CONSULAR AGENCY   H-HONORARY CONSULAR STATUS

STATE* RESIDENCE	NAME AND RANK	DATE OF RECOGNITION	STATE* RESIDENCE	NAME AND RANK	DATE OF RECOGNITION

MR. ROSSEN HRISTOV GENCHEV, — Jul. 18, 2006
  CONSUL

FLORIDA

BOCA RATON (HC) 2000 GLADES RD., SUITE 110, 33431.
(561) 750-1800
  MR. STEPHEN FRANKLIN BEINER, — Jun. 23, 2005
    HONORARY CONSUL

ILLINOIS

CHICAGO (CG) 737 N. MICHIGAN AV., SUITE 2105, 60611.
(312) 867-1901, FAX (312) 867-1906
  MR. IVAN IORDANOV SOTIROV, — Oct. 17, 2005
    CONSUL GENERAL
  MR. ALEXANDER M. PEYTCHEV, — Jul. 11, 2006
    CONSUL

MARYLAND

BALTIMORE (HC) 20 S. CHARLES ST., SUITE 304, 21201.
(301) 651-9605
  DR. ROBERT SCOTT TARGAN, — Mar. 31, 2005
    HONORARY CONSUL

MASSACHUSETTS

BOSTON (HC) 101 FEDERAL ST., FLOOR 30, 02110.
(617) 646-2000
  MR. FRANK JOSEPH BAILEY, — Sep. 01, 2006
    HONORARY CONSUL

NEVADA

LAS VEGAS (HC) 3773 S. HOWARD HUGHES PW., FLOOR 3, 89109.
(702) 862-2953
  MR. ROBERT JOSEPH MILLER, — Feb. 22, 2005
    HONORARY CONSUL

NEW YORK

NEW YORK (CG) 121 E. 62ND ST., 10021.
(212) 935-4646
  MR. NIKOLAY MILKOV MILKOV, — Oct. 04, 2005
    CONSUL GENERAL
  MRS. NATALIYA EVGENIEVA UZUNOVA, — Nov. 04, 2005
    CONSUL
  MR. VALENTIN STOYANOV STOEV, — Apr. 20, 2005
    VICE CONSUL
  MS. VANYA ILIYANOVA ILIEVA, — Mar. 03, 2006
    VICE CONSUL
  MS. VICTORIA ELLEN SCHONFELD, — Feb. 24, 2004
    HONORARY CONSUL

PENNSYLVANIA

MEDIA (HC) 201 W. FRONT ST., 19063.
(610) 565-9191
  MR. STEPHEN JOSEPH , JR MC EWEN, — Jun. 29, 2004
    HONORARY CONSUL

BURKINA FASO

CALIFORNIA

LOS ANGELES (HCG) 214 23RD ST., SANTA MONICA 90402.
(310) 393-2531, FAX (310) 393-0181
  MR. ALLEN I. NEIMAN, — Aug. 20, 1980
    HONORARY CONSUL GENERAL

LOUISIANA

NEW ORLEANS (HC) 1527 ROBERT E. LEE BL., 70112.
(504) 284-6351
  MR. JOHN WILLIAM ORMOND, — Oct. 04, 1968
    HONORARY CONSUL

BURMA

NEW YORK

NEW YORK (CG) 10 E. 77TH ST., 10021.
(212) 535-1310, FAX (212) 737-2421

BURUNDI

CALIFORNIA

LOS ANGELES (HC) 8318 WILSHIRE BL., BEVERLY HILLS 90211.
(310) 274-2793
  DR. NIGISTI AZEBE TESFAI, — Aug. 02, 1999
    HONORARY CONSUL

CAMBODIA

WASHINGTON

SEATTLE (HC) 1818 WESTLAKE AV., N, SUITE 315, 98109.
(206) 217-0830
  MR. DARAVUTH HUOTH, — Mar. 02, 2001
    HONORARY CONSUL

CAMEROON

CALIFORNIA

SAN FRANCISCO (HC) 147 TERRA VISTA ., 94115.
(415) 921-5372
  MR. DONALD LOW, — Apr. 18, 1986
    HONORARY CONSUL

TEXAS

HOUSTON (HC) 1319 GAMMA ., CROSBY 77532.
(713) 499-3502
  MR. CHARLES R. GREENE, — Apr. 18, 1986
    HONORARY CONSUL

CANADA

ALASKA

ANCHORAGE (CON) 310 K ST., SUITE 220, 99501.
(907) 264-6733
  MS. KAREN JOAN ARIEL MATTHIAS, — Oct. 05, 2004
    CONSUL

ARIZONA

PHOENIX (CG) 2415 E. CAMELBACK RD., SUITE 700, 85016.
(602) 508-3573

STATE* RESIDENCE	NAME AND RANK	DATE OF RECOGNITION	STATE* RESIDENCE	NAME AND RANK	DATE OF RECOGNITION
	MR. GORDON DOUGLAS PATERSON, CONSUL	Jan. 25, 2005	**COLORADO**		
			DENVER (CG) 1625 BROADWAY ST., SUITE 2600, 80202. (303) 626-0640		
CONSULATE TUCSON (CON) 1840 E. RIVER RD., SUITE 200, 85718.	MR. RICHARD J. STEPHENSON, CONSUL	Mar. 17, 2006		MR. MICHAEL AARON FINE, CONSUL GENERAL	Oct. 19, 2004
				MR. MARC BOUCHER, CONSUL	Oct. 19, 2004
CALIFORNIA				MS. MONICA JANET HERON, CONSUL	Nov. 08, 2005
LOS ANGELES (CG) 550 S. HOPE ST., SUITE 900, 90071. (213) 346-2700				MR. ANDREW FRANKLIN RAYBURN, CONSUL	Sep. 27, 2006
	MR. ALAIN DUDOIT, CONSUL GENERAL	Sep. 29, 2004		MS. KIM ONEIL, CONSUL	Sep. 27, 2006
	MR. JAMES FEIR, DEPUTY CONSUL GENERAL	Oct. 17, 2005		MS. SHELLEY ELIZABETH WHITING, CONSUL	Nov. 17, 2006
	MS. JENNIFER PRICE, CONSUL	Jul. 10, 2002		MR. PHILIPPE TAILLON, VICE CONSUL	Sep. 27, 2006
	MR. SYED ZULFIQUER SADEQUE, CONSUL	Aug. 14, 2003			
	MR. GERALD EARL LISK, CONSUL	Sep. 15, 2004	**DISTRICT OF COLUMBIA**		
	MR. JOHN JONG CHAN CHOI, CONSUL	Sep. 15, 2004	WASHINGTON (CHN) 501 PENNSYLVANIA AV., NW, 20001. (202) 682-1740, FAX (202) 682-7726		
	MR. DAVID WILLIAM LUPUL, CONSUL	Sep. 23, 2004		MRS. MARGERY ELAINE LANDERYOU, CONSUL GENERAL	Oct. 23, 2006
	MRS. MYRA PASTYR LUPUL, CONSUL	Sep. 23, 2004		MS. B. JILL MORRELL, CONSUL	Oct. 23, 2006
	MR. CHRISTOPHER JOHN VEENSTRA, CONSUL	Oct. 11, 2005		MRS. ANNE CATHERINE PETERS, CONSUL	Jul. 13, 2007
	MR. ERIC HOLDRINET, CONSUL	Nov. 08, 2005			
	MR. JOHN DONALD ROSE, CONSUL	Nov. 08, 2005	**FLORIDA**		
	MR. MAURICE YVES BERNIER, CONSUL	Nov. 08, 2005	MIAMI (CG) 200 S. BISCAYNE BL., SUITE 1600, 33131. (305) 579-1600		
	MS. CHANTAL GORDON RAMSAY, CONSUL	Apr. 27, 2006		MRS. MARCY L. GROSSMAN, CONSUL GENERAL	Oct. 05, 2005
	MR. CARL BEVAN HARTILL, CONSUL	May. 04, 2007		MRS. HELENE FOREST, CONSUL	Jun. 24, 2004
				MRS. MARIE JOSEE DUBE, CONSUL	Sep. 07, 2004
CONSULATE GENERAL SAN DIEGO (CG) 402 W. BROADWAY UN., FLOOR 4, 92101. (619) 615-4286				MR. REX EARL BRASNETT, CONSUL	Aug. 22, 2006
	MR. SUNIL SHARMA, CONSUL	Sep. 10, 2004		MR. OLIVIER JACQUES, CONSUL	Sep. 27, 2006
	MR. SEAN DAVID BARR, CONSUL	Nov. 03, 2005		MR. RICHARD STEINBURG, CONSUL	Sep. 27, 2006
				MR. BRIAN ROBERT PAUL MOREAU, CONSUL	May. 07, 2007
SAN FRANCISCO (CG) 580 CALIFORNIA ST., FLOOR 14TH, 94104. (415) 834-3180				MR. JAN STEFAN SCAZIGHINO, CONSUL	Aug. 01, 2007
	MR. MARC AUGUSTE JOSEPH LEPAGE, CONSUL GENERAL	Oct. 06, 2005			
	MRS. BARBARA TERESA GIACOMIN, CONSUL	Nov. 08, 2005	TAMPA (HC) 101 E. KENNEDY BL., SUITE 2000, 33602. (813) 229-2111		
	MS. STEFANIE MCCOLLUM, CONSUL	Jan. 23, 2006		MR. ANDREW LOCHLAN MCINTOSH, HONORARY CONSUL	Oct. 14, 2005
	MR. TRISTAN EMMANUEL LANDRY, CONSUL	Mar. 16, 2006			
			GEORGIA		
SAN JOSE (CON) 333 W. SAN CARLOS ST., SUITE 945, 95110. (408) 289-1157			ATLANTA (CG) 1175 PEACHTREE ST., SUITE 1700, 30361. (404) 532-2000		
	MR. ANDREW JOHN KEENAN, CONSUL	Oct. 29, 2003		MR. GEORGE BRIAN OAK, CONSUL GENERAL	Mar. 02, 2006
				MR. STEVEN J. GAWRELETZ, DEPUTY CONSUL GENERAL	Aug. 10, 2006

STATE* RESIDENCE	NAME AND RANK	DATE OF RECOGNITION	STATE* RESIDENCE	NAME AND RANK	DATE OF RECOGNITION

MS. CHRISTINE LYNN PAPPAS,
CONSUL — May. 26, 2005

MR. RICHARD ANTHONY CLEGG,
CONSUL — Sep. 27, 2006

ILLINOIS

CHICAGO (CG) 180 N. STETSON AV., SUITE 2400, 60601.
(312) 616-1860

MR. GEORGES LOUIS RIOUX,
CONSUL GENERAL — Sep. 26, 2006

MR. PAUL MAURICE EGAN,
DEPUTY CONSUL GENERAL — Oct. 17, 2005

MR. JAMES O'NEIL LYNCH,
CONSUL — Oct. 20, 2003

IOWA

MUSCATINE (HCG) 301 IOWA AV., SUITE 400, 52761.
(563) 264-5000

MR. ROGER LEE LANDE,
HONORARY CONSUL GENERAL — Sep. 28, 2006

LOUISIANA

NEW ORLEANS (HC) 210 BARONNE ST., SUITE 1108, 70112.
(504) 561-1191

MRS. PATRICIA DENECHAUD,
HONORARY CONSUL — Mar. 03, 2004

MAINE

PORTLAND (HC) 1 CANAL PZ., FLOOR 10, 04101.
(207) 775-1547

MR. PERRY BART NEWMAN,
HONORARY CONSUL — Mar. 03, 2004

MASSACHUSETTS

BOSTON (CG) 3 COPLEY PL., SUITE 400, 02116.
(617) 262-3760

MR. NEIL JOSEPH LEBLANC,
CONSUL GENERAL — Sep. 07, 2006

MR. MICHEL CHARLES TETU,
DEPUTY CONSUL GENERAL — Sep. 10, 2004

MS. MARIE-LOUISE HANNAN,
DEPUTY CONSUL GENERAL — Oct. 12, 2005

MR. STEPHEN GODDARD,
CONSUL — Oct. 01, 2004

MR. JACQUES RUEL,
CONSUL — Apr. 22, 2005

MRS. PATRICIA FORTIER,
CONSUL — Dec. 16, 2005

MR. NEAL BURNHAM,
CONSUL — Sep. 27, 2006

MICHIGAN

DETROIT (CG) 600 RENAISSANCE CTR. ., SUITE 1100,R650, 48243-1798.
(313) 567-2340

MR. ROBERT B. NOBLE,
CONSUL GENERAL — Jan. 25, 2007

MR. DOUGLAS R. BINGEMAN,
CONSUL — Sep. 19, 2002

MR. RAYMOND M. GABIN,
CONSUL — Oct. 06, 2005

MS. GIOSEPPINA PARROTTA MARCK,
CONSUL — Nov. 08, 2005

MS. JULI SYMATA STONEBERG,
VICE CONSUL — Mar. 15, 2007

MINNESOTA

MINNEAPOLIS (CG) 701 4TH AV., S, FLOOR 9TH, 55415.
(612) 333-4641

MR. KIM PERRY BUTLER,
CONSUL GENERAL — Sep. 14, 2004

MR. RICHARD WARREN ULRICH,
CONSUL — Sep. 14, 2004

MR. MURRAY S. HARDIE,
CONSUL — Oct. 01, 2004

MR. RICCARDO SAVONE,
CONSUL — Nov. 08, 2005

MR. ROBERT W. TREMAYNE PENGELLY,
CONSUL — Nov. 08, 2005

MR. ANDREW ALFRED MELNYK,
CONSUL — May. 09, 2007

MISSOURI

SAINT LOUIS (HCG) 12555 MANCHESTER RD., FLOOR 7TH, 63131.

MR. JOHN WILLIAM BACHMANN,
HONORARY CONSUL GENERAL — Sep. 26, 2006

MONTANA

NASHUA (HC) HC 81 BALL RD., 59248.
(406) 785-4731

MS. SHIRLEY ANN BALL,
HONORARY CONSUL — May. 09, 2006

NEBRASKA

OMAHA (HC) 1321 JONES ST., 68102.
(402) 341-2020

MR. JOHN J. CAVANAUGH,
HONORARY CONSUL — Apr. 30, 2004

NEW JERSEY

PRINCETON (CON) 10 SKYFIELD DR., 08540.
(609) 333-9940, FAX (609) 333-9943

NEW YORK

BUFFALO (CG) 3000 HSBC CENTER ., FLOOR 30TH&31ST, 14203-2884.
(716) 858-9500

MR. STEPHEN JOHN BRERETON,
CONSUL GENERAL — Oct. 12, 2005

MR. RANDY ORR,
CONSUL — Sep. 23, 2002

MS. LAURENCE MARIE CASSANDRE COUTURE,
CONSUL — Mar. 16, 2006

MR. RICHARD BURKE THORNTON,
CONSUL — Aug. 10, 2006

MR. TERRANCE DENNIS VENERUS,
CONSUL — Aug. 10, 2006

MS. DANECA RENE WORKMAN,
CONSUL — Aug. 10, 2006

STATE* RESIDENCE	NAME AND RANK	DATE OF RECOGNITION
	MR. MICHAEL CLIFFORD FLAHERTY, CONSUL	Sep. 27, 2006
NEW YORK (CG) 1251 AVE. OF THE AMERICAS UN., 10020. (212) 596-1600		
	MR. DANIEL FRANCIS SULLIVAN, CONSUL GENERAL	Jan. 25, 2007
	MR. JOHN ALEXANDER MCNAB, DEPUTY CONSUL GENERAL	Sep. 14, 2006
	MR. DAVID MURCHISON, CONSUL	Sep. 25, 2002
	MR. ZAHIR LALANI, CONSUL	Nov. 18, 2002
	MR. LOUIS POISSON, CONSUL	Sep. 29, 2003
	MR. ALAN HENRY MINZ, CONSUL	Nov. 07, 2003
	MS. KAREN ANN POULTER, CONSUL	Jun. 22, 2004
	MR. PETER ALLAN LILIUS, CONSUL	Sep. 07, 2004
	MS. GEORGIA GASS, CONSUL	Sep. 10, 2004
	MS. GAYLE FOSTER, CONSUL	Mar. 04, 2005
	MS. DARCEE MUNROE, CONSUL	Oct. 06, 2005
	MR. ALAN LAWRENCE BUDDE, CONSUL	Nov. 08, 2005
	MRS. DINA MARIA SANTOS, CONSUL	Nov. 08, 2005
	MR. CHARLES GODFREY, CONSUL	Jun. 29, 2006
	MS. ANNE MALEPART, CONSUL	Oct. 10, 2006
	MR. MICHAEL GORDON BROOKER, VICE CONSUL	Oct. 06, 2005
	MS. LAURA MEI WOON KO, VICE CONSUL	Oct. 06, 2005
	MR. OWEN TEO, VICE CONSUL	Oct. 12, 2005
	MR. DONALD ALLENBY O'NEILL, VICE CONSUL	Aug. 10, 2006
	MR. SCOTT CLIFFORD KNOWLES, VICE CONSUL	Aug. 10, 2006

NORTH CAROLINA

STATE* RESIDENCE	NAME AND RANK	DATE OF RECOGNITION
HUNTERSVILLE (HC) 16516 RANGER TR., 28078. (704) 904-9416		
	MR. DANA MINTER , III HICKS, HONORARY CONSUL	Dec. 07, 2005
RALEIGH (CON) 3737 GLENWOOD AV., 27612. (919) 573-1808		
	MR. KEVIN PETER SINNOTT, CONSUL	Aug. 10, 2006
	MR. WILLIAM JAMES NORTON, CONSUL	Aug. 10, 2006

OHIO

CLEVELAND (HC) 30650 SUMMIT LA., 44124. (216) 831-1392

STATE* RESIDENCE	NAME AND RANK	DATE OF RECOGNITION
	MR. HENRY THOMAS , JR KING, HONORARY CONSUL	Jun. 07, 2004

OREGON

STATE* RESIDENCE	NAME AND RANK	DATE OF RECOGNITION
PORTLAND (HC) 805 S.W. BROADWAY AV., SUITE 1900, 97205. (503) 224-5560		
	MR. JAMES MARTIN BAUMGARTNER, HONORARY CONSUL	Mar. 18, 2005

PENNSYLVANIA

STATE* RESIDENCE	NAME AND RANK	DATE OF RECOGNITION
PHILADELPHIA (CON) 1650 MARKET ST., FLOOR 36TH, 19103. (267) 207-2721		
	MR. DAVID BRUCE WEINER, CONSUL	Oct. 19, 2004
	MR. DANIEL TREMBLAY, CONSUL	Oct. 03, 2005
PITTSBURGH (HC) 425 SIXTH AV., FLOOR 11, 15219. (412) 392-4555		
	MR. ROGER OWEN CRANVILLE, HONORARY CONSUL	Mar. 08, 2004

PUERTO RICO

STATE* RESIDENCE	NAME AND RANK	DATE OF RECOGNITION
SAN JUAN (HC) 268 PONCE DE LEON AV., SUITE 515, 00918. (789) 759-6629, FAX (787) 294-1205		
	MR. REX DOUGLAS KEITH SEYMOUR, HONORARY CONSUL	Nov. 29, 1995

TENNESSEE

STATE* RESIDENCE	NAME AND RANK	DATE OF RECOGNITION
MEMPHIS (HC) 4294 SWINNEA RD., 38118. (901) 370-4352		
	MR. BARTON LEE , III MALLORY, HONORARY CONSUL	Apr. 05, 2004

TEXAS

STATE* RESIDENCE	NAME AND RANK	DATE OF RECOGNITION
DALLAS (CG) 750 N. SAINT PAUL ST., SUITE 1700, 75201. (214) 922-9806		
	MR. NORRIS MCKENZIE PETTIS, CONSUL GENERAL	Sep. 28, 2006
	MR. DAVID FREDERICK JOHN MARSHALL, CONSUL	Sep. 15, 2004
	MS. DIANE BELLON, CONSUL	Sep. 16, 2004
	MR. DAVID CECIL DIX, CONSUL	Nov. 26, 2004
	MR. RODNEY B. JOHNSON, CONSUL	Nov. 08, 2005
CONSULATE **HOUSTON (CON)** 5847 SAN FELIPE ST., SUITE 1700, 77057. (713) 821-1442		
	MR. GILLES JOSEPH LOUIS GAUDET, CONSUL	Oct. 04, 2005
	MR. DAVID RICHARD MCGREGOR, CONSUL	Sep. 26, 2006
SAN ANTONIO (HCG) 106 S. ST. MARY'S ST., SUITE 800, 78205. (210) 299-3525		
	MR. J. TULLOS WELLS, HONORARY CONSUL	Jun. 13, 2005

STATE* RESIDENCE	NAME AND RANK	DATE OF RECOGNITION	STATE* RESIDENCE	NAME AND RANK	DATE OF RECOGNITION

UTAH

BOUNTIFUL (HC) 757 WOODMOOR CI., 84010.
(801) 292-8181
    MR. SCOTT S. PARKER, — Oct. 14, 2005
      HONORARY CONSUL

VIRGINIA

RICHMOND (HC) 1021 E. CARY ST., FLOOR 17TH, 23219.
(804) 783-6402
    MR. WILLIAM JOHN BENOS, — Aug. 11, 2004
      HONORARY CONSUL

WASHINGTON

SEATTLE (CG) 1501 4TH AV., SUITE 600, 98101.
(206) 443-1777
    MR. PETER MORRIS LLOYD, — Mar. 19, 2007
      CONSUL GENERAL
    MR. JOHN PEARCE, — Oct. 12, 2004
      CONSUL
    MRS. KIMBERLEY LEE BLANCHETTE, — Apr. 18, 2007
      CONSUL
    MR. BRYAN FOYE, — Apr. 30, 2007
      CONSUL
    MR. MICHAEL GARNETT VIRR, — Apr. 30, 2007
      CONSUL
    MS. RITA AGNES BEAUCHAMP, — Apr. 30, 2007
      CONSUL
    MR. JESS WILLIAM BOSSERT, — Jul. 27, 2006
      VICE CONSUL

<h2 style="text-align:center">CAPE VERDE</h2>

MASSACHUSETTS

BOSTON (CG) 607 BOYLSTON ST., 02116.
(617) 353-0014
    MRS. MARIA DE JESUS VEIGA MASCARENHAS, — Mar. 28, 2006
      CONSUL GENERAL

<h2 style="text-align:center">CENTRAL AFRICAN REPUBLIC</h2>

CALIFORNIA

LOS ANGELES (HCG) 901 N. CAMDEN DR., BEVERLY HILLS 90210.
(310) 278-1095
    MR. CLARK E., SR PARKER, — Jun. 07, 2001
      HONORARY CONSUL GENERAL

NEW YORK

NEW YORK (HC) 51 E. 42ND ST., 10017.
    MR. HOWARD A. HIRSCHFELD, — Mar. 07, 1994
      HONORARY CONSUL

<h2 style="text-align:center">CHILE</h2>

CALIFORNIA

LOS ANGELES (CG) 6100 WILSHIRE BL., SUITE 1240&1260, 90048.
(323) 933-3697, FAX (323) 933-3842
    MR. JOSE MANUEL LIRA OVALLE, — Feb. 01, 2007
      CONSUL GENERAL

    MS. VIVIANA ARANEDA, — Oct. 11, 2006
      CONSULAR AGENT

SAN DIEGO (HC) 550 WEST "C" ST., SUITE 1820, 92101-3509.
(619) 232-6361, FAX (619) 696-0991
    MR. GEORGE L. GILDRED, — Jan. 20, 1976
      HONORARY CONSUL

SAN FRANCISCO (CG) 870 MARKET ST., SUITE 1058, 94102.
(415) 982-7662, FAX (415) 982-2384
    MR. CESAR ALBERTO RUIZ ASMUSSEN, — Mar. 24, 2004
      CONSUL GENERAL
    MR. FERNANDO ALEGRIA, — Jan. 15, 1992
      HONORARY CONSUL

SANTA CLARA (HCA) 1376 JOHNSON ST., MENLO PARK 94025.
(650) 543-3847, FAX (650) 322-6403
    MR. CARLOS LOPEZ, — Nov. 29, 1976
      HONORARY CONSULAR AGENT

DISTRICT OF COLUMBIA

WASHINGTON (CHN) 1732 MASSACHUSETTS AV., NW, 20036.
(202) 785-1746, FAX (202) 887-5579
    MR. ALEJANDRO PABLO ARRIARAN, — Mar. 02, 2004
      CONSUL
    MR. FELIPE COUSINO DONOSO, — Mar. 15, 2005
      CONSUL
    MR. SERGIO TORO MENDOZA, — Mar. 07, 2006
      CONSUL
    MR. RODRIGO ENRIQUE ARCOS CASTRO, — May. 23, 2007
      CONSUL

FLORIDA

MIAMI (CG) 800 BRICKELL AV., SUITE 1230, 33131.
(305) 371-3219, FAX (305) 379-6613
    MR. SAMUEL GERARDO FERNANDEZ, — Aug. 10, 2006
      CONSUL GENERAL
    MR. JORGE CARLOS VALDES ORTIZ, — Jul. 07, 2005
      CONSUL

COMMERCIAL OFFICE
MIAMI (CONA) 1101 BRICKELL AV., SUITE M-103, 33133.
(305) 599-2224

GEORGIA

ATLANTA (HC) 2876 SEQUOYAH DR., NW, 30327.
(404) 355-7923
    MRS. ERIKA M. MONCKEBERG, — Jun. 10, 1998
      HONORARY CONSUL

HAWAII

HONOLULU (HC) 1329 LUSITANIA ST., SUITE 206, 96813.
(808) 550-4985
    MS. GLADYS VERNOY, — Oct. 17, 2002
      HONORARY CONSUL

ILLINOIS

CHICAGO (CG) 875 N. MICHIGAN AV., SUITE 3352, 60611.
(312) 654-8780, FAX (312) 654-8948

STATE* RESIDENCE	NAME AND RANK	DATE OF RECOGNITION

MR. JOSE MIGUEL CRUZ,   Jul. 26, 2006
   CONSUL GENERAL

LOUISIANA

NEW ORLEANS (HC) 1350 PORT OF NEW ORLEANS PL., 70130.
(504) 528-3364, FAX (504) 524-4156
   MR. ANGEL PELAYO CARRERAS,   Aug. 14, 1992
      HONORARY CONSUL

MASSACHUSETTS

BOSTON (HC) 1 BERNARDO O'HIGGINS CI., BRIGHTON 02135-7840.
(617) 232-0416, FAX (617) 232-0817
   MR. PAUL WILLIAM GARBER,   Jun. 26, 1974
      HONORARY CONSUL
   MR. PHILIP C. GARBER,   Feb. 22, 1982
      HONORARY CONSUL

MISSOURI

KANSAS CITY (HC) 4153 BROADWAY ., 64111.
(816) 531-2345
   MR. ROBERT WILLIAM EVANS,   Aug. 20, 2001
      HONORARY CONSUL

NEVADA

LAS VEGAS (HC) P.O. BOX 371216 UN., 89137.
(702) 456-9965
   MS. PAULINA ELENA BIGGS,   May. 08, 2002
      HONORARY CONSUL

NEW YORK

NEW YORK (CG) 866 UNITED NATIONS PZ., SUITE 601, 10017.
(212) 355-0612, FAX (212) 688-5879
   MR. BENJAMIN CONCHA,   Jan. 11, 2005
      CONSUL GENERAL
   MR. DIEGO RIVERA,   Feb. 23, 2006
      CONSUL
   MR. JUAN A. SOMAVIA SANTA CRUZ,   Sep. 18, 2002
      CONSULAR AGENT
   MS. ELBA FUENTES,   Aug. 05, 1970
      HONORARY CONSUL

PENNSYLVANIA

PHILADELPHIA (CG) 446 6TH & CHESTNUT ST., SUITE 1030, 19106.
(215) 829-9520, FAX (215) 829-0594
   MR. ALDEN LEAVENWORTH,   Sep. 29, 2005
      HONORARY CONSUL

PUERTO RICO

SAN JUAN (CG) 1509 LOPEZ LANDRON ., SUITE 1101, 00911.
(809) 725-6365, FAX (809) 725-7295

SOUTH CAROLINA

CHARLESTON (HC) 948 EQUESTRIAN DR., MOUNT PLEASANT
29464.
(843) 884-6224, FAX (843) 792-3212
   MR. CARLOS SALINAS,   Mar. 31, 1978
      HONORARY CONSUL

TEXAS

DALLAS (HC) 3500 OAK LAWN AV., APT 200, 75219-4343.
(214) 528-2731, FAX (214) 522-7167
   MS. DOROTHY J. REID,   Jun. 22, 1989
      HONORARY CONSUL

HOUSTON (CG) 1360 POST OAK BL., SUITE 1130, 77056.
(713) 963-9066, FAX (713) 961-3910
   MR. CARLOS VICENTE CHARME SILVA,   Jan. 21, 2003
      CONSUL GENERAL

UTAH

PROVO (HC) 3008 N. 175TH EAST UN., 84604.
(801) 375-0354
   MR. THOMAS EDGAR , JR LYON,   Mar. 16, 2006
      HONORARY CONSUL

WASHINGTON

OLYMPIA (HC) 700 SLEATER-KINNEY RD., SE, SUITE B-261, 98503.
(360) 754-8747
   MR. JORGE GILBERT,   Sep. 16, 1997
      HONORARY CONSUL

CHINA

CALIFORNIA

LOS ANGELES (CG) 443 SHATTO PL., 90020.
(213) 380-3105, FAX (213) 380-1961
   MR. YUN ZHANG,   May. 07, 2007
      CONSUL GENERAL
   MR. CHAO YOU XU,   Jul. 16, 2004
      DEPUTY CONSUL GENERAL
   MRS. XIAO JIAN HUANG,   Jul. 07, 2005
      DEPUTY CONSUL GENERAL
   MR. YAO SHENG LI,   Jun. 25, 2002
      CONSUL
   MR. KAI BIN ZHANG,   Nov. 26, 2002
      CONSUL
   MS. LI YING WANG,   Jul. 29, 2003
      CONSUL
   MR. WAN SHENG LIU,   Aug. 05, 2003
      CONSUL
   MR. ZHI XUE DONG,   Feb. 02, 2004
      CONSUL
   MR. HUAI ZHI CHEN,   Mar. 22, 2004
      CONSUL
   MR. LIAN ZHEN SONG,   May. 17, 2004
      CONSUL
   MR. SU FENG YAO,   Jun. 01, 2004
      CONSUL
   MR. XIAO MING ZOU,   Jun. 26, 2004
      CONSUL
   MR. GUANG MING GU,   Feb. 15, 2005
      CONSUL
   MR. TUO QIANG WANG,   Apr. 27, 2006
      CONSUL
   MR. XIANG DONG YE,   Jun. 05, 2006
      CONSUL
   MS. LUO WANG,   Jun. 29, 2006
      CONSUL
   MR. SHI JIE CHEN,   May. 04, 2007
      CONSUL
   MS. YAN QI HOU,   May. 04, 2007
      CONSUL

STATE* RESIDENCE	NAME AND RANK	DATE OF RECOGNITION	STATE* RESIDENCE	NAME AND RANK	DATE OF RECOGNITION
	MRS. AIDI YANG, CONSUL	May. 07, 2007		MR. AI MIN LI, CONSUL	Oct. 06, 2005
	MRS. XINTAO ZHENG, VICE CONSUL	Jan. 09, 2004		MRS. XIAOHONG OUYANG, CONSUL	Oct. 06, 2005
	MR. DAO SHENG LIU, VICE CONSUL	Apr. 20, 2004		MR. JIE MING TAO, CONSUL	Oct. 24, 2005
	MR. LEKANG CHEN, VICE CONSUL	Feb. 07, 2006		MR. FA MING YAO, CONSUL	Nov. 09, 2005
	MISS YUE CHEN, VICE CONSUL	Mar. 16, 2006		MR. YI GONG WANG, CONSUL	May. 23, 2006
	MR. YU ZHANG, VICE CONSUL	Feb. 16, 2007		MR. DONG JUN LIU, CONSUL	Jun. 05, 2006
	MR. YANG CHEN, VICE CONSUL	May. 07, 2007		MR. CHUANFENG TANG, CONSUL	Jun. 08, 2006
	MS. RAN WANG, VICE CONSUL	May. 07, 2007		MR. JIN LIN YAN, CONSUL	Apr. 30, 2007
				MR. QI PAN, CONSUL	Apr. 30, 2007
VISA OFFICE LOS ANGELES (CON) 500 SHATTO PL., 90020. (213) 807-8006, FAX (213) 380-0372				MS. XIANG BIN LIU, CONSUL	Apr. 30, 2007
				MR. JIAN HUA SUN, CONSUL	May. 04, 2007
SAN FRANCISCO (CG) 1450 LAGUNA ST., 94115. (415) 674-2905, FAX (415) 292-6523				MS. JIA QI ZHANG, CONSUL	May. 07, 2007
	MR. KE YU PENG, CONSUL GENERAL	Mar. 17, 2004		MS. SHU JIE CHEN, CONSUL	Jun. 19, 2007
	MR. WEI LIAN SHEN, DEPUTY CONSUL GENERAL	Apr. 18, 2005		MR. XIN BING HU, VICE CONSUL	Apr. 04, 2003
	MR. XIN PING WANG, DEPUTY CONSUL GENERAL	Nov. 09, 2005		MS. LIN TIAN, VICE CONSUL	Mar. 10, 2004
	MR. WEI MIN ZHU, DEPUTY CONSUL GENERAL	May. 11, 2006		MR. DONG WANG, VICE CONSUL	Mar. 22, 2004
	MS. JIN HUA XIN, CONSUL	Jun. 22, 2001		MR. PING CHEN, VICE CONSUL	Jul. 16, 2004
	MR. YONG PU WANG, CONSUL	Jul. 26, 2002		MR. ZHENG XING ZHOU, VICE CONSUL	Oct. 19, 2004
	MR. JI JIAN YANG, CONSUL	Sep. 04, 2002		MR. QIAO CUN LU, VICE CONSUL	Jan. 07, 2005
	MS. PEI FANG GU, CONSUL	Sep. 23, 2002		MR. XIA HONG, VICE CONSUL	Oct. 24, 2005
	MR. YANG SHEN, CONSUL	Apr. 04, 2003		MS. FANG LIU, VICE CONSUL	Nov. 09, 2005
	MR. SHIXUN YAN, CONSUL	Oct. 06, 2003		MS. MING JI SUN, VICE CONSUL	May. 23, 2006
	MS. JUBAO PU, CONSUL	Oct. 06, 2003		MR. YANG SONG, VICE CONSUL	May. 04, 2007
	MR. TAO WANG, CONSUL	Feb. 05, 2004		MS. WEN JUAN SHEN, VICE CONSUL	May. 07, 2007
	MR. XIAO YI CHEN, CONSUL	Feb. 10, 2004		MR. JI HUA ZHOU, VICE CONSUL	Jun. 06, 2007
	MR. XUE JUN TONG, CONSUL	Mar. 10, 2004		MR. HAIBIN LI, VICE CONSUL	Jul. 11, 2007
	MR. DA WEI LI, CONSUL	May. 05, 2004			
	MS. LI YAN, CONSUL	May. 05, 2004	**DISTRICT OF COLUMBIA**		
	MS. JIN KUN LIU, CONSUL	Jul. 28, 2004	WASHINGTON (CHN) 2300 CONNECTICUT AV., NW, 20008. (202) 328-2500, FAX (202) 328-2582		
	MR. ZHI QI WEI, CONSUL	Nov. 30, 2004		MR. ZENGBO GAO, VICE CONSUL	Oct. 12, 2006
	MR. DE FA TONG, CONSUL	Jan. 12, 2005	CONSULAR AFFAIRS		
	MRS. BO YAN, CONSUL	Jan. 12, 2005	WASHINGTON (CONA) 2300 CONNECTICUT AV., NW, 20008. (202) 328-2518		
	MR. TIAN LONG MIN, CONSUL	Mar. 07, 2005		MRS. LI YU WANG, CONSUL	Jan. 07, 2004

STATE* RESIDENCE	NAME AND RANK	DATE OF RECOGNITION	STATE* RESIDENCE	NAME AND RANK	DATE OF RECOGNITION
	MR. FU QING TAN, CONSUL	May. 01, 2007		MS. CHU YUN ZHANG, CONSUL	May. 23, 2006
	MR. SHI TONG WANG, DEPUTY CONSUL	Mar. 28, 2007		MR. XIAO CE YAN, VICE CONSUL	Apr. 10, 2003
				MR. BIN XUN, VICE CONSUL	Oct. 24, 2005
ILLINOIS				MS. LIN LI, VICE CONSUL	Jan. 18, 2006
CHICAGO (CG) 100 W. ERIE ST., 60610. (312) 803-0095, FAX (312) 803-0105					
	MR. PING HUANG, CONSUL GENERAL	Jul. 26, 2007	**NEW YORK**		
	MR. MAO MING CHU, DEPUTY CONSUL GENERAL	Aug. 01, 2007	NEW YORK (CG) 520 12TH AV., 10036. (212) 279-4275		
	MR. XIAO DONG FAN, CONSUL	Jul. 01, 2003		MR. BI WEI LIU, CONSUL GENERAL	Sep. 15, 2003
	MR. XIN JIE LI, CONSUL	Jul. 31, 2003		MR. AI MIN CUI, DEPUTY CONSUL GENERAL	Feb. 10, 2004
	MR. GANG LIANG, CONSUL	Apr. 06, 2004		MR. WEILIN KUANG, DEPUTY CONSUL GENERAL	Feb. 15, 2005
	MR. HUI XUN ZHANG, CONSUL	Oct. 01, 2004		MS. XIAO FEI HAO, DEPUTY CONSUL GENERAL	Jul. 10, 2007
	MR. JUN LIU, CONSUL	Feb. 15, 2005		MR. ER JUN LIANG, CONSUL	Nov. 07, 1996
	MR. XIN HUI GUO, CONSUL	Jun. 27, 2005		MR. KANG LIN YU, CONSUL	Nov. 05, 1997
	MR. LIANG ZHANG, CONSUL	Oct. 04, 2005		MR. XIONG FENG CHEN, CONSUL	Nov. 16, 1998
	MR. GUANG MING MENG, CONSUL	May. 23, 2006		MR. LI BIN SHEN, CONSUL	Feb. 19, 1999
	MR. YI MU PENG, CONSUL	May. 23, 2006		MR. YUE CHENG LI, CONSUL	Jun. 11, 1999
	MR. XU QIN LI, CONSUL	Sep. 14, 2006		MRS. JING BO LIU, CONSUL	Aug. 12, 1999
	MS. ZHI YUAN JI, CONSUL	Nov. 28, 2006		MS. GUI ZHI TANG, CONSUL	Nov. 26, 1999
	MR. DE MIN WU, CONSUL	Feb. 01, 2007		MS. JIN LAN SHI, CONSUL	Mar. 28, 2000
	MR. ZONG GUANG GUO, CONSUL	Apr. 30, 2007		MR. SHU JING SUN, CONSUL	Jan. 10, 2001
	MR. HAI XIA YU, CONSUL	May. 04, 2007		MR. SHAO ZONG XU, CONSUL	Mar. 05, 2001
	MR. WEI JIA WANG, VICE CONSUL	Jul. 07, 2005		MR. XIANG YANG ZHANG, CONSUL	Mar. 05, 2001
	MRS. JIAN ZHONG SHI, VICE CONSUL	May. 04, 2007		MR. GUANG YI LIU, CONSUL	Apr. 16, 2001
				MR. WEI WEN HE, CONSUL	May. 23, 2001
EDUCATION OFFICE CHICAGO (CONA) 3322 W. PETERSON AV., 60659. (312) 463-9187				MR. FANG LIN AI, CONSUL	Jan. 07, 2002
	MR. WEI ZHONG WANG, CONSUL	Feb. 18, 2004		MR. MING SHENG LU, CONSUL	Apr. 10, 2002
	MR. SHENG XIONG, CONSUL	Apr. 13, 2004		MS. YI LIU, CONSUL	Jun. 27, 2002
	MR. TONG ZENG BAO, CONSUL	Jul. 16, 2004		MR. GANG WEI, CONSUL	Jul. 12, 2002
	MR. JIA JIE JIANG, CONSUL	Oct. 08, 2004		MR. LONG LI, CONSUL	Feb. 07, 2003
	MR. JI YUAN, CONSUL	Nov. 09, 2005		MR. XING BAO ZHU, CONSUL	May. 05, 2003
				MR. ZHANLING YUAN, CONSUL	May. 05, 2003
VISA OFFICE CHICAGO (CONA) 1 E. ERIE ST., SUITE 500, 60611. (312) 573-3072, FAX (312) 803-0121				MS. DONG YANG, CONSUL	Aug. 05, 2003
	MS. HONG ZHU, CONSUL	Apr. 10, 2003		MRS. CHUN FANG, CONSUL	Sep. 03, 2003
				MR. FENG HE QIAO, CONSUL	Nov. 10, 2003

STATE* RESIDENCE	NAME AND RANK	DATE OF RECOGNITION	STATE* RESIDENCE	NAME AND RANK	DATE OF RECOGNITION
	MR. LI YAN LI, CONSUL	Jan. 08, 2004		MS. XU MING LIU, CONSUL	May. 17, 2007
	MR. YU MING XIA, CONSUL	Apr. 07, 2004		MR. JIAN WEI ZHANG, CONSUL	Jul. 19, 2007
	MR. XU HUI ZHONG, CONSUL	May. 16, 2004		MR. LEI LIU, CONSUL	Jul. 26, 2007
	MS. ZHEN JIE GAO, CONSUL	Jun. 16, 2004		MS. YUAN ZHI LI, VICE CONSUL	Nov. 24, 1997
	MR. GUO ZAO LI, CONSUL	Sep. 07, 2004		MR. SHAO QIANG GUO, VICE CONSUL	Apr. 30, 1998
	MR. JIE CHEN, CONSUL	Sep. 14, 2004		MR. LI ZHANG, VICE CONSUL	Aug. 07, 1998
	MR. SHUO YI CHEN, CONSUL	Sep. 14, 2004		MS. RUI YU, VICE CONSUL	Nov. 26, 1999
	MR. JIAN LIN, CONSUL	Nov. 05, 2004		MR. FEI PENG, VICE CONSUL	Dec. 03, 1999
	MR. HUI CHUN SUN, CONSUL	Feb. 15, 2005		MS. LU SHENG FAN, VICE CONSUL	Mar. 03, 2000
	MR. WU QIANG LI, CONSUL	Mar. 09, 2005		MR. JIAN QUAN ZHANG, VICE CONSUL	Nov. 14, 2000
	MR. YING WANG, CONSUL	Apr. 15, 2005		MR. XIAO JUN KONG, VICE CONSUL	Jan. 09, 2001
	MR. BIN HE, CONSUL	Jul. 07, 2005		MS. HONG LIU, VICE CONSUL	Aug. 28, 2001
	MR. DONG BO FANG, CONSUL	Aug. 10, 2005		MR. WEI ZHANG, VICE CONSUL	Apr. 15, 2002
	MR. PENG YU LIU, CONSUL	Oct. 14, 2005		MR. XI ZOU, VICE CONSUL	Feb. 28, 2003
	MRS. HUA WU, CONSUL	Nov. 10, 2005		MR. CHANG ZHONG HE, VICE CONSUL	Apr. 09, 2003
	MR. DE YU ZHAI, CONSUL	Feb. 07, 2006		MR. YI HU, VICE CONSUL	Nov. 10, 2003
	MS. HUA YANG, CONSUL	Feb. 07, 2006		MR. GANG MA, VICE CONSUL	Sep. 07, 2004
	MR. LIU ZHU, CONSUL	Mar. 16, 2006		MS. HONG LI, VICE CONSUL	Sep. 07, 2004
	MR. XIUKUAN CUI, CONSUL	Mar. 16, 2006		MR. ZHUANG SONG LI, VICE CONSUL	Sep. 14, 2004
	MS. XUE WANG, CONSUL	May. 23, 2006		MR. XUAN ZHENG, VICE CONSUL	Oct. 27, 2004
	MS. GUI ZHI LI, CONSUL	May. 24, 2006		MR. XIANG JUN MU, VICE CONSUL	Dec. 03, 2004
	MR. DA YAO, CONSUL	Aug. 10, 2006		MR. TAO TAO, VICE CONSUL	Dec. 07, 2005
	MR. JIANG HONG FAN, CONSUL	Sep. 14, 2006		MR. HANG TIAN XU, VICE CONSUL	Feb. 07, 2006
	MR. GANG LUO, CONSUL	Nov. 13, 2006		MR. KAI KANG, VICE CONSUL	Feb. 07, 2006
	MRS. HONG WEN LI, CONSUL	Dec. 15, 2006		MS. WEI WEI, VICE CONSUL	Feb. 07, 2006
	MR. ZHIXIONG DUAN, CONSUL	Feb. 20, 2007		MR. XIANG HUANG, VICE CONSUL	May. 16, 2006
	MR. WEN QI GAO, CONSUL	Apr. 27, 2007		MS. CHUN MEI LI, VICE CONSUL	May. 16, 2006
	MS. XIAO XIA SHI, CONSUL	Apr. 30, 2007		MR. CHANG GAO LI, VICE CONSUL	May. 23, 2006
	MR. GUANG YI ZHANG, CONSUL	May. 04, 2007		MS. YING GAO, VICE CONSUL	May. 24, 2006
	MR. CAN WANG, CONSUL	May. 07, 2007		MS. LI LIN, VICE CONSUL	Aug. 10, 2006
	MR. HAI TAO ZHANG, CONSUL	May. 07, 2007		MR. HAI FENG ZHENG, VICE CONSUL	Sep. 27, 2006
	MR. YONG JUN WANG, CONSUL	May. 07, 2007		MR. LIN LIN MA, VICE CONSUL	Oct. 10, 2006
	MR. JUN HUA LIU, CONSUL	May. 17, 2007		MR. SHOU XIANG ZHANG, VICE CONSUL	Nov. 01, 2006

* DEPENDENCIES SUCH AS GUAM, PUERTO RICO, AND THE VIRGIN ISLANDS ARE LISTED HERE.
CG-CONSULATE GENERAL   C-CONSULATE   VC-VICE CONSULATE   CA-CONSULAR AGENCY   H-HONORARY CONSULAR STATUS

STATE* RESIDENCE	NAME AND RANK	DATE OF RECOGNITION	STATE* RESIDENCE	NAME AND RANK	DATE OF RECOGNITION
	MS. YING JUN WANG, VICE CONSUL	Jan. 26, 2007		MRS. JI PING LI, CONSUL	Jun. 16, 2006
	MR. JIN XIAO GAO, VICE CONSUL	May. 07, 2007		MR. LI QING WEI, CONSUL	Jul. 18, 2006
	MR. YONG HUA DING, VICE CONSUL	May. 07, 2007		MR. QIN LING ZHAO, CONSUL	Jul. 27, 2006
	MS. SHAN ZI GAO, VICE CONSUL	May. 07, 2007		MR. DONG WANG, CONSUL	Sep. 14, 2006
	MR. GANG YU, VICE CONSUL	May. 17, 2007		MR. WENLIANG YAO, CONSUL	Feb. 19, 2007
	MR. YU LIU, VICE CONSUL	May. 17, 2007		MR. HUO WANG ZOU, CONSUL	Feb. 20, 2007
	MS. YING ZHANG, VICE CONSUL	May. 17, 2007		MR. QIJUN RAN, CONSUL	May. 04, 2007
	MR. RUI LI, VICE CONSUL	Jun. 06, 2007		MR. BING XIAO, CONSUL	May. 22, 2007
	MR. XIAO BO WANG, VICE CONSUL	Jun. 19, 2007		MS. JING GAO, VICE CONSUL	Dec. 10, 2004
	MR. XING ZHANG, VICE CONSUL	Jul. 05, 2007		MR. GUANGDA CHEN, VICE CONSUL	Aug. 19, 2005
	MR. DE WANG FU, VICE CONSUL	Jul. 10, 2007		MS. QI LAN TONG, VICE CONSUL	Sep. 28, 2005
	MR. QING ZHAN LI, VICE CONSUL	Jul. 26, 2007		MR. QIAN ZHANG, VICE CONSUL	Oct. 12, 2005
	MS. TING YAN LAI, VICE CONSUL	Aug. 09, 2007		MRS. REN HONG LU, VICE CONSUL	Dec. 07, 2005
	MR. XIAO ZHONG ZHU, CONSULAR AGENT	May. 23, 2006		MR. JINYU GAO, VICE CONSUL	Mar. 16, 2006
	MS. JING ZHONG, CONSULAR AGENT	May. 23, 2006		MR. XUE JUN WANG, VICE CONSUL	May. 23, 2006
				MISS YI WANG, VICE CONSUL	May. 22, 2007

TEXAS

HOUSTON (CG) 3417 MONTROSE BL., SUITE 700, 77006.
(713) 524-0780

STATE* RESIDENCE	NAME AND RANK	DATE OF RECOGNITION
	MRS. HONG QIAO, CONSUL GENERAL	May. 22, 2007
	MR. BO REN YU, DEPUTY CONSUL GENERAL	Jul. 26, 2007
	MR. WEI PING ZHA, CONSUL	Jan. 07, 2004
	MR. ZHI PING HAO, CONSUL	Nov. 12, 2004
	MR. CHONG JUN BAI, CONSUL	Dec. 10, 2004
	MR. CHANG SONG REN, CONSUL	Jan. 05, 2005
	MR. DING ZHOU, CONSUL	Jan. 06, 2005
	MR. SHI XING WU, CONSUL	Feb. 18, 2005
	MR. JI JUN FU, CONSUL	Mar. 08, 2005
	MS. JIA LIU, CONSUL	May. 26, 2005
	MR. HEPING CHEN, CONSUL	Nov. 09, 2005
	MR. GUOSHENG ZHANG, CONSUL	Feb. 07, 2006
	MS. LIJUAN GAO, CONSUL	Feb. 07, 2006
	MR. YIBIN CHEN, CONSUL	Mar. 16, 2006
	MRS. AI PING SUN, CONSUL	May. 23, 2006
	MS. LI WEI FENG, CONSUL	May. 23, 2006

EDUCATION OFFICE
HOUSTON (CONA) 811-817 HOLMAN ST., 77002.

COLOMBIA

CALIFORNIA

BEVERLY HILLS (CG) 8383 WILSHIRE BL., SUITE 420, 90211.
(323) 653-9863

| | MR. GABRIEL JAIME RESTREPO, CONSUL GENERAL | Apr. 30, 2007 |
| | MS. MARIA FERNANDA MELO, VICE CONSUL | May. 04, 2007 |

SAN FRANCISCO (CG) 595 MARKET ST., SUITE 2130, 94105.
(415) 795-7195

| | MR. JOSE MIGUEL CASTIBLANCO, CONSUL GENERAL | Feb. 01, 2007 |
| | MRS. ALICIA TERESA D'AMBROSIO HADDAD, CONSUL | Apr. 30, 2007 |

DISTRICT OF COLUMBIA

CONSULATE GENERAL
WASHINGTON (CG) 1101 17TH ST., NW, SUITE 1007, 20036.
(202) 332-7476, FAX (202) 332-7180

| | MR. CARLOS ANDRES HURTADO PEREZ, VICE CONSUL | Sep. 26, 2006 |

FLORIDA

MIAMI (CG) 280 ARAGON AV., 33134.
(305) 448-5558

STATE* RESIDENCE	NAME AND RANK	DATE OF RECOGNITION	STATE* RESIDENCE	NAME AND RANK	DATE OF RECOGNITION
	MR. LUIS IGNACIO GUZMAN, CONSUL GENERAL	Aug. 14, 2007		MR. JOSE IVAN AGUILAR CASTANEDA, CONSUL	Sep. 16, 2004
	MS. LUZ ESTELA PENA HERRERA, CONSUL	Nov. 09, 2005		MR. JUAN CARLOS CAIZA ROSERO, CONSUL	Oct. 01, 2004
	MR. PAULO CESAR MINA, CONSUL	Aug. 14, 2007		MR. JAVIER ERNESTO BETANCOURT VALLE, CONSUL	Apr. 22, 2005
	MRS. MARIA DAZA CASTRO, VICE CONSUL	May. 09, 2003		MS. SAMIRA SILVA YOUNES, CONSUL	Nov. 09, 2005
	MR. ALFREDO A. SAADE DIAZGRANADOS, VICE CONSUL	Mar. 08, 2004		MR. FRANCISCO ALBERTO GONZALEZ, CONSUL	Mar. 16, 2006
	MRS. JESSIE ANN HASTIE, VICE CONSUL	Apr. 22, 2005		MS. NIDIA MARIA PIRAQUIVE LONDONO, CONSUL	Mar. 16, 2006
	MR. LUIS FERNANDO OROZCO BARRERA, VICE CONSUL	May. 23, 2006		MR. JOSE FERNANDO URUENA GONZALEZ, CONSUL	Apr. 25, 2006
	MRS. ANA LUCIA MADRID, VICE CONSUL	Jun. 06, 2007		MRS. ANA LUCIA LALINDE ANZOLA, CONSUL	Apr. 16, 2007
	MRS. ANDREA MARCELA ALARCON, VICE CONSUL	Aug. 14, 2007		MS. MARIA MILENE ANDRADE GARCIA, CONSUL	May. 04, 2007
				MS. MARIA PAULA GUERRA LOPEZ, CONSUL	May. 04, 2007

TRADE OFFICE
MIAMI (CONA) 601 BRICKELL KEY DR., SUITE 801, 33131.
(305) 374-3144

MR. MAURICIO GOMEZ ORDONEZ, DEPUTY CONSUL GENERAL	Sep. 10, 2001

GEORGIA

ATLANTA (CG) 5901 B PEACHTREE-DUNWOODY RD., SUITE 405,
30328.
(770) 668-0451, FAX (770) 668-0763

MR. CAMILO DE BEDOUT HERRERA, CONSUL GENERAL	May. 27, 2005
MRS. LUZ MARLENY ACOSTA SUAREZ, VICE CONSUL	Apr. 15, 2004

ILLINOIS

CHICAGO (CG) 500 N. MICHIGAN AV., SUITE 2040, 60611.
(312) 923-1196, FAX (312) 923-1197

MS. PAULINA MARIA GOMEZ, CONSUL GENERAL	Sep. 26, 2006
MRS. SARA INES VALENCIA VASQUEZ, DEPUTY CONSUL	Nov. 09, 2005

LOUISIANA

NEW ORLEANS (CG) 2 CANAL ST., SUITE 2302, 70130.
(504) 525-5580

MASSACHUSETTS

BOSTON (CG) 535 BOYLSTON ST., FLOOR 3RD, 02116.
(617) 303-4656, FAX (617) 536-9372

MS. BIBIANA D. GOMEZ JARAMILLO, CONSUL	Mar. 16, 2006
MS. ADRIANA M. GUTIERREZ CASTANEDA, VICE CONSUL	Oct. 31, 2003
MR. PEDRO ISIDRO LOPEZ, VICE CONSUL	Sep. 27, 2006

NEW YORK

NEW YORK (CG) 10 E. 46TH ST., 10017.
(212) 949-9898

MR. FRANCISCO A. NOGUERA ROCHA, CONSUL GENERAL	Apr. 13, 2007

PUERTO RICO

SAN JUAN (CG) 814 PONCE DE LEON AV., SUITE 814, HATO REY
00918.
(809) 754-6885

MS. ROSA CLARA PARDO RODRIGUEZ, CONSUL GENERAL	Apr. 30, 2007

TRADE OFFICE OF COLOMBIA
SAN JUAN (CONA) 1510 ESQ. SAN PATRICIO PZ., 00968.
(787) 273-1444, FAX (787) 273-7006

TEXAS

HOUSTON (CG) 5851 SAN FELIPE UN., SUITE 300, 77057.
(713) 527-8919

MS. MARIA CRISTINA CHIROLLA, CONSUL GENERAL	Mar. 02, 2006

CONGO, DEMOCRATIC REPUBLIC OF

NEW YORK

NEW YORK (HCG) 529 5TH AV., 10017.

MR. MAURICE TEMPELSMAN, HONORARY CONSUL GENERAL	Mar. 03, 1977

CONGO, REPUBLIC OF

LOUISIANA

NEW ORLEANS (HC) 201 ST. CHARLES AV., SUITE 2500, 70170.
(504) 568-9376

MR. NORBERT SIMMONS, HONORARY CONSUL	Jun. 26, 2000

COOK ISLANDS

CALIFORNIA

LOS ANGELES (HC) 6033 W. CENTURY BL., SUITE 690, 90045.
(310) 216-2872

MR. METUA NGARUPE, HONORARY CONSUL	Feb. 22, 1995

---

* DEPENDENCIES SUCH AS GUAM, PUERTO RICO, AND THE VIRGIN ISLANDS ARE LISTED HERE.
CG-CONSULATE GENERAL   C-CONSULATE   VC-VICE CONSULATE   CA-CONSULAR AGENCY   H-HONORARY CONSULAR STATUS

STATE* RESIDENCE	NAME AND RANK	DATE OF RECOGNITION	STATE* RESIDENCE	NAME AND RANK	DATE OF RECOGNITION

HAWAII

HONOLULU (HC) 144 KE ALA OLA RD., 96817.
(808) 847-6377

MR. ROBERT E. WORTHINGTON,   Mar. 19, 1985
HONORARY CONSUL

COSTA RICA

ARIZONA

TUCSON (HC) 3567 E. SUNRISE DR., SUITE 235, 85718.
(520) 577-5559

MS. CARMEN BERMUDEZ,   Nov. 14, 2002
HONORARY CONSUL

CALIFORNIA

LOS ANGELES (CG) 1605 W. OLYMPIC BL., SUITE 400, 90015.
(213) 380-7915, FAX (213) 380-5639

MS. XINIA VARGAS MORA,   May. 07, 2007
CONSUL GENERAL
MS. CYNTHIA SOLIS LIZANO,   May. 01, 2006
CONSUL
MS. PAULA COTO RAMIREZ,   May. 24, 2006
CONSUL

SAN FRANCISCO (CG) 870 MARKET ST., ROOM 645, 94102.
(415) 392-8488

COLORADO

DENVER (HC) 3356 S. XENIA ST., 80231-4542.
(303) 696-8211, FAX (303) 696-1110

MR. TITO CHAVERRI,   Sep. 05, 1964
HONORARY CONSUL

DISTRICT OF COLUMBIA

WASHINGTON (CHN) 2114 S ST., NW, 20008.
(202) 234-2945, FAX (202) 265-4795

MR. ROLANDO MADRIGAL GUTIERREZ,   Jun. 28, 2006
CONSUL GENERAL
MR. ROBERTO AVENDANO SANCHO,   Jan. 10, 2006
CONSUL

FLORIDA

MIAMI (CG) 1101 BRICKELL AV., SUITE 401 N, 33131.
(305) 871-7485, FAX (305) 871-0860

MRS. ANA LORENA SANCHEZ URPI,   Sep. 14, 2006
CONSUL GENERAL
MISS SUSSI JIMENEZ NUNEZ,   May. 07, 2004
CONSUL
MS. FLORA LEAH VENEGAS CORRALES,   Jul. 26, 2006
CONSUL
MR. WALTER FONSECA,   Apr. 30, 2007
CONSUL
MR. CARLOS ALBERTO PAEZ PIZARRO,   Jul. 25, 2002
CONSULAR AGENT

COMMERCIAL OFFICE
MIAMI (CONA) 5201 BLUE LAGOON DR., SUITE 864, 33126.
(305) 347-5153

MR. JORGE ARTURO ZAMORA MONTOYA,   May. 02, 2007
CONSUL

GEORGIA

ATLANTA (CG) 1870 THE EXCHANGE UN., SUITE 100, 30339.
(770) 951-7025, FAX (770) 951-7073

MS. EMILIA MARIA TREJOS CASTRO,   Jul. 15, 2003
CONSUL GENERAL
MR. MANUEL JAVIER DOBLES MORA,   May. 04, 2007
CONSUL GENERAL
MR. RODOLFO RODRIGUEZ CAMBRONERO,   Nov. 09, 2005
CONSUL

ILLINOIS

CHICAGO (CG) 203 N. WABASH AV., SUITE 702, 60601.
(312) 263-2772, FAX (312) 263-5807

MR. JUAN SALAS,   Dec. 29, 1998
CONSUL GENERAL

LOUISIANA

NEW ORLEANS (CG) 2 CANAL ST., SUITE 2334, 70130.
(504) 581-6800, FAX (504) 581-6850

MRS. JOANNE LEIGH NORIEGA,   Jul. 08, 2005
VICE CONSUL

MASSACHUSETTS

BOSTON (HCG) 175 MCCLELLAN HW., 02128-9114.
(617) 561-2444, FAX (617) 561-2461

MR. LEONARD FLORENCE,   Sep. 29, 1999
HONORARY CONSUL GENERAL

MINNESOTA

MINNEAPOLIS (HC) 2424 TERRITORIAL RD., ST. PAUL 55114.
(651) 645-4103, FAX (651) 645-4684

MR. ANTHONY L. ANDERSEN,   Nov. 02, 1983
HONORARY CONSUL

NEW YORK

NEW YORK (CG) 225 W. 34TH ST., SUITE 1202, 10122.
(212) 509-3066, FAX (212) 509-3068

MRS. ALEJANDRA SOLANO,   Jun. 29, 2006
CONSUL GENERAL
MR. EDUARDO SALGADO RETANA,   Jul. 28, 2004
CONSUL
MR. ARMANDO E. HEILBRON,   Sep. 15, 1997
CONSULAR AGENT
MS. MARIA DEL PILAR MADRIGAL,   Aug. 04, 1999
CONSULAR AGENT
MR. ELIECER FEINZAIG MINTZ,   Jan. 13, 2003
CONSULAR AGENT
MR. C. JOSEPH, JR HALLINAN,   Oct. 20, 1993
HONORARY CONSUL

PUERTO RICO

SAN JUAN (CG) 1413 FERNANDEZ JUNCOS AV., SUITE 2D, 00909.
(787) 723-6227, FAX (787) 723-6226

MRS. NAZARETH A DE INCERA,   May. 04, 2007
CONSUL GENERAL
MR. MARIO ALBERTO VEGA HERNANDEZ,   Jul. 29, 2005
CONSUL
MR. MAYKOL ANTONIO LOPEZ ROJAS,   Jul. 07, 2005
CONSULAR AGENT

STATE* RESIDENCE	NAME AND RANK	DATE OF RECOGNITION	STATE* RESIDENCE	NAME AND RANK	DATE OF RECOGNITION

TEXAS

AUSTIN (CON) 1730 E. O HORF ., 78741.
(512) 445-0023

DALLAS (HC) 7777 FORREST LA., SUITE B-445, 75230.
(972) 566-7020, FAX (972) 566-7943
    MR. JAIME ABRAHAM DAVIDSON,   Jun. 15, 1999
      HONORARY CONSUL

HOUSTON (CG) 3000 WILCREST DR., SUITE 112, 77042.
(713) 266-0484, FAX (713) 266-1527
    MR. SERGIO ALONSO VALVERDE ALPIZAR,   Aug. 23, 2005
      CONSUL GENERAL
    MRS. MARIA GABRIELA BOLANOS,   Jul. 30, 1999
      CONSUL
    MISS DANIA LORENA GARCIA DIAZ,   Jun. 05, 2006
      CONSUL
    MRS. ANGELA VANESSA ZUNIGA SOLANO,   Jun. 08, 2006
      CONSUL

COTE D'IVOIRE

CALIFORNIA

LOS ANGELES (HC) 4221 WILSHIRE BL., SUITE 290-06, 90010.
(323) 931-5036
    MR. AMOIFO KOFFI,   Dec. 12, 2006
      HONORARY CONSUL

SAN FRANCISCO (HCG) X PIER 23 UN., 94111.
(415) 310-0812, FAX (415) 928-0512
    MR. EDGAR DE PUE OSGOOD,   Oct. 09, 1981
      HONORARY CONSUL GENERAL

CONNECTICUT

STAMFORD (HC) 1055 WASHINGTON BL., 06901.
(203) 348-7580
    MR. GEORGE GHASSAN TALISSE,   Sep. 13, 2001
      HONORARY CONSUL

FLORIDA

ORLANDO (HC) 1650 CHAFFEE DR., TITUSVILLE 32781.
(321) 269-4193
    MR. HUGH M. BROWN,   Sep. 13, 2001
      HONORARY CONSUL

MICHIGAN

DETROIT (HC) 615 GRISWOLD ., SUITE 320, 48226.
(313) 962-2100, FAX (313) 962-3225
    MR. HAROLD RICHARD VARNER,   May. 22, 1991
      HONORARY CONSUL

TEXAS

HOUSTON (HCG) 412 HAWTHORNE UN., 77006.
(713) 529-4928
    MS. MARLENE DENESE MCCLINTON,   Aug. 14, 2002
      HONORARY CONSUL GENERAL

CROATIA

CALIFORNIA

LOS ANGELES (CG) 11766 WILSHIRE BL., SUITE 1250, 90025.
(310) 477-1009
    MR. ANTE BARBIR,   Feb. 07, 2006
      CONSUL GENERAL
    MS. BRANKA SOMEN,   Mar. 24, 2005
      CONSUL
    MS. ALIDA VALIC,   May. 07, 2007
      CONSUL

ILLINOIS

CHICAGO (CG) 737 N. MICHIGAN AV., SUITE 1030, 60611.
(312) 482-9902
    MS. MARICA MATKOVIC,   Feb. 13, 2004
      CONSUL GENERAL
    MS. SILVIJA GRGIC,   Sep. 11, 2006
      VICE CONSUL

KANSAS

KANSAS CITY (HC) 408 N. 5TH ST., 66101.
(913) 371-2525
    DR. JUDITH K. VOGELSANG,   Jun. 18, 2003
      HONORARY CONSUL

LOUISIANA

NEW ORLEANS (HC) 321 ST. CHARLES AV., FLOOR 10TH, 70130.
(504) 586-1979
    MR. JAMES O. COLEMAN,   Jan. 09, 2002
      HONORARY CONSUL

NEW YORK

NEW YORK (CG) 369 LEXINGTON AV., FLOOR 11TH, 10017.
    MR. PETAR LJUBICIC,   Sep. 15, 2004
      CONSUL GENERAL
    MRS. RUZICA IVANKOVIC,   Aug. 26, 2003
      CONSUL
    MS. ZDENKA KARDUM,   Jan. 13, 2004
      CONSUL
    MR. JASMIN DEVLIC,   Oct. 13, 2005
      CONSUL

PENNSYLVANIA

PITTSBURGH (HC) 100 DELANEY DR., 15235.
(412) 351-3909
    DR. MARION M. VUJEVICH,   Dec. 31, 2001
      HONORARY CONSUL

WASHINGTON

SEATTLE (HC) 7547 S. LAUREL ST., 98178.
(206) 772-2968, FAX (206) 772-3487
    DR. FRANK WALTER BROZOVICH,   Jan. 09, 2002
      HONORARY CONSUL

CYPRUS

ARIZONA

PHOENIX (HC) 1277 E. MISSOURI ., 85014.
(602) 264-9701
    MR. STANLEY J. DRU,   Aug. 26, 1980
      HONORARY CONSUL

STATE* RESIDENCE	NAME AND RANK	DATE OF RECOGNITION	STATE* RESIDENCE	NAME AND RANK	DATE OF RECOGNITION

CALIFORNIA

LOS ANGELES (HCG) 4219 COOLIDGE AV., 90066.
(310) 397-0771
    MR. ANDREAS C. KYPRIANIDES,   Jun. 05, 1987
       HONORARY CONSUL GENERAL

SAN FRANCISCO (HC) 75 SILVERWOOD DR., LAFAYETTE 94549.
(925) 284-1060
    MR. NICOLAOS COSTAS THEOPHANOUS,   Aug. 20, 2001
       HONORARY CONSUL

DISTRICT OF COLUMBIA

WASHINGTON (CHN) 2211 R ST., NW, 20008.
(202) 462-5772, FAX (202) 483-6710
    MR. ANDREAS NICOLAIDES,   Feb. 15, 2005
       CONSUL

GEORGIA

ATLANTA (HC) 895 SOMERSET DR., 30327.
(404) 231-3698, FAX (404) 841-6537
    MR. KYRIAKOS M. MICHAELIDES,   Oct. 23, 1985
       HONORARY CONSUL

ILLINOIS

CHICAGO (HC) 1875 DEMPSTER ST., SUITE 555, PARK RIDGE 60068.
(847) 698-9500, FAX (847) 685-1182
    DR. CHARLES, JR KANAKIS,   Mar. 13, 1995
       HONORARY CONSUL

LOUISIANA

NEW ORLEANS (HC) 2 CANAL ST., SUITE 2146, 70130.
(504) 568-9300
    MR. THOMAS MANTIS,   May. 02, 2002
       HONORARY CONSUL

MASSACHUSETTS

BOSTON (HC) 70-7 KIRKLAND ST., CAMBRIDGE 02138.
(617) 497-0219
    MR. JOHN C. PAPAJOHN,   Aug. 11, 1987
       HONORARY CONSUL

MICHIGAN

DETROIT (HC) 15706 MICHIGAN AV., DEARBORN 48126.
(313) 582-1411, FAX (313) 582-6791
    MR. STEVE G. STYLIANOU,   Aug. 26, 1987
       HONORARY CONSUL

NEW YORK

NEW YORK (CG) 13 E. 40TH ST., 10016.
(212) 686-6016
    MR. CLEANTHIS ORPHANOS,   Sep. 08, 2004
       CONSUL
    MS. EMMANUELA MARIA KOUROS,   Mar. 31, 2000
       VICE CONSUL

TOURIST OFFICE
NEW YORK (CONA) 13 E. 40TH ST., 10016.
(212) 683-5280

MARITIME OFFICE
NEW YORK (CONA) 13 E. 40TH ST., FLOOR 5TH, 10016.
(212) 447-1790

NORTH CAROLINA

JACKSONVILLE (HC) 412 COUNTRY CLUB DR., 28546.
(910) 353-4970, FAX (910) 353-0126
    DR. TAKEY CRIST,   Sep. 12, 1997
       HONORARY CONSUL

OREGON

PORTLAND (HC) 1130 MORRISON ST., SW, SUITE 510, 97205.
(503) 227-1411
    MR. ALEXANDER CHRISTY,   Mar. 29, 1985
       HONORARY CONSUL

TEXAS

HOUSTON (HCG) 320 S. 66TH ST., 77011.
(713) 928-2264
    MR. WILLIAM C. CRASSAS,   May. 01, 1995
       HONORARY CONSUL GENERAL

WASHINGTON

SEATTLE (HC) 5555 LAKEVIEW DR., SUITE 200, KIRKLAND 98033.
(206) 827-1700
    MR. VASSOS MICHAEL DEMETRIOU,   Jun. 04, 1996
       HONORARY CONSUL

CZECH REPUBLIC

ALASKA

ANCHORAGE (HC) 310 K ST., SUITE 601, 99501.
(907) 274-2602
    DR. FRANCIS JOHN NOSEK,   Oct. 07, 1999
       HONORARY CONSUL

CALIFORNIA

LOS ANGELES (CG) 10990 WILSHIRE BL., SUITE 1100, 90024.
(310) 473-0889, FAX (310) 473-9813
    MR. DANIEL KUMERMANN,   Jan. 24, 2007
       CONSUL GENERAL
    MS. LUDMILA KUNDRATOVA,   Aug. 24, 2005
       CONSUL
    MR. TOMAS KADLEC,   Apr. 06, 2006
       CONSUL

SAN FRANCISCO (HCG) 500 SANSOME ST., FLOOR 8TH, 94111.
(415) 772-9603, FAX (415) 772-9670
    MR. RICHARD JOSEPH PIVNICKA,   Jun. 20, 2000
       HONORARY CONSUL GENERAL

FLORIDA

FT. LAUDERDALE (HCG) 3111 STIRLING RD., 33312.
(954) 985-4178, FAX (954) 985-4176

STATE* RESIDENCE	NAME AND RANK	DATE OF RECOGNITION
MR. ALAN S. BECKER, HONORARY CONSUL GENERAL		Feb. 09, 2004
GEORGIA		
ATLANTA (HCG) 4 CONCOURSE PW., SUITE 215, 30328. (678) 587-9198, FAX (770) 395-1655		
MR. GEORGE A. NOVAK, HONORARY CONSUL GENERAL		Mar. 04, 2004
ILLINOIS		
CHICAGO (CG) 205 N. MICHIGAN AV., SUITE 1680, 60601. , FAX (312) 861-1944		
MR. MAREK SKOLIL, CONSUL GENERAL		Jan. 06, 2006
DR. BOREK LIZEC, CONSUL		Oct. 31, 2005
MS. KATERINA KULHANKOVA, VICE CONSUL		Mar. 03, 2006
LOUISIANA		
NEW ORLEANS (HC) 3800 FLORIDA AV., SUITE 202, KENNER 70065. (504) 456-1336, FAX (504) 455-1565		
MR. KENNETH H. ZEZULKA, HONORARY CONSUL		Aug. 26, 1998
MASSACHUSETTS		
WELLESLEY (HC) 28 HOWE ST., 02482. (781) 249-2896		
MR. IGOR LUKES, HONORARY CONSUL		Aug. 24, 2005
MISSOURI		
KANSAS CITY (HC) 105 W. 113TH ST., 64114. (816) 363-6827		
MS. SHARON KAY VALASEK, HONORARY CONSUL		Feb. 13, 2003
NEW YORK		
BUFFALO (HC) 10545 MAIN ST., CLARENCE 14031. (716) 759-6078, FAX (716) 759-7925		
MR. B. JOHN ZAVREL, HONORARY CONSUL		Feb. 02, 1995
NEW YORK (CG) 1109-1111 MADISON AV., FLOOR 1ST, 10028. (212) 717-5643, FAX (212) 717-5064		
MS. HALKA KAISEROVA, CONSUL GENERAL		Sep. 14, 2006
MISS ALICE MARIE SVOBODOVA, CONSUL		Mar. 09, 2005
MR. DAVID OLSA, CONSULAR AGENT		Jun. 04, 2003
OREGON		
PORTLAND (HC) 10260 S. W. GREENBURG RD., SUITE 560, 97223. (503) 293-9547, FAX (503) 293-9546		
MRS. MARIE ROSE AMICCI, HONORARY CONSUL		Feb. 02, 1995

STATE* RESIDENCE	NAME AND RANK	DATE OF RECOGNITION
PENNSYLVANIA		
PHILADELPHIA (HCG) 921 BETHLEHEM PK., SUITE 102, SPRING HOUSE 19477. (215) 646-7777, FAX (215) 646-7770		
MR. PETER A. RAFAELI, HONORARY CONSUL GENERAL		Jun. 20, 2000
PITTSBURGH (HC) 425 SIXTH AV., SUITE 11, 15219. (412) 855-6581		
MS. CAROL HOLLY HOCHMAN, HONORARY CONSUL		Dec. 05, 2006
PUERTO RICO		
SAN JUAN (HC) 62 SAN FRANCISCO ST., 00901. (787) 722-2467, FAX (787) 723-5787		
MS. JUDITH ANN CONDE, HONORARY CONSUL		Aug. 20, 2001
TEXAS		
HOUSTON (HCG) 11748 HERITAGE PW., WEST 76691. (713) 629-6963, FAX (254) 826-7727		
MR. RAYMOND SNOKHOUS, HONORARY CONSUL GENERAL		Aug. 01, 2006

DENMARK

STATE* RESIDENCE	NAME AND RANK	DATE OF RECOGNITION
ALABAMA		
MOBILE (HC) 205 ST. LOUIS ST., 36602. (251) 432-4636, FAX (251) 432-8675		
MR. MARTIN HORST CUNNINGHAM, HONORARY CONSUL		Dec. 16, 1987
ALASKA		
ANCHORAGE (HC) 425 G ST., SUITE 610, 99501. (907) 276-1221		
MR. WILLIAM GRANT , II CALLOW, HONORARY CONSUL		Mar. 22, 2006
ARIZONA		
SCOTTSDALE (HC) 9280 E. RAINTREE DR., SUITE 101, 85260. (480) 922-0290		
MR. JOHN LARSEN, HONORARY CONSUL		Jan. 27, 2005
CALIFORNIA		
SAN DIEGO (HC) 7705 WHITEFIELD PL., LA JOLLA 92037. (858) 459-5205		
MR. CRAIG S. ANDREWS, HONORARY CONSUL		May. 28, 1998
SAN FRANCISCO (HC) 1 CALIFORNIA ST., SUITE 330, 94111. (415) 391-0100		
MR. FINN MARTENSEN, HONORARY CONSUL		May. 19, 2003
MS. ANNE GRETHE MARTENSEN, HONORARY VICE CONSUL		Jul. 29, 2005

STATE* RESIDENCE	NAME AND RANK	DATE OF RECOGNITION	STATE* RESIDENCE	NAME AND RANK	DATE OF RECOGNITION

STUDIO CITY (HC) 10877 WILSHIRE BL., SUITE 1402, LOS ANGELES 90024.
(310) 481-0391, FAX (310) 481-0390
   MR. STIG STENHOJ,   Nov. 08, 2002
     HONORARY CONSUL

COLORADO

DENVER (HC) 5353 W. DARTMOUTH AV., SUITE 508, 80227.
(303) 980-9100
   MRS. NANNA NIELSEN SMITH,   Jun. 25, 1996
     HONORARY CONSUL

FLORIDA

HOLLYWOOD (HC) 3230 STIRLING RD., SUITE 1, 33021--2041.
(954) 322-0065
   MR. JONATHAN H. ROSENTHAL,   Jun. 10, 2005
     HONORARY CONSUL

JACKSONVILLE (HC) 9620 DAVE RAWLS BL., BLOUNT ISLAND 32226.
(904) 696-7750, FAX (904) 696-7760
   MR. LARRY JOE WARREN,   Sep. 01, 1995
     HONORARY CONSUL

TAMPA (HC) 1803 EASTPORT DR., 33605.
(813) 247-4550, FAX (813) 247-4256
   MR. ARTHUR RENFRO SAVAGE,   Nov. 04, 1998
     HONORARY CONSUL

GEORGIA

ATLANTA (HC) 1100 SPRING ST., SUITE 550, 30309-2848.
(404) 876-5511, FAX (404) 875-2629
   MR. STEPHEN SELIG,   Oct. 20, 1997
     HONORARY CONSUL

MACON (HC) 130 N. CREST DR., SUITE B, 31210.
(478) 477-8145
   MR. CHRISTOPHER NOLAN SMITH,   Mar. 13, 2006
     HONORARY CONSUL

HAWAII

HONOLULU (HC) 285 SAND ISLAND ACCESS RD., 96819.
(808) 852-6716
   MR. LAURENCE VOGEL,   Sep. 27, 1993
     HONORARY CONSUL

ILLINOIS

CHICAGO (CG) 211 EAST ONTARIO ST., SUITE 1800, 60611-3242.
(312) 787-8780, FAX (312) 787-8744
   MR. MADS MIKKELSEN,   Oct. 05, 2005
     CONSUL GENERAL

INDIANA

INDIANAPOLIS (HC) ONE AMERICAN SQ., SUITE 1700, 46282.
(317) 639-1210
   MR. STEVEN LESLIE TUCHMAN,   Jan. 16, 2003
     HONORARY CONSUL

IOWA

DES MOINES (HC) 4653 NE 46TH ST., 50317-4722.
(515) 263-0044, FAX (515) 266-3000
   MR. LOWELL BERNARD KRAMME,   Apr. 23, 1997
     HONORARY CONSUL

LOUISIANA

NEW ORLEANS (HC) 321 ST. CHARLES AV., 70130.
(504) 586-8300
   MR. THOMAS KENDALL WININGDER, Nov. 21, 1989
     HONORARY CONSUL

MARYLAND

BALTIMORE (HC) 217 E. REDWOOD ST., 21202-3316.
(410) 685-3116, FAX (410) 625-3801
   MR. TIMOTHY CONNOR MCNAMARA, Mar. 09, 1982
     HONORARY CONSUL

MASSACHUSETTS

BOSTON (HC) 60 STATE ST., 02109.
(617) 542-1415, FAX (617) 482-6201
   MR. JACOB FRIIS,   Sep. 20, 2000
     HONORARY CONSUL

MICHIGAN

DETROIT (HC) 5510 WOODWARD AV., 48202.
(313) 875-9856, FAX (313) 875-9857
   MR. DAVID W. CHRISTENSEN,   Oct. 03, 1995
     HONORARY CONSUL

MINNESOTA

MINNEAPOLIS (HC) 1417 EAST RIVER PW., 55414.
(612) 338-7283
   MS. ANELISE SAWKINS,   Jun. 09, 1995
     HONORARY CONSUL

MISSOURI

KANSAS CITY (HC) 1700 W. 12TH ST., 64101.
(800) 821-2702
   MS. KAREN ELAINE NIELSEN,   Oct. 23, 1996
     HONORARY CONSUL

SAINT LOUIS (HC) 16486 HOLLISTER CROSSING DR., WILDWOOD 63011.
(314) 603-2470
   MR. NIELS C. ANDERSEN,   Jan. 14, 2000
     HONORARY CONSUL

NEBRASKA

OMAHA (HC) 1620 DODGE ST., 68102.
(402) 633-3033
   MR. BRUCE R. LAURITZEN,   Dec. 01, 1995
     HONORARY CONSUL

NEW YORK

NEW YORK (CG) 885 2ND AV., FLOOR 18, 10017-2201.
(212) 223-4545

STATE* RESIDENCE	NAME AND RANK	DATE OF RECOGNITION
	MR. TORBEN ANTONIO GETTERMANN, CONSUL GENERAL	Oct. 06, 2005
	MRS. ANETTE STEENBERG WILLIAMS, DEPUTY CONSUL GENERAL	Sep. 27, 2006
	MRS. HELLE MEINERTZ, CONSUL	Oct. 09, 2002
	MS. BETTINA KAREN PEDERSEN, CONSUL	Dec. 13, 2006

OHIO

CLEVELAND (HC) 13400 GLENSIDE RD., 44110.
(216) 541-0500

	MR. J. CHRISTIAN LANGMACK, HONORARY CONSUL	Oct. 07, 1998

OKLAHOMA

OKLAHOMA CITY (HC) 9400 BROADWAY EXTENSION ., SUITE 130, 73114-7499.
(405) 606-0335

	MR. WILLIAM W., II TALLEY, HONORARY CONSUL	Jul. 11, 1988

OREGON

PORTLAND (HC) 888 S.W. 5TH AV., 97204.
(503) 802-2131, FAX (503) 972-3813

	MR. INGOLF NOTO, HONORARY CONSUL	Feb. 27, 1989

PENNSYLVANIA

PHILADELPHIA (HC) 123 S. BROAD ST., 19109.
(215) 772-1500, FAX (215) 772-7620

	MR. ALFRED J. KUFFLER, HONORARY CONSUL	Nov. 20, 1991

PITTSBURGH (HC) 104 SHANOR HEIGHTS UN., BUTLER 16001.
(724) 283-2274

	MS. EVA MARIANNE ROBINSON, HONORARY CONSUL	Jan. 24, 2006

PUERTO RICO

SAN JUAN (HC) 360 SAN FRANCISCO ST., 00901.
(787) 725-2532, FAX (787) 724-0339

	MR. JOSE O. BUSTO, HONORARY CONSUL	Sep. 15, 1983

SOUTH CAROLINA

CHARLESTON (HC) 205 KING ST., SUITE 400, 29401.
(843) 577-9440

	MR. BRADISH JOHNSON WARING, HONORARY CONSUL	Apr. 25, 2007

TENNESSEE

NASHVILLE (HC) 2200 CHILDREN'S WAY ., N, SUITE 1424, 37232.
(615) 936-4952, FAX (615) 936-4944

	MR. RICHARD M. HELLER, HONORARY CONSUL	Sep. 14, 1981

TEXAS

DALLAS (HC) 2100 MCKINNEY AV., SUITE 700, 75201.
(214) 661-8399, FAX (214) 661-8036

	MR. HARLAN R. CROW, HONORARY CONSUL	May. 28, 1984

HOUSTON (HC) 4545 POST OAK PL., SUITE 347, 77027.
(713) 622-9018, FAX (713) 622-7512

	MR. RAY JENS DAUGBJERG, HONORARY CONSUL	Feb. 09, 1990
	MRS. ANNA D. STOTTRUP HOLLIDAY, HONORARY VICE CONSUL	Oct. 01, 1998

UTAH

SALT LAKE CITY (HC) 524 S. 600RD ., E, 84102.
(801) 531-7061, FAX (801) 531-9850

	MR. NIELS ERIK VALENTINER, HONORARY CONSUL	Apr. 07, 1993

VIRGIN ISLANDS

ST. THOMAS (HC) 9003 HAVENSIGHT MALL ., 3, ST.THOMAS 00801.
(340) 776-0656, FAX (340) 774-6642

	MR. SOREN BLAK, HONORARY CONSUL	Apr. 06, 1994

VIRGINIA

NORFOLK (HC) 1800 NATIONS BANK CENTER ., 23510-2197.
(757) 628-5568

	MR. WILLIAM EDWARD, JR RACHELS, HONORARY CONSUL	Mar. 03, 1978

WASHINGTON

SEATTLE (HC) 6204 E. MERCER WA., MERCER ISLAND 98040.
(206) 230-0888

	MR. ERIK D. LAURSEN, HONORARY CONSUL	Nov. 15, 1993
	MRS. KIRSTEN VILHOLM, HONORARY VICE CONSUL	Feb. 11, 1999

WISCONSIN

MILWAUKEE (HC) 19335A MCALLISTER LA., BROOKFIELD 53045.
(262) 253-1717, FAX (262) 253-2277

	MR. BARRY N. JAMES, HONORARY CONSUL	Apr. 25, 1983

DOMINICA

NEW YORK

NEW YORK (CG) 800 2ND AV., SUITE 400H, 10017.
(212) 599-8478, FAX (212) 661-0979

	MS. ZILPHA THEODORE, VICE CONSUL	Jul. 21, 1997

DOMINICAN REPUBLIC

CALIFORNIA

SUN VALLEY (CG) 9001 LAUREL CANYON BL., SUITE 204, 91352.
(818) 504-6605

STATE* RESIDENCE	NAME AND RANK	DATE OF RECOGNITION	STATE* RESIDENCE	NAME AND RANK	DATE OF RECOGNITION

MRS. CELESTE JIMENEZ PENA DE AMARANTE,   Apr. 25, 2006
    CONSUL GENERAL

FLORIDA

MIAMI (CG) 1038 BRICKELL AV., 33131.
(305) 358-3221

   MR. MANUEL FELIPE ALMANZAR CASTILLO,   Apr. 17, 2007
     CONSUL GENERAL
   MR. NELSON AHMED CHABEBE BAEZ,   Sep. 18, 1998
     VICE CONSUL
   MR. MARCOS JOSE PEREYRA JORGE,   Nov. 19, 2001
     VICE CONSUL

ILLINOIS

CHICAGO (CG) 25 E. WASHINGTON ST., SUITE 1400, 60602.
(312) 469-8350, FAX (312) 469-8386

   MRS. GISSELLE D. CASTILLO VEREMIS,   May. 29, 2007
     CONSUL GENERAL

LOUISIANA

NEW ORLEANS (CG) 2 CANAL ST., SUITE 2100, 70130.
(504) 522-1843, FAX (504) 522-1007

   MR. JOAQUIN A. BALAGUER RICARDO,   Dec. 05, 1990
     CONSUL GENERAL

MASSACHUSETTS

BOSTON (CG) 20 PARK PZ., SUITE 601, 02116.
(617) 482-8121, FAX (617) 482-8133

   MR. DOMINICO CABRAL ABAD,   Nov. 21, 2005
     CONSUL GENERAL
   MR. FRANCISCO LIZARDO DE LEON,   Jan. 04, 2006
     VICE CONSUL
   MR. CLAUDIO A. PEREZ DIAZ,   Jan. 26, 2006
     VICE CONSUL

NEW YORK

NEW YORK (CG) 1501 BROADWAY ., SUITE 410, 10036.
(212) 768-2480, FAX (212) 768-2677

   MR. RAFAEL EDUARDO SELMAN HASBUN,   May. 07, 2007
     CONSUL GENERAL
   MR. LUIS PRINCE RODRIGUEZ,   Jul. 31, 2006
     VICE CONSUL
   MR. ROMAN OCTAVIO JAQUEZ HERNANDEZ,   Jan. 29, 2007
     VICE CONSUL
   MS. RAMONA ANTONIA ABREU DE LOPEZ,   May. 04, 2007
     VICE CONSUL
   MR. NELSON MANUEL BALCACER ABREU,   May. 08, 2007
     VICE CONSUL

PUERTO RICO

MAYAGUEZ (CG) 30 CALLE MCKINLEY ST., FLOOR 2ND, 00680.
(809) 833-0007

   MR. MAXIMO CARMELO TAVERAS,   Jan. 06, 2006
     CONSUL GENERAL

SAN JUAN (CG) 1612 AVENIDA PONCE DELEON UN., FLOOR 7,
00907.
(809) 725-9550

   MR. JOSE NAZARIO FONDEUR ALMANZAR,   Apr. 19, 2007
     CONSUL GENERAL

ECUADOR

CALIFORNIA

LOS ANGELES (CG) 8484 WILSHIRE BL., SUITE 540, 520, BEVERLY
HILLS 90211.
(323) 658-6020

   MR. EDDIE RAINIERO BEDON ORBE,   Jun. 06, 2007
     CONSUL GENERAL
   MR. FERNANDO ARIAS,   Sep. 09, 1999
     DEPUTY CONSUL GENERAL
   MR. IVAN MICHEL MALDONADO VACA,   Jul. 28, 2004
     CONSUL
   MS. MERCEDES S. MANRIQUEZ SAMPEDRO,   Jul. 29, 2005
     CONSULAR AGENT
   MS. ALBA RUBIO,   May. 04, 2007
     CONSULAR AGENT

SAN FRANCISCO (CG) 235 MONTGOMERY ST., SUITE 944, 94104.
(415) 957-5921, FAX (415) 957-5923

   MR. JUAN MIGUEL LEORO ALMEIDA,   Jul. 31, 2007
     CONSUL GENERAL
   MRS. MAGDALENA C. NARANJO MANCERO,   Nov. 14, 2005
     CONSULAR AGENT
   MRS. XIMENA CORDOVEZ ANGOTTI,   Jan. 31, 1984
     HONORARY CONSUL
   MR. JACOB RATINOFF,   Aug. 01, 2006
     HONORARY CONSUL

DISTRICT OF COLUMBIA

WASHINGTON (CHN) 2535 15TH ST., NW, 20009.
(202) 234-7200, FAX (202) 667-3482

   MS. MARIA GUADALUPE RIOS BAYAS,   Mar. 30, 2007
     CONSULAR AGENT

CONSULAR AFFAIRS OFFICE
WASHINGTON (CA) 2535 15TH ST., NW, 20009.
(202) 234-7166

FLORIDA

MIAMI (CG) 1101 BRICKELL AV., SUITE M-102, 33131.
(305) 539-8214, FAX (305) 539-8313

   MR. JUAN CARLOS TOLEDO GRADIN,   May. 23, 2007
     CONSUL GENERAL
   MRS. CYNTHIA MARIE MAYER ZAVALA,   Aug. 10, 2006
     DEPUTY CONSUL GENERAL
   MRS. MARTHA GUADALUPE CARRERA AGREDA,   Apr. 25, 2007
     CONSUL

VISA OFFICE OF ECUADOR
MIAMI (CONA) 3785 N.W. 82ND AV., SUITE 317, 33166.
(305) 716-5252, FAX (305) 716-9296

TAMPA (HC) 8104 N. HALE AV., 33614.
(813) 884-8985

   MR. AGUSTIN FABRIZIO VERA,   Oct. 14, 2005
     HONORARY CONSUL

---

* DEPENDENCIES SUCH AS GUAM, PUERTO RICO, AND THE VIRGIN ISLANDS ARE LISTED HERE.
CG-CONSULATE GENERAL   C-CONSULATE   VC-VICE CONSULATE   CA-CONSULAR AGENCY   H-HONORARY CONSULAR STATUS

STATE* RESIDENCE	NAME AND RANK	DATE OF RECOGNITION	STATE* RESIDENCE	NAME AND RANK	DATE OF RECOGNITION

GEORGIA

ATLANTA (HC) 5505 ROSWELL RD., SUITE 350, 30342.
(404) 252-2211, FAX (404) 252-8580
  MRS. PATRICIA BOEZIO,   Mar. 29, 2000
    HONORARY CONSUL

ILLINOIS

CHICAGO (CG) 30 S. MICHIGAN AV., SUITE 204, 60603.
(312) 338-1003, FAX (312) 338-1004
  MS. ELSA LOPEZ MOLINA,   May. 04, 2007
    CONSUL
  MS. EVELYN PAOLA INIGUEZ RODRIGUEZ,   Nov. 14, 2005
    VICE CONSUL
  MRS. MARIA ENMA VIZCAINO BUSTAMANTE,   Apr. 28, 2006
    CONSULAR AGENT
  MR. HERNAN MARCELO VELA HERVAS,   Feb. 26, 2001
    HONORARY CONSUL

LOUISIANA

NEW ORLEANS (CG) 2 CANAL ST., SUITE 2338, 70130.
(504) 523-3229
  MR. JUAN CARLOS AROSEMENA MARMOL,   Oct. 11, 2005
    VICE CONSUL

MASSACHUSETTS

BOSTON (HC) 52 CRANBERRY LA., NEEDHAM 02492.
(781) 444-0213
  MRS. BEATRIZ STEIN,   Nov. 13, 2002
    HONORARY CONSUL

MINNESOTA

EDEN PRAIRIE (HC) 1304 E. LAKE ST., SUITE 200, MINNEAPOLIS
55407.
(612) 721-6468, FAX (612) 625-1955
  MR. JUAN CARLOS MORENO,   Nov. 08, 2004
    HONORARY CONSUL

NEVADA

LAS VEGAS (HC) 630 S. 10TH ST., 89101.
(702) 869-4351, FAX (702) 869-4352
  MR. GERARDO EFREN MEJIA CAMPODONICO,   Sep. 03, 2004
    HONORARY CONSUL

NEW JERSEY

NEWARK (CG) 400 MARKET ST., FLOOR 4TH, 07105.
(973) 344-6900, FAX (973) 344-0008
  MRS. PATRICIA PELAEZ MORA,   Oct. 06, 2003
    CONSULAR AGENT
  MS. ELSA MARIANA VILLALBA AREQUIPA,   Jun. 30, 2006
    CONSULAR AGENT
  MRS. PAULINA SYLVA CRUZ,   Apr. 30, 2007
    CONSULAR AGENT

NEW YORK

NEW YORK (CG) 800 2ND AV., SUITE 600, 10017.
(212) 808-0170
  MR. JORGE WASHINGTON LOPEZ AMAYA,   Jul. 26, 2007
    CONSUL GENERAL
  MS. GLORIA ESPINEL CHIRIBOGA,   Aug. 18, 1997
    CONSUL

  MS. IVONNE GARCES ALMEIDA,   Jun. 03, 2004
    CONSUL
  MS. NELLY M. NAVARRETE TORRES,   May. 04, 2007
    CONSUL
  MS. MARIA EUGENIA AVILES ZEVALLOS,   May. 30, 2007
    CONSUL
  MR. JUAN GRANADOS PALADINES,   Dec. 07, 2001
    VICE CONSUL
  MR. SANTIAGO DANILO CHIRIBOGA ACOSTA,   Apr. 11, 2005
    VICE CONSUL
  MR. OSCAR FUERTES JIMENEZ,   Sep. 29, 2003
    CONSULAR AGENT
  MRS. VICTORIA GENOVEVA PEREZ CARVAJAL,   Nov. 14, 2005
    CONSULAR AGENT
  MR. EDWIN RUBEN ANDRADE DELGAGO,   Feb. 23, 2006
    CONSULAR AGENT
  MRS. AMERICA YOLANDA VACA MORALES,   Oct. 16, 2006
    CONSULAR AGENT

COMMERCIAL OFFICE
NEW YORK (CONA) 399 PARK AV., SUITE 28B, 10022.
(212) 888-7229

PUERTO RICO

SAN JUAN (HC) 65 INF CALLE ABAD- VEB CLUB MANOR ., RIO
PIEDROS 00924.
(787) 999-5226, FAX (787) 999-5243
  MR. ANDRES VITOLA,   Feb. 21, 2002
    HONORARY CONSUL

TEXAS

DALLAS (HCG) 7510 ACORN LA., FRISCO 75034.
(972) 712-9107, FAX (253) 369-7475
  MR. RICARDO M. BOWEN GRIMMER,   Feb. 05, 2007
    HONORARY CONSUL GENERAL

HOUSTON (CG) 4200 WESTHEIMER ., SUITE 218, 77027.
(713) 622-1787
  MRS. VERONICA PENA MONTERO,   May. 19, 2006
    CONSUL GENERAL
  MR. LENIN AMARO ARCOS CADENA,   May. 02, 2005
    CONSULAR AGENT
  DR. CARLOS E. ROMERO,   May. 06, 1985
    HONORARY CONSUL

EGYPT

CALIFORNIA

SAN FRANCISCO (CG) 3001 PACIFIC AV., 94115.
(415) 346-9700
  MR. ABDERAHMAN SALAH ELDIN ABDERAHMAN,   Sep. 29, 2004
    CONSUL GENERAL
  MR. YASSER MAHMOUD ABED,   Oct. 04, 2005
    CONSUL
  MR. KHALED FADI MAHMOUD EL SHAZLY,   May. 07, 2007
    DEPUTY CONSUL
  MR. HESHAM ELDAHSHAN,   Dec. 29, 2004
    VICE CONSUL
  MR. NABIL AHMED MOHAMED ELGENDY,   Aug. 10, 2006
    VICE CONSUL

STATE* RESIDENCE	NAME AND RANK	DATE OF RECOGNITION	STATE* RESIDENCE	NAME AND RANK	DATE OF RECOGNITION

EGYPTIAN PRESS OFFICE
SAN FRANCISCO (CONA) 1255 POST ST., SUITE 1034, 94109.
(415) 346-3427, FAX (415) 346-3430

MR. ATTIYA ALI ATTIYA SHAKRAN, CONSUL	Nov. 14, 2005	

ECONOMIC AND COMMERCIAL OFFICE
SAN FRANCISCO (CONA) 1255 POST ST., SUITE 300, 94109.
(415) 771-1995

MR. AMIN SABRY ABDEL MEGUD, CONSUL	Oct. 09, 2002
MR. AHMED SEIF ELNASR OMAR MOHAMED, VICE CONSUL	Mar. 17, 2006
MR. SOBHY ELSAYED ABDEL MOHSEN, VICE CONSUL	Apr. 30, 2007

ILLINOIS

CHICAGO (CG) 500 N. MICHIGAN AV., SUITE 1900, 60611.
(312) 828-9162

MS. HODA ABDOU MOHAMED GOUDA, CONSUL GENERAL	Sep. 29, 2004
MR. MAHMOUD FAROUK YOUSSEF AMER, DEPUTY CONSUL GENERAL	Aug. 10, 2006
MR. SALAHELDIN MOHAMED ZAKI, VICE CONSUL	May. 11, 2005
MR. AMR A. M. HALIM, VICE CONSUL	Jul. 08, 2005
MR. MAHMOUD LABIB MOHAMED ABDOU, VICE CONSUL	Nov. 14, 2005

COMMERCIAL OFFICE
CHICAGO (CONA) 500 N. MICHIGAN AV., SUITE 1030, 60611.
(312) 840-9033, FAX (312) 840-9035

MR. ABDEL MONEIM A. MOUSSA, CONSUL	Jul. 10, 2006
MR. AHMED FADEL ABDEL RAZEK BEDEWI, VICE CONSUL	Mar. 17, 2006

NEW YORK

NEW YORK (CG) 1110 2ND AV., SUITE 201, 10022.
(212) 759-7120

AMBASSADOR SHERIF RIAD ELKHOLI, CONSUL GENERAL	Sep. 23, 2004
MR. KHALED FATHY YOUSSEF, DEPUTY CONSUL GENERAL	Sep. 10, 2004
MR. MOHAMED MOHAMED KHALIL MORSI, CONSUL	Jul. 31, 2006
MR. SAMY AHMED MORSY YONIS, CONSUL	Apr. 25, 2007
MR. ATEF GALAL ABDEL MAWGOOD, VICE CONSUL	Aug. 14, 1996
MR. MOANES A. K. ALI, VICE CONSUL	Sep. 17, 1996
MR. HUSSEIN A. H. HUSSEIN, VICE CONSUL	Sep. 23, 1996
MR. HASSAN MAHMOUD HAMED EL DEEB, VICE CONSUL	Aug. 12, 1999
MR. AHMED BAYOUMI, VICE CONSUL	Aug. 30, 2004
MR. AHMED FOUAD AHMED AMER, VICE CONSUL	Dec. 16, 2004
MR. MANSOUR ABDEL MONEIM AMIN EMAM, VICE CONSUL	Nov. 14, 2005

MR. METWALLY ABOU EL SEOUD, VICE CONSUL	Nov. 14, 2005
MS. FAYZA M. A. S. AHMED, VICE CONSUL	Nov. 06, 2006
MR. FAHMY MOHAMED SAMIR M. RAMDAN, VICE CONSUL	Apr. 25, 2007

TOURIST OFFICE OF EGYPT
NEW YORK (CONA) 630 5TH AV., SUITE 2305, 10111.
(212) 332-2570, FAX (212) 956-6439

MR. AYDEN S. NOUR, CONSUL	Nov. 13, 1998
MR. ELSAYED MEHREZ KHALIFA, CONSUL	May. 07, 2007

ECONOMIC AND COMMERCIAL OFFICE OF EGYPT
NEW YORK (CONA) 10 ROCKEFELLER PZ., SUITE 715, 10020.
(212) 399-9898, FAX (212) 399-9899

MR. AHMED M. A. HOSNI, CONSUL	Jun. 27, 2005
MR. MOHAMED ABDEL KADER, VICE CONSUL	Mar. 08, 2004
MR. WALEED WAGIH SAMI EL ZOMOR, VICE CONSUL	Oct. 14, 2005
MR. GAMEEL FAHEEM ELSAYED, VICE CONSUL	Aug. 11, 2006

TEXAS

HOUSTON (CG) 1990 POST OAK BL., SUITE 2180, 77056.
(713) 961-4915

MR. EL HUSSEINI MOHAMED ABDEL WAHAB, CONSUL GENERAL	Sep. 14, 2006
MR. KHALED AHMED TAHA M. ABOUZEID, CONSUL	Sep. 30, 2003
MRS. MAGDA EZZAT KHALIL GHALI, VICE CONSUL	Oct. 15, 2004
MR. KAMAL MAHMOUD OSMAN HAMED, VICE CONSUL	May. 11, 2005
MR. AHMED ABDEL AZIZ FAHMY, VICE CONSUL	Sep. 29, 2006

EL SALVADOR

ARIZONA

NOGALES (CG) 840 N. GRAND AV., SUITE 3, 85621.
(520) 287-9405

MR. LEOCADIO JOSE J. CHACON CORADO, CONSUL GENERAL	May. 03, 2005
MS. SYLVIA ROSA HILDALGO ALVAYERO, CONSUL	Aug. 10, 2006

CALIFORNIA

CHULA VISTA (HC) 353 CHURCH AV., SUITE A, 91910.
(619) 585-8883

DR. GREGORY J. WIENER, HONORARY CONSUL	Apr. 30, 2004

COSTA MESA (HC) 32562 CRETE RD., DANA POINT 92629.
(949) 351-6319

MR. HARVEY ALEXANDER SMITH, HONORARY CONSUL	Aug. 11, 2004

STATE* RESIDENCE	NAME AND RANK	DATE OF RECOGNITION

LOS ANGELES (CG) 3450 WILSHIRE BL., SUITE 250, 90010.
(213) 383-8580

MR. HUGO HERRERA ESPINOZA, CONSUL GENERAL		Jul. 08, 2005
MS. RINA YOLANDA MEDINA NAVARRETE, CONSUL		Mar. 17, 2006
MR. JOSE R. GARCIA PRIETO ESQUIVEL, CONSUL		Feb. 16, 2007
MISS ANNA MARIA DE LA GASCA, VICE CONSUL		Feb. 27, 2004
MR. WILLIAM BENJAMIN JARQUIN MARENCO, VICE CONSUL		Sep. 07, 2004
MS. YOLANDA LYZ ANGULO AGUIRRE, VICE CONSUL		Jul. 07, 2005
MS. EVELYN R. DE CANDEL, VICE CONSUL		Jun. 05, 2006
MS. AIDA GRISELDA ALAS ARTEAGA, VICE CONSUL		Feb. 21, 2007
MRS. GINA C. LEVY, HONORARY CONSUL		Nov. 10, 1999

OAKLAND (HC) 10550 INTERNATIONAL BL., SUITE 2B, 94603--3804.
(510) 635-1700

MR. ANTHONY A., JR BATARSE, HONORARY CONSUL — Apr. 25, 2006

SAN FRANCISCO (CG) 870 MARKET ST., SUITE 508, 94102.
(415) 781-7924

MR. RAFAEL ANTONIO CARBALLO LACAYO, CONSUL GENERAL — Jan. 06, 2006
MR. LUIS ROBERTO CASTELLANOS ALVAREZ, VICE CONSUL — Mar. 26, 2003

SANTA ANA (CG) 203 N. GOLDEN CIRCLE DR., SUITE 103, 92705.
MS. ANA BESSIE MILLA DE RECINOS, CONSUL — Jul. 07, 2005

DISTRICT OF COLUMBIA

CONSULATE GENERAL
WASHINGTON (CG) 1724 20TH ST., NW, 20009.
(202) 331-4032, FAX (202) 331-4036

MS. ANA MARGARITA CHAVEZ ESCOBAR, CONSUL GENERAL — Jul. 01, 2005
MRS. FLORENCIA VILANOVA DE VON OEHSEN, CONSUL — Jun. 22, 2005
MRS. ROSA ANGELA VALENCIA DE ARGUMEDO, CONSUL — May. 01, 2007
MS. ANGELA MARIA RUBIO MARTINEZ, VICE CONSUL — Dec. 29, 2006

FLORIDA

MIAMI (CG) 2600 DOUGLAS RD., SUITE 104, CORAL GABLES 33134.
(305) 774-0840, FAX (305) 774-0850

MR. LUIS MONTES BRITO, CONSUL GENERAL — Jul. 26, 2006
MS. PAOLA BARRERA RUBIO, CONSUL — Jun. 05, 2007
MRS. ANA MARIA ESERSKI, VICE CONSUL — Jun. 15, 1999
MR. ROBERTO ALAS ENGELHARD, VICE CONSUL — Feb. 16, 2000
MS. FLORENCE KRIETE AVILA, VICE CONSUL — Jan. 08, 2002

MR. RAUL J. VALDES FAULI, HONORARY CONSUL — Dec. 14, 1998

GEORGIA

DULUTH (CG) 3505 DULUTH PARK LA., SUITE 320, 30096.
(770) 623-8891

MR. LUCAS ASDRUBAL AGUILAR ZEPEDA, CONSUL GENERAL — Jun. 07, 2005
MR. MARCIAL VELA RAMOS, CONSUL — Jul. 07, 2005

ILLINOIS

CHICAGO (CG) 104 S. MICHIGAN AV., SUITE 816, 60603.
(312) 332-1393, FAX (312) 332-4446

MS. PATRICIA MAZA PITTSFORD, CONSUL GENERAL — May. 13, 2002
MS. PATRICIA H. FERNANDEZ MONTALVO, VICE CONSUL — Dec. 30, 2005

LOUISIANA

NEW ORLEANS (HCG) 315 W. WM. DAVID PW., METAIRIE 70005.
(504) 828-1727, FAX (504) 831-7404

DR. PATRICIA ELENA MOLINA, HONORARY CONSUL GENERAL — Jun. 28, 2001

MASSACHUSETTS

BOSTON (CON) 20 MERIDIAN ST., FLOOR 4TH, 02128.
(617) 567-8484

MS. ROXANA PATRICIA ABREGO GRANADOS, CONSUL GENERAL — Oct. 23, 2006
MR. PEDRO A. ANGEL ORELLANA, VICE CONSUL — Jun. 05, 2003

MISSOURI

KANSAS CITY (HC) 608 W. 101ST TE., 64114.
(816) 941-6648

MR. JOHN H. FISHER, HONORARY CONSUL — Feb. 21, 2002

SAINT LOUIS (HC) 7730 FORSYTH ., SUITE 200, ST. LOUIS 63105.
(314) 862-0300

MR. MICHAEL JAY BOBROFF, HONORARY CONSUL — Oct. 13, 1976

NEVADA

LAS VEGAS (CG) 765 NELLIS AV., SUITE C-5, 89110.
(702) 437-5339

MR. OSCAR S. BENAVIDES GUTIERREZ, CONSUL GENERAL — Mar. 10, 2004
MR. JUAN ANTONIO SALAMANCA ESCOLERO, VICE CONSUL — Feb. 01, 2006

NEW JERSEY

ELIZABETH (CON) 333 N. BROAD ST., SUITE 2&3, 07208.
(908) 820-0881

MR. CARLOS WILFREDO LOPEZ, CONSUL — Mar. 26, 2006

---

* DEPENDENCIES SUCH AS GUAM, PUERTO RICO, AND THE VIRGIN ISLANDS ARE LISTED HERE.
CG-CONSULATE GENERAL   C-CONSULATE   VC-VICE CONSULATE   CA-CONSULAR AGENCY   H-HONORARY CONSULAR STATUS

STATE* RESIDENCE	NAME AND RANK	DATE OF RECOGNITION	STATE* RESIDENCE	NAME AND RANK	DATE OF RECOGNITION

NEW YORK

NEW YORK (CG) 46 PARK AV., 10016.
(212) 889-3608

    MS. LORENA SOL DE POOL,   Jul. 22, 2002
      CONSUL GENERAL
    MRS. ANA VILMA AVILA DE SOLER,   Jan. 30, 1996
      CONSUL
    MRS. SILVIA GERALDINA SOMOZA,   Jun. 19, 2007
      CONSUL

CONSULATE GENERAL
NEW YORK (CG) 1090 SUFFOLK AV., BRENTWOOD 11717.
(631) 273-1355

    MR. OSCAR E. LANDAVERDE CONTRERAS,   Apr. 27, 2007
      CONSUL GENERAL

PENNSYLVANIA

PHILADELPHIA (HC) 119 BLEDDYN RD., ARDMORE 19003.
    MRS. ANA MARIA KEENE,   May. 02, 1983
      HONORARY CONSUL

PUERTO RICO

BAYAMON (HCG) 22 GONZALEZ GISUTI ., SUITE 224, GUAYNABO
00968.
(787) 793-7577, FAX (787) 793-7578

    MS. MARIA TERESA DE ESTEVEZ,   Jun. 04, 1992
      HONORARY CONSUL GENERAL

TEXAS

DALLAS (CG) 1555 W. MOCKINGBIRD LA., SUITE 216, 75235.
    MR. MARIO ROGER HERNANDEZ CALDERON,   Aug. 16, 2006
      CONSUL GENERAL
    MRS. ANA MARIA PEREZ DE LOPEZ,   Feb. 20, 2003
      VICE CONSUL
    MRS. ALMA LORENA VELASQUEZ,   Aug. 24, 2005
      VICE CONSUL

HOUSTON (CG) 1702 HILLENDAHL BL., 77055.
(713) 270-6239

    MR. LUIS ERNESTO CARRANZA,   Aug. 15, 2000
      CONSUL GENERAL
    MRS. ANA SILVIA ARCE DE GALLO,   Jul. 21, 2006
      CONSUL
    MS. MARLENE E. ORANTES DE SALAZAR,   Oct. 26, 1987
      VICE CONSUL
    MS. XOCHITL MENJIVAR,   Feb. 28, 2006
      VICE CONSUL
    MR. FRANCISCO E. CARTAGENA VAQUERO,   Sep. 29, 2006
      VICE CONSUL

UTAH

SALT LAKE CITY (HC) 2530 S. WEST TEMPLE UN., 84115.
(801) 631-0843

    MRS. VERONICA FLORES VAN LEEUWEN,   May. 14, 2002
      HONORARY CONSUL

VIRGINIA

WOODBRIDGE (CG) 14572 POTOMAC MILLS RD., SUITE 12, 22192.
(703) 490-4300

    MISS MIRIAN E. VARGAS CASTILLO,   Apr. 05, 2006
      CONSUL

    MRS. ALICIA C. VILLAMARIONA,   Dec. 21, 2006
      VICE CONSUL

ERITREA

CALIFORNIA

OAKLAND (CG) 409 13TH ST., FLOOR 14TH, 94612.
(510) 986-1991

    MR. AHMED MOHAMED IMAN,   Jun. 04, 2002
      CONSUL GENERAL

ESTONIA

CALIFORNIA

LOS ANGELES (HC) 5273 TENDILLA AV., WOODLAND HILLS 91364.
(818) 340-5766, FAX (805) 552-8733

    MR. JAAK TREIMAN,   Mar. 26, 1986
      HONORARY CONSUL

SAN FRANCISCO (HC) 2004 GOUGH ST., 94109.
(415) 931-5420

    DR. JOHN NEWMEYER,   Mar. 31, 2004
      HONORARY CONSUL

ILLINOIS

CHICAGO (HC) 410 N. MICHIGAN AV., 60611.
(312) 595-2527

    MR. ERIC HARKNA,   Mar. 31, 2004
      HONORARY CONSUL

NEW HAMPSHIRE

PORTSMOUTH (HC) 181 PLEASANT ST., 03801.
(603) 433-0929

    MRS. IRJA CILLUFFO NURMET,   Nov. 23, 2005
      HONORARY CONSUL

NEW YORK

NEW YORK (CG) 600 3RD AV., FLOOR 26TH, 10016.
(212) 883-0636, FAX (212) 883-0648

    MR. PEETER RESTSINSKI,   Jun. 20, 2003
      CONSUL GENERAL
    MRS. CELIA KUNINGAS SAAGPAKK,   Mar. 22, 2002
      CONSUL
    MS. SIGNE MATTEUS,   May. 11, 2004
      CONSUL

WASHINGTON

SEATTLE (HC) 9133 VIEW AV., NW, 98117.
    MR. PAUL AARNE RAIDNA,   Jan. 24, 2007
      HONORARY CONSUL

ETHIOPIA

CALIFORNIA

LOS ANGELES (CG) 3460 WILSHIRE BL., SUITE 308, 90010.
(213) 365-6651

    MR. TAYE ATSKE SELASSIE,   Oct. 21, 2002
      CONSUL GENERAL

STATE* RESIDENCE	NAME AND RANK	DATE OF RECOGNITION	STATE* RESIDENCE	NAME AND RANK	DATE OF RECOGNITION

| | | | **FINLAND** | | |

MR. ANWAR KEDIR ABDO, CONSUL — Oct. 09, 2002

MR. ATAKLTI HAGEGE HAILU, CONSUL — Nov. 26, 2004

MR. ENDALEW METIKU ZELEKE, CONSUL — Jun. 05, 2006

MR. TEKLU HABTEWOLD WOLDEMARIAM, VICE CONSUL — May. 07, 2007

NEW YORK

NEW YORK (CON) 866 2ND AV., FLOOR 3RD, 10017.
(212) 421-1830

MRS. ALGANESH MELESE MESHESHA, CONSUL — Jul. 26, 2007

MS. YEMISRATCH HUNEGNAW ISHETTE, VICE CONSUL — Jun. 27, 2002

TEXAS

HOUSTON (HC) 9301 SOUTHWEST FW., SUITE 250, 77074.
(713) 271-7567

MR. GEZAHEGN KEBEDE, HONORARY CONSUL — Mar. 27, 2001

WASHINGTON

SEATTLE (HCG) 2200 ALASKAN WA., SUITE 300, 98121.
(206) 239-0184, FAX (206) 224-4344

MR. SOLOMON TADESSE, HONORARY CONSUL GENERAL — Sep. 23, 2003

FIJI

CALIFORNIA

EL SEGUNDO (HC) 2301 ROSECRANS AV., SUITE 3185, 90245.
(310) 531-8784, FAX (310) 531-8789

DR. DONALD E. VINSON, HONORARY CONSUL — Dec. 18, 1996

SAN FRANCISCO (HC) 521 ROCCA AV., SOUTH SAN FRANCISCO 94080.
(650) 225-0666

DR. NARAYAN R. RAJU, HONORARY CONSUL — Dec. 18, 1996

OREGON

PORTLAND (HC) 2153 N. E. SANDY BL., 97232.
(503) 231-4222

MR. JAMES W. BOSLEY, HONORARY CONSUL — Dec. 18, 1996

TEXAS

DALLAS (HC) 3400 CARLISLE ST., SUITE 310, 75204.
(214) 954-9993

MR. ROBERT TUCKER HAYES, HONORARY CONSUL — Jun. 14, 2007

ALABAMA

BIRMINGHAM (HC) 2000 INTERNATIONAL PARK DR., 35243.
(205) 972-6655, FAX (205) 972-6779

MR. THOMAS MICHAEL GOODRICH, HONORARY CONSUL — Jun. 26, 2003

ALASKA

ANCHORAGE (HC) 1529 P ST., 99501-4923.
(907) 274-6607, FAX (907) 279-2060

MR. WAYNE ALLAN STOLT, HONORARY CONSUL — May. 25, 1983

ARIZONA

PHOENIX (HC) 8601 N. 64TH PL., PARADISE VALLEY 85253.
(480) 998-7121, FAX (480) 998-7121

MRS. GLORIA J. JACKSON, HONORARY CONSUL — Feb. 21, 2001

CALIFORNIA

LOS ANGELES (CG) 1801 CENTURY PARK EAST ., SUITE 2100, 90067.
(310) 203-9903, FAX (310) 203-9186

MR. MANU VIRTAMO, CONSUL GENERAL — Mar. 17, 2004

MR. RENE SODERMAN, DEPUTY CONSUL GENERAL — Oct. 17, 2005

PORTOLA VALLEY (HC) 108 TYNAN WA., 94028.
(650) 529-1052

DR. LIISA JOHANNA VALIKANGAS, HONORARY CONSUL — Sep. 17, 2004

SAN DIEGO (HC) 1059 10TH AV., 92101.
(619) 236-9202, FAX (619) 993-4436

MS. KATHRIN S. MAUTINO, HONORARY CONSUL — Apr. 19, 2001

COLORADO

DENVER (HC) 11002 MAIN RANGE TRAIL ., LITTLETON 80127.
(303) 972-3790, FAX (303) 948-8390

MR. DANIEL L. KAMUNEN, HONORARY CONSUL — May. 03, 1989

CONNECTICUT

NORWICH (HC) 82 CHELSEA HARBOR DR., 06360.
(860) 886-8845, FAX (860) 886-7276

MR. CARL DENNIS ANDERSON, HONORARY CONSUL — May. 25, 1977

FLORIDA

LAKE WORTH (HC) 523 LAKE AV., 33460.
(561) 582-2335, FAX (561) 586-7996

MR. PETER MAKILA, HONORARY CONSUL — Jul. 31, 2001

MIAMI (HC) 3399 PONCE DE LEON BL., SUITE 200, 33134.
(305) 444-0004, FAX (305) 444-9057

MS. SUSAN P. KELLEY, HONORARY CONSUL — Oct. 30, 2002

STATE* RESIDENCE	NAME AND RANK	DATE OF RECOGNITION	STATE* RESIDENCE	NAME AND RANK	DATE OF RECOGNITION

GEORGIA

ATLANTA (HC) 1230 PEACHTREE ST., NE, SUITE 3100, 30309-3592.
(404) 815-3682, FAX (404) 685-6982

   MR. JOHN DEVAUGHN, SR SAUNDERS,   May. 28, 1996
      HONORARY CONSUL

HAWAII

HONOLULU (HC) 1650 ALA MOANA BL., APT 813, 96815.
(808) 943-2640

   MR. ERKKI E. INKINEN,   Jan. 21, 1982
      HONORARY CONSUL

ILLINOIS

CHICAGO (HC) 362 E. BURLINGTON ST., RIVERSIDE 60546.
(708) 442-0635, FAX (708) 442-6884

   MR. FREDERICK CHARLES NIEMI,   Feb. 18, 1975
      HONORARY CONSUL

LOUISIANA

NEW ORLEANS (HC) 365 CANAL ST., SUITE 2000, 70130.
(504) 584-9223, FAX (504) 568-9130

   MR. PHILIP DEVILLIERS CLAVERIE,   Sep. 27, 2002
      HONORARY CONSUL

MARYLAND

BALTIMORE (HC) 2200 BROENING HW., SUITE 230, 21224.
(410) 633-4666

   MR. DONALD W., JR CARROLL,   Jul. 11, 2000
      HONORARY CONSUL

MASSACHUSETTS

BOSTON (HCG) 101 ARCH ST., FLOOR 12TH, 02110.
(617) 654-1800, FAX (617) 654-1735

   MR. LEONARD KOPELMAN,   Nov. 28, 1990
      HONORARY CONSUL GENERAL

MICHIGAN

FARMINGTON (HC) 23629 LIBERTY UN., SUITE 100, 48335.
(248) 478-3450

   MR. PAUL NOAH POTTI,   Apr. 26, 2007
      HONORARY CONSUL

MARQUETTE (HC) 601 QUINCY ST., HANCOCK 49930.
(906) 487-7200, FAX (906) 487-7366

   DR. ROBERT ALLEN UBBELOHDE,   Sep. 13, 2002
      HONORARY CONSUL

MINNESOTA

MINNEAPOLIS (HC) 2429 GIRARD AV., S, 55405.
(612) 374-2718, FAX (612) 377-5030

   MS. K. MARIANNE WARGELIN,   Feb. 18, 1999
      HONORARY CONSUL

VIRGINIA (HC) 307 1ST ST., N, 55792.
(218) 741-2595

   MR. JAMES L. JOHNSON,   Jun. 28, 1999
      HONORARY CONSUL

NEW JERSEY

NEWARK (HC) 1151 RATTLESNAKE BRIDGE RD., BEDMINSTER 07921.
(908) 439-2222

   MRS. HELEN WINTER MARX,   Jun. 11, 2003
      HONORARY CONSUL

NEW MEXICO

ALBUQUERQUE (HC) 1005 STUART RD., 87114.
(505) 898-2079

   MR. ALAN B. CLARK,   Oct. 03, 1983
      HONORARY CONSUL

NEW YORK

NEW YORK (CG) 866 UNITED NATIONS PZ., SUITE 250, 10017.
(212) 750-4400, FAX (212) 750-4418

   MR. OSMO ANTERO LIPPONEN,   Nov. 05, 2004
      CONSUL GENERAL
   MS. LAURA JOHANNA KAMRAS,   Oct. 17, 2005
      DEPUTY CONSUL GENERAL
   MS. ULLA MARKETTA AHONEN,   Oct. 02, 2006
      VICE CONSUL

OREGON

PORTLAND (HC) 2730 S.W. CEDAR HILLS ., BEAVERTON 97005.
(503) 641-7447, FAX (503) 526-0902

   MR. PAUL MCCORD NISKANEN,   Aug. 14, 1980
      HONORARY CONSUL

PUERTO RICO

SAN JUAN (HC) CALLE D D URB. TORREMOLINOS ST., ROOM G6, GUAYBANO 00969.
(787) 720-0098, FAX (787) 720-0098

   MR. GUSTAVO ADOLFO BENITEZ BADRENA,   Nov. 07, 1973
      HONORARY CONSUL

SAN JUAN (HVC) 18 CAMINO DEL LAGO UN., 00926.
(787) 760-6378

   MR. GARY WILLIAM TUOMINEN,   Jul. 13, 2007
      HONORARY VICE CONSUL

TEXAS

DALLAS (HC) 1601 ELM ST., SUITE 3000, 75201.
(214) 999-4672

   MR. KENNETH MICHAEL NIESMAN,   Sep. 13, 2006
      HONORARY CONSUL

HOUSTON (HC) 14 GREENWAY PZ., SUITE 22R, 77046.
(713) 552-1722, FAX (713) 522-1676

   MR. RONALD A. KAPCHE,   Oct. 21, 1992
      HONORARY CONSUL

VIRGINIA

NORFOLK (HC) 100 ELM ST., SUITE 300, 23510.
(757) 627-6286, FAX (757) 627-3948

STATE* RESIDENCE	NAME AND RANK	DATE OF RECOGNITION	STATE* RESIDENCE	NAME AND RANK	DATE OF RECOGNITION

MR. DAVID F. HOST,   Aug. 20, 1996
 HONORARY CONSUL

WASHINGTON

SEATTLE (HC) 17102 N.E. 37TH PL., BELLEVUE 98008.
(425) 451-3983
 MR. MATTI SUOKKO,   Nov. 29, 2000
  HONORARY CONSUL

FRANCE

ALABAMA

AUBURN UNIVERSITY (HC) 6066 HALEY CENTER UN., 36849.
(334) 844-6374
 DR. SAMIA I. SPENCER,   Nov. 19, 2004
  HONORARY CONSUL

ALASKA

ANCHORAGE (HCA) 2606 C ST., SUITE 3, 99503.
(907) 222-6232
 MR. ROY MARC LA ROSE, Jun. 26, 2003
  HONORARY CONSULAR AGENT

ARIZONA

PHOENIX (HC) 2 N. CENTRAL AV., SUITE 1600, 85004-2393.
(602) 262-5846
 MR. GERRIT MARK STEENBLIK, Feb. 23, 2000
  HONORARY CONSUL

ARKANSAS

LITTLE ROCK (HC) 21 MONARCH DR., MAUMELLE 72113-6112.
(501) 450-1350
 MRS. MARY LOU MARTIN, Oct. 08, 1998
  HONORARY CONSUL

CALIFORNIA

LOS ANGELES (CG) 10990 WILSHIRE BL., SUITE 300, 90024.
(310) 235-3200
 MR. PHILIPPE LARRIEU,   Sep. 29, 2004
  CONSUL GENERAL
 MR. FRANCOIS XAVIER MARIE TILLIETTE, Sep. 14, 2006
  DEPUTY CONSUL GENERAL
 MS. REGINE DENISE ANTOINETTE LOPEZ, Oct. 02, 2006
  DEPUTY CONSUL

FRENCH TOURISM OFFICE
LOS ANGELES (CONA) 9454 WILSHIRE BL., SUITE 210, BEVERLY
HILLS 90212.
(310) 271-6665

CULTURAL DIVISION OF FRANCE
LOS ANGELES (CONA) 10990 WILSHIRE BL., SUITE 300, 90024.
(310) 235-3280

INVEST IN FRANCE AGENCY OFFICE OF FRANCE
LOS ANGELES (CONA) 1801 AVENUE OF THE STARS UN., SUITE
1248, 90067.
(310) 785-9735, FAX (310) 785-9213

SACRAMENTO (HCA) 1831 ROCKWOOD DR., 95864.
(916) 488-7659
 MRS. JANE R. WHEATON, Feb. 28, 1984
  HONORARY CONSULAR AGENT

SAN DIEGO (HC) 3219 CLAIREMONT MESA DR., 92117.
(858) 273-3940
 MR. ANDRE PHILIPPE BORDES, Sep. 10, 2003
  HONORARY CONSUL

SAN FRANCISCO (CG) 540 BUSH ST., 94108.
(415) 397-4330
 MR. FREDERIC DESAGNEAUX, Jul. 31, 2003
  CONSUL GENERAL
 MR. PIERRE HENRI MATTOT, Sep. 24, 2004
  DEPUTY CONSUL

CULTURAL AND SCIENTIFIC OFFICES OF FRANCE
SAN FRANCISCO (CONA) 540 BUSH ST., 94108.

COMMERCIAL OFFICE TRADE COMMISSION OF FRANCE
SAN FRANCISCO (CONA) 88 KEARNY ST., SUITE 700, 94108.
(415) 781-0986

SAN JOSE (HC) 2 N. 2ND ST., SUITE 300, 95113.
(408) 971-1751, FAX (831) 459-4880
 MR. HERVE LE MANSEC, Feb. 12, 1985
  HONORARY CONSUL

COLORADO

DENVER (HCA) 899 LOGAN ST., 80203.
(303) 832-5588
 MR. JEFFREY JACOB RICHARDS, Apr. 19, 2007
  HONORARY CONSULAR AGENT

CONNECTICUT

HARTFORD (HC) 250 SHADDUCK RD., MIDDLEBURY 06762.
(203) 758-2042
 MRS. YOLANDE DIANNE BOSMAN, Oct. 12, 1995
  HONORARY CONSUL

DISTRICT OF COLUMBIA

WASHINGTON (CHN) 4101 RESERVOIR RD., NW, 20007.
(202) 944-6000, FAX (202) 944-6166
 MR. JEAN PIERRE ALLEX LYOUDI, Jan. 28, 2004
  CONSUL GENERAL
 MR. PHILIPPE EMILE TISSIER, Sep. 09, 2004
  DEPUTY CONSUL
 MR. ERIC NAVEL,   Sep. 11, 2006
  DEPUTY CONSUL
 MR. GERARD MARCEL CAMILLE BILLET, Oct. 18, 2006
  DEPUTY CONSUL

FLORIDA

CLEARWATER (HC) 3158 HYDE PARK DR., 33761.
(727) 791-1617, FAX (727) 791-1613
 MR. JEAN CHARLES FAUST, Nov. 10, 2003
  HONORARY CONSUL

STATE* RESIDENCE	NAME AND RANK	DATE OF RECOGNITION	STATE* RESIDENCE	NAME AND RANK	DATE OF RECOGNITION

MIAMI (CG) 1395 BRICKELL AV., SUITE 1050, 33131.
(305) 403-4150, FAX (305) 403-4151

   MR. PHILIPPE CHRISTIAN VINOGRADOFF, — Oct. 17, 2005
     CONSUL GENERAL

   MISS SYLVIE FRANCOISE CLASQUIN, — Sep. 15, 2004
     DEPUTY CONSUL GENERAL

   MR. ASHOK ADICEAM, — May. 04, 2007
     CONSUL

   MR. JACKY TRINEL, — Oct. 10, 2006
     VICE CONSUL

COMMERCIAL OFFICE OF FRANCE
MIAMI (CONA) 2 S. BISCAYNE BL., SUITE 1750, 33131.

TOURISM OFFICE OF FRANCE
MIAMI (CONA) 2 S. BISCAYNE BL., SUITE 1710, 33131.
(305) 373-8177

ORLANDO (HC) 7657 MOUNT CARMEL DR., 32835.
(407) 292-1142, FAX (407) 924-5844

   MS. BRIGITTE MARTHE BROWN DAGOT, — Feb. 24, 1995
     HONORARY CONSUL

GEORGIA

ATLANTA (CG) 3475 PIEDMONT RD., NE, SUITE 1840, 30305.
(404) 495-1660, FAX (404) 495-1661

   MR. PHILIPPE PATRICK ARDANAZ, — Oct. 17, 2005
     CONSUL GENERAL

   MR. MICHEL H. BESSON, — Jul. 07, 2005
     CONSUL

   MR. AURELIEN PIERRE MAILLET, — Oct. 06, 2004
     VICE CONSUL

COMMERCIAL OFFICE TRADE COMMISSION OF FRANCE
ATLANTA (CONA) 3475 PIEDMONT RD., NE, SUITE 1840, 30305.
(404) 495-1660, FAX (404) 495-1661

SAVANNAH (HC) 17 E. JOHNS ST., 31404.
(912) 236-0818

   MR. HUBERT FRANCOIS MILLET, — Jan. 16, 2001
     HONORARY CONSUL

GUAM

TAMUNING (HCA)   ., 96931.
(671) 649-7277

   MS. JOELLE LILIANE WAINER, — May. 14, 2002
     HONORARY CONSULAR AGENT

HAWAII

HONOLULU (HC) 1099 ALAKEA ST., SUITE 1800, 96813.
(808) 547-5625

   MRS. PATRICIA Y. LEE, — Jun. 30, 1997
     HONORARY CONSUL

IDAHO

BOISE (HCA) 5796 MILLSTREAM WA., 83711.
(208) 323-7953

   MS. GABRIELLE APPLEQUIST, — Jul. 17, 2003
     HONORARY CONSULAR AGENT

ILLINOIS

CHICAGO (CG) 205 N. MICHIGAN AV., SUITE 3700, 60601.
(312) 787-5359

   MR. JEAN BAPTISTE MAIN DE BOISSIERE, — May. 04, 2007
     CONSUL GENERAL

   MRS. ISABELLE GROSS MARQUES, — Aug. 24, 2005
     DEPUTY CONSUL GENERAL

   MR. CHRISTOPHE RENAUD JOEL ALAMELAMA, — Nov. 22, 2005
     VICE CONSUL

COMMERICAL OFFICE TRADE OFFICE OF FRANCE
CHICAGO (CONA) 205 N. MICHIGAN AV., FLOOR 37TH, 60601.
(312) 661-1880

   MR. DANIEL MARIE GALLISSAIRES, — May. 29, 2007
     CONSUL

CULTURAL AND SCIENTIFIC OFFICES OF FRANCE
CHICAGO (CONA) 205 N. MICHIGAN AV., FLOOR 37TH, 60601.
(312) 664-3525

INVEST IN FRANCE AGENCY
CHICAGO (CONA) 205 N. MICHIGAN AV., FLOOR 37TH, 60601.
(312) 661-1640

INDIANA

INDIANAPOLIS (HC) 4330 MICHIGAN RD., 46208.
(317) 923-1951

   MR. ALAIN WEBER, — Sep. 01, 2006
     HONORARY CONSUL

IOWA

INDIANOLA (HC) 115 S. HOWARD ST., 50125.
(515) 961-2509

   MR. MARK FREDERICK SCHLENKER, — Mar. 18, 2005
     HONORARY CONSUL

KENTUCKY

LOUISVILLE (HC) 1602 GREENSBROOK PL., 40245.
(502) 245-6325

   MR. JOHN A. LINA, — Feb. 14, 2000
     HONORARY CONSUL

LOUISIANA

LAFAYETTE (HC) 407 N. MARKET ST., OPELOUSAS 70570.
(337) 942-5766

   MR. CHRISTIAN MARC GOUDEAU, — Dec. 06, 2000
     HONORARY CONSUL

NEW ORLEANS (CG) 1340 POYDRAS ST., SUITE 1710, 70112.
(504) 523-5772

   MR. PIERRE LEBOVICS, — Oct. 17, 2005
     CONSUL GENERAL

STATE* RESIDENCE	NAME AND RANK	DATE OF RECOGNITION	STATE* RESIDENCE	NAME AND RANK	DATE OF RECOGNITION

MAINE

PORTLAND (HC) 443 CONGRESS ST., 04101-3590.
(207) 775-5831
    MR. SEVERIN M. BELIVEAU, — Jun. 11, 1992
        HONORARY CONSUL

MASSACHUSETTS

BOSTON (CG) 31 ST. JAMES AV., SUITE 750, 02116.
(617) 542-7374, FAX (617) 542-8054
    MR. FRANCOIS JEROME GAUTHIER, — Oct. 17, 2005
        CONSUL GENERAL
    MISS MIREILLE ANDREA MAKANDA, — Nov. 06, 2002
        DEPUTY CONSUL
    MR. JEAN FRANCOIS LABORIE, — Oct. 01, 2004
        VICE CONSUL
    MR. JEAN JACQUES CHARLES PIERRAT, — Jul. 08, 2005
        VICE CONSUL

TRADE OFFICE
BOSTON (CONA) 535 BOYLSTON ST., FLOOR 9, 02116.
(617) 585-9900

MICHIGAN

DETROIT (HC) 500 WOODWARD AV., SUITE 3500, 48226-3435.
(313) 965-8256, FAX (313) 965-8252
    MR. ROBERT L. WEYHING, — Oct. 10, 1997
        HONORARY CONSUL

MINNESOTA

MINNEAPOLIS (HC) 150 S. FIFTH ST., SUITE 2300, 55402.
(612) 338-6868, FAX (612) 338-6878
    MR. ALAIN J-C FRECON, — Apr. 01, 1994
        HONORARY CONSUL

MISSISSIPPI

JACKSON (HC) 4400 OLD CANTON RD., SUITE 400, 39211.
(601) 914-5236, FAX (601) 969-1116
    MR. SILAS WOOD MCCHAREN, — May. 02, 1997
        HONORARY CONSUL

MISSOURI

KANSAS CITY (HCA) 4401 WORNALL RD., 64111.
(816) 932-2575, FAX (816) 932-9819
    MR. ARTHUR JULIUS ELMAN, — Nov. 18, 2002
        HONORARY CONSULAR AGENT

SAINT LOUIS (HC) 112 S. HANLEY RD., ST. LOUIS 63105.
(314) 726-2800, FAX (314) 863-3821
    MR. JAMES F. MAUZE', — Jan. 03, 1991
        HONORARY CONSUL

MONTANA

MISSOULA (HCA) 636 W. ARTEMOS UN., 59803.
(406) 543-1075
    MRS. CHANTAL DAVOINE MOSER, — May. 08, 2002
        HONORARY CONSULAR AGENT

NEVADA

LAS VEGAS (HC) 9625 CLIFF VIEW WA., 89117.
(702) 242-3811
    MR. ANDRE YVES PORTAL, — Dec. 11, 1997
        HONORARY CONSUL

NEW HAMPSHIRE

MANCHESTER (HC) 110 BRIDGE ST., 03101.
(603) 627-1574, FAX (603) 625-6437
    MRS. ADELE BOUFFORD BAKER, — May. 08, 2002
        HONORARY CONSUL

NEW JERSEY

PRINCETON (HC) 604 PRINCETON KINGSTON RD., 08540.
(609) 430-1690
    MRS. ISABELLE EDITH WILHELM, — Nov. 10, 2003
        HONORARY CONSUL

NEW MEXICO

ALBUQUERQUE (HCA) 201 3RD ST., NW, SUITE 1700, 87102.
(505) 724-9564
    MR. PERRY EDWARD , III BENDICKSEN, — Apr. 19, 2007
        HONORARY CONSULAR AGENT

NEW YORK

BUFFALO (HC) 32 ADMIRAL RD., 14216.
(716) 832-7740
    MR. PASCAL R. SOARES, — Mar. 12, 2004
        HONORARY CONSUL

NEW YORK (CG) 934 5TH AV., 10021.
(212) 606-3688
    MR. FRANCOIS DELATTRE, — Sep. 14, 2004
        CONSUL GENERAL
    MS. CHANTAL ANITA CHAUVIN, — Oct. 06, 2005
        DEPUTY CONSUL GENERAL
    MR. PATRICK PIERRE RUDOLPH LE MENES, — Oct. 06, 2004
        DEPUTY CONSUL
    MR. MICHEL OLIVIER BESSE, — Oct. 26, 2004
        DEPUTY CONSUL
    MR. YANN RENE PIERRE BATTEFORT, — Nov. 22, 2005
        DEPUTY CONSUL
    MR. FABRICE ARNAUD DE SAINT ETIENNE, — Oct. 12, 2006
        DEPUTY CONSUL

FRENCH GOVERNMENT TOURIST OFFICE
NEW YORK (CONA) 825 3RD AV., FLOOR 29TH, 10022.
(212) 838-7800, FAX (212) 838-7855

COMMERCIAL OFFICE TRADE COMMISSION
NEW YORK (CONA) 810 7TH AV., FLOOR 38TH, 10019.
(212) 307-8800
    MR. HERVE GEORGES OCHSENBEIN, — Oct. 17, 2005
        DEPUTY CONSUL GENERAL

CULTURAL SERVICES OF FRANCE
NEW YORK (CONA) 972 5TH AV., 10021.
(212) 439-1447
    MR. JEAN JACQUES VICTOR, — Oct. 02, 2006
        DEPUTY CONSUL GENERAL

STATE* RESIDENCE	NAME AND RANK	DATE OF RECOGNITION	STATE* RESIDENCE	NAME AND RANK	DATE OF RECOGNITION

MS. KAREEN GERALDINE MARIE RISPAL,
   DEPUTY CONSUL GENERAL — Nov. 28, 2006

VISA SECTION OF FRANCE
NEW YORK (CONA) 10 E. 74TH ST., 10021.
(212) 606-3644

PRESS SECTION OF FRANCE
NEW YORK (CONA) 10 E. 74TH ST., 10021.
(212) 606-3685

FINANCIAL SERVICE (FRENCH TREASURY OFFICE)
NEW YORK (CONA) 810 7TH AV., FLOOR 38TH, 10019.
(212) 432-1820, FAX (212) 432-1822
   MR. BRUNO XAVIER ZANGHELLINI, — Sep. 15, 2004
      CONSUL
   MR. STEPHANE MICHEL PAILLAUD, — Mar. 30, 2006
      DEPUTY CONSUL

SOCIAL SERVICE OF FRANCE
NEW YORK (CONA) 10 E. 74TH ST., 10021.
(212) 606-3605

INVEST IN FRANCE AGENCY
NEW YORK (CONA) 810 7TH AV., FLOOR 38TH, 10019.
(212) 757-9340, FAX (212) 245-1568

NORTH CAROLINA

CHARLOTTE (HC) 1440 CARMEL RD., 28226.
(704) 943-4566
   MRS. MILDRED D. COX, — Oct. 11, 1991
      HONORARY CONSUL

OHIO

CINCINNATI (HC) 9253 VILLAGE GREEN DR., 45242.
(513) 791-5970
   MRS. ANNE CAPPEL, — Jan. 14, 2000
      HONORARY CONSUL

CLEVELAND (HC) 3300 BP AMERICA BUILDING ., 44114.
(216) 621-0150
   MR. STEPHEN KNERLY, — Jun. 16, 1995
      HONORARY CONSUL

OKLAHOMA

OKLAHOMA CITY (HC) 315 N.W. 39TH ST., 73118.
(405) 524-1776
   MRS. BARBARA IRENE THOMPSON, — Mar. 22, 2000
      HONORARY CONSUL

OREGON

PORTLAND (HCA) 393 NEUBERGER HALL ., 97207-0751.
(503) 725-5298
   MRS. CLAUDINE FISHER, — Oct. 22, 1998
      HONORARY CONSULAR AGENT

PENNSYLVANIA

PHILADELPHIA (HC) 1617 JFK BL., SUITE 1500, 19103.
(215) 557-2975
   MR. MICHAEL E. SCULLIN, — Dec. 02, 2005
      HONORARY CONSUL

PITTSBURGH (HC) 800 PRESQUE ISLE DR., 15239.
(412) 327-2911
   MR. JEAN-PIERRE COLLET, — Aug. 08, 1991
      HONORARY CONSUL

PUERTO RICO

SAN JUAN (HC) 206 CALLE ROSARIO ST., 00911.
(787) 725-2527
   MR. MARC CHARLES PASSERIEU, — Feb. 04, 2005
      HONORARY CONSUL

RHODE ISLAND

PROVIDENCE (HC) 100 WESTMINSTER ST., SUITE 136, 02903.
(401) 278-5213
   MR. ROGER N. BEGIN, — Nov. 06, 1998
      HONORARY CONSUL

SOUTH CAROLINA

COLUMBIA (HC) 1004 ROCKWOOD RD., 29209.
(803) 783-3708, FAX (775) 249-0419
   MR. PHILIPPE GERARD FELSENHARDT, — Aug. 04, 1997
      HONORARY CONSUL

TENNESSEE

MEMPHIS (HC) 81 MONROE BLDG. ., 38103.
(901) 525-7744, FAX (901) 529-9816
   MR. CHARLES METCALF, JR CRUMP, — Apr. 01, 1991
      HONORARY CONSUL

TEXAS

AUSTIN (HC) 515 CONGRESS ., 78701.
(512) 480-5605
   MR. JOHN M. HARMON, — Mar. 20, 1989
      HONORARY CONSUL

DALLAS (HC) 12720 HILLCREST RD., SUITE 730, 75230.
(972) 789-9305
   MR. ROBERT LAVIE, — Jun. 08, 2005
      HONORARY CONSUL

HOUSTON (CG) 777 POST OAK BL., SUITE 600, 77056.
(713) 572-2799, FAX (713) 572-2911
   MR. PATRICK OLIVIER BERRON, — Oct. 18, 2005
      CONSUL GENERAL
   MR. RENE JERUSEL, — Sep. 15, 2004
      DEPUTY CONSUL GENERAL
   MR. JOEL FRANCOIS MARIE SAVARY, — Nov. 14, 2002
      DEPUTY CONSUL
   MR. BERNARD ROBERT RIEHL, — Dec. 23, 2003
      DEPUTY CONSUL

CULTURAL AND SCIENTIFIC OFFICE
HOUSTON (CONA) 777 POST OAK BL., FLOOR 6TH, 77056.
(713) 572-2799, FAX (713) 572-2911

STATE* RESIDENCE	NAME AND RANK	DATE OF RECOGNITION	STATE* RESIDENCE	NAME AND RANK	DATE OF RECOGNITION

GAMBIA

CALIFORNIA

LOS ANGELES (HCG) 10777 BELLAGIO RD., 90077.
(310) 476-0532
  MS. AIMEE KLAUS,
    HONORARY CONSUL GENERAL — Dec. 15, 1995

COMMERCIAL OFFICE TRADE COMMISSION OF FRANCE
HOUSTON (CONA) 777 POST OAK BL., FLOOR 6TH, 77056.
(713) 572-2799, FAX (713) 572-2911

FLORIDA

MIAMI (HCG) 12875 N.E. 14TH AV., 33161.
(305) 895-9600
  MR. RONY DESVARENNES,
    HONORARY CONSUL GENERAL — Jan. 24, 2006

SAN ANTONIO (HC) X ROUTE 1 UN., 78209.
(210) 659-3101
  MR. JOHN L. COLLET,
    HONORARY CONSUL — Feb. 08, 1986

UTAH

SALT LAKE CITY (HC) 975 N. BONNEVILLE DR., 84103.
(801) 364-6083
  MRS. MARIE HELENE CONCEPTION GLON,
    HONORARY CONSUL — May. 31, 2007

GEORGIA

ALABAMA

MOBILE (HC) 5 DAUPHIN ST., SUITE 101, 36602.
(251) 432-2600, FAX (251) 433-4478
  MR. MATTHEW SPURGEON METCALFE,
    HONORARY CONSUL — Jul. 30, 1999

VERMONT

ESSEX JUNCTION (HC) 16 PEACHAM LA., 05452.
(802) 878-0992
  MR. PATRICK HONORE BUFFET,
    HONORARY CONSUL — Jan. 16, 2004

CALIFORNIA

ORANGE (HC) 1800 W. KATELLA AV., SUITE 400, 92867.
(714) 744-7140
  MR. FRANK PAUL GREINKE,
    HONORARY CONSUL — May. 02, 2007

VIRGIN ISLANDS

ST. THOMAS (HC) 42 FORTUNA ST., SAINT THOMAS 00804.
(340) 776-1140, FAX (340) 776-7381
  MRS. ODILE RITA DE LYROT,
    HONORARY CONSUL — Sep. 11, 2000

DISTRICT OF COLUMBIA

WASHINGTON (CHN) 2209 MASSACHUSETTS AV., NW, 20008.
(202) 387-2390, FAX (202) 387-0864
  MR. ALEXANDER LATSABIDZE,
    CONSUL — Nov. 30, 2006

VIRGINIA

NORFOLK (HC) 417 PIN OAK RD., NEWPORT NEWS 23601.
(804) 596-2754
  MS. NICOLE YANCEY,
    HONORARY CONSUL — Aug. 08, 1991

MASSACHUSETTS

BOSTON (HC) 17 BERKELEY ST., 02138.
(617) 492-0727
  MR. RICHARD PIPES,
    HONORARY CONSUL — May. 29, 1997

WASHINGTON

SEATTLE (HCA) 2200 ALASKAN WA., SUITE 490, 98121.
(206) 256-6184, FAX (206) 448-4218
  MR. JACK ALBERT COWAN,
    HONORARY CONSULAR AGENT — Jul. 21, 1998

NEW YORK

NEW YORK (CG) 144 E. 44TH ST., FLOOR 5TH, 10017.
(212) 867-3617, FAX (212) 867-3654
  MR. IRAKLI JORDANIA,
    CONSUL GENERAL — Mar. 19, 2007
  MR. ZURAB TINIKASHVILI,
    CONSUL — May. 02, 2007

WYOMING

DUBOIS (HCA) 9 MEDILL CT., 82513.
(307) 455-3775
  MRS. SEVERINE CHRISTINE MURDOCH,
    HONORARY CONSULAR AGENT — Mar. 16, 2006

PUERTO RICO

SAN JUAN (HC) PIER 15 MIRAFLORES ST., FLOOR 2, MIRAMAR 00907.
(787) 724-8070, FAX (787) 977-1660
  MR. ROBERT LEITH,
    HONORARY CONSUL — Jun. 29, 1998

GABON

NEW YORK

NEW YORK (CON) 18 E. 41ST ST., FLOOR 9TH, 10017.
(212) 686-9720
  MRS. YVONNE WALKER BOROBO,
    CONSULAR AGENT — Aug. 22, 1995

TEXAS

HOUSTON (HC) 3040 POST OAK BL., SUITE 700, 77056.
(281) 633-3500
  MR. LAN CHASE BENTSEN,
    HONORARY CONSUL — Jun. 20, 1997

---

* DEPENDENCIES SUCH AS GUAM, PUERTO RICO, AND THE VIRGIN ISLANDS ARE LISTED HERE.
CG-CONSULATE GENERAL   C-CONSULATE   VC-VICE CONSULATE   CA-CONSULAR AGENCY   H-HONORARY CONSULAR STATUS

STATE* RESIDENCE	NAME AND RANK	DATE OF RECOGNITION	STATE* RESIDENCE	NAME AND RANK	DATE OF RECOGNITION

GERMANY, FED. REP. OF

ALABAMA

BIRMINGHAM (HC) 500 BEACON PW., W, 35209.
(205) 943-4772, FAX (205) 257-7546

MR. J. BRUCE JONES, HONORARY CONSUL	Nov. 09, 2001

ALASKA

ANCHORAGE (HC) 425 G ST., SUITE 650, 99501.
(907) 274-6537

MR. BERND CARL GUETSCHOW, HONORARY CONSUL	Oct. 23, 1978

ARIZONA

PHOENIX (HC) 1007 E. MISSOURI AV., 85014.
(602) 264-2545, FAX (602) 265-4428

MR. BERNARD OTTO M. OTREMBA BLANC, HONORARY CONSUL	Aug. 06, 2002

CALIFORNIA

CARLSBAD (HC) 1947 CAMINO VIDA ROBLE ., SUITE 108, 92008.
(760) 918-0265, FAX (760) 918-0404

MS. ANNETTE IRIS ZILLGENS GOLDMAN, HONORARY CONSUL	Jan. 31, 2006

LOS ANGELES (CG) 6222 WILSHIRE BL., SUITE 500, 90048.
(323) 930-2703, FAX (323) 930-2805

DR. CHRISTIAN STOCKS, CONSUL GENERAL	Aug. 10, 2005
MR. DIETMAR ANTON BOCK, DEPUTY CONSUL GENERAL	Jul. 12, 2007
MR. PAUL HARMEL, CONSUL	Jun. 28, 2004
MR. LARS GERRIT LEYMANN, CONSUL	Jul. 07, 2005
MR. SOENKE LENUWEIT, VICE CONSUL	Jul. 31, 2002
MR. THOMAS SCHERER, VICE CONSUL	Oct. 14, 2003
MRS. CHRISTINE KEOUGH, VICE CONSUL	Jun. 02, 2004
MRS. ANGELIKA DRESEN, VICE CONSUL	Jun. 27, 2005
MS. DANIELA LOTZEN, VICE CONSUL	Jul. 29, 2005
MRS. CAROLIN SCHWARZ, VICE CONSUL	Jul. 18, 2006

SAN FRANCISCO (CG) 1960 JACKSON ST., 94109.
(415) 775-1061

MR. ROLF SCHUETTE, CONSUL GENERAL	Oct. 14, 2005
DR. CHRISTIAN F. A. SEEBODE, DEPUTY CONSUL GENERAL	May. 17, 2004
MR. KARSTEN TIETZ, CONSUL	Jul. 06, 2006
MR. ROBERT FERDINAND HALLEN, CONSUL	May. 04, 2007
MR. WERNER ARTHUR LEHMANN, CONSUL	Jun. 29, 2007
MR. HANSJOERG DENG, VICE CONSUL	Aug. 29, 2003
MS. STEFANIE MEYER, VICE CONSUL	Oct. 06, 2005

MRS. EDELTRAUD ANNA HARGREAVES, VICE CONSUL	Jul. 18, 2007
MR. THOMAS MARIO VOGELBACHER, VICE CONSUL	Aug. 01, 2007
MR. STEFAN BUSCH, CONSULAR AGENT	Sep. 14, 2004
MR. RUEDIGER WOZNIAK, CONSULAR AGENT	Oct. 11, 2005
MRS. BRITTA ANGELA JACOB, CONSULAR AGENT	Oct. 11, 2005

COLORADO

DENVER (HC) 621 17TH ST., SUITE 811, 80293.
(303) 292-5922, FAX (303) 295-0072

DR. BERNHARD JURGEN BLEISE, HONORARY CONSUL	Dec. 19, 2001

DISTRICT OF COLUMBIA

WASHINGTON (CHN) 4645 RESERVOIR RD., NW, 20007.
(202) 298-4000, FAX (202) 298-4249

MR. THOMAS JOHANNES RAINER PROEPSTL, CONSUL GENERAL	Jun. 21, 2005
MR. JOHANNES MOOSBURNER, CONSUL	Oct. 10, 2005
MRS. KIRSTEN HEIKE MOOSBURNER, CONSUL	Dec. 20, 2005
MR. JUERGEN KIELING, VICE CONSUL	Aug. 02, 2002
MRS. WALTRAUD BREUER GLEIN, VICE CONSUL	May. 06, 2004
MR. ANDREAS GOTTFRIED RUEMPLER, VICE CONSUL	Jan. 31, 2007

FLORIDA

MIAMI (CG) 100 N. BISCAYNE BL., SUITE 2200, 33132.
(305) 358-0290

COUNTESS EVA ALEXANDRA KENDEFFY, CONSUL GENERAL	Sep. 23, 2004
MR. HELMUT WILHELM LOERSCH, CONSUL	Nov. 25, 2005
MR. PETER HEINRICH PIETZOWSKY, VICE CONSUL	Nov. 13, 2003
MS. STEFANIE ANGELIKA KESTLER, VICE CONSUL	Jul. 16, 2004
MRS. STEFANIE ELISABETH DEHNER, VICE CONSUL	Aug. 24, 2005
MR. KARL OTTO MOEGLICH, VICE CONSUL	Jan. 30, 2006
MRS. PETRA RENNER, VICE CONSUL	Oct. 03, 2006
MS. ULRIKE WENIG, VICE CONSUL	May. 04, 2007
MR. THOMAS A. BUSCH, VICE CONSUL	Aug. 01, 2007
MRS. ANDJELKA BUSCH, VICE CONSUL	Aug. 01, 2007

NAPLES (HC) 4500 EXECUTIVE DR., SUITE 210, 34119.
(239) 596-6020, FAX (239) 596-6051

MRS. NORMA BRENNE HENNING, HONORARY CONSUL	Jan. 16, 2003

STATE* RESIDENCE	NAME AND RANK	DATE OF RECOGNITION

GEORGIA

ATLANTA (CG) 285 PEACHTREE CENTER AV., NE, SUITE 901, 30303.
(404) 659-4760

DR. LUTZ H. GOERGENS, DEPUTY CONSUL GENERAL		Oct. 03, 2006
MR. SONKE LORENZ, DEPUTY CONSUL GENERAL		Aug. 01, 2007
MR. REINHOLD FRIEDRICH KRICKL, CONSUL		Apr. 18, 2007
MRS. MONIKA REUTER, VICE CONSUL		Jul. 12, 2004
MR. THOMAS ERICH KUHN, VICE CONSUL		Jul. 16, 2004
MRS. ROSA MARIA KUHN, VICE CONSUL		Jul. 16, 2004
MS. UTE GREUL, VICE CONSUL		Jul. 18, 2007

ILLINOIS

CHICAGO (CG) 676 N. MICHIGAN AV., SUITE 3200, 60611.
(312) 580-1199

MR. WOLFGANG DRAUTZ, CONSUL GENERAL		Oct. 14, 2005
MR. ROLAND HERRMANN, DEPUTY CONSUL GENERAL		Jul. 11, 2006
MR. BERND RUDENZ HAUSDORF, CONSUL		Nov. 19, 2003
MR. JOHANNES NIKLAS HARMS, CONSUL		Oct. 03, 2006
MR. EDUARD SCHROEDER, VICE CONSUL		Nov. 07, 2003
MR. KLAUS STEITZ, VICE CONSUL		Jul. 28, 2004
MS. ANJA WILMA SEIFERT, VICE CONSUL		Sep. 02, 2004
MR. VOLKER HABERLANDT, VICE CONSUL		Oct. 27, 2004
MS. SUSAN HABERLANDT NEVISI, VICE CONSUL		Oct. 27, 2004
MS. NADINE DOERTHE LAHAYNE, VICE CONSUL		Jul. 26, 2006
MR. WINFRIED VOELKERING, VICE CONSUL		Oct. 03, 2006

INDIANA

INDIANAPOLIS (HC) 4330 MICHIGAN RD., 46208.

MR. ALAIN WEBER, HONORARY CONSUL		Sep. 13, 2006

IOWA

INDIANOLA (HC) 115 S. HOWARD ST., 50125.
(515) 961-2509

MR. MARK FREDERICK SCHLENKER, HONORARY CONSUL		Jun. 29, 1994

KANSAS

KANSAS CITY (HC) 8014 STATE LINE ., LEAWOOD 66208.
(913) 642-5134

MR. WILLARD BREIDENTHAL SNYDER, HONORARY CONSUL		Sep. 27, 1972

KENTUCKY

LOUISVILLE (HC) 500 W. JEFFERSON ST., SUITE 2500, 40202.
(502) 562-7296, FAX (502) 589-0309

MR. MARK C. BLACKWELL, HONORARY CONSUL		Mar. 17, 2003

LOUISIANA

NEW ORLEANS (HC) 1100 POYDRAS ST., SUITE 1700, 70163.
(504) 585-7500

MR. W. PAUL ANDERSSON, HONORARY CONSUL		Oct. 18, 1999

MAINE

PORTLAND (HC) 415 CONGRESS ST., FLOOR 5TH, 04101.
(207) 774-7000

MR. ADRIAN PETER KENDALL, HONORARY CONSUL		May. 14, 2007

MASSACHUSETTS

BOSTON (CG) 3 COPLEY PL., SUITE 500, 02116.
(617) 536-4414

MR. WOLFGANG KURT VORWERK, CONSUL GENERAL		Sep. 09, 2004
MR. BERND RINNERT, DEPUTY CONSUL GENERAL		Jun. 27, 2005
MR. GERHARD KUENTZLE, CONSUL		Nov. 14, 2003
MR. ARMIN HUBERT MATHEIS, CONSUL		Jul. 26, 2007
MRS. KATJA HOFMANN, VICE CONSUL		Jun. 27, 2005
MR. RAYNER APPELRATH, VICE CONSUL		Jul. 06, 2006
MS. DANIELA AGNES LOPEZ SANDOVAL, VICE CONSUL		Jul. 06, 2006
MS. KIRSTEN HARDT, VICE CONSUL		Jul. 18, 2006
MR. GUNNAR HELMKE, VICE CONSUL		Jun. 20, 2007
MS. HEINRIKE CHARLOTTE KRUCK, CONSULAR AGENT		May. 04, 2007

MICHIGAN

AUBURN HILLS (HC) 1000 CHRYSLER DR., E, 48326.
(248) 512-3352

MR. FREDERICK W. HOFFMAN, HONORARY CONSUL		Jan. 22, 2003

MINNESOTA

MINNEAPOLIS (HC) 1000 LASALLE AV., 55403-2205.
(651) 962-4000

DR. HEINO A. P. BECKMANN, HONORARY CONSUL		Dec. 18, 1996

MISSISSIPPI

JACKSON (HC) 49 EASTBROOK ST., 39216.
(601) 354-8283, FAX (601) 982-0608

MR. EMERSON BARNEY, JR ROBINSON, HONORARY CONSUL		Apr. 18, 1990

---

* DEPENDENCIES SUCH AS GUAM, PUERTO RICO, AND THE VIRGIN ISLANDS ARE LISTED HERE.
CG-CONSULATE GENERAL   C-CONSULATE   VC-VICE CONSULATE   CA-CONSULAR AGENCY   H-HONORARY CONSULAR STATUS

STATE* RESIDENCE	NAME AND RANK	DATE OF RECOGNITION

MISSOURI

SAINT LOUIS (HC) 330 WENNEKER DR., 63124.
(314) 567-4601, FAX (314) 567-1101

MR. LANSING GERVIG HECKER, HONORARY CONSUL		Aug. 17, 2004

NEVADA

LAS VEGAS (HC) 4815 W. RUSSELL RD., SUITE 10J, 89118.

MR. ANDREAS ROLF ADRIAN, HONORARY CONSUL		Apr. 17, 2007

NEW MEXICO

ALBUQUERQUE (HC) 4801 LANG ., NE, SUITE 110, 87109.
(505) 798-2567, FAX (505) 796-9601

MR. LANNY DEE MESSERSMITH, HONORARY CONSUL		May. 29, 1981

NEW YORK

BUFFALO (HC) ONE M&T PZ., SUITE 2000, 14203.
(716) 848-1256

MR. CHRISTIAN GERARD , III KOELBL, HONORARY CONSUL		Sep. 15, 2003

NEW YORK (CG) 871 UNITED NATIONS PZ., 10017.
(212) 610-9700, FAX (212) 610-9702

MR. HANS JUERGEN RANJIT HEIMSOETH, CONSUL GENERAL	Aug. 10, 2005
DR. STEPHAN HEINRICH LORENZ GRABHERR, DEPUTY CONSUL GENERAL	Jun. 29, 2007
MR. ALEXANDER PAUL CHRISTIAN NOWAK, CONSUL	Nov. 25, 2005
MR. TILMAN ULRICH HANCKEL, CONSUL	Jul. 31, 2006
MRS. CORNELIA MARIE JARASCH, CONSUL	Jun. 19, 2007
MR. HANS RAINER ESS, VICE CONSUL	Jun. 29, 2004
MR. EGBERT SCHMIDT, VICE CONSUL	Aug. 24, 2005
MRS. KATJA ALEXANDRA BAUTZ, VICE CONSUL	Feb. 02, 2006
MR. STEPHAN SEBASTIEN FAGO, VICE CONSUL	Jul. 06, 2006
MS. ANDREA SABINE AKPOTOWHO, VICE CONSUL	Jul. 06, 2006
MR. SWEN JANKE, VICE CONSUL	Aug. 11, 2006
MS. JULIA BAUER, VICE CONSUL	May. 05, 2007
MR. JOHANNES SCHARLAU, VICE CONSUL	Jun. 12, 2007
MR. WINFRIED WERNER WOLF, VICE CONSUL	Jun. 29, 2007

DEUTSCHE BUNDESBANK
NEW YORK (CONA) 499 PARK AV., 10022.
(212) 688-3680

MR. MARTIN ROESCH, DEPUTY CONSUL GENERAL	Dec. 20, 2005
MR. BERND KALTENHAEUSER, CONSUL	Aug. 30, 2004

NORTH CAROLINA

CHARLOTTE (HC) 1910 ABBOTT ST., SUITE 201, 28203.
, FAX (253) 423-8142

MR. KURT G. WALDTHAUSEN, HONORARY CONSUL	May. 06, 2002

OHIO

CINCINNATI (HC) 733 OLD CHEMISTRY BLDG. ., ROOM ML0372, 45221-0372.
(513) 556-2752, FAX (513) 556-1991

DR. RICHARD ERICH SCHADE, HONORARY CONSUL	Jul. 08, 1996

CLEVELAND (HC) 925 EUCLID ST., 44115-1475.
(216) 696-1100

MS. DIANA MARIE THIMMIG, HONORARY CONSUL	May. 25, 1989

OKLAHOMA

OKLAHOMA CITY (HC) 5801 N. BROADWAY ., SUITE 120, 73118.
(405) 842-0100

MR. CHARLES E. WIGGIN, HONORARY CONSUL	Mar. 08, 1995

OREGON

PORTLAND (HC) 200 S.W. MARKET ST., SUITE 1695, 97201.
(503) 222-0490

MR. GUENTHER HEINZ HOFFMANN, HONORARY CONSUL	Jan. 30, 1981

PENNSYLVANIA

PHILADELPHIA (HC) 1600 JOHN F. KENNEDY BL., SUITE 200, 19103.
(215) 568-5573

MS. BARBARA AFANASSIEV, HONORARY CONSUL	Feb. 21, 2002

PITTSBURGH (HC) 535 SMITHFIELD ST., SUITE 1500, 15222.
(412) 355-6472

MR. DAVID A. MURDOCH, HONORARY CONSUL	Nov. 08, 2001

SOUTH CAROLINA

GREER (HC) 1784 POPLAR DR., 29651.
(864) 879-9334

MR. WOLF DIETRICH STROMBERG, HONORARY CONSUL	Jun. 23, 2005

TENNESSEE

NASHVILLE (HC) 201 4TH AV., N, SUITE 1420, 37219.
(615) 251-5444

MR. DOUGLAS BERRY, HONORARY CONSUL	Oct. 19, 2004

TEXAS

CORPUS CHRISTI (HC) 615 N. UPPER BROADWAY UN., SUITE 630, 78477.
(361) 884-7766

MR. ERICH E. WENDL, HONORARY CONSUL	Oct. 31, 1980

STATE* RESIDENCE	NAME AND RANK	DATE OF RECOGNITION	STATE* RESIDENCE	NAME AND RANK	DATE OF RECOGNITION

GHANA

DISTRICT OF COLUMBIA

DALLAS (HC) 325 N. ST. PAUL ST., SUITE 2300, 75201.
(214) 748-8500
   MR. WILLIAM HAYES HART, — Mar. 16, 2006
      HONORARY CONSUL

WASHINGTON (CHN) 3512 INTERNATIONAL DR., NW, 20008.
(202) 686-4520, FAX (202) 686-4527
   MR. CHRIS OBENG, — Nov. 04, 2004
      VICE CONSUL

HOUSTON (CG) 1300 POST OAK BL., SUITE 1850, 77056.
(713) 627-7770
   MR. RAINER KONRAD MUENZEL, — Aug. 22, 2005
      CONSUL GENERAL
   MR. KAI UWE H. SPICHER, — Oct. 03, 2005
      DEPUTY CONSUL GENERAL
   MR. THORSTEN GOTTFRIED, — Aug. 01, 2007
      CONSUL
   MR. STEPHAN WUENSCH, — Jul. 07, 2005
      VICE CONSUL
   MR. MARKUS ALEXANDER LAQUE, — Nov. 25, 2005
      VICE CONSUL
   MR. DANIEL ROMAN KLEMP, — Jun. 16, 2006
      VICE CONSUL
   MRS. DAGMAR KIRCHHOFF, — Jun. 16, 2006
      VICE CONSUL
   MRS. MONIKA BERCHER PETTERSEN, — Jul. 26, 2006
      VICE CONSUL
   MR. KLAUS MARTIN GUENTHER, — May. 05, 2007
      VICE CONSUL

NEW YORK

NEW YORK (CG) 19 E. 47TH ST., 10017.
(212) 832-1300
   MR. OBENG GYAN BUSIA, — Apr. 14, 2005
      CONSUL GENERAL
   MR. SIDNEY RUDOLPH YAW BIMPONG, — Mar. 28, 2005
      DEPUTY CONSUL GENERAL
   MR. GILBERT TSATSU TAMAKLOE, — May. 31, 1996
      CONSUL
   MR. ANDREW BINEY, — Feb. 01, 2001
      CONSUL
   MR. JOSEPH NGMINEBAYIHI, — Mar. 03, 2006
      CONSUL
   MS. ADRIANA ARTHIABAH, — May. 04, 2007
      CONSUL
   MS. JOSEPHINE AIDOO, — Feb. 20, 2004
      VICE CONSUL

SAN ANTONIO (HC) 310 S. ST. MARY'S ., 78205.
(210) 226-1788
   MR. BERNARD JOHN BUECKER, — Feb. 22, 2001
      HONORARY CONSUL

TEXAS

HOUSTON (HCG) 3434 LOCKE LA., 77027-8806.
(713) 960-8806, FAX (713) 960-8833
   MR. JACK M. WEBB, — Nov. 28, 2006
      HONORARY CONSUL GENERAL

TRUST TERRITORIES OF THE PACIFIC ISLANDS

MANILA, PHILIPPINES (CON) 777 PASEO DE ROXAS ., 00000.
   MR. CONRAD CAPPELL, — Dec. 11, 1989
      CONSUL

GREECE

CALIFORNIA

LOS ANGELES (CG) 12424 WILSHIRE BL., SUITE 800, 710, 90025.
(310) 826-5555, FAX (310) 826-8670
   MR. DIMITRIS CARAMITSOS TZIRAS, — Oct. 17, 2005
      CONSUL GENERAL

WELLINGTON, NEW ZEALAND (CON) 90-92 HOBSON ST., FLOOR
23RD, WELLINGTON 00000.
   MR. JOERG ZIMMERMANN, — Jan. 19, 2006
      CONSUL GENERAL

GREEK TOURIST OFFICE OF GREECE
LOS ANGELES (CONA) 611 W. 6TH ST., SUITE 2198, 90017.
(213) 626-6696, FAX (213) 489-9744

ECONOMIC AND COMMERCIAL OFFICE OF GREECE
LOS ANGELES (CONA) 11835 W. OLYMPIC BL., SUITE 405, 90064.
(310) 914-3434, FAX (310) 914-4577

UTAH

SALT LAKE CITY (HC) 60 E. SOUTH TEMPLE ., SUITE 1800, 84111.
(801) 321-4807
   MR. CHARLES WINSTON, II DAHLQUIST, — Dec. 20, 1999
      HONORARY CONSUL

SAN FRANCISCO (CG) 2441 GOUGH ST., 94123.
(415) 775-2102, FAX (415) 776-6815
   MRS. POLYXENI STEFANIDOU, — Oct. 17, 2005
      CONSUL GENERAL

VIRGINIA

VIRGINIA BEACH (HC) 536 VIKING DR., 23450.
(757) 486-9166
   MR. PETER KONRAD MUELLER, — Dec. 16, 2005
      HONORARY CONSUL

OFFICE OF EDUCATIONAL AFFAIRS OF GREECE
SAN FRANCISCO (CONA) 870 MARKET ST., SUITE 616, 94102.
(415) 788-2727, FAX (415) 788-4252

WASHINGTON

SPOKANE (HC) 1047 W. GARLAND UN., 99205.
(509) 624-5242
   MR. HUBERTUS P. GUENTHER, — Sep. 30, 1987
      HONORARY CONSUL

DISTRICT OF COLUMBIA

WASHINGTON (CHN) 2217 MASSACHUSETTS AV., NW, 20008.
(202) 939-1300, FAX (202) 939-1324
   MR. DIMITRI ANGHELAKIS, — Oct. 18, 2005
      CONSUL

STATE* RESIDENCE	NAME AND RANK	DATE OF RECOGNITION

| | MR. CONSTANTINOS ALEXANDRIS, CONSUL | Jan. 20, 2007 |

FLORIDA

TAMPA (CG) 601 BAYSHORE BL., SUITE 800, 33606.

| | MR. ANDREAS PSYCHARIS, CONSUL GENERAL | Feb. 18, 2005 |
| | MR. GRIGORIOS RIGAS, VICE CONSUL | Oct. 04, 2005 |

GEORGIA

ATLANTA (CON) 3340 PEACHTREE RD., NE, SUITE 1670, 30326.
(404) 261-3313, FAX (404) 262-2798

| | MR. LAMBROS KAKISSIS, CONSUL | Sep. 29, 2003 |
| | MR. GEORGIOS TSONIS, VICE CONSUL | Sep. 20, 1999 |

ILLINOIS

CHICAGO (CG) 650 N. SAINT CLAIR ST., 60611.
(312) 335-3915, FAX (312) 335-3958

| | MS. ALIKI HADJI, CONSUL GENERAL | Nov. 12, 2003 |
| | MRS. VASSILIKI MARIA GRIVITSOPOULOU, VICE CONSUL | Feb. 20, 2004 |

OFFICE FOR ECONOMIC AND COMMERCIAL AFFAIRS
CHICAGO (CONA) 211 E. ONTARIO ST., SUITE 560, 60611.
(312) 332-1716

| | MR. KONSTANTINOS DASKALOPOULOS, VICE CONSUL | Mar. 15, 2007 |

OFFICE OF EDUCATIONAL AFFAIRS
CHICAGO (CONA) 151 N. MICHIGAN AV., SUITE 1003, 60601.
(312) 228-9516

| | MRS. ELENI FREZADOU, CONSUL | Jan. 20, 2006 |

LOUISIANA

NEW ORLEANS (CON) 2 CANAL ST., SUITE 2318, 70130.
(504) 523-1167, FAX (504) 524-3610

OFFICE OF MERCANTILE MARINE OF GREECE
NEW ORLEANS (CONA) 2 CANAL ST., SUITE 2707, 70130.
(504) 529-5288

MASSACHUSETTS

BOSTON (CG) 86 BEACON ST., 02108.
(617) 523-0100, FAX (617) 523-0511

	MR. CONSTANTINOS ORPHANIDES, CONSUL GENERAL	Apr. 06, 2006
	MRS. CATHERINE ECONOMOU DEMETER, VICE CONSUL	Nov. 01, 1999
	MS. CHRISTINA GEORGOPOULOU KALATHAKI, CONSULAR AGENT	Jul. 30, 2002
	MR. NICOLAS DRACOPOULOS, CONSULAR AGENT	Dec. 12, 2005

NEW YORK

NEW YORK (CG) 69 E. 79TH ST., 10021.
(212) 988-5500, FAX (212) 734-8492

	MRS. CATHERINE BOURA, CONSUL GENERAL	Mar. 04, 2004
	MS. IRENE PENTZAROPOULOU, CONSUL	Mar. 17, 2003
	MR. GEORGIOS VLIKIDIS, CONSUL	Dec. 21, 2005
	MS. SOFIA VEVE, CONSUL	Feb. 28, 2007
	MR. CHRISTOS DIMOPOULOS, CONSUL	Jun. 18, 2007
	MRS. ERIKETI ABATIS, VICE CONSUL	May. 24, 2005
	MR. IOANNIS NIKOLAIDIS, VICE CONSUL	Oct. 18, 2005
	MRS. EKATERINI ERGATI, CONSULAR AGENT	Jul. 03, 1997

OFFICE OF TOURISM
NEW YORK (CONA) 645 5TH AV., FLOOR 9TH, 10022.
(212) 421-5777, FAX (212) 826-6940

| | MR. GEORGIOS TAMBAKIS, CONSUL | Aug. 14, 2001 |

OFFICE OF THE COMMERCIAL COUNSELOR
NEW YORK (CONA) 150 E. 58TH ST., SUITE 1715A, 10155.
(212) 751-2404, FAX (212) 593-2278

| | MR. NIKOLAOS BELIAS, CONSUL | Mar. 28, 2007 |
| | MS. GARIFALIA PAPANASTASIOU, VICE CONSUL | Feb. 02, 2004 |

MERCANTILE MARINE DEPARTMENT OF GREECE
NEW YORK (CONA) 29 BROADWAY UN., SUITE 2300, 10006.
(212) 425-5764, FAX (212) 425-3795

| | CAPTAIN PELOPIDAS ANGELOPOULOS, CONSUL | Nov. 22, 1996 |
| | MR. KONSTANTINOS KARAMPAMPAS, CONSUL | Jun. 06, 2006 |

TEXAS

HOUSTON (CON) 520 POST OAK BL., SUITE 450, 77027.
(713) 840-7522, FAX (713) 840-0614

| | MR. STYLIANOS GAVRIIL, CONSUL | Nov. 14, 2003 |
| | MR. KONSTANTINOS MASTORAKIS, VICE CONSUL | Jun. 06, 2006 |

GRENADA

CALIFORNIA

POMONA (HCA) 2530 SUPPLY ST., 91767.
(909) 596-6668

| | MR. FEI DU, HONORARY CONSULAR AGENT | May. 18, 2007 |

FLORIDA

FT. LAUDERDALE (HC) 201 S. BISCAYNE BL., SUITE 2800, MIAMI 33131.
(305) 913-7555, FAX (954) 538-9615

STATE* RESIDENCE	NAME AND RANK	DATE OF RECOGNITION	STATE* RESIDENCE	NAME AND RANK	DATE OF RECOGNITION

MR. RICHARD ALLAN. NIXON,
  HONORARY CONSUL — Feb. 13, 2003

ILLINOIS

CHICAGO (HC) 438 W. ST. JAMES PL., 60614.
, FAX (773) 472-2809
  DR. ALVIN J. SCHONFELD,
    HONORARY CONSUL — Nov. 16, 1993

MICHIGAN

NORTHVILLE (HC) 17445 PARKSHORE DR., 48168.
(248) 305-8080, FAX (815) 327-2441
  MR. ROBERT G. DAVID,
    HONORARY CONSUL — Aug. 23, 2004

NEW YORK

NEW YORK (CG) 800 2ND AV., SUITE 400K, 10017.
(212) 599-0301
  MR. ALLEN MORGAN MCGUIRE,
    CONSUL GENERAL — Aug. 29, 2005

GUATEMALA

ALABAMA

MONTGOMERY (HC) 2153 MEADOW LANE DR., 36106.
(205) 269-2756
  MR. JOSE ROBERTO ORTEGA-LOPEZ,
    HONORARY CONSUL — Feb. 05, 1981

ARIZONA

PHOENIX (CG) 4747 N. 7TH ST., SUITE 410, 85014.
(602) 200-3660
  MR. OSCAR ADOLFO PADILLA LAM,
    CONSUL GENERAL — Mar. 03, 2006
  MS. PATRICIA MEIGHAM,
    VICE CONSUL — Apr. 07, 2006
  MR. PERSY RALDA,
    VICE CONSUL — May. 08, 2007

CALIFORNIA

LOS ANGELES (CG) 1625 W. OLYMPIC BL., SUITE 1000, 90015.
(213) 365-9251
  MR. MILTON EDUARDO ALVAREZ VELA,
    CONSUL GENERAL — Oct. 14, 2005
  MRS. GUADALUPE DE MURGA,
    VICE CONSUL — Jan. 14, 1999
  MS. ANA GABRIELA DUARTE DE SARTI,
    VICE CONSUL — Nov. 25, 2005
  MS. ANA LORENA LEIVA LUTTMANN,
    VICE CONSUL — Apr. 06, 2006
  MR. LEONARDO SALVADOR RAMOS SURIA,
    CONSULAR AGENT — Jan. 21, 2005
  MS. KARIN VIOLETA RAYMUNDO RODRIGUEZ,
    CONSULAR AGENT — Feb. 15, 2005
  MR. JUAN PABLO FRANCISCO,
    CONSULAR AGENT — Mar. 07, 2005
  MR. ANGEL MANUEL SALAZAR ANLEU,
    CONSULAR AGENT — Aug. 10, 2006
  MR. JORGE GONZALO CABRERA JUAREZ,
    CONSULAR AGENT — Oct. 03, 2006

MR. JOHN L. ULMEN,
  HONORARY CONSUL — Mar. 06, 1989
MR. HUGO W. MERIDA,
  HONORARY VICE CONSUL — Nov. 04, 2004

SAN DIEGO (HC) 10405 SAN DIEGO MISSION RD., SUITE 205, 92108.
(619) 282-8127
  MR. EUGENE HERBERT SAPPER,
    HONORARY CONSUL — Jul. 26, 1974

SAN FRANCISCO (CG) 870 MARKET ST., SUITE 667, 94102.
(415) 788-5651
  MS. ANA PATRICIA RAMIREZ MORALES,
    CONSUL GENERAL — Apr. 26, 2007
  MS. VERONICA ELIZABETH JIMENEZ TOBAR,
    VICE CONSUL — Jun. 06, 2006
  MR. FRANS J. KETELAAR MOLINA,
    VICE CONSUL — Jul. 16, 2007
  MR. BAYRON VINICIO MORALES LOPEZ,
    CONSULAR AGENT — Apr. 30, 2007
  MR. CARLOS ARMANDO AFRE,
    HONORARY CONSUL — Dec. 16, 1991

COLORADO

DENVER (CG) 820 16TH ST., SUITE 615, 80202.
  MR. ALFREDO VASQUEZ RIVERA,
    CONSUL GENERAL — Jan. 21, 2003
  MS. ROSA MARIA GALLARDO,
    VICE CONSUL — May. 26, 2005
  MS. BLANCA LIDIA DE LEON DIGHERO,
    VICE CONSUL — Apr. 26, 2007

DISTRICT OF COLUMBIA

WASHINGTON (CHN) 2220 R ST., NW, 20008.
(202) 745-4952, FAX (202) 745-1908
  MR. HECTOR PALACIOS LIMA,
    CONSUL — Jun. 30, 2004

FLORIDA

FT. LAUDERDALE (HC) 2601 OAKLAND PARK BL., E, APT 200, 33306.
(954) 467-1700, FAX (954) 764-1700
  MR. JOHN P. BAUER,
    HONORARY CONSUL — Aug. 24, 1990

JUPITER (HCG) 106 MILITARY TR., 33458.
(561) 745-9199
  MR. JERONIMO CAMPOSECO,
    HONORARY CONSUL GENERAL — Sep. 01, 2006

MIAMI (CG) 1101 BRICKELL AV., SUITE 1003-S, 33131.
(305) 679-9945
  MRS. JULIA BEATRIZ ILLESCAS PUTZEYS,
    CONSUL GENERAL — May. 25, 2006
  MS. DUNIA MIRANDA,
    VICE CONSUL — Aug. 01, 1997
  MS. ANA MARIA COREA VILLEDA,
    VICE CONSUL — Feb. 01, 2006
  MR. OSCAR BERGER WIDMANN,
    VICE CONSUL — Feb. 03, 2006
  MS. KARLA MARIA CRUZ REYES,
    VICE CONSUL — Apr. 07, 2006

---

* DEPENDENCIES SUCH AS GUAM, PUERTO RICO, AND THE VIRGIN ISLANDS ARE LISTED HERE.
CG-CONSULATE GENERAL   C-CONSULATE   VC-VICE CONSULATE   CA-CONSULAR AGENCY   H-HONORARY CONSULAR STATUS

STATE* RESIDENCE	NAME AND RANK	DATE OF RECOGNITION	STATE* RESIDENCE	NAME AND RANK	DATE OF RECOGNITION
	MR. RICARDO JOSE ORTIZ ALTENBACH, VICE CONSUL	Apr. 10, 2006		DR. JOSEPH PETER SPALITTO, HONORARY CONSUL	Sep. 13, 2002
	MS. DORIS QUEZADA GUZMAN, CONSULAR AGENT	Feb. 27, 2003	**NEVADA**		
	MR. GEORGE L. COMBALUZIER, HONORARY CONSUL	Mar. 24, 1969	N. LAS VEGAS (HC) 2987 N. LAS VEGAS BL., NORTH LAS VEGAS 89030. (702) 499-9442		
GEORGIA				MR. ARACELICA PAREDES, HONORARY CONSUL	May. 27, 2005
ATLANTA (CG) 2750 BUFORD HW., NE, 30324. (404) 320-8804, FAX (404) 320-8806				DR. ALDO ADRIAN AGUIRRE, HONORARY VICE CONSUL	May. 27, 2008
	MR. HUGO HAROLDO HUN ARCHILA, CONSUL GENERAL	Feb. 13, 2006	**NEW YORK**		
	MS. NIVIA ROSEMARY ARAUZ MONZON, VICE CONSUL	Jun. 06, 2006	NEW YORK (CG) 57 PARK AV., 10016. (212) 686-3837		
	MS. CRISTY ANDRINO, VICE CONSUL	May. 04, 2007		MS. ROSA MARIA MERIDA DE MORA, CONSUL GENERAL	Jun. 13, 2000
ATLANTA (HC) 4772 E. CONWAY DR., NW, 30327. (404) 255-7019, FAX (404) 255-0023				MRS. MARIA LUZ ZYRIEK, CONSUL	Jun. 02, 2000
	MRS. MARIA TERESA FRASER, HONORARY CONSUL	Dec. 26, 1964		MRS. MARGARITA SIMEONIDIS, VICE CONSUL	Jun. 19, 1998
	MR. CARLOS ENRIQUE CHANG, HONORARY VICE CONSUL	Jul. 29, 2005		MR. ROBERTO ROSENBERG, VICE CONSUL	May. 23, 2000
ILLINOIS				MRS. DINA BEATRIZ MOGOLLON VARGAS, VICE CONSUL	Sep. 18, 2006
CHICAGO (CG) 203 N. WABASH AV., SUITE 910, 60601. (312) 332-1587, FAX (312) 322-4256				MRS. CLAUDIA DE FERNANDEZ, CONSULAR AGENT	Aug. 27, 1999
	MR. GUSTAVO ADOLFO LOPEZ, CONSUL GENERAL	Nov. 30, 2004		MR. PEDRO TZUNUN, CONSULAR AGENT	Mar. 09, 2001
	MISS IVONNE SANCHEZ ARDON, VICE CONSUL	Jul. 20, 2004		MRS. CLAUDIA GATICA MORENO, CONSULAR AGENT	Mar. 09, 2001
	MR. JORGE RAFAEL ARCHILA RUIZ, VICE CONSUL	Apr. 07, 2006		MRS. EUGENIA BARRIOS ESCALANTE, CONSULAR AGENT	Mar. 28, 2005
	MS. T. ROXANA RIEPELE, CONSULAR AGENT	Jun. 15, 2000	**NORTH CAROLINA**		
	MR. SERMINIO SANCHINEL, CONSULAR AGENT	Jun. 18, 2001	CHARLOTTE (HC) 201 S. DOTGER AV., 28207. (704) 333-5958, FAX (704) 333-5959		
	MRS. LILLIAN GLEASON DE MAGNUSON, HONORARY VICE CONSUL	Jun. 04, 1968		MR. STEVEN HOWARD KROPP, HONORARY CONSUL	Sep. 29, 2005
LOUISIANA			**OREGON**		
LAFAYETTE (HC) 735 RUE JEFFERSON ., 70501. (318) 268-5474			PORTLAND (HC) 821 N.W. 11TH AV., SUITE 323, 97209. (503) 224-4193, FAX (503) 224-4886		
	MR. ENRIQUE HERRERA, HONORARY CONSUL	Sep. 17, 1996		MR. SERGE D'ROVENCOURT, HONORARY CONSUL	Jun. 15, 1999
NEW ORLEANS (HC) 1001 HOWARD AV., SUITE 2504, 70113. (504) 558-3777			**PENNSYLVANIA**		
	MS. MARGARITA LOURDES JEREZ, HONORARY CONSUL	Jun. 10, 1998	PHILADELPHIA (HC) 1245 HIGHLAND AV., SUITE 301, ABINGTON 19001. (215) 885-5551		
MINNESOTA				DR. ROBERTO RENDON MALDONADO, HONORARY CONSUL	Jun. 06, 1983
MINNEAPOLIS (HC) 2105 1ST AV., S, 55404. (612) 870-3459			**PUERTO RICO**		
	MR. ALEX EDMUND S. DAHINTEN, HONORARY CONSUL	Dec. 03, 1998	SAN JUAN (HC) 530 PONCE DE LEON ATRIUM OFFICE CENTER AV., 00901. (787) 289-7871, FAX (787) 289-8779		
MISSOURI				MR. ALBERTO M. PEREZ NEGRONI, HONORARY CONSUL	May. 10, 1996
KANSAS CITY (HC) 400 E. RED BRIDGE RD., SUITE 107, 64131. (816) 942-6990, FAX (816) 942-4301					

STATE* RESIDENCE	NAME AND RANK	DATE OF RECOGNITION

RHODE ISLAND

PROVIDENCE (CG) 754 BRANCH AV., SUITE 201, 02904.
(401) 210-6345

MR. CARLOS ENRIQUE AVILA SANDOVAL, CONSUL GENERAL		Nov. 22, 2006
MISS DANIELA SANCHEZ, VICE CONSUL		Jun. 06, 2006

TENNESSEE

MEMPHIS (HC) 147 JEFFERSON AV., 38103.
(901) 527-8466, FAX (901) 527-8469

MR. GEORGE E. WHITWORTH, HONORARY CONSUL — Feb. 14, 1968

TEXAS

HOUSTON (CG) 3013 FOUNTAIN VIEW UN., SUITE 210, 77057.
(713) 953-9531

MR. JOSE BARILLAS TRENNERT, CONSUL GENERAL		Jun. 21, 2002
MS. MARA E. MEJIA GARCIA, VICE CONSUL		May. 17, 2004
MS. ANA PAULINA SPINDLER BAUER, VICE CONSUL		Jul. 15, 2004
MISS MARIA EUGENIA MALDONADO, VICE CONSUL		May. 05, 2007
MR. JASSON ALDANA BENAVENTE, CONSULAR AGENT		Jun. 06, 2006
MR. DAVID TIRADO, CONSULAR AGENT		May. 09, 2007
DR. CARLOS HUGO MONSANTO, HONORARY CONSUL		Mar. 29, 1989
MR. JOSE RAFAEL ESPADA, HONORARY CONSUL		Feb. 17, 1994

SAN ANTONIO (HVC) 4840 WHIRLWIND ., 78217.

MR. CARLOS FERREYRO LUCERO, HONORARY VICE CONSUL — Apr. 09, 1992

WASHINGTON

SEATTLE (HC) 2100 5TH AV., 98121.
(206) 728-5920

MRS. ELSA OSBORNE SMITH, HONORARY CONSUL — Jan. 18, 1991

GUINEA

FLORIDA

JACKSONVILLE (HC) 24 E. 6TH ST., 32206.

MR. ARNETT E. GIRARDEAU, HONORARY CONSUL — Apr. 19, 1994

OHIO

CLEVELAND (HC) 39 S. MAIN ST., SUITE 404, AKRON 44308.
(330) 252-1795, FAX (330) 252-1874

MR. ABDOUL RAHIM ABDOULKARIM, HONORARY CONSUL — Sep. 13, 1996

PENNSYLVANIA

PHILADELPHIA (HC) 2 PENN CENTER ., SUITE 200, 19102.
(215) 842-0860

MR. STANLEY L. STRAUGHTER, HONORARY CONSUL — Mar. 01, 1992

GUYANA

CALIFORNIA

LOS ANGELES (HC) 222 W. FLORANCE AV., INGLEWOOD 90301.
(310) 641-3688, FAX (310) 641-6980

MR. JOSEPH GABRIEL D'OLIVEIRA, HONORARY CONSUL — Aug. 03, 1994

FLORIDA

MIAMI (HC) 795 N.W. 72ND ST., 33150.
(786) 235-0431, FAX (305) 693-9313

MR. RAMZAN ROSHANALI, HONORARY CONSUL — Sep. 23, 2003

NEW YORK

NEW YORK (CG) 370 7TH AV., SUITE 402, 10001.

MR. BRENTNOLD FITZPATRICK EVANS, CONSUL GENERAL		Sep. 14, 1993
MR. MOHAMED RAHEEL KHAN, DEPUTY CONSUL GENERAL		Jun. 27, 2005

TEXAS

HOUSTON (HC) 1810 WOODLAND PARK DR., 77077.
(713) 497-4466

MS. TERRY A. REIS, HONORARY CONSUL — Mar. 26, 1997

HAITI

CALIFORNIA

SAN FRANCISCO (HC) 401 CHINA BASIN BL., SUITE 128, 94107.
(415) 543-1915

MR. GERALD JAY SANDERS, HONORARY CONSUL — Mar. 02, 2000

COLORADO

DENVER (HC) 621 17TH ST., SUITE 1741, 80293.
(303) 298-7392

MR. PAUL EDWARD VRANESIC, HONORARY CONSUL — Nov. 14, 1975

FLORIDA

MIAMI (CG) 259 S.W. 13TH ST., 33130.
(305) 377-3547

MR. JEAN BERNARD RALPH LATORTUE, CONSUL GENERAL		Apr. 11, 2006
MR. NICOLAS GERARD ALEX JOSPITRE, CONSUL		May. 01, 2006
MRS. MARIE SONIA DUBUISSON SATURNE, VICE CONSUL		Jun. 06, 2006
MS. ANDRELLE JEAN BAPTISTE, CONSULAR AGENT		Mar. 07, 2000
MRS. MIE ALTAGRACIA KETTLY METAYER B., CONSULAR AGENT		May. 28, 2002
MR. ROSARIO ALEXANDRE, CONSULAR AGENT		Dec. 12, 2005

---

* DEPENDENCIES SUCH AS GUAM, PUERTO RICO, AND THE VIRGIN ISLANDS ARE LISTED HERE.
CG-CONSULATE GENERAL   C-CONSULATE   VC-VICE CONSULATE   CA-CONSULAR AGENCY   H-HONORARY CONSULAR STATUS

STATE* RESIDENCE	NAME AND RANK	DATE OF RECOGNITION	STATE* RESIDENCE	NAME AND RANK	DATE OF RECOGNITION
ORLANDO (CON) 1616 E. COLONIAL DR., 32803. (407) 897-1262			**MICHIGAN**		
	MR. LAURENT P. PROSPER, CONSUL	Jun. 07, 2006	DETROIT (HC) X 1ST NATIONAL BLDG. UN., SUITE 2121, 48226. (313) 965-7962		
	MR. GREGORY MAX MENARD, CONSULAR AGENT	Jun. 07, 2006		MR. RALPH JENKINS OSBORNE, HONORARY CONSUL	Dec. 27, 1956
	MRS. PATRICE ANGELINE LUCIEN, CONSULAR AGENT	Jun. 07, 2006	**MISSOURI**		
	MS. MARJORIE ROMAIN, CONSULAR AGENT	Jun. 07, 2006	SAINT LOUIS (HC) 441 CLOISTERS WALK ., KIRKWOOD 63122. (314) 966-5280		
	MS. MONIQUE LOUIS JEAN, CONSULAR AGENT	Apr. 02, 2007		MR. NORMAN BRADFORD WEST, HONORARY CONSUL	Aug. 30, 1979
	MS. MONETTE ANDRESOL DUVIL, CONSULAR AGENT	May. 01, 2007	**NEW JERSEY**		
GEORGIA			TRENTON (HC) X P.O. BOX 1960 UN., PASSAIC 07055. (973) 777-2121		
ATLANTA (HC) ., 30366. (404) 455-3434				MR. JEAN CLAUDE SERGE LEVY, HONORARY CONSUL	Nov. 07, 1980
	MR. WILLIAM GILBERT BROWNING, HONORARY CONSUL	Sep. 14, 1979	**NEW YORK**		
ILLINOIS			NEW YORK (CG) 271 MADISON AV., FLOOR 17TH, 10016. (212) 697-9767		
CHICAGO (CG) 220 S. STATE ST., SUITE 2110, 60601. (312) 922-4004, FAX (312) 922-7122				MR. JOSEPH JOACHIM SIMON, CONSUL	Jun. 02, 2006
	MR. LESLIE LOUIS CONDE, CONSUL GENERAL	Jan. 24, 2006		MR. GUY GELIN, VICE CONSUL	Aug. 05, 1991
	MR. JEAN BUTEAUX CORIOLAN, CONSUL	Apr. 10, 2006		MR. JEAN YVES PERNIER, VICE CONSUL	Oct. 15, 2004
	MRS. CHARLES MYRIAME CHERY CARRENARD, VICE CONSUL	Jun. 06, 2006		MR. JACQUES LAROCHE, VICE CONSUL	Jun. 28, 2005
INDIANA				MS. STEPHANE FRANCK ETIENNE, VICE CONSUL	Jun. 20, 2006
EVANSVILLE (HC) ., 47711. (812) 423-8000, FAX (812) 426-6118				MS. MARIE MADELEINE PIARD, CONSULAR AGENT	Apr. 10, 2002
	MR. ALFRED DECALB VANHOOSE, HONORARY CONSUL	Jun. 16, 1969		MR. FRITZGERALD ALEXANDRE, CONSULAR AGENT	Jan. 27, 2006
				MRS. YVELANDE CLERMEUS CLAIRMEUS, CONSULAR AGENT	Jan. 27, 2006
LOUISIANA				MR. MARCEL NOEL, CONSULAR AGENT	Feb. 02, 2006
NEW ORLEANS (HC) 416 COMMON ST., 70130. (504) 586-8309				MR. ROBERT VON TAUBER, HONORARY CONSUL	Sep. 26, 1989
	MR. PIERRE BENJAMIN CLEMENCEAU, HONORARY CONSUL	Mar. 25, 1949	**OHIO**		
MASSACHUSETTS			CLEVELAND (HC) X STANDARD BLDG. UN., SUITE 1016, 44113. (216) 771-0280		
BOSTON (CG) 545 BOYLSTON ST., ROOM 201, 02116. (617) 266-3660				MR. HENRY P. KOSLING, HONORARY CONSUL	Apr. 15, 1975
	MR. JEAN ROLAND ELIE, CONSUL	Oct. 31, 2002	**PENNSYLVANIA**		
	MRS. GLADYS JOSEPH, CONSUL	Nov. 29, 2005	PHILADELPHIA (HC) 1600 MARKET ST., SUITE 3600, 19103. (215) 751-2516		
	MR. CHRISTIAN JEAN ROBERT VICTORIA, VICE CONSUL	Jun. 13, 1991		MR. ALBERT MOMJIAN, HONORARY CONSUL	Jun. 20, 1978
	MS. MARTINE GEORGES CASIMIR AMBROISE, VICE CONSUL	Jul. 30, 2003	POTTSVILLE (HC) 200 MAHANTONGO ST., 17901.		
	MS. NORDAMISE LAMOUR CLERVIL, VICE CONSUL	Nov. 29, 2005		MR. JOHN JOSEPH CURRAN, HONORARY CONSUL	Feb. 18, 1981
			PUERTO RICO		
			SAN JUAN (CG) 654 NUNOS RIVERA AV., SUITE 909, HATO REY 00918.		

STATE* RESIDENCE	NAME AND RANK	DATE OF RECOGNITION	STATE* RESIDENCE	NAME AND RANK	DATE OF RECOGNITION
	MR. RALPH VIARD, VICE CONSUL	Jan. 22, 1991	**FLORIDA**		
	MR. JERRY SAINDOUX, VICE CONSUL	Dec. 02, 1996	JACKSONVILLE (CON) 1914 BEACHWAY RD., SUITE 3-0, 33207. (904) 348-3550		
	MR. JOSPEH E. BINARD, HONORARY CONSUL	Nov. 12, 1980		MR. ANTONIO J. VALLADARES, CONSUL	Jun. 04, 1982

TEXAS

HOUSTON (HVC) 3535 SAGE RD., 77027.

	MR. RENATO F. PEREIRA, HONORARY VICE CONSUL	Jun. 17, 1983	MIAMI (CG) 7171 CORAL WA., SUITE 309, 33155. (305) 269-9399, FAX (305) 269-9445		
				MR. FERNANDO JOSE AGURCIA LEFEBVRE, CONSUL GENERAL	Jul. 26, 2006

HONDURAS

STATE* RESIDENCE	NAME AND RANK	DATE OF RECOGNITION	STATE* RESIDENCE	NAME AND RANK	DATE OF RECOGNITION
ARIZONA				MRS. MIRIAM BERNARDA YNESTROZA, CONSUL	Aug. 14, 2002
PHOENIX (CG) 4040 E. MC DOWELL RD., SUITE 305, 85008. (602) 273-0173, FAX (602) 273-0547				MS. NADIA GISELLE AGUILERA, VICE CONSUL	Oct. 05, 2006
	MRS. NORA ISABEL MONTOYA TORRES, CONSUL GENERAL	May. 25, 2006		MS. VIRGINIA BUESO, CONSULAR AGENT	Jul. 13, 1990
	MS. NOEMI PADILLA, CONSULAR AGENT	Oct. 06, 2005		MR. JUAN CARLOS VASQUEZ, CONSULAR AGENT	Feb. 09, 1999
	MS. KENIA MARIEL RAMOS, CONSULAR AGENT	May. 17, 2007		MR. ROBERTO A. MARTINEZ CASTELLANOS, CONSULAR AGENT	Jul. 15, 2004
	MR. REYES ANTONIO BANEGAS, HONORARY CONSUL	Mar. 24, 2006		MS. LIGIA ISABEL CASTILLO TURCIOS, CONSULAR AGENT	Jul. 26, 2006
CALIFORNIA				MR. AMILCAR MEDINA, CONSULAR AGENT	Oct. 05, 2006
LOS ANGELES (CG) 3550 WILSHIRE BL., SUITE 410, 90010. (213) 383-9244				MS. ANA CECILIA SALGADO GIRON, CONSULAR AGENT	Oct. 06, 2006
	MISS VIVIAN VERONICA PANTING GALO, CONSUL GENERAL	Aug. 27, 1998		MR. FEDERICO ALBERTO SMITH, HONORARY CONSUL	Mar. 31, 1992
	MR. OSCAR EDGARDO BENITEZ CABRERA, VICE CONSUL	Aug. 22, 2006		MR. OWEN S. FREED, HONORARY CONSUL	Mar. 17, 1997
	MS. AISSA ALEJANDRA ANTUNEZ, CONSULAR AGENT	Aug. 21, 1998	**GEORGIA**		
	MRS. RAFAELA E. ACOSTA, CONSULAR AGENT	Jul. 06, 2000	ATLANTA (CG) 600 HOUZE WA., SUITE 3-A, ROSWELL 30076. (770) 234-9560		
	MR. GEORGE V. CHILINGAR, HONORARY CONSUL	Oct. 07, 1991		MRS. ROSA PINEDA, CONSUL GENERAL	Sep. 18, 2006
	MRS. XIOMARA ALICIA FIELDS, HONORARY CONSUL	Nov. 04, 2004		DR. CECILIA CALLEJAS DE WILSON, VICE CONSUL	Sep. 18, 2006
	MR. MARIO FAUSTINO NUNEZ, HONORARY CONSUL	Jun. 27, 2006		MRS. LOURDES MAVEL SUMMERS, HONORARY CONSUL	Mar. 22, 2007
SAN DIEGO (HC) 525 B ST., SUITE 2002, 92101. (619) 533-4515			**HAWAII**		
			HONOLULU (HC) 1734 MALANAI ST., APT B, 96826. (808) 944-2811		
	MS. ELLA ISABEL FLORES-PARIS, HONORARY CONSUL	Apr. 29, 1966		MRS. LESBY PEREZ BILLAM-WALKER, HONORARY CONSUL	Mar. 10, 1972
SAN FRANCISCO (CG) 870 MARKET ST., SUITE 875, 94102. (415) 392-0076			**ILLINOIS**		
			CHICAGO (CG) 4439 W. FULLERTON AV., 60639. (773) 342-8281, FAX (773) 342-8293		
	MR. FRANCISCO VENEGAS, CONSUL GENERAL	Oct. 16, 2006		MR. JOSE ERAZMO MONTALVAN HERNANDEZ, CONSUL GENERAL	Jun. 20, 2006
	MS. JEANNY M. RODRIGUEZ MONDRAGON, CONSUL	Oct. 06, 2006		MS. SANDRA MIRIAM ROSALES ROBLES, VICE CONSUL	Nov. 29, 2005
	MRS. ADA ARGENTINA SANTOS MORALES, VICE CONSUL	Oct. 05, 2006		MRS. DIONISIA D. FUENTES PUERTO, CONSULAR AGENT	Apr. 18, 2006
	MS. SUYAPA ISABEL BARAHONA, CONSULAR AGENT	Apr. 09, 2007	**LOUISIANA**		
	MR. JUAN CARLOS FERRERA BULNES, CONSULAR AGENT	Jun. 19, 2007	BATON ROUGE (HC) 11017 N. OAK HILLS PW., 70810. (225) 766-4350, FAX (225) 766-7334		
	MR. HENRY LANGENBERG MC INTYRE, HONORARY VICE CONSUL	May. 03, 1972			

---

* DEPENDENCIES SUCH AS GUAM, PUERTO RICO, AND THE VIRGIN ISLANDS ARE LISTED HERE.
CG-CONSULATE GENERAL   C-CONSULATE   VC-VICE CONSULATE   CA-CONSULAR AGENCY   H-HONORARY CONSULAR STATUS

STATE* RESIDENCE	NAME AND RANK	DATE OF RECOGNITION
MS. VILMA CABRERA CALHOUN, HONORARY CONSUL		Apr. 23, 2003
MR. WILLIAM HUMPHREYS, HONORARY VICE CONSUL		Jun. 07, 2001

NEW ORLEANS (CG) 2 CANAL ST., SUITE 1641, 70130. (504) 522-3118

MISS ENA LILIANA CASTRO RICE, CONSUL GENERAL		Apr. 17, 2007
MISS MELISSA MARIA DISCUA BUEZO, CONSUL		Jul. 12, 2007
MS. VALENTINA MARIA SUAREZ, VICE CONSUL		Oct. 12, 2006
MS. GLENDA MARINA ROMERO VALLADARES, CONSULAR AGENT		Oct. 13, 2000
MR. JORGE VITANZA KATTAN, CONSULAR AGENT		May. 05, 2007

MARYLAND

BALTIMORE (HCG) 5803 LOCH RAVEN BL., 21239. (301) 435-6233

MR. RENE LICONA DUARTE, HONORARY CONSUL GENERAL		Oct. 16, 1978

MASSACHUSETTS

BOSTON (HC) 64 WELLAND RD., BROOKLINE 02445. (617) 731-3249

MS. GRACIELA SUAREZ, HONORARY CONSUL		Aug. 22, 2005

MISSOURI

SAINT LOUIS (HC) 6241 ALEXANDER DR., ST. LOUIS 63105. (314) 727-9179

MS. MARIA TAXMAN, HONORARY CONSUL		Mar. 29, 2001

NEVADA

RENO (HC) 5250 NEIL RD., SUITE 303, 89502-6503. (775) 829-1209

DR. RUDOLF GUNNERMAN, HONORARY CONSUL		Mar. 29, 2001

NEW YORK

NEW YORK (CG) 35 WEST 35TH ST., FLOOR 6, 10001.

MR. JAVIER HERNANDES MEJIA, CONSUL GENERAL		Dec. 06, 2006
MR. FRANCISCO QUEZADA LOBO, CONSULAR AGENT		Jul. 29, 2003

TEXAS

HOUSTON (CG) 5433 WESTHEIMER RD., SUITE 325, 77056. (713) 667-4693

MRS. LASTENIA PINEDA, CONSUL GENERAL		Aug. 19, 2002
MR. OSCAR A. ALVAREZ GUERRERO, VICE CONSUL		Jun. 12, 2006
MS. YOLANI DUBON, CONSULAR AGENT		Oct. 05, 2006
MRS. MAYRA O. SIMON, HONORARY CONSULAR AGENT		Mar. 11, 1985

HUNGARY

CALIFORNIA

LOS ANGELES (CG) 11766 WILSHIRE BL., SUITE 410, 90025. (310) 473-9344

MR. BALAZS BOKOR, CONSUL GENERAL		Jun. 29, 2007
MR. GABOR KALETA, CONSUL		Mar. 09, 2007
MR. GEZA VASS, CONSUL		Apr. 24, 2007

SAN FRANCISCO (HCG) 205 DE ANZA BL., SAN MATEO 94402. (650) 573-7351, FAX (650) 573-7355

MRS. EVA E. VOISIN, HONORARY CONSUL GENERAL		Sep. 20, 2005

COLORADO

DENVER (HCG) 1700 BROADWAY ST., SUITE 1700, 80290. (303) 861-8013, FAX (303) 832-3804

MR. EUGENE, JR FELEGYHAZY-MEGYESY, HONORARY CONSUL GENERAL		May. 14, 2002

DISTRICT OF COLUMBIA

WASHINGTON (CHN) 3910 SHOEMAKER ST., NW, 20008. (202) 362-6730, FAX (202) 966-8135

FLORIDA

MIAMI (HCG) 2655 LE JEUNE RD., SUITE 303, 33134. (305) 448-2131, FAX (305) 448-3184

MR. ALEXANDER S. TAR, HONORARY CONSUL GENERAL		Oct. 28, 1997
MR. GEORGE DEPOZSGAY, HONORARY CONSUL		Aug. 14, 2001

GEORGIA

MORROW (HC) 1115 MT. ZION RD., SUITE H, 30260. (404) 715-6937

MR. JOHN EMBRY , JR PARKERSON, HONORARY CONSUL		Apr. 02, 2007

HAWAII

HONOLULU (HC) 6710 HAWAII KAI DR., SUITE 1110, 96825. (808) 377-3637, FAX (808) 396-2605

MS. EMESE ROZALIA KOMJATHY, HONORARY CONSUL		Sep. 01, 1994

ILLINOIS

CHICAGO (CG) 600 N. STATE ST., 60610. (312) 943-3800

DR. ISTVAN GYULA MEZEI, CONSUL GENERAL		Jun. 07, 2007
MRS. MAGDOLNA EGRI, CONSUL		Jun. 07, 2007
MS. BRITA KAARINA KOSKENALUSTA, HONORARY CONSUL		Nov. 29, 2000

STATE* RESIDENCE	NAME AND RANK	DATE OF RECOGNITION	STATE* RESIDENCE	NAME AND RANK	DATE OF RECOGNITION

LOUISIANA

NEW ORLEANS (HC) 1417 BORDEAUX ST., 70115.
(504) 842-4604
  DR. STEPHEN GERGATZ,   Sep. 28, 1999
    HONORARY CONSUL

MASSACHUSETTS

BOSTON (HCG) 111 HUNTINGTON AV., FLOOR 26, 02199.
(617) 342-4022, FAX (617) 342-4001
  MR. GABOR GARAI,   May. 29, 2007
    HONORARY CONSUL GENERAL

MISSOURI

SAINT LOUIS (HCG) 7733 FORSYTH BL., SUITE 730, 63105.
  MR. JULIUS JOE ADORJAN,   Nov. 23, 2005
    HONORARY CONSUL GENERAL

NEW YORK

NEW YORK (CG) 223 E. 52ND ST., 10022.
(212) 752-0661, FAX (212) 755-5986
  MR. GABOR FOLDVARI,   Oct. 12, 2005
    DEPUTY CONSUL GENERAL

OHIO

CLEVELAND (HCG) 11312 FITZWATER RD., 44144.
(440) 717-0238, FAX (440) 717-0238
  MR. LASZLO BOJTOS,   Oct. 30, 1997
    HONORARY CONSUL GENERAL

PUERTO RICO

MAYAGUEZ (HC) 637 S. POST ST., 00682.
(787) 831-2010, FAX (787) 834-8380
  MR. DENNIS BECHARA,   Mar. 14, 1997
    HONORARY CONSUL

TEXAS

HOUSTON (HCG) 2221 POTOMAC UN., B, 77057.
(713) 977-8604
  MR. PHILLIP A. ARONOFF,   Jul. 11, 2005
    HONORARY CONSUL GENERAL

UTAH

SANDY (HC) 7641 MARY ESTHER CI., 84093.
(801) 733-6717
  MR. STEVEN GEORGE SIMON,   Jun. 01, 2007
    HONORARY CONSUL

WASHINGTON

SEATTLE (HC) 703 4TH AV., SUITE 103, KIRKLAND 98033.
(425) 576-8997, FAX (425) 739-6931
  MRS. HELEN M. SZABLYA,   Aug. 12, 1993
    HONORARY CONSUL

ICELAND

ALASKA

ANCHORAGE (HC) 3211 PROVIDENCE DR., SUITE 310, 99508.
(907) 786-1366

  MR. BJARTMAR SVEINBJORNSSON,   Apr. 05, 2000
    HONORARY CONSUL

ARIZONA

PHOENIX (HC) 2999 N. 44TH ST., SUITE 650, 85018.
(602) 952-1200, FAX (602) 956-8474
  DR. OMER K. REED,   May. 29, 1997
    HONORARY CONSUL

CALIFORNIA

LOS ANGELES (HCG) 155 N. ANITA AV., 90049.
(310) 440-3494, FAX (310) 440-9565
  MR. SIGURJON SIGHVATSSON,   Oct. 07, 1998
    HONORARY CONSUL GENERAL
  MRS. SIGRIDUR J. THORISDOTTIR,   Nov. 06, 1998
    HONORARY VICE CONSUL

SAN DIEGO (HC) 5910 PACIFIC CENTER BL., SUITE 100, 92121.
(858) 777-5164
  MR. ROBERT STEVEN HOROWITZ,   Sep. 11, 2003
    HONORARY CONSUL

SAN FRANCISCO (HCG) 222 FRONT ST., FLOOR 5TH, 94111.
(415) 433-3103, FAX (415) 433-0449
  MR. ROBERT E., JR CARTWRIGHT,   Sep. 21, 2006
    HONORARY CONSUL GENERAL
  MS. DOROTHY CARTWRIGHT,   Sep. 05, 1997
    HONORARY VICE CONSUL

COLORADO

ENGLEWOOD (HC) 4 CANTITOTE LA., 80110.
(303) 771-5842
  MR. EDWARD PHILLIPS CONNORS,   Mar. 22, 2001
    HONORARY CONSUL

FLORIDA

ORLANDO (HC) 6573 AUTUMN COVE DR., 32822.
  DR. KRISTJAN INGVARSSON,   Jul. 24, 2007
    HONORARY CONSUL

PLANTATION (HCG) 1820 S.W. 73RD AV., 33317.
(954) 792-4750, FAX (954) 920-6977
  MR. THORIR SIGURDSSON GRONDAL,   May. 02, 2001
    HONORARY CONSUL GENERAL

TALLAHASSEE (HCG) 1486 ST. CHARLES PLACE UN., 32308.
(850) 878-1144, FAX (850) 878-3862
  MR. HILMAR S. SKAGFIELD,   Dec. 24, 1985
    HONORARY CONSUL GENERAL

GEORGIA

ATLANTA (HCG) 191 PEACHTREE ST., NE, FLOOR 16, 30303.
(404) 572-6670, FAX (404) 572-6999
  MR. MAURICE KARL HOROWITZ,   Jan. 21, 1987
    HONORARY CONSUL GENERAL
  MR. MARC DOUGLAS GLENN,   Jan. 16, 2003
    HONORARY VICE CONSUL

STATE* RESIDENCE	NAME AND RANK	DATE OF RECOGNITION	STATE* RESIDENCE	NAME AND RANK	DATE OF RECOGNITION

ILLINOIS

CHICAGO (HCG) 15750 S. HARLEM AV., SUITE 28, ORLAND PARK 60611.
(708) 429-1126, FAX (708) 429-9972

MR. EDWARD J. DERWINSKI, HONORARY CONSUL GENERAL		Sep. 06, 1994
MR. ARISTOTLE P. HALIKIAS, HONORARY VICE CONSUL		Sep. 28, 1994

KENTUCKY

LOUISVILLE (HC) 2600 HIGHWAY 146 ., E, LA GRANGE 40031.
(502) 222-1441, FAX (502) 222-1445

MR. JON S. GUDMUNDSSON, HONORARY CONSUL		Jan. 30, 1989
MR. ORN EGGERT, SR GUDMUNDSSON, HONORARY CONSUL		Jun. 24, 2005

LOUISIANA

NEW ORLEANS (HC) 210 BARONNE ST., SUITE 1022, 70112.
(504) 524-3342, FAX (504) 524-3344

MR. GREG J. BEUERMAN, HONORARY CONSUL		Feb. 16, 1994

MASSACHUSETTS

BOSTON (HC) 33 BROAD ST., 02109.
(617) 227-4300, FAX (617) 227-5505

MR. ELISHA FLAGG LEE, HONORARY CONSUL		Jul. 26, 1996
MR. JAMES FRANCIS, III GERRITY, HONORARY VICE CONSUL		Aug. 14, 1996

MICHIGAN

DETROIT (HC) 73 KERCHEVAL AV., SUITE 201, GROSSE POINTE FARMS 48236.
(313) 886-7070, FAX (313) 886-7150

MR. EDWARD K. CHRISTIAN, HONORARY CONSUL		Sep. 03, 1997

MINNESOTA

MINNEAPOLIS (HCG) 6428 NORDIC CI., EDINA 55439.
(952) 942-5745

DR. ORN ARNAR, HONORARY CONSUL GENERAL		Feb. 29, 2000
MR. JOHN SWANHOLM, JR MAGNUSSON, HONORARY CONSUL		Jun. 30, 2000
MS. MARY LEOLA JOSEFSON, HONORARY VICE CONSUL		Apr. 07, 2000

MISSOURI

GRANDVIEW (HC) 7100 E. 131ST ST., 64030.
(816) 763-2046

MRS. VIGDIS ADALSTEINSDOTTIR TAYLOR, HONORARY CONSUL		May. 21, 1985

NEW YORK

NEW YORK (CG) 800 THIRD AV., FLOOR 36TH, 10022.
(212) 593-2700, FAX (212) 593-6269

MR. HLYNUR GUDJONSSON, CONSUL		Jul. 14, 2006

MR. PETUR THORSTEINN OSKARSSON, VICE CONSUL		Feb. 27, 2004
MR. MAGNUS MAR GUSTAFSSON, HONORARY CONSUL		Aug. 22, 2006

NORTH DAKOTA

GRAND FORK (HC) 12963 87TH ST., NE, MOUNTAIN 58262.
(701) 993-8282

MRS. LORETTA KAY BERNHOFT, HONORARY CONSUL		Apr. 19, 2001

OREGON

PORTLAND (HC) 724 S.W. HARRISON UN., ROOM 239, 97207.
(503) 725-9705, FAX (503) 725-9174

MR. LESLIE SWANSON, HONORARY CONSUL		Feb. 03, 2001

PENNSYLVANIA

HARRISBURG (HC) 2015-D SOUTH POINT DR., HUMMELSTOWN 17036.
(717) 566-7791, FAX (717) 566-7792

MR. HUBERT JONAS GEORGES, HONORARY CONSUL		Apr. 21, 1980

PUERTO RICO

SAN JUAN (HC) 2 ISLANDIA ST., BAYAMON 00960.
(787) 780-4323, FAX (787) 740-2888

MR. ANTONIO RUIZ OCHOA, HONORARY CONSUL		Mar. 11, 1992

SOUTH CAROLINA

CHARLESTON (HC) 241 E. BAY ST., 29401.
(843) 577-5100, FAX (843) 722-4688

MR. MARK CHARLES TANENBAUM, HONORARY CONSUL		Sep. 10, 2003

TEXAS

DALLAS (HC) 17910 WINDFLOWER WA., APT 2201, 75252.
(214) 540-9135, FAX (214) 969-5162

MS. PAMELA KAY BAUER, HONORARY CONSUL		Sep. 28, 1990

HOUSTON (HC) 2348 W. SETTLER'S WAY ., THE WOODLANDS 77380.
(713) 367-2777, FAX (281) 362-4385

MR. OLAFUR A. ASGEIRSSON, HONORARY CONSUL		Aug. 06, 1993

UTAH

SALT LAKE CITY (HC) 818 CANYON RD., SPRINGVILLE 84663.
(801) 378-3337, FAX (801) 378-7860

MR. J. BRENT HAYMOND, HONORARY CONSUL		Apr. 05, 2001

VIRGINIA

NORFOLK (HC) 500 E. MAIN ST., SUITE 1000, 23510.
(757) 640-5360

---

* DEPENDENCIES SUCH AS GUAM, PUERTO RICO, AND THE VIRGIN ISLANDS ARE LISTED HERE.
CG-CONSULATE GENERAL   C-CONSULATE   VC-VICE CONSULATE   CA-CONSULAR AGENCY   H-HONORARY CONSULAR STATUS

STATE* RESIDENCE	NAME AND RANK	DATE OF RECOGNITION	STATE* RESIDENCE	NAME AND RANK	DATE OF RECOGNITION
	MR. JOHN E. HOLLOWAY, HONORARY CONSUL	Mar. 22, 2001		MR. KRISHAN KUMAR PAHEL, VICE CONSUL	Oct. 10, 2006
	MRS. SESSELJA SEIFERT, HONORARY VICE CONSUL	Mar. 22, 2001			

LOUISIANA

NEW ORLEANS (HC) 1525 WEBSTER ST., 70118.

MR. GEORGE DENEGRE, HONORARY CONSUL	Mar. 14, 1977

WASHINGTON

SEATTLE (HCG) 5610 20TH AV., NW, 98107.
(206) 783-4100, FAX (206) 784-8916

MR. JON MARVIN JONSSON, HONORARY CONSUL GENERAL	Aug. 02, 1990
MR. GEIR T. JONSSON, HONORARY VICE CONSUL	Feb. 27, 2003

WISCONSIN

MADISON (HC) 1364 VAN HISE HALL AV., 53706.
(608) 262-2090

MR. RICHARD N. RINGLER, HONORARY CONSUL	Nov. 24, 2003

INDIA

CALIFORNIA

SAN FRANCISCO (CG) 540 ARGUELLO BL., 94118.
(415) 668-0662

MR. PRAKASH BELLUR SHAMARAO, CONSUL GENERAL	Mar. 28, 2005
MR. GOURANGALAL DAS, CONSUL	Oct. 06, 2004
MR. PRABHAT KUMAR SINGH, CONSUL	Apr. 20, 2005
MR. SOUMENDU BAGCHI, CONSUL	Dec. 05, 2005
MR. MACHINGAL VIJAYAN, VICE CONSUL	Jul. 13, 2004

GEORGIA

ATLANTA (HC) 1201 W. PEACHTREE ST., SUITE 2000, 30309-3400.
(404) 898-8172, FAX (404) 881-0470

MR. KENNETH ANDREW CUTSHAW, HONORARY CONSUL	Dec. 20, 2000

HAWAII

HONOLULU (HCG) 2051 YOUNG ST., 96826.
(808) 732-7692

MRS. SHEILA H. WATUMULL, HONORARY CONSUL GENERAL	Oct. 02, 1990

ILLINOIS

CHICAGO (CG) 455 N. CITYFRONT PLAZA DR., SUITE 850, 60611.
(312) 595-0405, FAX (312) 595-0416

MR. ASHOK KUMAR ATTRI, CONSUL GENERAL	Jul. 12, 2007
MR. JAGDISH RAI, CONSUL	Oct. 26, 2004
MR. RAJINDER SINGH BADWAL, CONSUL	Jul. 08, 2005
MR. RAVINDRAN GOPALAKRISHNAN, VICE CONSUL	Nov. 24, 2004
MR. ASHOK KUMAR SAWHNEY, VICE CONSUL	Dec. 05, 2005

NEW YORK

NEW YORK (CG) 3 E. 64TH ST., 10021.
(212) 879-7800

MRS. NEELAM DEO, CONSUL GENERAL	Dec. 16, 2005
MR. SURINDER K. NANGIA, CONSUL	Jul. 22, 2002
MR. SANDEEP MOHAN BHATNAGAR, CONSUL	Oct. 22, 2003
MR. AJJAMPUR RANGAIAH GHANASHYAM, CONSUL	Jul. 12, 2004
MR. PUTHENVEETTIL S. SASI KUMAR, CONSUL	Mar. 31, 2006
MS. NEENA MALHOTRA, CONSUL	Jun. 08, 2006
MR. PANACHIKKUTH PRAKASH, CONSUL	May. 11, 2007
MR. P. K. KEERIKAT GOVINDAPILLAI, CONSUL	Apr. 30, 2009
MR. SUBHASH CHANDER, VICE CONSUL	May. 15, 2002
MR. RAJESH KUMAR, VICE CONSUL	Jul. 22, 2005
MR. CHERIAN THOMAS, VICE CONSUL	Oct. 06, 2006
MR. RAMESH CHANDER CHADHA, VICE CONSUL	Oct. 06, 2006

TEXAS

HOUSTON (CG) 1990 POST OAK BL., SUITE 600, 77056.
(713) 626-2148

MR. SHASHISHEKHAR MADHUKAR GAVAI, CONSUL GENERAL	Oct. 17, 2005
MR. JITENDRA NATH MISRA, DEPUTY CONSUL GENERAL	Aug. 18, 1998
MR. KUNJURAMAN PRESENNAN PILLAI, CONSUL	Aug. 19, 2005
MR. BAL KRISHAN ASEEJA, VICE CONSUL	Sep. 24, 2004
MR. NARINDER KUMAR KARIR, VICE CONSUL	Apr. 12, 2005
MRS. NITA KAMAL GHAI, VICE CONSUL	Jul. 18, 2007

INDONESIA

CALIFORNIA

LOS ANGELES (CG) 3457 WILSHIRE BL., 90010.
(213) 383-5126

MR. SUBIJAKSONO SUJONO, CONSUL GENERAL	May. 05, 2007
MR. HANGGIRO SETIABUDI, CONSUL	Mar. 09, 2004
MR. HERRY HOTMA, CONSUL	Nov. 08, 2004

---

* DEPENDENCIES SUCH AS GUAM, PUERTO RICO, AND THE VIRGIN ISLANDS ARE LISTED HERE.
CG-CONSULATE GENERAL C-CONSULATE VC-VICE CONSULATE CA-CONSULAR AGENCY H-HONORARY CONSULAR STATUS

STATE* RESIDENCE	NAME AND RANK	DATE OF RECOGNITION	STATE* RESIDENCE	NAME AND RANK	DATE OF RECOGNITION

MR. BUDHI HARMANTO,
   CONSUL — Nov. 26, 2004
MR. AGUSTI ANWAR,
   CONSUL — Apr. 26, 2007
MR. WANDI ADRIANO,
   VICE CONSUL — Jul. 08, 2004

INDONESIAN TRADE PROMOTION CENTER
LOS ANGELES (CONA) 3457 WILSHIRE BL., SUITE 101, 90010.
(213) 387-7041

SAN FRANCISCO (CG) 1111 COLUMBUS AV., 94133.
(415) 474-9571
MR. YUDHISTIRANTO SUNGADI,
   CONSUL GENERAL — May. 05, 2007
MR. DEDDY SAIFUL HADI,
   CONSUL — Dec. 08, 2004
MR. ANDI RAHADIAN,
   CONSUL — Apr. 13, 2006
MR. OKTO DORINUS MANIK,
   CONSUL — May. 04, 2007
MR. KHASAN ASHARI,
   VICE CONSUL — Apr. 13, 2006

HAWAII

HONOLULU (HC) 1001 BISHOP ST., SUITE 2970, 96813.
(808) 531-3017
MR. PATRICK KEVIN SULLIVAN,
   HONORARY CONSUL — Aug. 20, 2001

ILLINOIS

CHICAGO (CG) 211 W. WACKER DR., SUITE 800, 60606.
(312) 595-1777, FAX (312) 595-9952
MR. HIDAYAT KARTA HADIMADJA,
   CONSUL GENERAL — Jan. 21, 2005
MS. ENDANG DEWI MARDEYANI,
   CONSUL — Feb. 24, 2004
MR. STEPHANUS MARIA SUWARYANTO,
   CONSUL — Jun. 08, 2006
MR. YUDHO SASONGKO,
   VICE CONSUL — Sep. 07, 2004
MS. RNAWATI ,
   VICE CONSUL — Jun. 08, 2006

NEW YORK

NEW YORK (CG) 5 E. 68TH ST., 10021.
(212) 879-0600
MRS. TRIE EDI MULYANI,
   CONSUL GENERAL — Apr. 27, 2007
MR. IWANSHAH WIBISONO,
   CONSUL — Jan. 08, 2004
MR. EEK SLAMET,
   CONSUL — Aug. 19, 2004
MR. WIWIT WIRSATYO,
   CONSUL — Dec. 28, 2006
MR. BAMBANG ANTARIKSO,
   CONSUL — May. 30, 2007
MR. YOHPY ICHSAN WARDANA,
   VICE CONSUL — Nov. 10, 2003
MRS. MEINARTI FAUZIE,
   VICE CONSUL — Oct. 10, 2006

TRADE PROMOTION CENTER OF INDONESIA
NEW YORK (CONA) 1328 BROADWAY AV., SUITE 510, 10001.

TEXAS

HOUSTON (CG) 10900 RICHMOND AV., 77042.
MR. KRIA FAHMI PASARIBU,
   CONSUL GENERAL — May. 05, 2007
MR. BASYIRUDDIN AHMAD HIDAYAT,
   CONSUL — Dec. 22, 2003
MR. RUSMAN K. UTOMO,
   CONSUL — Jun. 17, 2004
MR. CALDERON DALIMUNTHE,
   CONSUL — Dec. 05, 2005
MR. ANAK AGUNG GDE ALIT SANTHIKA,
   CONSUL — Mar. 31, 2006
MR. HERU PRAYITNO,
   CONSUL — Mar. 31, 2006

IRELAND

CALIFORNIA

LOS ANGELES (HC) 1631 BEVERLY BL., 90026.
(714) 658-9832
MR. MICHAEL FINBAR HILL,
   HONORARY CONSUL — Aug. 27, 2002

SAN FRANCISCO (CG) 100 PINE ST., FLOOR 33, 94111.
(415) 392-4214, FAX (415) 392-0885
MS. EMER FIONNUALA DEANE,
   CONSUL GENERAL — Nov. 30, 2005
MRS. UNA MARIE FANNON,
   VICE CONSUL — Oct. 01, 2004

FLORIDA

NAPLES (HC) 400 5TH AV., S, SUITE 301, 34102.
(239) 649-1001, FAX (239) 649-1972
MRS. CYNTHIA BYRNE HALL,
   HONORARY CONSUL — Sep. 17, 2004

GEORGIA

ATLANTA (HC) 191 PEACHTREE ST., NE, SUITE 1320, 30303.
(404) 332-6401, FAX (404) 332-4299

ILLINOIS

CHICAGO (CG) 400 N. MICHIGAN AV., SUITE 911, 60611.
(312) 337-1868
MR. SEAN FARRELL,
   CONSUL GENERAL — Sep. 28, 2006
MS. HILARY OBRIEN,
   VICE CONSUL — Nov. 02, 2005

MASSACHUSETTS

BOSTON (CG) 535 BOYLSTON ST., FLOOR 5TH, 02116.
(617) 267-9330
MR. DAVID BARRY,
   CONSUL GENERAL — Oct. 17, 2005
MRS. MARIANNE BOLGER,
   VICE CONSUL — Sep. 15, 2004

STATE* RESIDENCE	NAME AND RANK	DATE OF RECOGNITION	STATE* RESIDENCE	NAME AND RANK	DATE OF RECOGNITION

MISSOURI

SAINT LOUIS (HC) 65 BROADVIEW ., CLAYTON 63105.
(618) 274-0886

MR. JOSEPH BERNARD MCGLYNN,   Oct. 31, 1977
HONORARY CONSUL

NEVADA

RENO (HC) 920 SCHELLBOURNE ST., 89511.
(775) 853-4497

DR. BERNARD NOEL BRADY,   Nov. 06, 1998
HONORARY CONSUL

NEW YORK

NEW YORK (CG) 345 PARK AV., FLOOR 17, 10154.
(212) 319-2552

MR. NIALL ANTHONY BURGESS,   May. 09, 2007
CONSUL GENERAL
MR. BREANDAN O CAOLLAI,   Sep. 14, 2006
DEPUTY CONSUL GENERAL
MR. DAVID PATRICK HEALY,   Dec. 12, 2005
VICE CONSUL
MS. YVONNE GILBRIDE,   Feb. 24, 2006
CONSULAR AGENT

TEXAS

HOUSTON (HC) 2630 SUTTON CT., 77027.
(713) 961-5263, FAX (713) 961-3850

MR. JOHN B. KANE,   Nov. 09, 1990
HONORARY CONSUL

ISRAEL

CALIFORNIA

LOS ANGELES (CG) 6380 WILSHIRE BL., SUITE 1700, 90048.
(213) 852-5500, FAX (213) 852-5555

MR. EHUD DANOCH,   Nov. 02, 2004
CONSUL GENERAL
MR. YARON GAMBURG,   Jul. 07, 2005
DEPUTY CONSUL GENERAL
MR. SHAI AIZIN,   Apr. 08, 2005
CONSUL
MR. GILAD MILLO,   Oct. 06, 2005
CONSUL
MR. MENASHE MIZRAHI,   Jun. 08, 2006
CONSUL
MR. RAMI LEVI,   Aug. 16, 2006
CONSUL
MR. ODED GELFER,   Oct. 05, 2006
CONSUL
MRS. SIGAL YAVETS,   Dec. 29, 2006
CONSUL
MR. YUVAL ELNER,   Apr. 05, 2006
VICE CONSUL
MR. ROI SHIMON AVISHAY,   Apr. 13, 2006
VICE CONSUL
MR. ERAN BARZILY,   Jun. 14, 2006
VICE CONSUL
MR. SHLOMO YEHEZKEL,   Apr. 25, 2007
VICE CONSUL

ECONOMIC MISSION OF ISRAEL
LOS ANGELES (CONA) 6404 WILSHIRE BL., SUITE 1150, 90048.
(213) 658-7924, FAX (213) 651-0572

SAN FRANCISCO (CG) 456 MONTGOMERY ST., FLOOR 21ST, 94104.
(415) 398-8885, FAX (415) 398-8589

MR. DAVID MORDECHAI AKOV,   Oct. 26, 2004
CONSUL GENERAL
MR. ISMAIL KHALDI,   May. 04, 2007
CONSUL
MR. ZIV YOASH,   Jun. 16, 2004
VICE CONSUL
MR. ALON SAMUEL,   May. 04, 2007
VICE CONSUL

DISTRICT OF COLUMBIA

WASHINGTON (CHN) 3514 INTERNATIONAL DR., NW, 20008.
(202) 364-5500, FAX (202) 364-5607

MR. MOSHE FOX,   Sep. 14, 2000
CONSUL GENERAL
MR. ROGEL RACHMAN,   May. 31, 2007
CONSUL

FLORIDA

MIAMI (CG) 100 N. BISCAYNE BL., SUITE 1800-1801, 33132.
(305) 358-8111, FAX (305) 371-5034

MR. ELIYAHU YIFRACH,   Oct. 06, 2005
CONSUL
MR. IDO KAZAZ,   Apr. 10, 2006
VICE CONSUL
MR. MICHAEL TZACH,   Oct. 06, 2006
VICE CONSUL

GEORGIA

ATLANTA (CG) 1100 SPRING ST., NW, SUITE 440, 30309.
(404) 487-6500, FAX (404) 487-6555

AMBASSADOR REDA MANSOUR,   Sep. 28, 2006
CONSUL GENERAL
MR. OREN ROZENBLAT,   Feb. 06, 2006
DEPUTY CONSUL GENERAL
MR. SHAHAR OVED,   Jul. 12, 2007
VICE CONSUL

TOURIST OFFICE OF ISRAEL
ATLANTA (CONA) 1100 SPRING ST., ROOM 440, 30309--2823.
(404) 875-9924

ECONOMIC MISSION OF ISRAEL
ATLANTA (CONA) 1100 SPRING ST., SUITE 440, 30309--2823.
(404) 487-6500, FAX (404) 487-6555

ILLINOIS

CHICAGO (CG) 111 E. WACKER DR., SUITE 1308, 60601.
(312) 565-3300, FAX (312) 565-3871

MR. BARUKH BINAH,   Oct. 04, 2005
CONSUL GENERAL
MR. ANDY DAVID,   Sep. 07, 2004
CONSUL
MR. ELIAHU LEVY,   Sep. 07, 2004
CONSUL
MR. YARON HAMISH AVRHAM,   Oct. 01, 2004
VICE CONSUL
MR. YORAM OZER,   Sep. 06, 2006
VICE CONSUL

STATE* RESIDENCE	NAME AND RANK	DATE OF RECOGNITION	STATE* RESIDENCE	NAME AND RANK	DATE OF RECOGNITION
				MR. ARIEL SHLEZINGER, VICE CONSUL	Jul. 26, 2006
OFFICE OF TOURISM OF ISRAEL CHICAGO (CONA) 111 E. WACKER DR., SUITE 1230, 60601. (312) 938-3885, FAX (312) 938-3668				MR. BOAZ MECILATY, VICE CONSUL	Jul. 26, 2006
				MR. EYAL ENCAOUA, VICE CONSUL	Feb. 08, 2007
ECONOMIC MISSION OF ISRAEL CHICAGO (CONA) 111 E. WACKER DR., SUITE 1230, 60601. (312) 332-2160, FAX (312) 332-2163				MR. SHAHAR AVRAHAMI, VICE CONSUL	Feb. 08, 2007
	MS. NOA ASHER, CONSUL	Apr. 24, 2007		MR. SHAY MIZRAHY, VICE CONSUL	May. 08, 2007
MASSACHUSETTS			DEFENSE PROCUREMENT MISSION OF ISRAEL NEW YORK (CONA) 800 2ND AV., FLOOR 10,11,12, 10017. (212) 551-0444, FAX (212) 551-0482		
BOSTON (CG) 20 PARK PZ., SUITE 1020, 02116. (617) 542-0041, FAX (617) 338-4995				MR. YEKUTIEL MOR, CONSUL	Aug. 05, 2003
	MR. NADAV TAMIR, CONSUL GENERAL	Dec. 15, 2006		MR. AMIR YAHAV, VICE CONSUL	Aug. 02, 2002
	MS. RONY YEDIDIA, CONSUL	Apr. 24, 2007		MR. DORON SHOOR, VICE CONSUL	Aug. 02, 2002
	MR. YOSSI TWITO, VICE CONSUL	Oct. 04, 2005		MR. ADRIAN SCHWARTZ, VICE CONSUL	Aug. 12, 2002
	MR. OFER PERRY, VICE CONSUL	Apr. 26, 2007		MR. AVRAHAM MASHIAH, VICE CONSUL	Jul. 27, 2003
				MRS. NECHAMA SHECHNER, VICE CONSUL	Jul. 29, 2003
NEW YORK				MRS. YONINA STRIKOVSKI, VICE CONSUL	Jul. 29, 2003
NEW YORK (CG) 800 2ND AV., FLOOR 13,14,15, 10017. (212) 499-5477, FAX (212) 499-5465				MR. MOSHE AISH, VICE CONSUL	Jul. 31, 2003
	MR. ARYE MEKEL, CONSUL GENERAL	Apr. 26, 2005		MR. ROBI MAROM, VICE CONSUL	Jul. 31, 2003
	MRS. IRIT DEGANI STOPPER, CONSUL	Sep. 10, 2004		MRS. RINA ZITSER, VICE CONSUL	Jul. 31, 2003
	MR. BENJAMIN KRASNA, CONSUL	Dec. 05, 2005		MR. DOV HAIM KEDEM, VICE CONSUL	Jul. 20, 2004
	MR. DAVID SARANGA, CONSUL	Dec. 05, 2005		MR. MILIAN MARAM, VICE CONSUL	Jul. 20, 2004
	MR. YORAM YIZHAK MORAD, CONSUL	Jul. 11, 2006		MR. SHAUL GOLDKIND GAL, VICE CONSUL	Jul. 20, 2004
	MRS. SHARON REGEV, CONSUL	Apr. 26, 2007		MR. SHLOMO BARTAL, VICE CONSUL	Jul. 20, 2004
	MR. DANNY ZALEWSKI, VICE CONSUL	Aug. 22, 2002		MR. ZVI LEV, VICE CONSUL	Jul. 20, 2004
	MR. ILAN YEHUDA, VICE CONSUL	Jul. 15, 2004		MR. SHAI SPINZI, VICE CONSUL	Jul. 28, 2004
	MR. RON ROTTENBERG, VICE CONSUL	Jul. 20, 2004		MRS. AYALA AVIRAM, VICE CONSUL	Jul. 28, 2004
	MR. MOTI ELKAIM, VICE CONSUL	Sep. 09, 2004		MRS. MICHAL MORIEL, VICE CONSUL	Jul. 28, 2004
	MR. YOGEV SHLOMI SISO, VICE CONSUL	Sep. 10, 2004		MR. MEIR MOSCOVITS, VICE CONSUL	Jul. 29, 2004
	MR. ELI SHUSHAN, VICE CONSUL	Dec. 03, 2004		MR. ABRAHAM KEREN, VICE CONSUL	Nov. 10, 2005
	MR. LEON SMULAKOWSKI, VICE CONSUL	Feb. 14, 2005		MR. ALON HORESH, VICE CONSUL	Nov. 10, 2005
	MR. IDAN KFIR, VICE CONSUL	Apr. 12, 2005		MR. YORAM ABECASIS, VICE CONSUL	Nov. 10, 2005
	MR. SHLOMO NEUMAN, VICE CONSUL	Nov. 15, 2005		MRS. ESTHER DAR DYCHOVSKY, VICE CONSUL	Nov. 10, 2005
	MR. ILAN PINHAS FEINGOLD, VICE CONSUL	Dec. 05, 2005		MR. AVISHAY HERTZ, VICE CONSUL	Nov. 14, 2005
	MR. OLEG KREIMER, VICE CONSUL	Jun. 02, 2006		MR. AVRAHAM SHARKA, VICE CONSUL	Nov. 14, 2005
	MR. YANIV AMIR, VICE CONSUL	Jun. 02, 2006		MR. SAMUEL ADMON ROYTER, VICE CONSUL	Nov. 14, 2005

STATE* RESIDENCE	NAME AND RANK	DATE OF RECOGNITION	STATE* RESIDENCE	NAME AND RANK	DATE OF RECOGNITION

MR. SHARON NAGEL,
  VICE CONSUL — Nov. 14, 2005
MR. SHAUL GILBOA,
  VICE CONSUL — Nov. 14, 2005
MR. SHLOMO BAR,
  VICE CONSUL — Nov. 14, 2005
MR. TZAFRIR SOLOMON,
  VICE CONSUL — Nov. 14, 2005
MR. GIL MELAMED,
  VICE CONSUL — Nov. 21, 2005
MS. HILA SHASHO HARRAM,
  VICE CONSUL — Dec. 01, 2005
MR. MENACHEM CHAIM GERSKOVICH,
  VICE CONSUL — Dec. 05, 2005
MR. ADIR MOVSHOVITZ,
  VICE CONSUL — Aug. 11, 2006
MR. DAVID AVRAHAM,
  VICE CONSUL — Aug. 11, 2006
MR. HAIM RUBINSTEIN,
  VICE CONSUL — Aug. 11, 2006
MR. ILAN AVIV,
  VICE CONSUL — Aug. 11, 2006
MS. FABIANA STEINBERG,
  VICE CONSUL — Aug. 11, 2006
MS. VERED VILENKO,
  VICE CONSUL — Aug. 11, 2006
MR. MOSHE ENGEL,
  VICE CONSUL — Aug. 16, 2006
MR. PINCHAS HAVIV ONUNU,
  VICE CONSUL — Sep. 06, 2006
MR. ILAN MAZUSHAN,
  VICE CONSUL — Jul. 18, 2007
MR. ISRAEL GAM,
  VICE CONSUL — Jul. 30, 2007
MR. ITSHAK LEVI,
  VICE CONSUL — Jul. 30, 2007
MR. MEIR WOLTSOVITCH,
  VICE CONSUL — Jul. 30, 2007
MR. MICHAEL RAN,
  VICE CONSUL — Jul. 30, 2007
MR. REUVEN SOFER,
  VICE CONSUL — Jul. 30, 2007
MS. ILANA BERMAN,
  VICE CONSUL — Jul. 30, 2007
MS. LEA DORIT ZIL BAR,
  VICE CONSUL — Jul. 30, 2007

OFFICE OF TOURISM MISSION OF ISRAEL
NEW YORK (CONA) 800 SECOND AV., FLOOR 16, 10017.
(212) 499-5600, FAX (212) 499-5715
  MR. ARIE YEHIEL SOMMER,
    CONSUL — Apr. 07, 2006

ECONOMIC MISSION OF ISRAEL
NEW YORK (CONA) 800 2ND AV., FLOOR 17, 10017.
(212) 499-5716, FAX (212) 499-5715
  MR. ZVI CHALAMISH,
    CONSUL — Dec. 05, 2005
  MR. RAN ALON,
    CONSUL — Feb. 22, 2006
  MR. YAIR SHWARZBARD SHIRAN,
    CONSUL — Sep. 06, 2006

PENNSYLVANIA

PHILADELPHIA (CG) 230 S. 15TH ST., FLOOR 7-8, 19102.
(215) 546-5556, FAX (215) 545-3986
  MR. URIEL PALTI,
    CONSUL GENERAL — Sep. 29, 2004
  MR. LEO VINOVEZKY,
    VICE CONSUL — Oct. 05, 2006

TEXAS

HOUSTON (CG) 24 GREENWAY PZ., SUITE 1500, 77046.
(713) 627-3780, FAX (713) 627-0149
  MR. ASHER YARDEN,
    CONSUL GENERAL — Mar. 21, 2006
  MR. JOSEPH ABRAHAM,
    CONSUL — Sep. 23, 2004
  MR. LEONID KALMANOVICH,
    VICE CONSUL — Feb. 11, 2004
  MS. BELAYNESH ZEVADIA ADIGEH,
    VICE CONSUL — Nov. 02, 2005
  MRS. TAMAR YARDEN,
    VICE CONSUL — Jul. 11, 2006

ITALY

ALASKA

ANCHORAGE (HCA) 12840 SILVER SPRUCE DR., 99516.
(907) 345-6419
  MR. VITTORIO M. MONTEMEZZANI,
    HONORARY CONSULAR AGENT — Feb. 09, 1990

ARIZONA

PHOENIX (HVC) 2525 E. CAMELBACK RD., SUITE 840, 85016.
(602) 956-5800
  MR. ANTHONY ALBERT BONACCI,
    HONORARY VICE CONSUL — Jun. 10, 1998

CALIFORNIA

FRESNO (HVC) 2125 MERCED ST., 93721.
(559) 268-8776, FAX (559) 268-5701
  MR. EDWARD LEROY FANUCCHI,
    HONORARY VICE CONSUL — May. 20, 1976

LOS ANGELES (CG) 12400 WILSHIRE BL., SUITE 300&360, 90025.
(310) 826-5998, FAX (310) 820-0727
  MR. DIEGO BRASIOLI,
    CONSUL GENERAL — Aug. 04, 2003
  MRS. MARIELLA SALVATORI,
    CONSULAR AGENT — Oct. 25, 2001
  MR. FERNANDO CURATOLO,
    CONSULAR AGENT — Oct. 27, 2003
  MS. CLARA CELATI,
    CONSULAR AGENT — Oct. 27, 2003
  MS. MONICA PESCATORI,
    CONSULAR AGENT — Apr. 04, 2007

ITALIAN CULTURAL INSTITUTE
LOS ANGELES (CONA) 1023 HILGARD AV., 90024.
(310) 443-3250
  MRS. FRANCESCA VALENTE GORJUP,
    CONSUL — Apr. 29, 2005
  MS. GIUSEPPINA CANDIA,
    CONSULAR AGENT — Oct. 14, 2004

STATE* RESIDENCE	NAME AND RANK	DATE OF RECOGNITION	STATE* RESIDENCE	NAME AND RANK	DATE OF RECOGNITION

TRADE PROMOTION SECTION OF ITALY
LOS ANGELES (CONA) 1801 AVENUE OF THE STARS UN., SUITE 700, 90067.
(323) 879-0950

    MS. PAOLA BELLUSCI,   Aug. 11, 2006
        CONSULAR AGENT

SACRAMENTO (HVC) 1420 54TH ST., SUITE 4, 95819.
(916) 456-1950

    MR. ANTHONY UMBERTO VIRGADAMO,   Feb. 27, 1976
        HONORARY VICE CONSUL

SAN FRANCISCO (CG) 2590 WEBSTER ST., 94115.
(415) 931-4924

    MR. ROBERTO FALASCHI,   May. 27, 2005
        CONSUL GENERAL
    MR. DIEGO ENRICO MARINO,   Jul. 15, 2003
        CONSULAR AGENT
    PROFESSOR TERENZIO SCAPOLLA,   Jul. 17, 2003
        CONSULAR AGENT
    MR. VITTORIO PALLADINO,   Nov. 22, 2004
        CONSULAR AGENT

ITALIAN CULTURAL INSTITUTE
SAN FRANCISCO (CON) 425 WASHINGTON ST., SUITE 200, 94111.

    MS. VALERIA RUMORI,   Jul. 25, 2003
        CONSULAR AGENT
    MR. ONOFRIO SPECIALE,   Jan. 24, 2006
        CONSULAR AGENT

SAN JOSE (HVC) 95 S. MARKET ST., SUITE 300, 95113.
(408) 971-9170

    MS. SILVIA RAVIOLA,   Apr. 01, 1995
        HONORARY VICE CONSUL

COLORADO

DENVER (HVC) 7325 S. JACKSON ST., LITTLETON 80122.
(303) 224-9927

    MRS. MARIA ELIZABETH SCORDO ALLEN,   Dec. 03, 1998
        HONORARY VICE CONSUL

CONNECTICUT

HARTFORD (HVC) 70 VERNON ST., 06106.
(860) 297-2123

    MR. ALFONSO E. PANICO,   Jul. 20, 2004
        HONORARY VICE CONSUL

FLORIDA

MIAMI (CG) 4000 PONCE DE LEON BL., SUITE 590, 33146.
(305) 374-6322, FAX (305) 374-7945

    MR. GIANFRANCO COLOGNATO,   Aug. 29, 2003
        CONSUL GENERAL
    MR. MARCO ROCCA,   Jul. 06, 2007
        CONSUL GENERAL
    MR. PIETRO DE SANTI,   Nov. 21, 2001
        CONSULAR AGENT
    MR. GIORGIO IMPARATO,   Nov. 29, 2002
        CONSULAR AGENT
    MR. GIOVANNI TURTURIELLO,   Jul. 10, 2003
        CONSULAR AGENT

    MR. VALTER FAVALLI,   Jul. 07, 2005
        CONSULAR AGENT
    MR. CARLO FERRARI,   Feb. 14, 2006
        CONSULAR AGENT
    MR. ANTONINO MENDOLIA,   Oct. 06, 2006
        CONSULAR AGENT

ORLANDO (HVC) 109 WEEPING ELM LA., LONGWOOD 32779.
(407) 869-9702, FAX (404) 869-9702

    MS. CARMELA LOREDANA CICCHETTI,   Oct. 03, 1995
        HONORARY VICE CONSUL

SARASOTA (HVC) 707 S. GULFSTREAM AV., SUITE 307, 34236.
(941) 957-0851, FAX (941) 954-0111

    MR. RICHARD HAROLD STORM,   Dec. 08, 1995
        HONORARY VICE CONSUL

GEORGIA

ATLANTA (HC) 133 N.W. LUCKIE ST., 30305.
(404) 239-0226

    MRS. ANGELA DELLA COSTANZA TURNER,   Apr. 19, 2005
        HONORARY CONSUL

SAVANNAH (HCA) 235 KENSINGTON DR., 31405.
(912) 232-1276, FAX (912) 233-4478

    MR. JOSEPH MOSE CAFIERO,   May. 05, 1976
        HONORARY CONSULAR AGENT

HAWAII

HONOLULU (HVC) 735 BISHOP ST., SUITE 419, 96813.

    MRS. CARMEN THERESA DI AMORE-SIAH,   Mar. 16, 1994
        HONORARY VICE CONSUL

ILLINOIS

CHICAGO (CG) 500 N. MICHIGAN AV., SUITE 1850, 60611.
(312) 467-1550

    MS. LIDIA RAMOGIDA,   Apr. 17, 2002
        CONSULAR AGENT
    MR. LUCIANO ODDO,   Dec. 15, 2005
        CONSULAR AGENT
    MR. GIOVANNI BUCOLO,   Oct. 10, 2006
        CONSULAR AGENT

ITALIAN CULTURAL INSTITUTE
CHICAGO (CONA) 500 N. MICHIGAN AV., SUITE 1450,1450, 60611.
(312) 822-9545, FAX (312) 822-9622

    MRS. PATRIZIA GAMBAROTTA,   Jul. 31, 2003
        CONSULAR AGENT
    MRS. ANNUNZIATA CERVONE PAPA,   Oct. 03, 2005
        CONSULAR AGENT

TRADE PROMOTION SECTION OF ITALY
CHICAGO (CONA) 401 N. MICHIGAN AV., SUITE 3030, 60611.
(312) 670-4360

    MR. PASQUALE BOVA,   Feb. 27, 2007
        CONSULAR AGENT

INDIANA

INDIANAPOLIS (HVC) 107 N. PENNSYLVANIA ST., SUITE 900, 46204.
(317) 634-4356

STATE* RESIDENCE	NAME AND RANK	DATE OF RECOGNITION	STATE* RESIDENCE	NAME AND RANK	DATE OF RECOGNITION

MR. PAUL GERALD ROLAND,
   HONORARY VICE CONSUL — May. 11, 1999

KANSAS

KANSAS CITY (HVC) 754 STATE AV., SUITE 102, 66101.
(913) 281-2222, FAX (913) 321-6525
   MR. ROBERTO LEOPOLDO SERRA,
   HONORARY VICE CONSUL — Sep. 17, 1970

LOUISIANA

NEW ORLEANS (HC) 650 POYDRAS ST., SUITE 1400, 70130.
(504) 524-6887, FAX (504) 299-3411
   MR. ARNALDO PARTESOTTI,
   HONORARY CONSUL — Dec. 15, 1997

MARYLAND

BALTIMORE (HC) 9 W. MULBERRY ST., SUITE 400, 21201.
(410) 727-6550, FAX (410) 727-6563
   MR. FRANCESCO LUIGI LEGALUPPI,
   HONORARY CONSUL — Jul. 20, 1988

MASSACHUSETTS

BOSTON (CG) 600 ATLANTIC AV., FLOOR 17TH, 02210.
(617) 722-9201, FAX (617) 722-9407
   MR. LIBORIO STELLINO,
   CONSUL GENERAL — Oct. 05, 2006
   MR. CIRO MORRONI,
   CONSULAR AGENT — Oct. 23, 2002

WORCESTER (HCA) 6 SEWARD ST., 01604.
(508) 414-7111
   MR. SALVATORE MUSTICA,
   HONORARY CONSULAR AGENT — Oct. 27, 2004

MICHIGAN

DETROIT (CON) 535 GRISWOLD UN., SUITE 1840, 48226.
(313) 963-8560
   MR. CARLO ROMEO,
   CONSUL — Mar. 30, 2007
   MR. VINCENZO ZEPPA,
   CONSULAR AGENT — Nov. 20, 2001

MINNESOTA

ST. PAUL (HC) 1844 PORTLAND AV., SAINT PAUL 55104.
(651) 641-0207
   MS. JANE CALABRIA MCPEAK,
   HONORARY CONSUL — Aug. 20, 2001

MISSOURI

SAINT LOUIS (HVC) 211 N. BROADWAY, 1 METROPOLITAN SQ.,
SUITE 3800, ST. LOUIS 63102.
(314) 259-5930, FAX (314) 259-5985
   MR. JOSEPH, JR COLAGIOVANNI,
   HONORARY VICE CONSUL — Mar. 28, 1997

NEW JERSEY

NEWARK (VC) 1 GATEWAY CN., SUITE 100, 07102.
(973) 643-1448

MR. PAOLO TOSCHI,
   VICE CONSUL — Oct. 14, 2004
MR. ALESSANDRO SIVIERI,
   CONSULAR AGENT — Jul. 28, 2004
MR. VINCENZO NERI,
   CONSULAR AGENT — Dec. 05, 2005

TRENTON (HVC) 284 EDINBURG RD., 08619.
(609) 587-7000
   DR. GILDA LEONORA RORRO,
   HONORARY VICE CONSUL — Jun. 29, 1998

NEW YORK

BUFFALO (HVC) 160 COURT ST., 14202.
(716) 856-3626
   MS. LUCIA CARACCI CULLENS,
   HONORARY VICE CONSUL — Mar. 25, 1998

MINEOLA (HC) 1 WEST ST., 11501.
(516) 661-9129
   MR. ANTONIO TUFANO,
   HONORARY CONSUL — Sep. 08, 1998

MT. VERNON (HCA) 25 35 BEECHWOOD AV., MOUNT VERNON
10553.
(914) 669-2020
   MR. STEPHEN E. B. ACUNTO,
   HONORARY CONSULAR AGENT — Jan. 16, 2003

NEW YORK (CG) 690 PARK AV., 10021.
(212) 737-9100
   MS. PAOLA MUNZI,
   CONSUL — Nov. 21, 2003
   MR. MAURIZIO IVONA,
   VICE CONSUL — Aug. 16, 2004
   MR. GIOVANNI FAVILLI,
   VICE CONSUL — Oct. 06, 2005
   MR. MAURIZIO ANTONINI,
   VICE CONSUL — Oct. 06, 2006
   MR. ANGELO PALMIERI,
   CONSULAR AGENT — Oct. 09, 2002
   MRS. MARIA PIA BIANCONI,
   CONSULAR AGENT — Nov. 06, 2002
   MRS. ORIETTA RANUCCI DI GENNARO,
   CONSULAR AGENT — Dec. 03, 2004
   MRS. FRANCESCA AGNETA TOMMASOLI,
   CONSULAR AGENT — Dec. 05, 2005
   MRS. IRENE BUONGIORNO,
   CONSULAR AGENT — Dec. 05, 2005
   MS. EMILIA LUCIANI,
   CONSULAR AGENT — Dec. 05, 2005
   MRS. EVA BARONE,
   CONSULAR AGENT — Aug. 11, 2006

ITALIAN CULTURAL INSTITUTE
NEW YORK (CONA) 686 PARK AV., 10021.
(212) 879-4242
   MRS. MELITA PALESTINI,
   CONSULAR AGENT — Feb. 12, 2003
   MRS. AMELIA CARPENITO ANTONUCCI,
   CONSULAR AGENT — Sep. 23, 2003
   MR. CLAUDIO ANGELINI,
   CONSULAR AGENT — Oct. 29, 2004

---

* DEPENDENCIES SUCH AS GUAM, PUERTO RICO, AND THE VIRGIN ISLANDS ARE LISTED HERE.
CG-CONSULATE GENERAL   C-CONSULATE   VC-VICE CONSULATE   CA-CONSULAR AGENCY   H-HONORARY CONSULAR STATUS

STATE* RESIDENCE	NAME AND RANK	DATE OF RECOGNITION

MRS. RENATA SPERANDIO BASSO,
CONSULAR AGENT — Jul. 21, 2005
MS. SILVIA GIAMPAOLA,
CONSULAR AGENT — Dec. 20, 2005

TRADE PROMOTION SECTION OF ITALY
NEW YORK (CONA) 33 E. 67TH ST., 10021.
(212) 980-1500
MR. ANIELLO MUSELLA,
CONSULAR AGENT — Dec. 20, 2005

ROCHESTER (HVC) 2740 MONROE AV., 14618.
(585) 271-1111
MR. MARIO DANIELE,
HONORARY VICE CONSUL — Feb. 07, 2005

OHIO
CLEVELAND (HVC) 1422 EUCLID AV., 44115.
(216) 861-1585
MS. SERENA SCAIOLA ZISKA,
HONORARY VICE CONSUL — May. 18, 2007

OREGON
PORTLAND (HVC) 121 S.W. SALMON ST., SUITE 1030, 97204.
(503) 225-0702
MR. ANDREA BARTOLONI,
HONORARY VICE CONSUL — Apr. 02, 2003

PENNSYLVANIA
PHILADELPHIA (CG) 150 S. INDEPENDENCE MALL WEST UN., SUITE 1026, 19106.
(215) 592-1218
MR. STEFANO MISTRETTA,
CONSUL GENERAL — Mar. 09, 2005
MRS. RITA SCIARRETTA CONOSCIANI,
CONSULAR AGENT — Feb. 05, 2002
MRS. NADIA BRAMA NICOLI,
CONSULAR AGENT — Jan. 06, 2006
MR. RENZO OLIVA,
CONSULAR AGENT — Mar. 06, 2007

PITTSBURGH (HC) 600 FORBES AV., SUITE 401, 15282.
(412) 765-0273
MRS. CARLA E. LUCENTE,
HONORARY CONSUL — Feb. 28, 2000

PUERTO RICO
SAN JUAN (HC) 266 CALLE INTERAMERICANA UN., 00927.
(787) 767-5855, FAX (787) 767-5855
MR. ANGELO PIO SANFILIPPO,
HONORARY CONSUL — Jun. 01, 1993

RHODE ISLAND
PROVIDENCE (HVC) 49 WEYBOSSET ST., 02903.
(401) 454-1492, FAX (401) 421-9080
MR. RONALD W. DEL SESTO,
HONORARY VICE CONSUL — Oct. 30, 2000

SOUTH CAROLINA
CHARLESTON (HCA) 550 LONG POINT RD., MOUNT PLEASANT 29464.
(843) 971-4100, FAX (843) 971-1155
MR. SERGIO FEDELINI,
HONORARY CONSULAR AGENT — Jun. 20, 2000

TEXAS
DALLAS (HVC) 6255 W. NORTHWEST HW., APT 304, 75225.
(214) 368-4113
MR. VINCENZO ENRICO DE NARDO,
HONORARY VICE CONSUL — Feb. 12, 1992

HOUSTON (CG) 1300 POST OAK BL., SUITE 660, 77056.
(713) 850-7520
MR. CRISTIANO MAGGIPINTO,
CONSUL GENERAL — Mar. 21, 2006
MS. SUSANNA SGOIFO,
CONSULAR AGENT — Aug. 16, 2002
MR. LEOPOLDO SPOSATO,
CONSULAR AGENT — Oct. 04, 2005

UTAH
SALT LAKE CITY (HVC) 175 SOUTH WEST TEMPLE UN., SUITE 700, 84101.
(801) 254-7500, FAX (801) 254-7505
MR. GIOVANNI G. MASCHERO,
HONORARY VICE CONSUL — Feb. 09, 1990

VIRGINIA
NORFOLK (HC) 300 E. MAIN ST., SUITE 1180, 23510.
(575) 622-4898
MR. VITO PIRAINO,
HONORARY CONSUL — Aug. 29, 1994

WASHINGTON
SEATTLE (HVC) 211 14TH AV., W, 98112.
(206) 349-4411
MR. GIUSEPPE LEPORACE,
HONORARY VICE CONSUL — Dec. 04, 2003

JAMAICA

CALIFORNIA
LOS ANGELES (HC) 8703 LA TIJERA BL., SUITE 208, 90045.
(323) 756-4601
MRS. JUNE PAMELA ROYES,
HONORARY CONSUL — Dec. 18, 2002

SAN FRANCISCO (HC) 1001 PORTRERO AV., SUITE NH1N1S, 94110.
(415) 206-5717
DR. NEWTON CHARLES GORDON,
HONORARY CONSUL — Dec. 08, 1999

DISTRICT OF COLUMBIA
WASHINGTON (CHN) 1520 NEW HAMPSHIRE AV., NW, 20036.
(202) 452-0660, FAX (202) 452-0081
MISS CYETH CYLONIA ALLISON DENTON,
CONSUL — Feb. 03, 2006

STATE* RESIDENCE	NAME AND RANK	DATE OF RECOGNITION	STATE* RESIDENCE	NAME AND RANK	DATE OF RECOGNITION

FLORIDA

MIAMI (CG) 25 S.E. 2ND AV., SUITE 842, 33131.
(305) 374-8431

MR. CLEMENT PHILIP RICARDO ALLICOCK, CONSUL GENERAL	Oct. 04, 2002
MS. SUZANNE D. V. JONES, CONSUL	Jan. 06, 2004
MR. VANCE ANTHONY CARTER, VICE CONSUL	Mar. 27, 2000
MR. KARL ST AUBYN PLUMMER, VICE CONSUL	Oct. 06, 2005

JAMAICA CENTRAL LABOUR ORGANIZATION
MIAMI (CONA) 12175 N.W. 98TH AV., 33016.
(305) 823-1146

GEORGIA

ATLANTA (HC) 5405 MEMORIAL DR., H-1, STONE MOUNTAIN 30083.
(404) 297-7696

MR. VIN NEWTON MARTIN,   Mar. 28, 1997
HONORARY CONSUL

ILLINOIS

CHICAGO (HC) 4655 S. DR. MARTIN LUTHER KING JR. DR., SUITE 201, 60653.
(773) 373-8988, FAX (773) 373-2496

MR. LLOYD L. HYDE,   Jan. 25, 1991
HONORARY CONSUL

MASSACHUSETTS

BOSTON (HC) 351 MASSACHUSETTS AV., 02115.
(617) 266-8604

MR. KENNETH IRVIN GUSCOTT,   May. 02, 1991
HONORARY CONSUL

NEW HAMPSHIRE

MANCHESTER (HC) 235 MOUNTAIN RD., CONCORD 03301.
(603) 230-9843

MS. OFELIA SARA DUDLEY POLACK,   Oct. 30, 2002
HONORARY CONSUL

NEW YORK

NEW YORK (CG) 767 3RD AV., 10017.
(212) 935-9000

MR. BASIL K. BRYAN, CONSUL GENERAL	Apr. 13, 1998
MRS. LISA MICHELLE HARRIET BRYAN SMART, DEPUTY CONSUL GENERAL	Mar. 04, 2005
MS. DONNETTE EVANGELINE CHAMBERS, CONSUL	Dec. 20, 2004
MISS CECILE JULIET CHRISTIE, VICE CONSUL	May. 05, 2007
MR. DESMOND SAMUEL GRAHAM, VICE CONSUL	May. 07, 2007
MS. ELAINE GREEN, VICE CONSUL	May. 07, 2007

PENNSYLVANIA

PHILADELPHIA (HC) 3701 CHESTNUT ST., 19104.
(215) 313-9508, FAX (610) 436-0795

MR. ALSTON BANCROFT MEADE,   Sep. 04, 2002
HONORARY CONSUL

TEXAS

DALLAS (HC) 3068 FORREST LA., 75234.
(972) 396-7969

DR. VICTOR HOMER CHARLES WATT,   Dec. 09, 1998
HONORARY CONSUL

HOUSTON (HC) 7737 SOUTHWEST FW., SUITE 580, 77074.
(713) 541-3333

MRS. M. BEVERLY FORD,   May. 30, 1996
HONORARY CONSUL

VIRGINIA

RICHMOND (HC) 1631 WESTBROOK AV., 23227.
(804) 262-4453

MRS. BERYL ADASSA WALTERS RILEY,   Feb. 08, 1999
HONORARY CONSUL

WASHINGTON

SEATTLE (HC) 8223 S. 222ND ST., KENT 98032.
(206) 872-8950

MRS. ENID L. DWYER,   Nov. 29, 1995
HONORARY CONSUL

JAPAN

ALABAMA

BIRMINGHAM (HCG) 80 BULLDOG CI., CROPWELL 35054.
(205) 525-5655, FAX (205) 252-4417

MR. ELMER B. HARRIS,   Mar. 04, 2002
HONORARY CONSUL GENERAL

ALASKA

ANCHORAGE (CON) 3601 C ST., SUITE 1300, 99503-5925.
(907) 562-8424

MR. YOSHIO UCHIYAMA, CONSUL	Apr. 13, 2006
MR. SHUJI INOUE, VICE CONSUL	Mar. 10, 2004
MS. CHIEKO NODA, VICE CONSUL	May. 25, 2006
MR. YOSHINARI WATANABE, VICE CONSUL	May. 23, 2007

ARIZONA

TEMPE (HCG) 409 E. ERIE DR., 85282.
(480) 967-2928

MR. KELLY SIMS MOEUR,   Oct. 25, 2004
HONORARY CONSUL GENERAL

CALIFORNIA

LOS ANGELES (CG) 350 S. GRAND AV., SUITE 1700, 90071.
(213) 617-6700, FAX (213) 617-6727

MR. KAZUO KODAMA, CONSUL GENERAL	Jul. 05, 2006
MR. MASAHIRO KOHARA, DEPUTY CONSUL GENERAL	Apr. 29, 2005

STATE* RESIDENCE	NAME AND RANK	DATE OF RECOGNITION	STATE* RESIDENCE	NAME AND RANK	DATE OF RECOGNITION
	MR. MASARU DEKIBA, CONSUL	Sep. 28, 2004		MR. TOMIO TAKAHASHI, VICE CONSUL	Dec. 03, 2004
	MR. YASUHIKO KAMADA, CONSUL	Apr. 11, 2005		MR. AKIHIRO MANABE, VICE CONSUL	Apr. 28, 2005
	MR. YOSHIKI NAKAMATA, CONSUL	Jun. 30, 2005		MS. ERIKA OI, VICE CONSUL	Apr. 13, 2006
	MR. TAKASHI HIRANAKA, CONSUL	Jul. 18, 2006		MS. MAYUMI AOKI, VICE CONSUL	May. 25, 2006
	MR. TAKASHI SHIDOJI, CONSUL	Oct. 25, 2006		MR. MASAHIRO NAKASHIMA, VICE CONSUL	May. 23, 2007
	MR. HIROSHI FURUSAWA, CONSUL	May. 04, 2007		MR. FUMITAKE TAKAHASHI, VICE CONSUL	Jun. 19, 2007
	MR. KATSUMI MARUOKA, CONSUL	May. 23, 2007			
	MR. SHIGEAKI KANAYAMA, CONSUL	Jul. 06, 2007	**COLORADO**		
	MR. SHINICHI YAMAMOTO, VICE CONSUL	Oct. 06, 2005	DENVER (CG) 1225 17TH ST., SUITE 3000, 80202. (303) 534-1151, FAX (303) 534-3393		
	MR. KEIICHI ICHIKAWA, VICE CONSUL	Oct. 13, 2005		MR. YUZO OTA, CONSUL GENERAL	Apr. 09, 2004
	MS. MIEKO ISHIMARU, VICE CONSUL	Dec. 05, 2005		MR. HARUO YAMAGAMI, CONSUL	Feb. 09, 2006
	MR. ATSUSHI MIZUTANI, VICE CONSUL	May. 30, 2006		MR. FUMIYOSHI KASHIMA, CONSUL	May. 07, 2007
	MR. TAKASHI MITSUNAMI, VICE CONSUL	May. 17, 2007		MR. MAKOTO SHIMAMURA, VICE CONSUL	Jan. 12, 2006
	MR. NAOYUKI KAWAGOISHI, VICE CONSUL	Jun. 06, 2007		MR. KENJI YAMAMOTO, VICE CONSUL	May. 03, 2007
	MR. HIRONAO OKUI, VICE CONSUL	Jul. 06, 2007			
			CONNECTICUT		
SAN DIEGO (HCG) 5154 VIA PLAYA LOS SANTOS UN., 92124. (858) 576-6866			SIMSBURY (HCG) 200 HOPMEADOW ST., 06070. (860) 843-5597		
	DR. MICHAEL SHIGERU INOUE, HONORARY CONSUL GENERAL	Mar. 13, 2006		MR. GREGORY A. BOYKO, HONORARY CONSUL GENERAL	Jan. 28, 2005
			DISTRICT OF COLUMBIA		
SAN FRANCISCO (CG) 50 FREMONT ST., SUITE 2300, 94105. (415) 777-3533			WASHINGTON (CHN) 2520 MASSACHUSETTS AV., NW, 20008. (202) 238-6700, FAX (202) 328-2187		
	MR. MAKOTO YAMANAKA, CONSUL GENERAL	Apr. 16, 2004		MR. TOSHIAKI IGARASHI, CONSUL	Mar. 22, 2005
	MR. KAZUYOSHI YAMAGUCHI, DEPUTY CONSUL GENERAL	Apr. 16, 2004		MR. KOHEI MASUZAWA, CONSUL	Sep. 22, 2006
	MR. KIYOSHI ITOI, CONSUL	May. 30, 2003		MR. YASUTOSHI TANIMOTO, VICE CONSUL	Jul. 10, 2003
	MR. KAZUAKI NAKAKOSHI, CONSUL	Jul. 12, 2004			
	MR. TADASHI MOGI, CONSUL	Jul. 12, 2004	**FLORIDA**		
	MR. HITOSHI AOKI, CONSUL	Aug. 05, 2005	MIAMI (CG) 80 S.W. 8TH ST., SUITE 3200, 33130. (305) 530-9090		
	MR. TAKAKI TAKINAMI, CONSUL	Aug. 05, 2005		MR. HIROSHI YAMAGUCHI, CONSUL GENERAL	Jan. 26, 2007
	MS. MIDORI YAMAMITSU, CONSUL	Oct. 13, 2005		MR. HITOSHI KOGA, CONSUL	Jun. 30, 2005
	MS. MITSUKO KOIKE, CONSUL	May. 25, 2006		MR. MASAMI OHNO, CONSUL	Dec. 05, 2005
	MR. HIDEKI KAWASHIMA, CONSUL	May. 30, 2006		MR. KENICHI KOGUCHI, CONSUL	Feb. 08, 2006
	MR. TAKANORI OKUDA, CONSUL	Jul. 31, 2006		MR. MINORU HIGUCHI, CONSUL	May. 30, 2006
	MR. KATSUYA HIGUCHI, CONSUL	Jun. 19, 2007		MR. NAOHITO WATANABE, CONSUL	May. 30, 2006
	MR. YOSUKE KAWANA, VICE CONSUL	Nov. 01, 2004		MR. MASAKAZU MATSUDA, CONSUL	May. 05, 2007
				MR. KOICHI MURAMATSU, CONSUL	May. 08, 2007

STATE* RESIDENCE	NAME AND RANK	DATE OF RECOGNITION	STATE* RESIDENCE	NAME AND RANK	DATE OF RECOGNITION

GEORGIA

ATLANTA (CG) 3500 LENOX RD., SUITE 1600, 30326.
(404) 240-4300, FAX (404) 240-4311

MR. SHOJI OGAWA, CONSUL GENERAL	Apr. 28, 2005
MR. SHINICHI FUJIWARA, CONSUL	Apr. 26, 2005
MR. MASANOBU YOSHII, CONSUL	May. 25, 2006
MR. MASAHIRO KATAMOTO, CONSUL	May. 04, 2007
MR. MASAKATSU SUZUKI, CONSUL	May. 07, 2007
MR. TOSHINORI MATSUDA, VICE CONSUL	Jun. 30, 2005
MR. YOSHIHIKO MACHIDA, VICE CONSUL	Jun. 30, 2005
MR. SHIGETAKA FUJIKI, VICE CONSUL	May. 25, 2006
MS. TOMOMI SAKO, VICE CONSUL	May. 25, 2006

GUAM

AGANA (CG) 590 S. MARINE DR., SUITE 604, TAMUNING 96911.

MR. TAMIO TOMINO, CONSUL GENERAL	Jun. 06, 2007
MR. MASAYUKI TSUCHIKAWA, DEPUTY CONSUL	Feb. 08, 2006
MR. YASUAKI MURAKAWA, VICE CONSUL	Jun. 30, 2005
MR. KENJI YOSHIDA, VICE CONSUL	May. 25, 2006
MR. SHINICHI WADA, VICE CONSUL	Apr. 17, 2007

HAWAII

HILO (HCG) 708 KANOELEHUA AV., 96720.
(808) 935-5477

MR. THOMAS TOSHIO HIRANO, HONORARY CONSUL GENERAL	Sep. 17, 2004

HONOLULU (CG) 1742 NUUANU AV., 96817.
(808) 536-2226

MR. SHIGEO IWATANI, CONSUL GENERAL	Dec. 27, 2005
MR. MAKOTO HINEI, CONSUL	Apr. 22, 2003
MR. TOYONORI HAYASAKA, CONSUL	Jul. 30, 2004
MR. YOSHITAKA YAMADA, CONSUL	Oct. 13, 2005
MS. HARUMI KATSUMATA, CONSUL	Oct. 13, 2005
MR. EIICHI ARAI, CONSUL	Apr. 13, 2006
MR. HIDEAKI SUZUKI, CONSUL	Jun. 06, 2007
MS. YUKIE KAWAI, CONSUL	Jun. 06, 2007
MS. MIYAKO KAYAMORI, VICE CONSUL	Jul. 31, 2003

MS. KUNIKO NAKAMURA, VICE CONSUL	Mar. 22, 2007
MS. MAKIKO YOKOTA, VICE CONSUL	Jun. 06, 2007

ILLINOIS

CHICAGO (CG) 737 N. MICHIGAN AV., SUITE 1100, 60611.
(312) 280-0400

MR. KENJI SHINODA, CONSUL GENERAL	Oct. 06, 2006
MR. HACHIRO ISHIDA, DEPUTY CONSUL GENERAL	Oct. 04, 2005
MR. MASARU IGAWAHARA, CONSUL	Apr. 16, 2004
MS. HIROKO MATSUO, CONSUL	Mar. 08, 2005
MR. MATSUO NAOE, CONSUL	Oct. 13, 2005
MR. MASAAKI KAWAHARA, CONSUL	Oct. 14, 2005
MR. OSAMU MINAKAWA, CONSUL	Jul. 18, 2006
MR. YASUNARI SAGA, CONSUL	Jul. 27, 2006
MR. YOSHIMITSU KAWATA, CONSUL	Sep. 14, 2006
MR. HIROYUKI KAMIMARU, CONSUL	Jul. 12, 2007
MS. FUMI IZUMITANI, VICE CONSUL	Feb. 08, 2006
MR. TAKANOBU AMEYA, VICE CONSUL	Jul. 26, 2006
MR. KEI UEHARA, VICE CONSUL	May. 09, 2007

JAPAN INFORMATION CENTER OF JAPAN
CHICAGO (CONA) 737 N. MICHIGAN AV., SUITE 1000, 60611.
(312) 280-0430

INDIANA

INDIANAPOLIS (HCG) 11 S. MERIDIAN ST., 46204.
(317) 231-7227

MR. ROBERT HUGH REYNOLDS, HONORARY CONSUL GENERAL	Jun. 09, 1999

KANSAS

SHAWNEE MISSION (HCG) 5319 MISSION WOODS TE., 66205.
(913) 236-5961

MR. MICHAEL BRAUDE, HONORARY CONSUL GENERAL	Aug. 29, 2005

KENTUCKY

LEXINGTON (HCG) 400 E. COLLEGE ST., GEORGETOWN 40324.
(502) 867-6600, FAX (502) 868-8887

MRS. MARTHA LAYNE COLLINS, HONORARY CONSUL GENERAL	Jun. 30, 1999

LOUISIANA

NEW ORLEANS (CG) 639 LOYOLA AV., SUITE 2050, 70113.
(504) 529-2101

---

* DEPENDENCIES SUCH AS GUAM, PUERTO RICO, AND THE VIRGIN ISLANDS ARE LISTED HERE.
CG-CONSULATE GENERAL   C-CONSULATE   VC-VICE CONSULATE   CA-CONSULAR AGENCY   H-HONORARY CONSULAR STATUS

STATE* RESIDENCE	NAME AND RANK	DATE OF RECOGNITION

NAME AND RANK	DATE OF RECOGNITION
MR. MASARU SAKATO, CONSUL GENERAL	May. 25, 2005
MR. KOICHI FUNAYAMA, CONSUL	Nov. 12, 2004
MR. KOZO KOJIMA, CONSUL	May. 16, 2005
MR. TAKESHI TOKAIRIN, CONSUL	May. 17, 2007
MISS YUKIKO OKAYASU, VICE CONSUL	Feb. 06, 2004
MS. YUKIKO NAKAZATO, VICE CONSUL	Apr. 13, 2006
MR. HIROSHI HIRAMATSU, VICE CONSUL	May. 30, 2006
MR. TAKESHI KODO, VICE CONSUL	Jul. 18, 2006
MISS KUMIKO ENOMOTO, VICE CONSUL	May. 09, 2007

MASSACHUSETTS

BOSTON (CG) 600 ATLANTIC AV., FLOOR 14TH, 02210.
(617) 973-9772

NAME AND RANK	DATE OF RECOGNITION
MR. YOICHI SUZUKI, CONSUL GENERAL	Nov. 30, 2005
MR. MASAYUKI TAKASHIMA, DEPUTY CONSUL GENERAL	Jul. 28, 2004
MR. YUZO SEKIGAWA, CONSUL	Feb. 14, 2005
MR. SHINICHI KOBAYASHI, CONSUL	Oct. 06, 2006
MR. KATSUMI MACHIDA, CONSUL	Jan. 26, 2007
MR. FUTOSHI YAMAZAKI, CONSUL	May. 05, 2007
MR. SHINJI YAMABE, VICE CONSUL	Jun. 01, 2006
MR. SHINKICHI TAKAHASHI, VICE CONSUL	Oct. 06, 2006
MS. MARIKO MORI, VICE CONSUL	Oct. 06, 2006
MR. HIROSHI FUJISHIMA, VICE CONSUL	May. 17, 2007

MICHIGAN

DETROIT (CG) 400 RENAISSANCE CENTER UN., SUITE 1600, 48243.
(313) 567-0120, FAX (313) 567-0274

NAME AND RANK	DATE OF RECOGNITION
MR. TAMOTSU SHINOTSUKA, CONSUL GENERAL	Dec. 05, 2006
MR. AKIHIKO FUJII, DEPUTY CONSUL GENERAL	May. 31, 2007
MR. TOSHIKAZU KOBAYASHI, CONSUL	Jun. 17, 2004
MR. NOBUYA KATO, CONSUL	Jun. 30, 2005
MR. MASAHIRO ISHIDA, CONSUL	May. 30, 2006
MR. YOSHIFUMI NAGAI, CONSUL	Jul. 18, 2006
MR. TAINOSUKE MATSUMURA, VICE CONSUL	Oct. 27, 2003
MR. ATSUO YATAKA, VICE CONSUL	Oct. 13, 2005

MINNESOTA

MINNEAPOLIS (HCG) 16 WOODLAND RD., 55424.
(952) 925-3807

NAME AND RANK	DATE OF RECOGNITION
MR. WILLIAM R. STRANG, HONORARY CONSUL GENERAL	Nov. 19, 2004

MISSOURI

SAINT LOUIS (HCG) 46 BRIARCLIFF ST., ST. LOUIS 63124.
(314) 994-1133, FAX (314) 994-1133

NAME AND RANK	DATE OF RECOGNITION
MR. BRUCE S. BUCKLAND, HONORARY CONSUL GENERAL	Aug. 26, 1992

NEBRASKA

OMAHA (HCG) 412 N. 85TH ST., 68114.
(402) 399-0928, FAX (402) 399-1796

NAME AND RANK	DATE OF RECOGNITION
DR. RONALD W. ROSKENS, HONORARY CONSUL GENERAL	Oct. 29, 1999

NEVADA

LAS VEGAS (HCG) 6583 PEACHTREE LA., 89103.
(702) 876-6716

NAME AND RANK	DATE OF RECOGNITION
MR. WAYNE NORIO TANAKA, HONORARY CONSUL GENERAL	Jul. 22, 2003

NEW YORK

BUFFALO (HCG) 45 TUDOR PL., 14222.
(716) 868-7899

NAME AND RANK	DATE OF RECOGNITION
MR. P. JOSEPH KOESSLER, HONORARY CONSUL GENERAL	May. 01, 2002

NEW YORK (CG) 299 PARK AV., FLOOR 18 & 19, 10171.
(212) 371-8222

NAME AND RANK	DATE OF RECOGNITION
MR. MOTOATSU SAKURAI, CONSUL GENERAL	Jun. 01, 2006
MR. MIKIO NUMATA, DEPUTY CONSUL GENERAL	May. 17, 2007
MR. MITSUO KAWAGUCHI, CONSUL	Sep. 16, 1994
MS. MIDORI TAKEUCHI, CONSUL	May. 03, 1995
MR. OSAMU SHIOZAKI, CONSUL	Sep. 17, 2002
MR. RYUTARO NAMBA, CONSUL	Sep. 28, 2004
MR. JIRO OKUYAMA, CONSUL	Nov. 01, 2004
MR. TSUGUYOSHI HADA, CONSUL	Jun. 21, 2005
MR. ICHIRO TAKAHASHI, CONSUL	Jun. 30, 2005
MR. MASAHIKO KURISHIMA, CONSUL	Jun. 30, 2005
MR. SHINJI URABAYASHI, CONSUL	Jun. 30, 2005
MS. MIKA HIROSAWA, CONSUL	Jun. 30, 2005
MR. KENYA OZAWA, CONSUL	Jul. 08, 2005
MR. ISSEI HATAKEYAMA, CONSUL	Aug. 04, 2005
MS. MIYUKI KURANISHI, CONSUL	Aug. 05, 2005

STATE* RESIDENCE	NAME AND RANK	DATE OF RECOGNITION	STATE* RESIDENCE	NAME AND RANK	DATE OF RECOGNITION
	MR. TAKASHI HAMADA, CONSUL	Oct. 06, 2005	**OKLAHOMA**		
	MR. KOICHI NAKAMOTO, CONSUL	Oct. 13, 2005	OKLAHOMA CITY (HCG) 211 N. ROBINSON AV., SUITE 1212N, 73102. (405) 235-4100		
	MR. MASAKI SUGAMIYA, CONSUL	Feb. 08, 2006		MR. LLOYD T. , JR HARDIN, HONORARY CONSUL GENERAL	May. 23, 2006
	MR. SHUJI UEMURA, CONSUL	Feb. 08, 2006			
	MS. NOBUKO HAMADA, CONSUL	Feb. 08, 2006	**OREGON**		
	MR. MUTSUMI ONOYAMA, CONSUL	Apr. 13, 2006	PORTLAND (CG) 1300 S.W. 5TH AV., SUITE 2700, 97201. (503) 221-1811		
	MR. ISAMU YAMADA, CONSUL	May. 25, 2006		MR. AKIO EGAWA, CONSUL GENERAL	Nov. 30, 2005
	MR. TOMIO TATSUKI, CONSUL	May. 25, 2006		MS. JUNKO OCHI, DEPUTY CONSUL GENERAL	May. 25, 2006
	MR. HIROTAKA ONO, CONSUL	May. 30, 2006		MS. TOSHIE TANAKA, CONSUL	Jun. 01, 1998
	MR. HIROYUKI OIKAWA, CONSUL	May. 30, 2006		MR. HIDEKI MAKINO, CONSUL	Oct. 04, 2004
	MR. KAZUYOSHI NINOMIYA, CONSUL	May. 30, 2006		MR. TATSUYA KUSAKA, CONSUL	May. 25, 2006
	MR. RYUICHI HOZUMI, CONSUL	May. 30, 2006		MR. HIDEHARU NAKASHIMA, CONSUL	Jul. 18, 2006
	MR. TAISHI NAKAMI, CONSUL	May. 30, 2006		MR. TAKASHI SATO, CONSUL	May. 23, 2007
	MR. HITOSHI SHIMURA, CONSUL	Jul. 18, 2006		MR. YU TAMURA, VICE CONSUL	Oct. 13, 2005
	MR. TETSUYA YAMAGATA, CONSUL	Jul. 18, 2006		MR. KENJI OKUHIRA, VICE CONSUL	May. 07, 2007
	MR. KEIICHIRO OGIYAMA, CONSUL	Oct. 06, 2006			
	MR. YUICHI MATSUURA, CONSUL	May. 07, 2007	**PENNSYLVANIA**		
	MS. KEIKO MATSUO, CONSUL	May. 07, 2007	PHILADELPHIA (HCG) 1701 MARKET ST., 19103. (215) 963-5513		
	MR. TAKANORI MAEDA, CONSUL	Jun. 06, 2007		MR. DENNIS J. MORIKAWA, HONORARY CONSUL GENERAL	Feb. 01, 2000
	MR. AKIRA NAITO, CONSUL	Jul. 30, 2007			
	MR. MASAYA UEDA, CONSUL	Aug. 01, 2007	**PUERTO RICO**		
	MS. YUKIKO HORI, VICE CONSUL	Aug. 11, 1993	SAN JUAN (HCG) 530 PONCE DE LEON AV., 00901. (787) 789-8725, FAX (787) 289-8726		
	MR. MASAHIKO NAKAZAWA, VICE CONSUL	Jun. 25, 1996		MR. MANUEL, JR MORALES, HONORARY CONSUL GENERAL	Jan. 06, 1997
	MR. SHOICHI NAGAYOSHI, VICE CONSUL	Sep. 03, 1999			
	MR. YUKIHIRO NOYORI, VICE CONSUL	Mar. 19, 2004	**TENNESSEE**		
	MS. KEIKO NAKANO, VICE CONSUL	Jun. 27, 2005	NASHVILLE (HCG) 3401 WEST END AV., SUITE 300, 37203. (615) 292-8787, FAX (615) 385-3150		
	MR. TAKUYA ODAWARA, VICE CONSUL	Jul. 18, 2006		MR. EDWARD G. NELSON, HONORARY CONSUL GENERAL	Oct. 05, 1988
	MS. MIHO OKI, VICE CONSUL	May. 05, 2007			
	MS. YUKO SUZUKI, VICE CONSUL	Jun. 29, 2007	**TEXAS**		
			DALLAS (HCG) 5819 EDINBURGH ST., 75252. (972) 713-8683		
				MR. JOHN MICHAEL STICH, HONORARY CONSUL GENERAL	Jan. 21, 2004
NORTH CAROLINA					
HIGH POINT (HCG) 510 EMERYWOOD DR., 27262. (336) 883-0392, FAX (336) 883-0392			HOUSTON (CG) 909 FANNIN SQ., SUITE 3000, 77010. (713) 652-2977		
	MR. O. WILLIAM, JR FENN, HONORARY CONSUL GENERAL	Apr. 09, 1999		MR. YOSHIHIKO KAMO, CONSUL GENERAL	Sep. 14, 2004
				MR. MITSURU MURASE, DEPUTY CONSUL GENERAL	May. 07, 2007
				MR. HIROSHI NOMURA, CONSUL	Aug. 05, 2005

STATE* RESIDENCE	NAME AND RANK	DATE OF RECOGNITION	STATE* RESIDENCE	NAME AND RANK	DATE OF RECOGNITION

MR. YUKIO TSUTSUMI,   Jul. 26, 2006
   CONSUL
MR. HIROKAZU HAYASHI,   Jun. 29, 2004
   VICE CONSUL
MR. KIYOMI WATANABE,   May. 25, 2006
   VICE CONSUL
MS. SEIKO WATANABE,   Jul. 26, 2006
   VICE CONSUL
MR. YOSHIHARU KATAYAMA,   May. 09, 2007
   VICE CONSUL

TRUST TERRITORIES OF THE PACIFIC ISLANDS

MARIANA ISLANDS (CON) MARINA HEIGHTS BUSINESS PARK UN.,
FLOOR 2, PUERTO RICO 96950.
(670) 323-7201, FAX (670) 323-8764
   MR. KENJI YAZAWA,   Aug. 11, 2006
      CONSUL
   MR. KIYOSHI MATSUKAI,   Aug. 11, 2006
      CONSUL

PAGO PAGO (HC) X ., PAGO PAGO, AM. SAMOA 96799.
   MR. OTTO VINCENT, JR. HALECK,   Dec. 23, 1993
      HONORARY CONSUL

WASHINGTON

SEATTLE (CG) 601 UNION ST., SUITE 500, 98101.
(206) 682-9107
   MR. KAZUO TANAKA,   Oct. 15, 2004
      CONSUL GENERAL
   MR. AYUMU KITAZAWA,   Nov. 04, 2004
      CONSUL
   MR. KOICHI SANO,   Oct. 06, 2005
      CONSUL
   MR. HIDEHIRO HOSAKA,   Apr. 13, 2006
      CONSUL
   MR. KENJI NAKAYAMA,   May. 25, 2006
      CONSUL
   MR. MASAYA TANIGAWA,   May. 30, 2006
      CONSUL
   MR. SHIGERU MATSUBARA,   Jul. 26, 2006
      CONSUL
   MR. HIROSHI SUGISAKI,   Jul. 31, 2006
      CONSUL
   MS. MEGUMI SAKURABA,   May. 05, 2007
      VICE CONSUL
   MR. TAKESHI YAMAUCHI,   May. 23, 2007
      VICE CONSUL

WYOMING

CASPER (HCG) 111 W. 14TH ST., 82601.
(307) 234-2317
   MRS. MARIKO T. MILLER,   Mar. 02, 1995
      HONORARY CONSUL GENERAL

JORDAN

CALIFORNIA

SAN FRANCISCO (HC) 972 MISSION ST., FLOOR 4, 94103.
(415) 546-1111
   MR. KAMEL J. AYOUB,   Oct. 09, 1997
      HONORARY CONSUL

ILLINOIS

CHICAGO (HCG) 12559 S. HOLIDAY DR., A, ALSIP 60803.
(708) 272-6665, FAX (708) 385-5894
   MR. IHSAN G. SWEISS,   Aug. 14, 2001
      HONORARY CONSUL GENERAL

MICHIGAN

DETROIT (HC) 28551 SOUTHFIELD RD., APT 203, LATHRUP 48076.
(248) 557-4377, FAX (248) 557-4517
   MR. HABIB I. FAKHOURI,   Feb. 06, 1997
      HONORARY CONSUL

KAZAKHSTAN

DISTRICT OF COLUMBIA

WASHINGTON (CHN) 1401 16TH ST., NW, 20036.
(202) 232-5488, FAX (202) 232-5845
   MS. RAUSHAN DYUSSEMBAYEVA,   Dec. 12, 2006
      VICE CONSUL

NEW YORK

NEW YORK (CON) 866 UNITED NATIONS PL., SUITE 586A, 10017.
(212) 888-3024

KENYA

CALIFORNIA

LOS ANGELES (CG) 4801 WILSHIRE BL., FLOOR MEZ, 90010.
   MS. MARY NYAMBURA KAMAU,   Nov. 04, 2004
      CONSUL GENERAL
   MRS. ALICENT KAMBURA ODIPO,   Jan. 25, 2005
      CONSUL
   MR. DAVID MUSEE SAMUEL,   Feb. 22, 2006
      DEPUTY CONSUL

NEW YORK

NEW YORK (CON) 866 UNITED NATIONS PZ., SUITE 4016, 10017.
(212) 421-4740
   MR. CHARLES MANTHI MUENDO,   May. 17, 2006
      CONSULAR AGENT

KIRIBATI

HAWAII

HONOLULU (HC) 95 NAKOLO PL., ROOM 265, 96734.
(808) 521-7703
   MR. WILLIAM E. PAUPE,   Apr. 26, 1990
      HONORARY CONSUL

KOREA

ALASKA

ANCHORAGE (HCG) 1127 W. 7TH AV., 99501.
(907) 263-7225
   MR. WILLIAM H. BITTNER,   Nov. 17, 1999
      HONORARY CONSUL GENERAL

---

* DEPENDENCIES SUCH AS GUAM, PUERTO RICO, AND THE VIRGIN ISLANDS ARE LISTED HERE.
CG-CONSULATE GENERAL   C-CONSULATE   VC-VICE CONSULATE   CA-CONSULAR AGENCY   H-HONORARY CONSULAR STATUS

STATE* RESIDENCE	NAME AND RANK	DATE OF RECOGNITION

CALIFORNIA

LOS ANGELES (CG) 3243-45 WILSHIRE BL., 90010.
(213) 385-9300, FAX (213) 384-5139

MR. BYUNG HYO CHOI, CONSUL GENERAL		Mar. 14, 2006
MR. SEONG JIN KIM, DEPUTY CONSUL GENERAL		May. 05, 2007
MR. MIN RYU, CONSUL		Mar. 21, 2002
MR. TAE HUN CHUNG, CONSUL		Oct. 14, 2004
MR. SE KEUN JANG, CONSUL		Apr. 12, 2005
MR. HONGKYOO KIM, CONSUL		Oct. 06, 2005
MR. YOUNG WOOK CHUN, CONSUL		Oct. 06, 2005
MR. BYUNG JUN MOON, CONSUL		Feb. 22, 2006
MR. HEEJUNG MOON, CONSUL		Feb. 22, 2006
MR. HEESANG YOON, CONSUL		Apr. 18, 2006
MR. SANGJIN PARK, CONSUL		Apr. 18, 2006
MR. JAEHUY PARK, CONSUL		Aug. 24, 2006
MR. SONG HWAN KWON, CONSUL		Oct. 12, 2006
MR. WIJIN PARK, CONSUL		Oct. 12, 2006
MR. YONGJU LEE, CONSUL		Oct. 13, 2006
MR. SANG SOO JUN, CONSUL		May. 05, 2007
MR. JONGYANG KIM, CONSUL		May. 07, 2007
MR. YOUNG CHUR SONG, CONSUL		May. 15, 2007
MR. BYEONG CHEOL MIN, VICE CONSUL		Apr. 14, 2006
MR. DAESUP CHUNG, VICE CONSUL		Apr. 14, 2006

CULTURAL CENTER OF KOREA
LOS ANGELES (CONA) 5505-5507 WILSHIRE BL., 90010.
(213) 936-7141

MR. JONGYUL KIM, CONSUL		Apr. 18, 2006

SAN FRANCISCO (CG) 3500 CLAY ST., 94118.
(415) 921-2251, FAX (415) 921-5946

MR. BON WOO KOO, CONSUL GENERAL		May. 15, 2007
MR. IN PIL CHUN, DEPUTY CONSUL GENERAL		Apr. 28, 2005
MR. SUWHAN CHOE, DEPUTY CONSUL GENERAL		May. 23, 2007
MR. JANG HYUN KIM, CONSUL		Apr. 28, 2005
MR. KYUNG HAN KIM, CONSUL		Apr. 28, 2005
MR. CHUL SOO KIM, CONSUL		Oct. 12, 2006
MRS. YOUNG MI KANG, VICE CONSUL		Sep. 15, 2004

MR. DONG RYUNG JANG, VICE CONSUL		May. 05, 2007

DISTRICT OF COLUMBIA

WASHINGTON (CHN) 2450 MASSACHUSETTS AV., NW, 20008.
(202) 939-5600, FAX (202) 387-0250

MR. TAEMYON KWON, CONSUL GENERAL		Mar. 08, 2006

FLORIDA

MIAMI (HCG) ONE S.E. THIRD AV., FLOOR 27TH, 33131.
(305) 982-5690, FAX (305) 374-5095

MR. BURTON A. LANDY, HONORARY CONSUL GENERAL		Jun. 24, 1999

GEORGIA

ATLANTA (CG) 229 PEACHTREE ST., NE, SUITE 500, 30303.
(404) 522-1611, FAX (404) 521-3169

MR. KWANG JAE LEE, CONSUL GENERAL		Jun. 07, 2005
MR. DONGGYOU CHOI, CONSUL		Aug. 18, 2004
DR. HEECHUL LEE, CONSUL		Oct. 12, 2006
MR. JAE EUNG LEE, CONSUL		Oct. 12, 2006
MR. YONG KIL KIM, CONSUL		May. 05, 2007
MR. HAE HONG PYUN, VICE CONSUL		Nov. 22, 2004

GUAM

AGANA (CG) 125C TUN JOSE CAMACHO ST., TAMUNING 96911.
(671) 647-6488, FAX (671) 649-1336

MR. CHONG IL LEE, CONSUL GENERAL		May. 07, 2007
MR. SEUNG MIN JEON, CONSUL		Oct. 05, 2004

HAWAII

HONOLULU (CG) 2756 PALI HWY. UN., 96817.
(808) 595-6109, FAX (808) 595-3046

MR. DAE HYUN KANG, CONSUL GENERAL		Oct. 05, 2005
MR. HYUN DUK KIM, DEPUTY CONSUL GENERAL		May. 05, 2007
MR. SOON JIN SUH, CONSUL		Sep. 28, 2004
MR. DONG WAN KIM, CONSUL		May. 26, 2005
MR. HYUNGKYU JOO, CONSUL		Nov. 30, 2006
MR. KEE YOUNG EOM, CONSUL		May. 05, 2007
MR. ICKWHEE SEO, VICE CONSUL		May. 05, 2007

ILLINOIS

CHICAGO (CG) 455 N. CITYFRONT PLAZA DR., SUITE 2700, 60611.
(312) 822-9485, FAX (312) 822-9849

STATE* RESIDENCE	NAME AND RANK	DATE OF RECOGNITION	STATE* RESIDENCE	NAME AND RANK	DATE OF RECOGNITION
	MR. SUNG HWAN SON, CONSUL GENERAL	May. 15, 2007		MR. BYUNG RAK HAN, DEPUTY CONSUL GENERAL	Oct. 04, 2005
	MR. HYEON GYU PARK, CONSUL	Oct. 06, 2005		MR. SUNG HYUN JIN, CONSUL	Oct. 04, 2004
	MR. SOON GU YOON, CONSUL	Oct. 06, 2005		MR. JEONG KU JIN, CONSUL	Oct. 14, 2004
	MR. HYUNSUK CHO, CONSUL	Nov. 23, 2005		MR. ILJUN PARK, CONSUL	Jun. 27, 2005
	MR. BYUNG GYU JUNG, CONSUL	Oct. 13, 2006		MR. CHANGJIN KIM, CONSUL	Apr. 14, 2006
	MR. JUNG IL HAN, CONSUL	May. 05, 2007		MR. SUKWOO KANG, CONSUL	Apr. 14, 2006
	MR. YONGHWAN KIM, CONSUL	May. 05, 2007		MR. TONG OP KIM, CONSUL	Apr. 17, 2006
	MR. INSUNG HWANG, VICE CONSUL	Oct. 06, 2005		MR. WAN JOONG KIM, CONSUL	Apr. 17, 2006
	MR. HEESUK KIM, VICE CONSUL	Jun. 08, 2006		MR. MYEONG KI BAEK, CONSUL	Apr. 18, 2006
				MR. SEUNG WOO PARK, CONSUL	Oct. 12, 2006
LOUISIANA				MR. MYUNG YUL LEE, CONSUL	Oct. 25, 2006
NEW ORLEANS (HCG) 321 ST. CHARLES AV., 70130. (504) 524-0757, FAX (504) 525-9464				MR. JONG HEON LEE, CONSUL	May. 05, 2007
	MR. JAMES JULIAN COLEMAN, HONORARY CONSUL GENERAL	Aug. 16, 1968		MR. JOOMIN LEE, CONSUL	May. 05, 2007
				MR. MYUNG JAE HAHN, CONSUL	May. 07, 2007
MASSACHUSETTS				MR. YUNJUN PARK, CONSUL	May. 15, 2007

LOUISIANA

NEW ORLEANS (HCG) 321 ST. CHARLES AV., 70130.
(504) 524-0757, FAX (504) 525-9464

MASSACHUSETTS

BOSTON (CG) 1 GATEWAY CN., FLOOR 2ND, NEWTON 02458.
(617) 641-2830, FAX (617) 641-2831

MS. YOUNG SUN JI, CONSUL GENERAL	May. 17, 2006
MR. DAL YOUNG MAENG, DEPUTY CONSUL GENERAL	Oct. 06, 2005
MS. MIN YOUNG HAN, CONSUL	Oct. 14, 2004
MR. HYUNG KUN LEE, CONSUL	Oct. 12, 2006
MR. KI SEOG LEE, CONSUL	May. 05, 2007

PASSPORT, VISA SECTION & CULTURAL SERVICE
NEW YORK (CON) 460 PARK AV., FLOOR 6TH, 10022.
(212) 759-9550

MR. JIN YUNG WOO, CONSUL	Oct. 04, 2005
MR. JONG CHUL JUNG, CONSUL	Oct. 13, 2006

MICHIGAN

DETROIT (HC) 40400 E. ANN ARBOR RD., SUITE 104B, PLYMOUTH 48170.
(734) 459-8770, FAX (734) 459-8799

MR. ALPHONSE V. TABAKA, HONORARY CONSUL	Sep. 12, 1991

OKLAHOMA

OKLAHOMA CITY (HC) 5400 N. GRAND BL., SUITE 220, 73112.

MR. RONALD JAMES NORICK, HONORARY CONSUL	Apr. 19, 2007

MONTANA

HELENA (HC) 1601 N. BENTON AV., 59625.
(406) 447-4331

MR. ROBERT RAY, JR SWARTOUT, HONORARY CONSUL	Oct. 27, 1998

OREGON

BEAVERTON (HCG) 4085 S.W. 109TH AV., 97005.
(503) 643-8909

PENNSYLVANIA

PHILADELPHIA (HCG) 1515 MARKET ST., SUITE 1200, 19102.
(215) 569-2800

MR. E. HARRIS BAUM, HONORARY CONSUL GENERAL	Oct. 02, 2006

NEW YORK

NEW YORK (CG) 335 E. 45TH ST., FLOOR 4,5,6, 10017.
(646) 674-6001

MR. BONG JOO MOON, CONSUL GENERAL	Oct. 18, 2004
MR. JOON IL LEE, DEPUTY CONSUL GENERAL	Nov. 15, 1996
MR. KIECHEON LEE, DEPUTY CONSUL GENERAL	Mar. 24, 2005

PUERTO RICO

SAN JUAN (HCG) 255 PONCE DE LEON AV., FLOOR 10TH, 00917.
(787) 777-8801, FAX (787) 765-4225

MR. HECTOR REICHARD, HONORARY CONSUL GENERAL	Nov. 04, 1996

STATE* RESIDENCE	NAME AND RANK	DATE OF RECOGNITION	STATE* RESIDENCE	NAME AND RANK	DATE OF RECOGNITION

SOUTH CAROLINA

COLUMBIA (HCG) 1705 COLLEGE ST., 29208.
(803) 777-9300

TEXAS

DALLAS (HC) 13111 N. CENTRAL EXPRESWAY ., 75243.
(214) 454-1112, FAX (214) 454-1212
   MR. KENNETH R. MARVEL,   Jun. 20, 1994
      HONORARY CONSUL

HOUSTON (CG) 1990 POST OAK BL., SUITE 1250, 77056.
(713) 961-0186, FAX (713) 961-3340
   MR. JUNG KEUN KIM,   Oct. 12, 2006
      CONSUL GENERAL
   MR. SEUNG KI SHIN,   Oct. 15, 2004
      CONSUL
   MR. IN SANG JUNG,   Oct. 06, 2005
      CONSUL
   MR. JONG SEON LIM,   Apr. 14, 2006
      CONSUL
   MR. JUNGJAE LEE,   May. 03, 2007
      CONSUL

KOREAN EDUCATION CENTER
HOUSTON (CONA) 1990 POST OAK BL., SUITE 750, 77056.
(713) 961-4104

WASHINGTON

SEATTLE (CG) 2033 6TH AV., SUITE 1125, 98121.
(206) 441-1011, FAX (206) 441-7912
   MR. CHAN HO KWON,   May. 17, 2006
      CONSUL GENERAL
   MR. YONG HO KIM,   Feb. 25, 2005
      CONSUL
   MR. WHEECHUL KIM,   Oct. 12, 2006
      CONSUL
   MR. JOOHOON KIM,   Oct. 13, 2006
      CONSUL
   MR. POK KEUN YUH,   Oct. 13, 2006
      CONSUL

KUWAIT

CALIFORNIA

LOS ANGELES (CG) 1801 AVENUE OF THE STARS UN., SUITE 1010, 90067.
(310) 402-1692
   MR. MUHYEE ALDEEN RASHEED ALFELAIJ,   Oct. 13, 2005
      CONSUL GENERAL
   MR. KHALED W A M A AL WAZZAN,   Feb. 22, 2006
      VICE CONSUL
   MR. MOHAMMAD I M H AL DORAEE,   Feb. 22, 2006
      VICE CONSUL

KYRGYZSTAN

CALIFORNIA

BUELLTON (HCG) 1320 COUGAR RIDGE RD., 93427.
(805) 688-2732
   MR. RICHARD GILBERT QUICK,   Apr. 06, 2004
      HONORARY CONSUL GENERAL

LOS ANGELES (HC) 800 W. 6TH ST., SUITE 1600, 90017.
(213) 891-9564, FAX (213) 891-9562
   MR. S. CHIC WOLK,   Aug. 20, 1996
      HONORARY CONSUL

DISTRICT OF COLUMBIA

WASHINGTON (CHN) 2360 MASSACHUSETTS AV., NW, 20008.
(202) 338-5141, FAX (202) 338-5139
   MR. EMIL KAIKIEV,   Nov. 27, 2002
      CONSUL

MONTANA

HELENA (HC) 6515 YORK RD., 59602.
   MR. ERNEST RAYMOND BRIDWELL,   Apr. 16, 2007
      HONORARY CONSUL

NEW JERSEY

SOUTH PLAINFIELD (HC) 2500 HAMILTON BL., 07080.
(908) 757-9800
   MR. BORIS SAVITSKY,   Apr. 18, 2007
      HONORARY CONSUL

NEW YORK

NEW YORK (CON) 866 UNITED NATIONS PZ., SUITE 514, 10017.
(212) 319-2836

TEXAS

HOUSTON (HCG) 15600 BARKERS LANDING RD., APT 1, 77079.
(281) 920-1841, FAX (281) 920-1823
   MR. DARRELL D. LUTHI,   Jan. 27, 1999
      HONORARY CONSUL GENERAL

UTAH

OREM (HCG) 800 W. UNIVERSITY PW., SUITE AD-217, 84058.
(801) 787-1708
   MS. DANIELLE BUTLER,   Mar. 10, 2004
      HONORARY CONSUL GENERAL

LATVIA

CALIFORNIA

COSTA MESA (HC) 2729 BRISTOL ST., 92626.
(714) 979-1700
   MR. JEFFREY ALAN YARCHEVER,   Dec. 12, 2006
      HONORARY CONSUL

LOS ANGELES (HC) 3013 PALOS VERDES DR., W, PALOS VERDES ESTATES 90274.
(310) 377-1784, FAX (310) 377-5235
   DR. ALFRED RAISTERS,   Feb. 29, 1996
      HONORARY CONSUL

CONNECTICUT

GREENWICH (HC) 22 PUTNAM PL., 06830.
(203) 531-1907
   MR. ROGER EDWARD ANDERSON,   Dec. 04, 2003
      HONORARY CONSUL

STATE* RESIDENCE	NAME AND RANK	DATE OF RECOGNITION	STATE* RESIDENCE	NAME AND RANK	DATE OF RECOGNITION
			MR. ANTHONY R. ABRAHAM, HONORARY CONSUL		Jan. 03, 2000
FLORIDA					
FT. LAUDERDALE (HC) 3501 SW DAVIE RD., SUITE 113, FORT LAUDERDALE 33314. (954) 201-6933			**MASSACHUSETTS**		
	DR. BARRY DONALD MOWELL, HONORARY CONSUL	Sep. 29, 2005	BOSTON (HC) 366 N. MAIN ST., ANDOVER 01810. (978) 470-0912, FAX (978) 470-0922		
				MR. IBRAHIM BECHARA HANNA, HONORARY CONSUL	Feb. 07, 2005
NEW YORK					
BUFFALO (HC) 5110 MAIN ST., SUITE 204, WILLIAMSVILLE 14221. (716) 568-8290, FAX (716) 568-8290			**MICHIGAN**		
	MR. AHMET MUCAHID OREN, HONORARY CONSUL	Feb. 01, 2005	DETROIT (CG) 3031 W. GRAND BL., SUITE 560, 48202. (313) 758-0753		
				MR. ALI AJAMI, CONSUL GENERAL	May. 28, 2004
NEW YORK (HC) 200 W. 79TH ST., APT 6F, 10024. (212) 496-2295				MR. BACHIR TAWK, CONSUL	Apr. 04, 2006
	MS. GERTA FEIGIN, HONORARY CONSUL	May. 01, 2002	**NEW YORK**		
			NEW YORK (CG) 9 E. 76TH ST., 10021. (212) 744-7905		
OHIO				MR. ANTOINE AZZAM, CONSUL	May. 19, 2004
CINCINNATI (HC) 251 SUNNY ACRES DR., 45255. (513) 231-1043					
	MR. KARLIS S. STEINMANIS, HONORARY CONSUL	Aug. 20, 2001	**NORTH CAROLINA**		
			RALEIGH (HC) 2501 BLUE RIDGE RD., SUITE 150, 27607. (919) 863-4306		
PENNSYLVANIA				MR. GHASSAN GEORGE ELDIRI, HONORARY CONSUL	Jul. 29, 2005
PHILADELPHIA (HC) 237 S. 18TH ST., SUITE 22C, 19103. (215) 985-9669					
	MR. JOHN JOSEPH MEDVECKIS, HONORARY CONSUL	May. 18, 2007	**TEXAS**		
			HOUSTON (HC) 2400 AUGUSTA DR., SUITE 308, 77057. (713) 268-1640, FAX (713) 268-1641		
TEXAS				MR. AMIN BOHSALI, HONORARY CONSUL	Jun. 25, 2001
HOUSTON (HC) 5847 SAN FELIPE ., SUITE 3400, 77057. (713) 785-0807					
	MR. STEPHEN P. PAYNE, HONORARY CONSUL	Aug. 16, 1999	**LESOTHO**		
WASHINGTON			**LOUISIANA**		
SNOHOMISH (HC) 13517 69TH AV., SE, 98296. (425) 773-0103			NEW ORLEANS (HCG) XX CANAL ST., SUITE 1937, 70130. (504) 581-1642, FAX (504) 581-4247		
	MR. STEPHEN LEE ZIRSCHKY, HONORARY CONSUL	Apr. 23, 2007		MR. MORRIS W. REED, HONORARY CONSUL GENERAL	Apr. 10, 2001
LEBANON			**TEXAS**		
CALIFORNIA			AUSTIN (HCG) 7400 VALBURN DR., 78731.		
LOS ANGELES (CG) 660 S. FIGUEROA ST., SUITE 1050, 90017. (213) 243-0999, FAX (213) 612-5070				MS. BERTHA E. MEANS, HONORARY CONSUL GENERAL	Aug. 18, 2006
			LIBERIA		
SAN DIEGO (HC) 148 E. 30TH ST., SUITE D, NATIONAL CITY 91950. (619) 336-4800			**CALIFORNIA**		
	MR. JEAN CLAUDE TURQUIEH, HONORARY CONSUL	Feb. 07, 2005	LOS ANGELES (HCG) 6127 RAMIREZ CYN RD., MALIBU 90265. (310) 457-1967, FAX (310) 457-9122		
				MR. ANDREW V. IPPOLITO, HONORARY CONSUL GENERAL	Feb. 06, 1985
FLORIDA					
MIAMI (HC) 6600 S.W. 57TH AV., SUITE 200, 33143. (305) 665-3004, FAX (305) 666-8905					

---

* DEPENDENCIES SUCH AS GUAM, PUERTO RICO, AND THE VIRGIN ISLANDS ARE LISTED HERE.
CG-CONSULATE GENERAL   C-CONSULATE   VC-VICE CONSULATE   CA-CONSULAR AGENCY   H-HONORARY CONSULAR STATUS

STATE* RESIDENCE	NAME AND RANK	DATE OF RECOGNITION

SAN FRANCISCO (HCG) 1101 EMBARCADERO UN., W, OAKLAND 94607.
(510) 452-6373, FAX (510) 444-3370
   MR. GARY SCHNITZER,
     HONORARY CONSUL GENERAL — Mar. 02, 1995

DISTRICT OF COLUMBIA

WASHINGTON (CHN) 5201 16TH ST., NW, 20011.
(202) 723-0437, FAX (202) 723-0436
   MR. ALEXANDER H. N., III WALLACE,
     CONSUL — Jan. 14, 1994
   MR. CHRISTOPHER J. , SR NIPPY,
     CONSUL — Apr. 20, 2005
   MRS. CATHERINE J. NMAH,
     VICE CONSUL — Jul. 22, 2003

FLORIDA

TAMPA (HC) 4401 W. KENNEDY BL., SUITE 150, 33609.
(813) 639-0155
   MR. DAVID A., JR STRAZ,
     HONORARY CONSUL — Nov. 22, 2004

GEORGIA

ATLANTA (HCG) 2265 CASCADE RD., SW, 30311.
(404) 753-4753, FAX (404) 753-4228
   DR. WALTER F. YOUNG,
     HONORARY CONSUL GENERAL — Mar. 07, 1985

ILLINOIS

CHICAGO (HCG) 7342 S. BENNETT AV., 60649.
(773) 643-8635
   MR. ALEXANDER POLEY GBAYEE,
     HONORARY CONSUL GENERAL — Mar. 28, 1979

LOUISIANA

NEW ORLEANS (HC) 1219 N. RENDON ST., 70119.
(504) 486-7800, FAX (504) 486-3200
   MS. VOYCE DURLING-JONES,
     HONORARY CONSUL — Jan. 25, 1982

MICHIGAN

DETROIT (HCG) 9602 GREENFIELD RD., 48227.
(313) 836-6331, FAX (313) 836-6375
   MR. MICHAEL MOHAMAD BAYDOUN,
     HONORARY CONSUL GENERAL — Aug. 18, 1994

NEW YORK

NEW YORK (CG) 820 2ND AV., 10017.
(212) 687-1025
   MR. JEFF GONGOER , SR DOWANA,
     CONSUL GENERAL — Jan. 19, 2006
   MRS. FAMATTA DELINE,
     DEPUTY CONSUL GENERAL — Nov. 17, 2004
   MR. VICTOR E., SR DOUGBA,
     CONSUL — Jun. 13, 1994

PENNSYLVANIA

PHILADELPHIA (HC) 204 GARNET LA., BALA CYNWYD 19004.

   MS. TETA V. BANKS,
     HONORARY CONSUL — Jan. 04, 1994

LIECHTENSTEIN

CALIFORNIA

LOS ANGELES (HC) 400 S. ROSSMORE AV., 90020.
   MR. LEODIS CLYDE MATTHEWS,
     HONORARY CONSUL — Jun. 04, 2007

GEORGIA

MACON (HC) 1338 OLD FORSYTH RD., 31210.
(478) 471-7788
   DR. BRUCE STUART ALLEN,
     HONORARY CONSUL — Jun. 11, 2007

LITHUANIA

ARIZONA

PHOENIX (HC) 1132 E. DRIFTWOOD DR., TEMPE 85283.
(480) 820-6335
   MR. KESTUTIS PAUL ZYGAS,
     HONORARY CONSUL — Feb. 03, 2001

CALIFORNIA

LAFAYETTE (HC) 674 SKY ITY CI., 94549.
(925) 284-3156
   MR. DENNIS LEE GARRISON,
     HONORARY CONSUL — Oct. 14, 2005

LOS ANGELES (HCG) 3236 N. SAWTOOTH CT., WESTLAKE VILLAGE 91362.
(805) 496-5324, FAX (805) 496-7435
   MR. VYTAUTAS CEKANAUSKAS,
     HONORARY CONSUL GENERAL — Oct. 06, 1977

FLORIDA

PALM BEACH (HC) 44 COCONUT ROW UN., SUITE T10, 33480.
(773) 582-8396, FAX (561) 832-7456
   MR. STANLEY BALZEKAS,
     HONORARY CONSUL — Jan. 28, 2000

ST. PETERSBURG (HC) 1101 1ST AV., S, 33705.
(727) 895-4811, FAX (727) 822-2252
   MR. ALGIMANTAS ALBINAS KARNAVICIUS,
     HONORARY CONSUL — Jan. 14, 2000

GEORGIA

MARIETTA (HC) 1202 LEXHAM DR., 30068.
   MS. ROMUALDA STASEVICIUS KLICIUS,
     HONORARY CONSUL — Sep. 13, 2006

ILLINOIS

CHICAGO (CG) 211 E. ONTARIO ST., SUITE 1500, 60611.
(312) 397-0382, FAX (312) 397-0885
   MR. ARVYDAS DAUNORAVICIUS,
     CONSUL GENERAL — Jul. 10, 2003

STATE* RESIDENCE	NAME AND RANK	DATE OF RECOGNITION	STATE* RESIDENCE	NAME AND RANK	DATE OF RECOGNITION

MRS. IRENA STRUMILIENE, CONSUL		Sep. 24, 2004
MRS. KRISTINA BABICIENE, VICE CONSUL		Oct. 13, 2006

MICHIGAN

LANSING (HC) 5 LOCUST LA., 48911.
(517) 394-9940

    MR. SAULIUS LINAS ANUZIS,   Oct. 27, 2004
       HONORARY CONSUL

MINNESOTA

STILLWATER (HC) 4290 NEAL AV., N, 55082.
(651) 430-4965

    MR. HEINZ OTTO VEINSREIDERIS,   May. 23, 2006
       HONORARY CONSUL

NEVADA

LAS VEGAS (HC) 2747 PARADISE RD., SUITE 106, 89109.
(702) 892-0499

    MS. ASTRA JULIANNA MICHELS,   Sep. 13, 2006
       HONORARY CONSUL

NEW HAMPSHIRE

MANCHESTER (HC) 18 COLE ST., SALEM 03079.
(603) 896-6350

    DR. THORSTEINN T. GISLASON,   Feb. 21, 2002
       HONORARY CONSUL

NEW JERSEY

MENDHAM (HC) 290 MOUNTAINSIDE RD., 07945.
(973) 543-7294

    MR. EUGENE CHARLES RAINIS,   Jun. 14, 2004
       HONORARY CONSUL

NEW YORK

NEW YORK (CG) 420 5TH AV., FLOOR 3RD, 10018.
(212) 354-7849, FAX (212) 354-7911

    MR. ALGIMANTAS MISEVICIUS,   Oct. 06, 2005
       CONSUL
    MS. RENATA DARULIENE,   Oct. 12, 2005
       CONSUL
    MS. DIANA KOPILEVIC,   Apr. 30, 2007
       VICE CONSUL

WEBSTER (HC) 140 REGATTA DR., 14580.
(585) 216-9254

    MR. RIMAS ANTANAS CHESONIS,   Jun. 14, 2004
       HONORARY CONSUL

OHIO

CLEVELAND (HCG) 18021 MARCELLA RD., SUITE 101, 44119.
(216) 486-8692

    MRS. INGRIDA BUBLYS,   May. 17, 2004
       HONORARY CONSUL GENERAL

OREGON

PORTLAND (HC) 1 PRODUCE ROW UN., 97208.
(503) 234-5600

    MR. RANDOLPH LATOURETTE MILLER,   Feb. 19, 2004
       HONORARY CONSUL

TEXAS

HOUSTON (HC) 4030 CASE ST., 77005.
(713) 665-4218

    MR. WILLIAM CARL ALTMAN,   Oct. 19, 2004
       HONORARY CONSUL

WASHINGTON

SEATTLE (HC) 5919 WILSON AV., S, 98118.
(206) 725-4576

    MR. VYTAUTAS VICTOR LAPATINSKAS,   Feb. 03, 2001
       HONORARY CONSUL

LUXEMBOURG

CALIFORNIA

SAN FRANCISCO (CG) 1 SANSOME ST., SUITE 830, 94104.
(415) 788-0816

    MR. ROBERT BIWER,   Sep. 13, 2001
       CONSUL GENERAL

WOODLAND HILLS (HC) 23143 CANZONET ST., 91367.
(818) 346-7045

    MR. PIERRE RENE BIWER,   Oct. 19, 2004
       HONORARY CONSUL

DISTRICT OF COLUMBIA

WASHINGTON (CHN) 2200 MASSACHUSETTS AV., NW, 20008.
(202) 265-4171, FAX (202) 328-8270

    MR. MARC HENRI GODEFROID,   Nov. 27, 2006
       CONSUL

GEORGIA

ATLANTA (HC) 1170 PEACHTREE ST., NE, SUITE 1750, 30309.
(404) 892-2100, FAX (404) 875-0798

    MR. GEORGES A. HOFFMANN,   Aug. 22, 1995
       HONORARY CONSUL

ILLINOIS

CHICAGO (HCG) 1417 BRAEBURN CT., WHEELING 60090-6933.
(847) 520-5995, FAX (847) 520-0842

    MR. DONALD JOHN HANSEN,   Aug. 19, 1999
       HONORARY CONSUL GENERAL

INDIANA

INDIANAPOLIS (HC) 8501 HARCOURT RD., 46260.
(317) 257-9197

    MR. JAMES B. STEICHEN,   Apr. 13, 1992
       HONORARY CONSUL

LOUISIANA

NEW ORLEANS (HC) 8012 OAK ST., 70118.
(504) 861-3743

STATE* RESIDENCE	NAME AND RANK	DATE OF RECOGNITION
	MR. GARY J. MANNINA, HONORARY CONSUL	Jun. 11, 1999
MASSACHUSETTS BOSTON (HC) 50 MILK ST., FLOOR 19TH, 02109. (617) 772-1399	MS. SUSAN C. LIVINGSTON, HONORARY CONSUL	Jan. 14, 2000
MICHIGAN DETROIT (HC) 2300 HARMON RD., AUBURN HILLS 48326. (810) 340-2200, FAX (810) 340-2308	MR. WILLIAM DAVIDSON, HONORARY CONSUL	Jul. 09, 1986
MINNESOTA EDINA (HC) 5012 NOB HILL UN., 55439. (612) 220-0404	MR. KEVIN MICHAEL RIES, HONORARY CONSUL	May. 02, 2007
MISSOURI KANSAS CITY (HCG) 325 WESTWOODS CI., LIBERTY 64068. (816) 792-0841, FAX (816) 792-4999	MR. ROBERT F. SCHAEFFER, HONORARY CONSUL GENERAL	Nov. 07, 1983
NEW YORK NEW YORK (CG) 17 BEEKMAN PL., 10022. (212) 888-6664, FAX (212) 888-6116	MR. GEORGES FABER, CONSUL GENERAL	Feb. 19, 2002
	MS. ANNE BASTIAN, CONSULAR AGENT	Jan. 25, 1977
	MR. JACQUES E. LENNON, HONORARY CONSUL	Sep. 20, 1977
OHIO CLEVELAND (HC) 925 EUCLID AV., SUITE 2000, 44115. (216) 696-4700	MR. JAMES R. BRIGHT, HONORARY CONSUL	Aug. 03, 1995
OREGON PORTLAND (HC) 1708 S.W. HAWTHORNE TE., 97201. (503) 224-5268	MR. WILLIAM L. FAILING, HONORARY CONSUL	Jul. 31, 2002
TEXAS FORT WORTH (HC) 48 VALLEY RIDGE RD., 76107-3109. (817) 738-8600	MRS. JOYCE PATE CAPPER, HONORARY CONSUL	May. 08, 2001

STATE* RESIDENCE	NAME AND RANK	DATE OF RECOGNITION
WASHINGTON SEATTLE (HC) 725 1ST ST., S, APT 202, KIRKLAND 98033. (425) 822-4607	MR. FRED R. CERF, HONORARY CONSUL	Oct. 10, 1980

MACEDONIA

STATE* RESIDENCE	NAME AND RANK	DATE OF RECOGNITION
DISTRICT OF COLUMBIA WASHINGTON (CHN) 2129 WYOMING AV., NW, 20008. (202) 667-0501, FAX (202) 667-2131	MR. ZORAN DABIK, CONSUL	Jan. 17, 2002
FLORIDA NAPLES (HC) 6525 CROWN COLONY PL., SUITE 101, 34108. (239) 591-3248	MR. LOUIS VLASHO, HONORARY CONSUL	Jul. 24, 2007
MICHIGAN SOUTHFIELD (CG) 2000 TOWN CN., SUITE 1130, 48075. (248) 354-5537	MR. JORDAN VESELINOV, CONSUL GENERAL	Jan. 11, 2006
	MR. DRAGAN JORDANOVSKI, CONSUL	Jan. 11, 2006
NEW JERSEY CLIFTON (HC) 164 GETTY AV., 07011. (973) 253-3633	MR. SLAVCO MADZAROV, HONORARY CONSUL	Jul. 27, 2007

MADAGASCAR

STATE* RESIDENCE	NAME AND RANK	DATE OF RECOGNITION
CALIFORNIA SAN DIEGO (HC) 124 LOMAS SANTA FE DR., SUITE 206-B, SOLANA BEACH 92075. (619) 755-5136	MRS. MONIQUE MARIE RODRIGUEZ, HONORARY CONSUL	Dec. 30, 1998
NEW YORK NEW YORK (CG) 801 2ND AV., ROOM 404, 10017. (212) 986-9491		
PENNSYLVANIA PHILADELPHIA (HC) 1235 WESTLAKE DR., SUITE 400, BERWYN 19312. (610) 640-7832	MR. JOHN B. HUFFAKER, HONORARY CONSUL	Mar. 13, 1984

MALAYSIA

STATE* RESIDENCE	NAME AND RANK	DATE OF RECOGNITION
CALIFORNIA LOS ANGELES (CG) 550 S. HOPE ST., SUITE 400, 90071. (213) 892-1238, FAX (213) 892-9031		

STATE* RESIDENCE	NAME AND RANK	DATE OF RECOGNITION	STATE* RESIDENCE	NAME AND RANK	DATE OF RECOGNITION

MR. AHMAD ANWAR BIN ADNAN,　Oct. 17, 2005
　CONSUL GENERAL
MR. MOHD RASLI BIN MUDA,　May. 26, 2005
　CONSUL
MRS. SHARIMAHTON BINTI MAT SALEH,　Oct. 12, 2005
　CONSUL
MR. AHMAD BIN ASMAWI,　Apr. 26, 2006
　CONSUL
MR. SHAH NIZAM BIN AHMAD,　Mar. 08, 2005
　VICE CONSUL
MS. HAMIDAH BINTI ABD KARIM,　Mar. 24, 2005
　VICE CONSUL
MR. NURUL SHAMS BIN RUSLI,　May. 03, 2007
　VICE CONSUL

HAWAII

HONOLULU (HC) 999 BISHOP ST., SUITE 2806, 96813.
(808) 525-7702, FAX (808) 525-5016
　MR. HERBERT E. WOLFF,　Oct. 11, 1985
　HONORARY CONSUL

NEW YORK

NEW YORK (CG) 313 E. 43RD ST., 10017.
(212) 682-0232, FAX (212) 983-1987
　MR. MOHAMAD SADIK BIN KETHERGANY,　Sep. 21, 2004
　CONSUL GENERAL
　MR. PRAKAS KIZHAKKE NAIR,　Mar. 04, 2004
　CONSUL
　MS. ZALINA BINTI ZAINOL,　Feb. 13, 2006
　VICE CONSUL
　MR. MOHD JAMIL BIN HAJI MUSTAPA,　Apr. 27, 2006
　VICE CONSUL

TRADE AND INVESTMENT OFFICE OF MALAYSIA
NEW YORK (CONA) 313 E. 43RD ST., FLOOR 2ND, 10017.
(212) 682-0232, FAX (212) 983-1987

OREGON

PORTLAND (HC) 6144 SW 37TH AV., 97221.
(503) 246-0707

TEXAS

HOUSTON (HC) 700 LOUISIANA UN., FLOOR 46TH, 77002.
(713) 222-1470
　MR. MONT P. HOYT,　Aug. 14, 2003
　HONORARY CONSUL

MALI

FLORIDA

FT. LAUDERDALE (HC) 1710 CYPRESS CREEK RD., W, 33309.
(954) 771-1795, FAX (954) 771-3281
　MR. MAYER SHIRAZIPOUR,　Mar. 23, 1995
　HONORARY CONSUL

GEORGIA

ATLANTA (HC) 1815 N. DECATUR RD., 30307.
　MR. VINCENT J. FARLEY,　Sep. 13, 2006
　HONORARY CONSUL

LOUISIANA

NEW ORLEANS (HC) 4232 WILLIAMS BL., SUITE 101, KENNER 70065.
(504) 465-0765
　MS. NANCY MARINOVIC SUTHERLAND,　Apr. 03, 1998
　HONORARY CONSUL

MASSACHUSETTS

BOSTON (HC) 339 UNION ST., 02370.
　MR. WARREN J. SCHJOLDEN,　Mar. 25, 1983
　HONORARY CONSUL

NEW MEXICO

ALBUQUERQUE (HC) 7600 AMERICAN HERITAGE DR., NE, 87109.
　MR. OLIVER C. REESE,　May. 02, 1983
　HONORARY CONSUL

MALTA

CALIFORNIA

LOS ANGELES (HC) 5449 ENDEAVOUR CT., MOORPARK 93021.
(805) 531-8898
　MR. HUGH R. CASSAR,　Sep. 20, 2000
　HONORARY CONSUL

SAN FRANCISCO (HCG) 2562 SAN BRUNO AV., 94134.
(415) 468-4321
　MR. CHARLES JOSEPH VASSALLO,　Mar. 21, 1989
　HONORARY CONSUL GENERAL
　MR. RAYMOND JOHN VASSALLO,　Oct. 19, 2004
　HONORARY CONSUL

DISTRICT OF COLUMBIA

WASHINGTON (CHN) 2017 CONNECTICUT AV., NW, 20008.
(202) 462-3611, FAX (202) 387-5470
　MS. CHRISTINE PACE,　Oct. 06, 2006
　CONSUL

FLORIDA

FT. LAUDERDALE (HC) 13829 VIA DAVINCI ., DELRAY BEACH 33446.
(561) 496-6942
　MR. JOHN F. GALEA,　Mar. 19, 1992
　HONORARY CONSUL

LOUISIANA

METAIRIE (HC) 3500 N. CAUSEWAY BL., SUITE 1500, 70002.
(504) 837-7700, FAX (504) 837-8482
　MR. ELIAS ANESTIS KATSAROS,　Jul. 02, 2002
　HONORARY CONSUL

MASSACHUSETTS

BELLMONT (HVC) 56 LANTERN RD., BELMONT 02478.
(617) 484-3333
　MRS. CHRISTINE JOSEPHINE SAIDNAWEY,　Jun. 09, 2006
　HONORARY VICE CONSUL

MICHIGAN

DETROIT (HCG) 26953 SHEAHAN DR., DEARBORN HEIGHTS 48127.
(313) 563-1779, FAX (313) 565-0103

STATE* RESIDENCE	NAME AND RANK	DATE OF RECOGNITION	STATE* RESIDENCE	NAME AND RANK	DATE OF RECOGNITION

MARSHALL ISLANDS

MR. LARRY J. ZAHRA, HONORARY CONSUL GENERAL	Mar. 21, 1989	
MR. JOHN CONSIGLIO MICALLEF, HONORARY CONSUL	Jun. 23, 1999	

GUAM

AGANA (HC) 111 CHALAN SANTO PAPA ., SUITE 701, 96910.
(671) 472-2922

MR. DANIEL A. ROLAND,
    HONORARY CONSUL — Oct. 20, 1997

MINNESOTA

ST. PAUL (HCG) 332 MINNESOTA ST., SUITE 3090, 55101.
(651) 224-1844, FAX (651) 224-3328

MR. JOSEPH STEPHEN MICALLEF,
    HONORARY CONSUL GENERAL — Sep. 19, 1988

HAWAII

HONOLULU (CG) 1888 LUSITANA ST., SUITE 301, 96813.

MR. PHILIP ANUNGAR,
    CONSUL GENERAL — Dec. 11, 2000

MR. LANNY L. KABUA,
    CONSUL — Mar. 08, 2007

NEW YORK

NEW YORK (CON) 249 E. 35TH ST., 10016.
(212) 725-2345

MR. WALTER MALLIA,
    CONSUL — Jun. 08, 2005

MAURITIUS

TOURISM OFFICE OF MALTA
NEW YORK (CONA) 65 BROADWAY AV., SUITE 823, 10006.
(212) 430-3799, FAX (212) 695-8229

ARIZONA

SUN CITY (HC) 9744 W. BELL RD., 85351--1343.
(623) 876-2718

MR. FRANK REID SMITH,
    HONORARY CONSUL — Sep. 04, 2003

PENNSYLVANIA

PHILADELPHIA (HC) 941 BRYN MAWR AV., PENN VALLEY 19072.
(610) 664-7475

MRS. SHEILA G. PARISH,
    HONORARY CONSUL — Mar. 14, 1997

CALIFORNIA

LOS ANGELES (HC) 2029 CENTURY PARK ., E, FLOOR 6TH, 90067.
(310) 557-2009, FAX (310) 551-0283

MR. BRUCE E. DIZENFELD,
    HONORARY CONSUL — Aug. 05, 1982

TENNESSEE

KINGSPORT (HC) 433 E. CENTER ST., SUITE 202, 37660.
(423) 246-8433

MR. DAVID BRUCE SHINE,
    HONORARY CONSUL — Jun. 03, 2004

SAN FRANCISCO (HC) 2844 GREENWICH ST., 94123.
(415) 693-9345

MR. JITU SOMAYA,
    HONORARY CONSUL — Apr. 11, 2000

MEXICO

TEXAS

AUSTIN (HC) 3925 W. BRAKER LA., SUITE 300, 78759.
(512) 305-0612

MR. SADA CUMBER,
    HONORARY CONSUL — Dec. 07, 2005

ALASKA

ANCHORAGE (HC) 3000 ROSALIND LP., 99507.
(907) 223-5544, FAX (907) 563-9152

MRS. LINA BENIGNA MARISCAL,
    HONORARY CONSUL — Oct. 29, 2001

DALLAS (HC) PO BOX 830688 UN., SM-24, RICHARDSON 75083.
(972) 883-4785, FAX (972) 883-4780

MR. GERALD H. HOAG,
    HONORARY CONSUL — Mar. 13, 1997

ARIZONA

DOUGLAS (CON) 1201 F ST., 85607.
(520) 364-3142

MR. OSCAR ANTONIO DE LA TORRE AMEZCUA,
    CONSUL — Oct. 05, 2006

MR. GUSTAVO MORALES CIRION,
    CONSUL — Apr. 24, 2007

HOUSTON (HCG) 2602 COMMONWEALTH UN., 77006.
(713) 654-7900

MR. JOHN D., JR ELLIS,
    HONORARY CONSUL GENERAL — Jul. 24, 2000

MR. RAUL CARLOS SAAVEDRA CINTA,
    DEPUTY CONSUL — Nov. 28, 2006

MR. OLIVERIO RAMIREZ AYALA,
    VICE CONSUL — May. 15, 2007

MS. ADRIANA SOTO YANEZ,
    VICE CONSUL — May. 15, 2007

WASHINGTON

SEATTLE (HC) 28817 N.E. 124TH ST., DUVALL 98019.
(425) 788-3120

MR. WILLIAM H., III WEISS,
    HONORARY CONSUL — Apr. 19, 2001

NOGALES (CG) 571 N. GRAND AV., 85621.
(602) 287-2521

MRS. MARIA LUISA B. LOPEZ GARGALLO,
    CONSUL GENERAL — Jun. 07, 2005

MR. FERNANDO VEGA MORA,
    CONSUL — Apr. 28, 2005

STATE* RESIDENCE	NAME AND RANK	DATE OF RECOGNITION
	MR. MARIO ENRIQUE FIGUEROA MATUZ, CONSUL	May. 23, 2006
	MS. DALYA SALINAS PEREZ, CONSUL	Apr. 26, 2007
	MISS MIRIAM VILLANUEVA AYON, DEPUTY CONSUL	Jan. 09, 2002
PHOENIX (CG) 1990 W. CAMELBACK RD., SUITE 110, 85015. (602) 249-2735		
	MR. CARLOS FLORES VIZCARRA, CONSUL GENERAL	Apr. 01, 2004
	MR. ALFONSO NAVARRO BERNACHI, DEPUTY CONSUL	Mar. 12, 2007
TUCSON (CON) 553 S. STONE AV., 85701.		
	MR. JUAN MANUEL CALDERON JAIMES, CONSUL	Mar. 09, 2004
	MR. ALEJANDRO RAMOS CARDOSO, CONSUL	Jun. 20, 2006
	MR. BERNARDO MENDEZ LUGO, DEPUTY CONSUL	Apr. 23, 2007
YUMA (CON) 600 W. 16TH ST., 85364. (928) 344-0066		
	MR. MIGUEL ESCOBAR VALDEZ, CONSUL	Jul. 19, 2006
	MS. NATALIA FORTUNY JEREZ, DEPUTY CONSUL	Jul. 07, 2005
	MR. JORGE LUIS HIDALGO PARTIDA, VICE CONSUL	May. 08, 2006
	MS. JUDITH ECHEVERRIA VILLA, VICE CONSUL	Apr. 24, 2007

ARKANSAS

STATE* RESIDENCE	NAME AND RANK	DATE OF RECOGNITION
LITTLE ROCK (CON) 3500 S. UNIVERSITY AV., 72204.		
	MR. ANDRES IMRE CHAO EBERGENYI, CONSUL	Oct. 06, 2006
	MR. ALEJANDRO LEON VARGAS, CONSUL	Feb. 01, 2007
	MR. ERIC LEVY WITEMBERG, CONSUL	Mar. 12, 2007

CALIFORNIA

STATE* RESIDENCE	NAME AND RANK	DATE OF RECOGNITION
CALEXICO (CON) 408 HEBER AV., 92231. (619) 357-3863		
	MR. LUIS GUILLERMO ROMERO PARRA, CONSUL	Dec. 04, 2002
	MS. ROSA CLEMENTINA CURTO PEREZ, CONSUL	Jun. 28, 2005
	MR. PABLO JESUS ARNAUD CARRENO, CONSUL	Feb. 23, 2006
	MR. SERGIO FRANCISCO SALINAS MEZA, VICE CONSUL	Jul. 08, 2005
FRESNO (CON) 2409 MERCED ST., 93721. (209) 233-4219		
	MRS. MARTHA ELVIA ROSAS RODRIGUEZ, CONSUL	Feb. 25, 2005
	MRS. SELENE BARCELO DE ALEXANDROU, DEPUTY CONSUL	May. 03, 2007
	MR. HERIBERTO GONZALEZ ESCAMILLA, VICE CONSUL	Feb. 23, 2006

STATE* RESIDENCE	NAME AND RANK	DATE OF RECOGNITION
LOS ANGELES (CG) 2401 W. 6TH ST., 90057. (213) 351-6815, FAX (213) 389-9186		
	MR. RUBEN ALBERTO BELTRAN GUERRERO, CONSUL GENERAL	Feb. 23, 2004
	MR. MARIO VELAZQUEZ SUAREZ, DEPUTY CONSUL GENERAL	Jul. 07, 2005
	MR. MARIO PEREZ RAMIREZ ZAMORA, CONSUL	Mar. 06, 2000
	MR. ALEJANDRO PELAYO RANGEL, CONSUL	May. 24, 2001
	MR. CARLOS ALFONSO VILLEDA TREJO, CONSUL	Sep. 17, 2002
	MR. ALEJANDRO CONTRERAS CASTANEDA, CONSUL	Sep. 26, 2002
	MR. MARGARITO JESUS OCAMPO MARTINEZ, CONSUL	Jul. 21, 2004
	MS. MIREYA MAGANA GALVEZ, CONSUL	Aug. 20, 2004
	MS. SYLVIA G. SEVILLA DE HEIMES, CONSUL	Nov. 09, 2004
	MR. LUIS ENRIQUE CASTRESANA RUBIO, CONSUL	Jun. 28, 2005
	MR. JOSE AGUILAR SALAZAR, CONSUL	May. 05, 2006
	MS. VANESSA CALVA RUIZ, CONSUL	Jun. 01, 2006
	MR. MARCO ANTONIO FRAIRE BUSTILLOS, CONSUL	Aug. 24, 2006
	MR. ROBERTO LUJAN GUTIERREZ, CONSUL	Jun. 06, 2007
	MR. MIGUEL ANGEL PERALTA VELASCO, VICE CONSUL	Feb. 17, 1998
	MS. MARIA DEL CARMEN REYES DIAZ, VICE CONSUL	Oct. 21, 2002
	MR. CARLOS LEOPOLDO MACEDO NUNEZ, VICE CONSUL	Oct. 03, 2003
COMMERICAL OFFICE OF MEXICO LOS ANGELES (CONA) 350 S. FIGUEROA ST., SUITE 296, 90071.		
	MR. ELIGIO SERNA NAJERA, VICE CONSUL	Apr. 12, 2005
OFFICE OF THE ATTORNEY GENERAL OF MEXICO LOS ANGELES (CONA) 3701 WILSHIRE BL., SUITE 1111, 90010. (213) 351-6820		
	MS. MILAGROS ALEJANDRA CANO, CONSUL	Mar. 21, 2003
	MR. GUILLERMO FONSECA LEAL, CONSUL	Jul. 29, 2005
TOURISM BOARD LOS ANGELES (CONA) 1880 CENTURY PARK UN., E, SUITE 511, 90067. (310) 282-9112		
	MR. JORGE ANTONIO GAMBOA PATRON, CONSUL	Jul. 07, 2005
	MS. MARIA L. GONZALEZ CADAVAL GUEDEA, VICE CONSUL	Mar. 08, 2005
FINANCE OFFICE LOS ANGELES (CONA) 600 WILSHIRE BL., SUITE 1210, 90017. (213) 538-1290		

STATE* RESIDENCE	NAME AND RANK	DATE OF RECOGNITION
OXNARD (CON) 3151 W. 5TH ST., SUITE E-100, 93030. (805) 984-8747, FAX (805) 984-8738		
	MR. FERNANDO GAMBOA, CONSUL	May. 09, 2002
	MR. ENRIQUE VALLE CARDENAS, CONSUL	Apr. 24, 2007
	MS. ROSA ELVA GARCIA FRANCO, CONSUL	Apr. 27, 2007
	MR. RAUL GARCIA ZENTLAPAL, CONSUL	Apr. 30, 2007
	MS. DULCE MARIA ZAMORA LEZAMA, DEPUTY CONSUL	Sep. 25, 2006
SACRAMENTO (CG) 1010 8TH ST., 95814. (916) 329-3526, FAX (916) 441-3147		
	MRS. ALEJANDRA BOLOGNA DE MORETT, CONSUL GENERAL	May. 18, 2004
	MR. EUCLIDES DEL MORAL ARBONA, DEPUTY CONSUL GENERAL	Jan. 05, 2007
	MRS. MARIA DE NURIA MARINE GONZALEZ, CONSUL	Jul. 07, 2005
	MR. VICTOR PELAEZ MILLAN, CONSUL	Feb. 23, 2006
SALINAS (HC) 333 SALINAS ST., 93901. (831) 422-0302		
	MS. BLANCA ESTELA DE LEON ZARAZUA, HONORARY CONSUL	Aug. 14, 2003
SAN BERNARDINO (CON) 293 NORTH D ST., 92401. (714) 889-9836		
	MR. CARLOS IGNACIO GIRALT CABRALES, CONSUL	Oct. 09, 2002
	MR. JOSE FEDERICO BASS VILLARREAL, CONSUL	May. 08, 2006
	MR. JEREMIAS GUZMAN BARRERA, DEPUTY CONSUL	May. 08, 2006
SAN DIEGO (CG) 1549 INDIA ST., 92101. (619) 231-8414, FAX (619) 231-4802		
	MR. LUIS CABRERA CUARON, CONSUL GENERAL	Mar. 03, 2004
	MR. RICARDO PINEDA ALBARRAN, DEPUTY CONSUL GENERAL	Oct. 06, 2005
	MR. MARIO CUEVAS ZAMORA, CONSUL	Dec. 06, 2001
	MR. JOSE FRANCISCO ANZA SOLIS, CONSUL	Aug. 16, 2002
	MR. ALBERTO LOZANO MERINO, CONSUL	Oct. 22, 2002
	MR. MARIO RICARDO PALMERIN VELASCO, CONSUL	Aug. 04, 2003
	MR. MIGUEL ANGEL MENDEZ BUENOS AIRES, CONSUL	Oct. 01, 2003
	MRS. LYDIA ANTONIO DE LA GARZA, CONSUL	Oct. 31, 2003
	MR. PEDRO ARATH OCHOA PALACIO, CONSUL	Dec. 05, 2004
	MS. ABIGAIL CALLEJA FERNANDEZ, CONSUL	May. 05, 2006
	MR. ANTONIO CURZIO GUTIERREZ, CONSUL	Jul. 19, 2006
	MR. MIGUEL F. ESCALANTE SANDOVAL, CONSUL	Apr. 24, 2007

STATE* RESIDENCE	NAME AND RANK	DATE OF RECOGNITION
	MRS. LAURA E. QUINTANILLA CASAS, VICE CONSUL	Sep. 13, 2001
OFFICE OF AGRICULTURE AND FORESTRY AFFAIRS OF MEXICO SAN DIEGO (CONA) 12625 HIGH BLUFF DR., 92130.		
OFFICE OF MEXICAN FISHERIES OF MEXICO SAN DIEGO (CONA) 2550 FIFTH ST., E, SUITE 101, 92103.		
OFFICE OF THE ATTORNEY GENERAL SAN DIEGO (CONA) 402 W. BROADWAY ST., SUITE 660, 92101. (619) 595-7881, FAX (619) 595-7883		
	MR. RUBEN GONZALEZ-BERMUDEZ, CONSUL	Jun. 16, 2006
SAN FRANCISCO (CG) 532 FOLSOM ST., 94105.		
	MR. ALFONSO DE MARIA Y CAMPOS, CONSUL GENERAL	Apr. 12, 2004
	MR. JAIME ARTURO MARTIN SERRANO, CONSUL	Dec. 20, 2002
	MS. CAROLINA AYALA ACEVES, CONSUL	Aug. 10, 2004
	MR. AGUSTIN EMILIO PRADILLO CUEVAS, CONSUL	Sep. 13, 2004
	MR. JONATHAN CHAIT AUERBACH, CONSUL	Nov. 10, 2004
	MR. CARLOS ALFREDO ZAMORA TREVINO, CONSUL	Dec. 06, 2006
	MS. ANDREA PANIAGUA BORREGO, CONSUL	Apr. 18, 2007
	MS. MARIA DEL CARMEN MORENO RODRIGUEZ, CONSUL	Jun. 06, 2007
	MRS. ALEJANDRA GARCIA WILLIAMS, DEPUTY CONSUL	Mar. 19, 2007
SAN JOSE (CG) 540 N. 1ST ST., 95112. (408) 294-3414		
	MR. JOSE EDUARDO LORETO MIRANDA, DEPUTY CONSUL GENERAL	Oct. 20, 2004
	MR. HUMBERTO TAMAYO CASTILLO, CONSUL	Dec. 08, 2004
	MR. ENRIQUE JAIME MORALES LOMELI, CONSUL	Feb. 23, 2006
CONSULAR ANNEX SAN JOSE (CONA) 115 N. FOURTH ST., SUITE 117, 95112. (408) 213-2255		
	MRS. ERIKA LOURDES GUZMAN SOSA, CONSUL	Apr. 25, 2005
SANTA ANA (CON) 828 N. BROADWAY ST., 92701.		
	MR. LUIS MIGUEL ORTIZ HARO AMIEVA, CONSUL	Oct. 04, 2002
	MR. MANUEL HERRERA RABAGO, CONSUL	Apr. 14, 2005
	MRS. CONCEPCION CAPULIN RAMIREZ, VICE CONSUL	Mar. 21, 2006

COLORADO

DENVER (CG) 5350 LEETSDALE DR., SUITE 100, 80246.
(303) 331-1110

STATE* RESIDENCE	NAME AND RANK	DATE OF RECOGNITION	STATE* RESIDENCE	NAME AND RANK	DATE OF RECOGNITION

MR. JUAN CARLOS MENDOZA SANCHEZ,   Sep. 14, 2006
    DEPUTY CONSUL GENERAL

MRS. LUCRECIA MARIA E. BARRERA ROMERO,   Jul. 16, 1999
    CONSUL

MRS. MARIANA AGUSTINA DIAZ NAGORE,   Apr. 01, 2003
    CONSUL

MR. JORGE A. GONZALEZ MAYAGOITIA,   Apr. 06, 2007
    CONSUL

MR. ISIDRO PIEDRA GARCIA,   Feb. 28, 2007
    VICE CONSUL

MR. JOSE LUIS GARCIA NOLASCO,   Apr. 30, 2007
    VICE CONSUL

FLORIDA

JACKSONVILLE (HC) 5991 CHESTER AV., SUITE 210, 32217.
(904) 448-1256

MIAMI (CG) 5975 S. W. 72ND ST., SUITE 301, 33143.
(786) 268-4900, FAX (786) 268-4895

    MS. SOFIA GARCIA CEJA,   Dec. 05, 1996
       CONSUL

    MR. RODRIGO ARTURO ORTEGA CAJIGAS,   Jun. 24, 2003
       CONSUL

    MR. EDGARDO BRIONES VELAZQUEZ,   Feb. 18, 2005
       CONSUL

    MR. ANTONIO ALFREDO LOMELI ITURBE,   Sep. 13, 2006
       CONSUL

    MS. CELIA ALCAIDE BLANCO,   Mar. 08, 2007
       CONSUL

    MR. ALONSO MARTIN GOMEZ FAVILA,   Apr. 24, 2007
       CONSUL

    MRS. MA DE LOS DOLORES ORTEGA AZUELA,   Jun. 27, 2005
       VICE CONSUL

COMMERCIAL OFFICE OF MEXICO
MIAMI (CONA) 5975 S.W. 72ND ST., SUITE 404, 33143.

TOURISM OFFICE OF MEXICO
MIAMI (CONA) 5975 SUNSET DR., SUITE 305, 33143.
(305) 443-9160

    MRS. MARIA T. VILLARREAL DE SAITCEVSKY,   Jun. 18, 2004
       CONSUL

MEXICAN TRADE COMMISSION
MIAMI (CONA) 444 BRICKELL AV., SUITE 450, 33131.
, FAX (305) 415-9361

ORLANDO (CON) 100 W. WASHINGTON ST., 32801.
    MR. JAIME PAZ Y PUENTE GUTIERREZ,   Jul. 29, 2005
       CONSUL

    MRS. JUANA MARIA RUIZ MARTINEZ,   Apr. 24, 2007
       CONSUL

    MRS. MARIA AURELIA MORALES GELAIN,   May. 13, 2003
       VICE CONSUL

    MR. GAMALIEL BUSTILLOS,   Apr. 23, 2007
       VICE CONSUL

GEORGIA

ATLANTA (CG) 2600 APPLE VALLEY RD., 30319.
(404) 266-2233, FAX (404) 266-2302
    MRS. REMEDIOS GOMEZ ARNAU,   Jul. 03, 2001
       CONSUL GENERAL

    MS. MARIA MARISELA QUIJANO HERRERO,   Jul. 10, 2003
       CONSUL

    MRS. MARIA DE LOS A. MEDINA VINALES,   Jul. 29, 2005
       CONSUL

    MR. ELIEL CAMPUZANO MENDIOLA,   Apr. 24, 2007
       CONSUL

COMMERCIAL OFFICE OF MEXICO
ATLANTA (CONA) 229 PEACHTREE ST., NE, SUITE 907, 30303.

TRADE COMMISSION
ATLANTA (CONA) 233 PEACHTREE ST., NE, SUITE 2205, 30303.
(404) 522-5373

HAWAII

HONOLULU (HC) 620 MCCULLY ST., SUITE 506, 96826.
(808) 947-0828
    MRS. LAURA ELENA ANGEL GUZMAN,   Feb. 05, 2004
       HONORARY CONSUL

ILLINOIS

CHICAGO (CG) 204 S. ASHLAND AV., 60607.
(312) 833-6331
    MR. MANUEL RODRIGUEZ ARRIAGA,   May. 08, 2007
       CONSUL GENERAL

    MR. ANIBAL GOMEZ TOLEDO,   Apr. 28, 2005
       DEPUTY CONSUL GENERAL

    MRS. EDURNE NEREA PINEDA AYERBE,   Aug. 16, 2002
       CONSUL

    MR. JULIO CESAR HUERTA GARCIA,   Oct. 09, 2002
       CONSUL

    MR. FELIPE ULISES CUELLAR SANCHEZ,   Dec. 10, 2002
       CONSUL

    MRS. RITA MARIA F. VARGAS TORREGROSA,   Dec. 10, 2002
       CONSUL

    MR. BRUNO HERNANDEZ PICHE,   Mar. 26, 2003
       CONSUL

    MRS. BEATRIZ MARGAIN CHARLES,   Jun. 23, 2003
       CONSUL

    MR. SANTIAGO ARDAVIN ITUARTE,   Dec. 02, 2004
       CONSUL

    MR. CESAR IGNACIO ROMERO JACOBO,   Dec. 29, 2004
       CONSUL

    MR. FRANCISCO J. VALDES ROA,   Feb. 23, 2006
       CONSUL

    MR. DANTE GOMEZ MARTINEZ,   May. 08, 2006
       CONSUL

    MR. EMILIO CARLOS BRACHO ARAGON,   Jul. 26, 2006
       CONSUL

    MR. JACOBO TELLEZ OCAMPO,   Jun. 03, 2003
       VICE CONSUL

    MR. ANTONIO A. PEREZ DE TEJADA ORTEGA,   Aug. 24, 2006
       VICE CONSUL

MEXICAN TOURISM BOARD
CHICAGO (CONA) 225 N. MICHIGAN AV., SUITE 1850, 60601.
(312) 606-0069
    MR. JOSE ALEJANDRO VALDEZ LUNA AMBIA,   May. 23, 2006
       CONSUL

    MS. MARIA HORTENSIA GUERRERO SOTELO,   Jul. 29, 2005
       VICE CONSUL

    MS. MARIA TERESA MATAMOROS MONTES,   May. 03, 2007
       VICE CONSUL

---

* DEPENDENCIES SUCH AS GUAM, PUERTO RICO, AND THE VIRGIN ISLANDS ARE LISTED HERE.
CG-CONSULATE GENERAL   C-CONSULATE   VC-VICE CONSULATE   CA-CONSULAR AGENCY   H-HONORARY CONSULAR STATUS

STATE* RESIDENCE	NAME AND RANK	DATE OF RECOGNITION

COMMERCIAL OFFICE
CHICAGO (CONA) 225 N. MICHIGAN AV., SUITE 1800, 60601.
(312) 856-0316

MR. MIGUEL ANGEL LEAMAN RIVAS, CONSUL		Sep. 13, 1996

INDIANA

CONSULATE
INDIANAPOLIS (CON) 39 W. JACKSON PL., SUITE 103, 46225.
(317) 951-0005

MR. JORGE CUAUHTEMOC ELIZONDO MEJIA, CONSUL		Sep. 17, 2002
MS. LORENA ALVARADO QUEZADA, CONSUL		Apr. 27, 2006
MR. MARTIN ALCALA SALGADO, DEPUTY CONSUL		Apr. 23, 2007
MS. ELSA VILLA MATA, VICE CONSUL		Nov. 08, 2002

MASSACHUSETTS

BOSTON (CG) 20 PARK PZ., SUITE 506,500, 02116.
(617) 426-4942

MR. RODRIGO MARQUEZ LARTIGUE, CONSUL		Jan. 23, 2002
MR. EDUARDO R. DE OLLOQUI GONZALEZ, CONSUL		Mar. 27, 2003
MS. AMPARO E. ANGUIANO RODRIGUEZ, CONSUL		Apr. 05, 2007
MR. GERMAN MURGUIA MIER, VICE CONSUL		Mar. 29, 2000

MICHIGAN

DETROIT (CON) 645 GRISWOLD AV., SUITE 830, 48226.
(313) 965-1868

MRS. MERCEDES ESQUIVEL DE ANTUNES, CONSUL		Nov. 27, 2002
MR. ANTONIO ORTEGA SAENZ, CONSUL		Mar. 18, 2004
MS. ADDA JACQUELINE MORAN ROSAS, CONSUL		May. 08, 2006
MR. VICENTE M. SANCHEZ VENTURA, CONSUL		Oct. 05, 2006
MS. ROCIO MAGALI MACIEL FRANCO, CONSUL		Apr. 30, 2007
MR. JORGE SANCHEZ CATANO, DEPUTY CONSUL		Apr. 24, 2007

COMMERCIAL OFFICE
DETROIT (CONA) 2000 TOWN CENTER ., SUITE 1900, SOUTHFIELD 48075.

MINNESOTA

ST. PAUL (CG) 797 E. 7TH ST., SAINT PAUL 55106.
(651) 379-4209

MR. NATHAN WOLF LUSTBADER, CONSUL		Jun. 02, 2005
MR. RICARDO F. HERNANDEZ LECANDA, CONSUL		Jun. 27, 2005
MS. MARIA EUGENIA SERRANO SALAZAR, VICE CONSUL		Jun. 27, 2005

MISSOURI

KANSAS CITY (CON) 1600 BALTIMORE AV., SUITE 100, 64108.
(816) 556-0800

MR. EVERARDO LUIS SUAREZ AMEZCUA, CONSUL		Dec. 31, 2002
MR. DANIEL AGUADO ORNELAS, CONSUL		May. 03, 2007
MRS. MARIA NOEMI HERNANDEZ TELLEZ, DEPUTY CONSUL		Nov. 29, 2002
MR. JUSTINIANO MENCHACA FUENTES, VICE CONSUL		May. 03, 2007

NEBRASKA

OMAHA (CON) 3552 DODGE ST., 68131.
(402) 595-1841, FAX (402) 595-1845

MR. JOSE LUIS CUEVAS HILDITCH, CONSUL		Aug. 29, 2000
MR. LUIS FERNANDO ALVA MARTINEZ, DEPUTY CONSUL		Oct. 27, 2000
MR. EDGAR REBOLLAR, CONSULAR AGENT		Apr. 24, 2007

NEVADA

LAS VEGAS (CON) 330 S. 4TH ST., 89101.
(702) 383-0623

MRS. MARIA LUISA SANTOS, CONSUL		Feb. 27, 2002
MR. MARIANO LEMUS GAS, CONSUL		Mar. 03, 2005
MR. FERNANDO DE LA TORRE GORRAEZ, CONSUL		Apr. 26, 2007
MR. JOHANNES JACOME CID, CONSUL		May. 15, 2007

NEW MEXICO

ALBUQUERQUE (CON) 1610 4TH ST., NW, SUITE 0, 87102.
(505) 247-2139

MR. JUAN MANUEL SOLANA MORALES, CONSUL		Jul. 11, 2001
MS. TANIA LIZETTE RION PENA, CONSUL		May. 02, 2006
MS. EMY KAMETA MIYAMOTO, CONSUL		Apr. 24, 2007
MR. ALBERTO BERNAL ACERO, DEPUTY CONSUL		Jan. 21, 2005
MR. OMAR A. RIVERA VALDERRABANO, VICE CONSUL		May. 08, 2006
MRS. IOANA NAVARRETE PELLICER, VICE CONSUL		Apr. 24, 2007

NEW YORK

NEW YORK (CG) 27-29 E. 39TH ST., 10016.
(212) 689-0456

MR. RAMON XILOTL, CONSUL GENERAL		Jul. 05, 2006
MR. GERARDO GUERRERO GOMEZ, CONSUL		Dec. 27, 1999
MR. GASPAR HERNAN OROZCO RIOS, CONSUL		Nov. 06, 2002

STATE* RESIDENCE	NAME AND RANK	DATE OF RECOGNITION	STATE* RESIDENCE	NAME AND RANK	DATE OF RECOGNITION

MR. JOSE ANTONIO LARIOS PONCE,   Jul. 26, 2006
    CONSUL

MS. IRMA OLIVIA LARIOS ALZUA,   Apr. 18, 2007
    CONSUL

MR. EDGAR DE JESUS TRUJILLO MUNOZ,   Apr. 19, 2007
    CONSUL

MS. NORMA EDITH AGUILAR ANDRADE,   Apr. 19, 2007
    CONSUL

MR. RAFAEL VASCONCELOS MORFIN,   Apr. 23, 2007
    CONSUL

MR. RAUL JAIME ZORRILLA ARREDONDO,   Aug. 09, 2007
    CONSUL

MRS. YOLANDA CASTRO ESCUDERO,   May. 08, 2006
    VICE CONSUL

COMMERCIAL OFFICE OF MEXICO
NEW YORK (CONA) 375 PARK AV., SUITE 1905, 10152.

TOURISM OFFICE OF MEXICO
NEW YORK (CONA) 400 MADISON AV., SUITE 11C, 10017.
(212) 308-2110, FAX (212) 308-9060

MS. MARIANA MORA PEDRERO,   Jul. 26, 2006
    CONSUL

MS. CLARA ADRIANA TORRES MARQUEZ,   Oct. 04, 2005
    VICE CONSUL

MEXICAN FOREIGN TRADE INSTITUTE OF MEXICO
NEW YORK (CONA) 375 PARK AV., SUITE 1905, 10152.
(212) 826-2916

MR. EDMUNDO F. GONZALEZ HERRERA,   Aug. 12, 2002
    CONSUL

MR. RODRIGO ESPONDA CASCAJARES,   Feb. 24, 2003
    CONSUL

NORTH CAROLINA

CHARLOTTE (HC) 4424 TAGGART CREEK RD., SUITE 101, 28208.
(704) 409-1416

MR. WAYNE P. COOPER,   May. 08, 1981
    HONORARY CONSUL

MR. PATRICK CVETKO BROWN,   Nov. 23, 2005
    HONORARY VICE CONSUL

RALEIGH (CON) 336 E. SIX FORKS RD., 29609.
(919) 754-0046, FAX (919) 754-1726

MR. ARMANDO ORTIZ ROCHA,   Dec. 16, 2002
    CONSUL

MR. JUAN CARLOS CARRILLO CABRERA,   Mar. 08, 2005
    CONSUL

MR. RODRIGO PINTADO COLLET,   May. 08, 2006
    CONSUL

MR. CARLOS PADILLA NORIEGA,   Jun. 07, 2007
    CONSUL

MRS. KARLA TATIANA ORNELAS LOERA,   Jul. 07, 2005
    DEPUTY CONSUL

OREGON

PORTLAND (CON) 1234 S.W. MORRISON ST., 97205.
(503) 274-1442

MS. URSULA AMANDA ROJAS WEISER,   Apr. 18, 2007
    CONSUL

MR. DAVID SIMON FIGUERAS,   Jan. 29, 2006
    DEPUTY CONSUL

MRS. ALICIA BEATRIZ BARBERENA HURTADO,   Apr. 18, 2007
    VICE CONSUL

PENNSYLVANIA

PHILADELPHIA (CON) 111 S. INDEPENDENCE MALL UN., E, SUITE
310, 19106.
(215) 922-4262

MS. MARIA DEL ROCIO VAZQUEZ ALVAREZ,   Jan. 23, 2002
    CONSUL

MISS CECILIA TREEMONISHA BARROS RUIZ,   May. 08, 2006
    CONSUL

MR. ENRIQUE RUIZ SANCHEZ,   May. 08, 2006
    CONSUL

MR. JOSE RAMON LORENZO DOMINGUEZ,   Feb. 04, 2005
    DEPUTY CONSUL

MS. BLANCA ILEANA VILLALON LOZANO,   Feb. 06, 2007
    VICE CONSUL

PUERTO RICO

SAN JUAN (CG) 654 AVENIDA MUNOZ RIVERA UN., SUITE 1837,
00918.
(809) 764-0258

MR. ROBERTO RODRIGUEZ HERNANDEZ,   Dec. 20, 2004
    CONSUL GENERAL

MR. JOSE ANTONIO AGUAYO VAZQUEZ,   Jul. 29, 2005
    DEPUTY CONSUL GENERAL

TEXAS

AUSTIN (CG) 800 BRAZOS ST., SUITE 330, 78701.
(512) 478-2803

MRS. ROSALBA OJEDA,   May. 22, 2007
    CONSUL GENERAL

MR. HUGO RENE OLIVA,   Jul. 26, 2006
    DEPUTY CONSUL GENERAL

MRS. ANGELES GOMEZ,   Nov. 19, 1999
    CONSUL

BROWNSVILLE (CON) 301 MEXICO BL., SUITE F-3, 78520.
(512) 542-4431

MR. MARCO ANTONIO CERRITOS MORENO,   Nov. 06, 2002
    CONSUL

MR. VICTOR MANUEL TREVINO ESCUDERO,   Nov. 02, 2005
    CONSUL

MR. LUIS CHAO PRATT,   Jul. 19, 2006
    CONSUL

MR. HECTOR JOSE AGUILAR MEZA,   Aug. 07, 2002
    DEPUTY CONSUL

CORPUS CHRISTI (CON) 800 SHORELINE BL., SUITE 410, 78401.

DALLAS (CG) 8855 N. STEMMONS FREEWAY ., 75247.
(214) 522-9740

MR. ENRIQUE HUBBARD URREA,   Sep. 07, 2006
    CONSUL GENERAL

MR. HUGO JUAREZ CARRILLO,   Jul. 08, 2005
    DEPUTY CONSUL GENERAL

MS. ANA VIRGINIA HERNANDEZ CARDENAS,   Jan. 07, 2003
    CONSUL

MS. CLAUDIA VELASCO OSORIO,   Dec. 21, 2004
    CONSUL

MR. MIGUEL EDUARDO REA FALCON,   Jan. 05, 2005
    CONSUL

---

* DEPENDENCIES SUCH AS GUAM, PUERTO RICO, AND THE VIRGIN ISLANDS ARE LISTED HERE.
CG-CONSULATE GENERAL   C-CONSULATE   VC-VICE CONSULATE   CA-CONSULAR AGENCY   H-HONORARY CONSULAR STATUS

STATE* RESIDENCE	NAME AND RANK	DATE OF RECOGNITION	STATE* RESIDENCE	NAME AND RANK	DATE OF RECOGNITION

MR. ADOLFO AYUSO AUDREY,
  CONSUL — May. 08, 2006

OFFICE OF THE COMMERCIAL COUNSELOR/TRADE COMMISSION
DALLAS (CONA) 2777 STEMMONS FW., SUITE 1622, 75207.
  MS. CONCEPCION VIRGINIA ARTEAGA SANZ,
  VICE CONSUL — Jul. 31, 2003

DEL RIO (CON) 2398 SPUR 239 ., 78840.
(830) 774-5031
  MR. RICARDO ANTONIO AHUJA HERNANDEZ,
  CONSUL — Oct. 05, 2006
  MS. INES BALTAZAR GUTIERREZ,
  CONSUL — Apr. 24, 2007
  MR. FERNANDO JAVIER VALDES VICENCIO,
  DEPUTY CONSUL — Aug. 12, 2004

EAGLE PASS (CON) 2252 E. GARRISON ST., 78852.
(512) 773-9255
  MR. JORGE ERNESTO ESPEJEL MONTES,
  CONSUL — May. 25, 2000
  MR. GERARD0 SERRANO GASCA,
  CONSUL — Apr. 24, 2007
  MR. JAIME JIMENEZ MORENO,
  DEPUTY CONSUL — Feb. 23, 2006

EL PASO (CG) 910 E. SAN ANTONIO AV., 79901.
(915) 533-3644
  MR. VICENTE COLMENARES SUMANO,
  CONSUL — Oct. 21, 2002
  MR. JOSE H. LOPEZ PORTILLO SANCHEZ,
  CONSUL — Apr. 23, 2007
  MS. GISELE FERNANDEZ LUDLOW,
  CONSUL — Apr. 24, 2007
  MRS. VIRGINIA S. ALVARADO MARCOS,
  CONSUL — Jul. 20, 2007
  MR. GUILLERMO REYES,
  DEPUTY CONSUL — Apr. 23, 2007
  MR. HECTOR AGUSTIN ORTEGA NIETO,
  VICE CONSUL — May. 17, 2006

HOUSTON (CG) 4507 SAN JACINTO ST., 77004.
(713) 271-6800, FAX (713) 271-3201
  MR. CARLOS I. GONZALEZ MAGALLON,
  CONSUL GENERAL — Jun. 14, 2005
  MS. CAROLINA ZARAGOZA FLORES,
  DEPUTY CONSUL GENERAL — Jul. 28, 2005
  MR. ARMANDO CAMARENA ARANDA,
  CONSUL — Apr. 09, 2001
  MR. JOSE LUIS AVILA SAAVEDRA,
  CONSUL — Sep. 17, 2002
  MR. CARLOS GARCIA DELGADO,
  CONSUL — Oct. 09, 2002
  MR. JOSE V. BORJON LOPEZ COTERILLA,
  CONSUL — Nov. 12, 2004
  MR. ROBERTO CANSECO MARTINEZ,
  CONSUL — Feb. 23, 2006
  MR. ARTURO BALDERAS RODRIGUEZ,
  CONSUL — Mar. 01, 2006
  MA ALFONSO SUMANO LAZCANO,
  CONSUL — Oct. 06, 2006
  MR. ROBERTO CAMPOS PADILLA,
  CONSUL — Feb. 01, 2007

MRS. MARIA DOLORES CABRERA PARKINSON,
  CONSUL — May. 31, 2007
MR. JOSE LUIS DIAZ MIRON HINOJOSA,
  VICE CONSUL — Apr. 24, 2007
MS. SILVANA GENOVEVA SANCHEZ LIRA,
  VICE CONSUL — May. 31, 2007

TRADE OFFICE OF MEXICO
HOUSTON (CONA) 5065 WESTHEIMER RD., SUITE 707, 77056.
(713) 965-0767

LAREDO (CG) 1612 FARRAGUT ST., 78040.
(512) 723-6369
  MR. RENE DAVID MEJIA QUINTANA,
  DEPUTY CONSUL GENERAL — Oct. 03, 2000
  MR. JAVIER ABUD OSUNA,
  DEPUTY CONSUL — Dec. 14, 2005
  MR. ALEJANDRO LOPEZ BAGO VILLARREAL,
  VICE CONSUL — Apr. 10, 2006

MCALLEN (CON) 600 S. BROADWAY ST., 78501.
(512) 686-0243
  MR. LUIS MANUEL LOPEZ MORENO,
  CONSUL — Jun. 13, 2001
  MR. ALEJANDRO SOUSA,
  CONSUL — May. 08, 2006
  MISS MIRIAM GABRIELA MEDEL GARCIA,
  CONSUL — Apr. 24, 2007
  MRS. SANDRA PATRICIA MENDOZA DURAN,
  VICE CONSUL — May. 08, 2006
  MR. ISRAEL CONSTANTINO LARA,
  VICE CONSUL — Apr. 24, 2007

MIDLAND (CON) 511 W. OHIO ST., SUITE 121, 79701.

CONSULATE
PRESIDIO (CON) 67 17 KELLEY ADDITION 1 HW., 79845.
(915) 229-2788, FAX (915) 229-2792
  MR. HECTOR RAUL ACOSTA FLORES,
  CONSUL — Apr. 19, 2007
  MR. ROBERTO RUELAS ANGELES,
  DEPUTY CONSUL — May. 08, 2006
  MR. FRANCISCO JAVIER JACOBI DURAN,
  VICE CONSUL — Apr. 16, 2003
  MR. CARLOS VLADIMIR RUBIO NOGUEROLA,
  VICE CONSUL — Jul. 26, 2006

SAN ANTONIO (CG) 127 NAVARRO ST., 78205.
(512) 227-9145
  MRS. MARTHA IRENE LARA,
  CONSUL GENERAL — Mar. 09, 2004
  MR. YURI SERGIO CAMARILLO MARTINEZ,
  CONSUL — Nov. 14, 2000
  MR. LUIS GABRIEL FERRER ORTEGA,
  CONSUL — Jul. 26, 2006
  MR. EVERARDO CORONA AGUILAR,
  CONSUL — Apr. 23, 2007
  MRS. LISELOTT REYES RUIZ,
  CONSULAR AGENT — Feb. 23, 2006

MEXICAN CULTURAL INSTITUTE OF MEXICO
SAN ANTONIO (CONA) 600 HEMIS FAIR PZ., 78205.

STATE* RESIDENCE	NAME AND RANK	DATE OF RECOGNITION	STATE* RESIDENCE	NAME AND RANK	DATE OF RECOGNITION

MISS GABRIELA FRANCO,   May. 15, 2007
   CONSUL

COMMERCIAL AFFAIRS OFFICE
SAN ANTONIO (CONA) 203 S. SAINT MARY'S ST., SUITE 450, 78213.

OFFICE OF MEXICAN ATTORNEY GENERAL
SAN ANTONIO (CONA) 613 N.W. LOOP 410 UN., SUITE 610, 78216.
(210) 344-1131
   MR. FERNANDO MORONES GONZALEZ,   Jun. 24, 2003
     CONSUL
   MR. CARLOS AGUSTO LAZOS CHAVEZ,   Oct. 06, 2003
     CONSUL
   MR. MANUEL EFREN CAMPOS ARMENDARIZ,   Oct. 06, 2003
     CONSUL
   MS. YURIKO LUISA GARCES,   Apr. 24, 2007
     CONSUL

UTAH

SALT LAKE CITY (CON) 155 S. 300 UN., W, FLOOR 3RD, 84101.
(801) 521-8502, FAX (801) 521-0534
   MR. SALVADOR JIMENEZ MUNOZ,   Mar. 07, 2005
     CONSUL
   MR. MANUEL JOSE MORODO FERNANDEZ,   Mar. 08, 2007
     CONSUL
   MR. EUSEBIO AUGUSTO ROMERO ESQUIVEL,   Feb. 23, 2006
     DEPUTY CONSUL

VIRGINIA

RICHMOND (HC) 2420 PEMBERTON RD., 23233.
(804) 747-9200
   MR. WALTER W. REGIRER,   Jan. 14, 1975
     HONORARY CONSUL

WASHINGTON

SEATTLE (CON) 2132 THIRD AV., 98121.
   MRS. M. DEL CARMEN CASTANEDA DE YUDIN,   May. 19, 2005
     CONSUL
   MR. SALVADOR TINAJERO ESQUIVEL,   May. 05, 2006
     CONSUL
   MS. VALERIA VALENTINA RODRIGUEZ MORA,   Apr. 18, 2007
     CONSUL
   MR. ROBERTO ASCENCION CALDERA ARROYO,   Aug. 30, 2000
     DEPUTY CONSUL

WISCONSIN

MADISON (HC) 141 NORTH HANCOCK ST., 53703.
(608) 283-6000
   DR. RUDOLPH CARO HECHT,   May. 30, 1974
     HONORARY CONSUL

MICRONESIA

GUAM

TAMUNING (CG) 590 S. MARINE DR., 96911.
(671) 646-9154, FAX (671) 649-6320
   MR. SAMSON E. PRETRICK,   Mar. 24, 2000
     CONSUL GENERAL

HAWAII

HONOLULU (CG) 3049 UALENA ST., SUITE 910, 96819.
(808) 836-4775, FAX (808) 836-6869
   MR. TADAO P. SIGRAH,   Mar. 04, 2005
     CONSUL GENERAL

MOLDOVA

DISTRICT OF COLUMBIA

WASHINGTON (CHN) 2101 S ST., NW, 20008.
(202) 667-1130, FAX (202) 667-1204
   MR. RADU CUCOS,   Oct. 14, 2004
     CONSUL

NEW YORK

NEW YORK (HC) 405 PARK AV., 10022.
(212) 888-6680
   MR. STEVEN A. SANDERS,   Oct. 30, 2001
     HONORARY CONSUL

NORTH CAROLINA

HICKORY (HC) 1117 2ND ST., 28601.
(828) 312-8980, FAX (828) 396-5579
   MR. FLORIN PINDIC BLAJ,   Apr. 03, 1998
     HONORARY CONSUL

PENNSYLVANIA

PHILADELPHIA (HC) 245 N. 15TH ST., 19102-1192.
(215) 762-4401
   MR. RICHARD ASTRO,   Mar. 14, 2000
     HONORARY CONSUL

VIRGINIA

NORFOLK (HC) 6350 CENTER DR., SUITE 112, 23502.
(757) 466-8899, FAX (757) 466-9481
   MR. ANTON SAMOILA,   Apr. 09, 1999
     HONORARY CONSUL

MONACO

CALIFORNIA

LOS ANGELES (HC) 100 UNIVERSAL CITY PZ., 2252, UNIVERSAL
CITY 91608.
(818) 777-3131, FAX (818) 866-1446
   MR. RICHARD A. WOLF,   Jan. 08, 1999
     HONORARY CONSUL

SAN FRANCISCO (HCG) 2643 UNION ST., 94123.
(415) 346-7766, FAX (415) 771-4842
   MRS. PAULA SULLIVAN ESCHER,   Nov. 12, 1992
     HONORARY CONSUL GENERAL

FLORIDA

MIAMI (HC) 3655 N.W. 87TH AV., FLOOR 6TH, 33178.
(305) 406-4688
   MR. ROBERT H. DICKINSON,   Jan. 08, 1999
     HONORARY CONSUL

STATE* RESIDENCE	NAME AND RANK	DATE OF RECOGNITION	STATE* RESIDENCE	NAME AND RANK	DATE OF RECOGNITION

ILLINOIS

CHICAGO (HC) 2337 N. COMMONWEALTH UN., APT 1E, 60614.
(773) 871-9059
   MR. ALBERT ANGE MANZONE,   Mar. 13, 2006
      HONORARY CONSUL

MASSACHUSETTS

BOSTON (HC) 200 SEAPORT BL., SUITE 50, 02210.
(617) 385-5360
   MR. JOHN E. DREW,   Jan. 16, 2003
      HONORARY CONSUL

NEW YORK

NEW YORK (CG) 565 5TH AV., FLOOR 23RD, 10017.
(212) 286-0500, FAX (212) 286-1574
   MRS. MAGUY J. DOYLE,   Jul. 23, 1997
      CONSUL GENERAL

TEXAS

DALLAS (HC) 8350 N. CENTRAL EXPRESSWAY UN., SUITE 1900, 75206.
(214) 234-4124
   MR. JOHN F. , III DAVIS,   May. 27, 2003
      HONORARY CONSUL

MONGOLIA

CALIFORNIA

CANOGA PARK (HC) 21601 VANOWEN ST., SUITE 201, 91303.
(818) 581-1667
   MRS. GRACE M. ROBERTS,   May. 30, 2006
      HONORARY CONSUL

SAN FRANCISCO (HCG) 909 MONTGOMERY ST., SUITE 400, 94133.
(415) 434-1111
   MR. RICHARD C. BLUM,   Jun. 28, 2001
      HONORARY CONSUL GENERAL

COLORADO

DENVER (HC) 1700 BROADWAY ., SUITE 1202, 80290-1201.
(303) 832-6511
   MR. JAMES FREDERICK WAGENLANDER,   Dec. 29, 1998
      HONORARY CONSUL

DISTRICT OF COLUMBIA

WASHINGTON (CHN) 2833 M ST., NW, 20007.
(202) 333-7117, FAX (202) 298-9227
   MR. GANBOLD GONCHIG,   Sep. 29, 2006
      CONSUL GENERAL

GEORGIA

ATLANTA (HC) 781 MARIETTA ST., 30318.
(404) 894-9451
   MR. JOHN EDGAR ENDICOTT,   Aug. 04, 2005
      HONORARY CONSUL

ILLINOIS

CHICAGO (HC) 4701 W. RICE ST., 60651.
(773) 626-8800, FAX (773) 626-1430
   MR. G. MICHAEL KENNY,   Feb. 07, 2005
      HONORARY CONSUL

MONTANA

BOZEMAN (HC) 108 S. BOZEMAN ST., 59715.
(406) 587-0125
   MR. KENT MADIN,   Mar. 26, 2007
      HONORARY CONSUL

NEW JERSEY

PLAINFIELD (HC) 805 SOUTH AV., 07062.
(908) 754-0355
   MR. CARMEN CABELL,   Jul. 29, 2005
      HONORARY CONSUL

NEW YORK

NEW YORK (CG) 6 E. 77TH ST., 10021.
   MR. JAGIR SUHEE,   Feb. 06, 1995
      CONSULAR AGENT

TEXAS

HOUSTON (HCA) 1221 LAMAR ., SUITE 1201, 77010.
(713) 759-1922
   MR. EDWARD T., JR STORY,   Jan. 06, 1997
      HONORARY CONSULAR AGENT

UTAH

SPRINGVILLE (HC) 1063 S.1650 UN., E, 84663.
(801) 489-8899
   MR. MALAN R. JACKSON,   Aug. 13, 2003
      HONORARY CONSUL

MONTENEGRO

NEW YORK

NEW YORK (CG) 801 SECOND AV., SUITE 7TH, 10017.
, FAX (212) 661-5466
   MR. BRANKO MILIC,   Jun. 19, 2007
      CONSUL GENERAL
   MR. DRAGAN SEKULOVIC,   Jun. 19, 2007
      CONSUL

MOROCCO

CALIFORNIA

LOS ANGELES (HC) 521 N. DAROCA ., 91775.
(818) 570-0318
   MR. ABDELHAK SAOUD,   Jul. 14, 1982
      HONORARY CONSUL

HAWAII

HONOLULU (HC) 796 ISENBERG ST., SUITE 19E, 96826.
(808) 383-2597
   MR. MOHAMMED JAN RUMI,   Jan. 28, 2005
      HONORARY CONSUL

STATE* RESIDENCE	NAME AND RANK	DATE OF RECOGNITION	STATE* RESIDENCE	NAME AND RANK	DATE OF RECOGNITION

KANSAS

KANSAS CITY (HC) 10777 BARKLEY UN., SUITE 200, OVERLAND
PARK 66211.
(913) 649-8021

    MR. HARRY MCLEAR,   Mar. 13, 1987
       HONORARY CONSUL

MASSACHUSETTS

CAMBRIDGE (HCG) 124 MT. AUBURN ST., SUITE 200, 02138.
(617) 495-6325

    MR. JOHN ANTHONY QUELCH,   May. 04, 2004
       HONORARY CONSUL GENERAL

NEW YORK

NEW YORK (CG) 10 E. 40TH ST., FLOOR 23RD, 10016.
(212) 758-2625

    MR. ABDERRAHIM BEYYOUDH,   Oct. 01, 2002
       DEPUTY CONSUL GENERAL
    MR. ABDELOUAHAB EL BOUHALI,   Oct. 12, 1977
       VICE CONSUL
    MR. MUSTAPHA EL ACHRAOUI,   May. 11, 1992
       VICE CONSUL
    MR. TALAL JENNANE,   Oct. 05, 2005
       VICE CONSUL
    MR. BENAISSA ROUIZEM,   May. 23, 2006
       VICE CONSUL

NAMIBIA

FLORIDA

ORLANDO (HCG) 200 S. ORANGE AV., SUITE 2600, 32801.
(407) 244-1112

    MR. STEPHEN WAYNE SNIVELY,   Jul. 25, 2007
       HONORARY CONSUL GENERAL

MICHIGAN

DETROIT (HC) 163 MADISON AV., SUITE 2000, 48226.
(313) 496-2900, FAX (313) 259-0154

    MR. DON H. BARDEN,   Dec. 02, 1996
       HONORARY CONSUL

TEXAS

HOUSTON (HC) 1330 POST OAK BL., SUITE 2200, 77056.
(713) 965-5119

    MR. JEAN MICHEL MALEK,   Apr. 25, 2007
       HONORARY CONSUL

NAURU

GUAM

AGANA (CON) MARINE DR., FLOOR 1ST, 96910.
    MR. MANFRED R. DEPAUNE,   Jun. 24, 1981
       CONSUL
    MR. KELLY D. EMIU,   May. 16, 1983
       CONSUL

HAWAII

HONOLULU (HC) 841 BISHOP ST., SUITE 506, 96813.
(808) 523-7821

    MR. ALFRED HINDMARSH STEPHEN,   May. 15, 1972
       HONORARY CONSUL
    MS. VALCINO H. BECKETT,   Mar. 30, 1981
       HONORARY CONSUL

TRUST TERRITORIES OF THE PACIFIC ISLANDS

PAGO PAGO (HC) X ., PAGO PAGO, AM. SAMOA 96799.
    MR. PETER TALI COLEMAN,   Dec. 02, 1985
       HONORARY CONSUL

NEPAL

CALIFORNIA

LOS ANGELES (HCG) 14920 ALVA DR., PACIFIC PALISADES 90272.
(310) 319-9559

    MR. GEORGE MARK PAPPAS,   Sep. 21, 1992
       HONORARY CONSUL GENERAL

SAN FRANCISCO (HCG) 909 MONTGOMERY ST., SUITE 400, 94133.
(415) 434-1111

    MR. RICHARD C. BLUM,   Aug. 02, 1983
       HONORARY CONSUL GENERAL

ILLINOIS

CHICAGO (HCG) 100 W. MONROE ST., SUITE 500, 60603.
(312) 263-1250, FAX (312) 263-3480

    MR. MARVIN A. BRUSTIN,   Mar. 10, 2004
       HONORARY CONSUL GENERAL

MASSACHUSETTS

BOSTON (HCG) 151 TREMONT ST., APT 21L, 02111.
(617) 948-9449

    MR. ROBERT C. SAGER,   May. 06, 2003
       HONORARY CONSUL GENERAL

NEW YORK

NEW YORK (CG) 820 2ND AV., SUITE 17B, 10017.
(212) 370-4188

NETHERLANDS

ARIZONA

PHOENIX (HC) 8149 N. 87TH PL., SCOTTSDALE 85258.
(480) 563-0092, FAX (602) 224-0620

    MR. SIEBE K. J. VAN DER ZEE,   May. 26, 1992
       HONORARY CONSUL

CALIFORNIA

LOS ANGELES (CG) 11766 WILSHIRE BL., SUITE 1150, 90025.
(310) 268-1598, FAX (310) 312-0989

    MRS. MAGDALINA ANNA JACOBA DE PLANQUE,   Oct. 17, 2005
       CONSUL GENERAL
    MR. LEENDERT JOHANNES VAN DEN DOOL,   Oct. 01, 2003
       DEPUTY CONSUL GENERAL
    MR. MAURITS WILLEM BELTGENS,   Oct. 11, 2006
       CONSUL
    MR. EDUARD MARCEL VAN DOORN,   Jan. 26, 2007
       VICE CONSUL

STATE* RESIDENCE	NAME AND RANK	DATE OF RECOGNITION

SAN FRANCISCO (HC) 901 MARINER'S ISLAND BL., SUITE 535, SAN MATEO 94404.
(650) 403-0073, FAX (415) 399-1249
- MR. DOUGLAS JOE ENGMANN, HONORARY CONSUL — Oct. 19, 2004
- MR. JOHAN P. SNAPPER, HONORARY VICE CONSUL — Jun. 29, 1993

COLORADO

DENVER (HC) 1625 BROADWAY UN., SUITE 680, 80202.
(303) 592-5362
- PROFESSOR MAXIMILIAAN PEETERS, HONORARY CONSUL — Oct. 14, 2005

DISTRICT OF COLUMBIA

WASHINGTON (CHN) 4200 LINNEAN AV., NW, 20008.
(202) 244-5300, FAX (202) 362-3430
- MR. HENDRIKUS GEBUIS, CONSUL — Sep. 12, 2003
- MRS. TERESA LOUISE VERBURG, VICE CONSUL — Sep. 07, 2005

FLORIDA

JACKSONVILLE (HC) 644 CESERY BL., SUITE 200, 32211.
(904) 744-0275, FAX (904) 744-3547
- MR. JEFFREY ROBERT LANDA, HONORARY CONSUL — Apr. 21, 1998

MIAMI (CG) 701 BRICKELL AV., FLOOR 5TH, 33131.
(786) 866-0480, FAX (786) 866-0498
- MRS. LUCITA C. G. N. MOENIRALAM, CONSUL GENERAL — Oct. 04, 2005
- MR. XAVIER CARLOS A. PRENS, CONSUL — Mar. 07, 2006
- MR. AREND CORNELIS GOUW, CONSUL — Feb. 08, 2007
- MS. JEANNETTE G. NIEUWENHUIJS, VICE CONSUL — Oct. 31, 2003

GEORGIA

ATLANTA (HC) 270 CARPENTER DR., SUITE 540, 30328.
(404) 943-0061
- MR. EWOUD NORBERT SWAAK, HONORARY CONSUL — Feb. 09, 2006

HAWAII

HONOLULU (HC) 700 BISHOP ST., SUITE 2100, 96813.
(808) 531-6897
- MR. GAYLORD G. TOM, HONORARY CONSUL — May. 02, 1991

ILLINOIS

CHICAGO (CG) 303 E. WACKER DR., SUITE 2600, 60601.
(312) 856-0110, FAX (312) 856-9218
- MR. DIRK WILLEM SCHIFF, CONSUL GENERAL — Oct. 05, 2005
- MR. CORNELIS WILHELMUS HERSBACH, CONSUL — Oct. 03, 2003

- MR. PETRUS JOHANNES VAN KLEEF, CONSUL — Apr. 06, 2007
- MRS. ELISABETH MARIA SMITS-WILMER, VICE CONSUL — Mar. 28, 2006

LOUISIANA

NEW ORLEANS (HC) 643 MAGAZINE ST., 70130.
(504) 596-2838
- MRS. CONSTANCE CHARLES WILLEMS, HONORARY CONSUL — Jul. 25, 1989

MASSACHUSETTS

BOSTON (CON) 20 PARK PZ., SUITE 524, 02116-4399.
(617) 542-8452, FAX (617) 542-3304
- MR. MARCO SMIT, CONSUL — Jun. 28, 2005

BOSTON (HC) 6 ST. JAMES AV., 02116-3800.
(617) 451-2330
- MR. HENRY PIETER MARCUS PAAP, HONORARY CONSUL — Jan. 16, 1998

MICHIGAN

DETROIT (HC) 535 GRISWOLD UN., SUITE 2400, 48226.
(313) 983-4999, FAX (313) 983-4350
- MR. JOHANNES H. J. PIJLS, HONORARY CONSUL — Apr. 27, 2000

GRAND RAPIDS (HC) 3250 28TH ST., SE, 49512.
(616) 285-9998
- MR. HENRY I. WITTE, HONORARY CONSUL — Jan. 11, 1991

MINNESOTA

MINNEAPOLIS (HC) 80 S. 8TH ST., SUITE 4200, 55402--2205.
(612) 371-5790
- MR. MARC ANDRE AL, HONORARY CONSUL — Sep. 11, 2003

MISSOURI

KANSAS CITY (HC) 5818 MANOR LA., PARKVILLE 64152-6063.
(816) 741-1152, FAX (816) 741-1152
- MR. ROBERT GODDIJN, HONORARY CONSUL — Sep. 03, 1996

SAINT LOUIS (HC) 562 N. WOODLAWN ., ST. LOUIS 63122.
(314) 965-3533
- MR. RICHARD WILLIAM LODGE, HONORARY CONSUL — Sep. 03, 1987

NEW YORK

NEW YORK (CG) 1 ROCKEFELLER PLAZA UN., FLOOR 11TH, 10020.
(212) 246-1429
- MRS. GABRIELLA SANCISI, CONSUL — Jul. 31, 2003
- MR. ALFRED WILLEM BELTGENS, CONSUL — Oct. 19, 2006

---

* DEPENDENCIES SUCH AS GUAM, PUERTO RICO, AND THE VIRGIN ISLANDS ARE LISTED HERE.
CG-CONSULATE GENERAL   C-CONSULATE   VC-VICE CONSULATE   CA-CONSULAR AGENCY   H-HONORARY CONSULAR STATUS

STATE* RESIDENCE	NAME AND RANK	DATE OF RECOGNITION	STATE* RESIDENCE	NAME AND RANK	DATE OF RECOGNITION

NEW ZEALAND

MR. MICHEL JEAN CHRISTIAN OOMS, CONSUL — Oct. 19, 2006

MS. JOSE ANTOINETTE AMSING, CONSUL — Jan. 25, 2007

NORTH CAROLINA

RALEIGH (HC) 5504 COMMERCIAL AV., SUITE 110, 27612.
(919) 645-1100, FAX (919) 719-2087

MR. GERARD TER WEE, HONORARY CONSUL — Aug. 14, 2001

OHIO

CLEVELAND (HC) 3200 NATIONAL CITY CENTER ., 44114-3485.
(440) 324-4164, FAX (440) 365-8326

MR. CHARLES A. DE LA PORTE, HONORARY CONSUL — Mar. 19, 1997

OREGON

PORTLAND (HC) 520 S.W. YAMHILL ., SUITE 600, 97204.
(503) 222-3531

MR. TED E. RUNSTEIN, HONORARY CONSUL — Feb. 10, 1997

PENNSYLVANIA

PHILADELPHIA (HC) 1030 E. LANCASTER AV., SUITE 1007, BRYN MAWR 19010.
(610) 520-9591, FAX (610) 520-1614

PUERTO RICO

RIO PIEDRAS (HC) 4 EXTENCION VILLA MAR EO 122 ., CAROLINA 00979.
(787) 726-7356, FAX (787) 759-9400

MR. FRANK F. HAACKE, HONORARY CONSUL — Feb. 16, 1989

TEXAS

HOUSTON (HC) 2200 POST OAK BL., SUITE 610, 77056.
(713) 622-8000

MR. GEERT CORNELIS VISSER, HONORARY CONSUL — Dec. 24, 2003

TRUST TERRITORIES OF THE PACIFIC ISLANDS

MANILA, PHILIPPINES (CG) 2129 PASONG TAMO, , KINGS CT., FLOOR 9TH, -.

UTAH

SALT LAKE CITY (HC) 230 WEST 700 SOUTH ., 84101.
(801) 364-1981, FAX (801) 355-2119

MR. LE GRANDE STEENBLIK, HONORARY CONSUL — Apr. 24, 1992

WASHINGTON

BELLEVUE (HC) 40 LAKE BELLEVUE DR., SUITE 100, 98005.
(425) 637-3050

MR. PETER PAUL HAGEMAN, HONORARY CONSUL — Mar. 13, 2006

CALIFORNIA

SACRAMENTO (HC) 44733 N. EL MACERO DR., EL MACERO 95618.
(530) 756-7016

DR. EDWARD J. HURLEY, HONORARY CONSUL — Sep. 14, 1998

SAN DIEGO (HC) 12555 HIGH BLUFF DR., SUITE 175, 92130.
(619) 677-1485, FAX (619) 677-1477

MR. ROBERT WILLIAM AYLING, HONORARY CONSUL — Dec. 28, 1994

SAN FRANCISCO (HC) P.O. BOX 330455 ., 94133-0455.
(415) 399-1255, FAX (415) 399-9775

MR. RICHARD COLLIER SEARS, HONORARY CONSUL — May. 04, 1994

SANTA MONICA (CG) 2425 OLYMPIC BL., SUITE 600E, 90404.
(310) 566-6555, FAX (310) 566-6556

MR. ROBERT JOHN TAYLOR, CONSUL GENERAL — May. 24, 2004

MR. PETER BLINMAN BULL, CONSUL — Feb. 23, 2006

NEW ZEALAND TOURISM BOARD
SANTA MONICA (CON) 501 SANTA MONICA BL., SUITE 300, 90401.
(310) 395-7840, FAX (310) 395-5453

DISTRICT OF COLUMBIA

WASHINGTON (CHN) 37 OBSERVATORY CI., NW, 20008.
(202) 328-4800, FAX (202) 667-5227

MR. WINTON ALEXANDER HOLMES, CONSUL GENERAL — Jan. 31, 2003

GEORGIA

ATLANTA (HC) 513 SEMINOLE AV., NE, 30307.
(404) 525-2495, FAX (404) 888-5147

MR. IAN LATHAM, HONORARY CONSUL — Mar. 26, 1996

GUAM

TAMUNING (HC) 290 SALAS ST., 96931.
(671) 646-7662, FAX (671) 646-1061

MR. JOHN W. SCRAGG, HONORARY CONSUL — Apr. 13, 1992

HAWAII

HONOLULU (HC) 900 RICHARDS ST., SUITE 414, 96813.
(808) 543-7900

MR. PETER CUSHMAN LEWIS, HONORARY CONSUL — Oct. 01, 1998

ILLINOIS

CHICAGO (HC) 8600 W. BRYN MAWR AV., SUITE 500N, 60631.
(773) 714-9461, FAX (773) 714-9483

MR. EDWARD BURKHARDT, HONORARY CONSUL — Feb. 22, 1995

STATE* RESIDENCE	NAME AND RANK	DATE OF RECOGNITION	STATE* RESIDENCE	NAME AND RANK	DATE OF RECOGNITION

NEW HAMPSHIRE

BOSTON (HC) 16 CENTRE ST., CONCORD 03301.
(603) 227-9935, FAX (603) 227-9935
   MR. SIMON CHARLES LEEMING, — Jan. 08, 2001
      HONORARY CONSUL

NEW YORK

NEW YORK (CG) 222 E. 41 ST., SUITE 2510, 10017.
(212) 832-4038, FAX (212) 832-7602
   MR. CHRISTOPHER TOZER, — Feb. 15, 2007
      CONSUL

TEXAS

HOUSTON (HC) 246 WARRENTON DR., 77024.
(713) 973-8680, FAX (713) 973-6679
   MRS. KATHLEEN D. KELLY, — Dec. 28, 1994
      HONORARY CONSUL

TRUST TERRITORIES OF THE PACIFIC ISLANDS

PAGO PAGO (CG) BEACH ROAD ., APIA, WESTERN SAMOA 00000.
   MR. JOHN STEWART ADANK, — Nov. 30, 2004
      CONSUL GENERAL

UTAH

SALT LAKE CITY (HC) 1379 NORTH BROOKHURST CI., CENTERVILLE
 84014.
(801) 296-2494, FAX (801) 296-1523
   MR. IAIN B. MCKAY, — May. 12, 1994
      HONORARY CONSUL

WASHINGTON

SEATTLE (HC) 10649 NORTH BEACH RD., BOW 98232.
(206) 624-8300
   MS. DELLA NEWMAN, — Aug. 08, 2000
      HONORARY CONSUL

NICARAGUA

CALIFORNIA

LOS ANGELES (CG) 3550 WILSHIRE BL., SUITE 200, 90010.
(213) 252-1170
   MRS. ADILIA SOMOZA ROMERO, — Jun. 14, 2004
      CONSULAR AGENT
   MS. MINA NELSON, — Oct. 01, 1991
      HONORARY CONSUL

SAN FRANCISCO (CG) 870 MARKET ST., SUITE 514-520, 94102.
(415) 765-6821

COLORADO

DENVER (HC) 1133 RACE ST., SUITE 17N, 80206.
(303) 320-0317
   DR. J. BRONWYN BATEMAN, — Sep. 13, 2006
      HONORARY CONSUL

DISTRICT OF COLUMBIA

WASHINGTON (CHN) 1627 NEW HAMPSHIRE AV., NW, 20009.
(202) 939-6570, FAX (202) 939-6545

FLORIDA

MIAMI (CG) 8532 S.W. 8TH ST., SUITE 270, 33144.
(305) 220-6900
   MR. LUIS ALBERTO MARTINEZ, — May. 18, 2007
      CONSUL GENERAL
   MR. RAFAEL ANGEL UBILLA SUAZO, — Jun. 29, 2004
      CONSUL

GEORGIA

ATLANTA (HC) 3161 LEMONS RIDGE DR., 30339.
(770) 319-1673
   MR. J. THOMAS, JR RATCHFORD, — Jan. 05, 1999
      HONORARY CONSUL

LOUISIANA

METAIRIE (HC) 4820 BURKE DR., 70003.
(504) 887-6498
   MR. CARLOS ALBERTO , JR SAMPSON, — Feb. 26, 2004
      HONORARY CONSUL

MASSACHUSETTS

SPRINGFIELD (HC) 52 MULBERRY ST., 01105.
(413) 781-5400
   DR. SHERMAN E. FEIN, — Apr. 18, 2000
      HONORARY CONSUL

NEW YORK

NEW YORK (CG) 820 SECOND AV., SUITE 802, 10017.
(212) 344-4491
   MR. CESAR MERCADO P., — Jun. 20, 2003
      CONSUL
   MRS. MARIA ROGELIA URCUYO DE ZARRUK, — Dec. 14, 2004
      HONORARY CONSUL GENERAL

NORTH CAROLINA

CHARLOTTE (HC) 5205 MONROE RD., SUITE C, 28205.
(704) 537-1230, FAX (704) 537-1326
   MR. GILBERTO BERGMAN, — Apr. 02, 2003
      HONORARY CONSUL

OKLAHOMA

TULSA (HC) 3233 E. 31ST ST., SUITE 103, 74105.
(918) 742-5617
   DR. JULIO C. CUADRA, — Aug. 13, 2003
      HONORARY CONSUL

PENNSYLVANIA

PHILADELPHIA (HC) 627 W. ERIE AV., 19140.
(215) 427-2570
   MS. MARTINA D. RUIZ BALLESTEROS, — May. 24, 2006
      HONORARY CONSUL

PITTSBURGH (HC) MOBAY RD., 15205.
(412) 777-2000
   DR. RICHARD L. WHITE, — Mar. 11, 1992
      HONORARY CONSUL

STATE* RESIDENCE	NAME AND RANK	DATE OF RECOGNITION	STATE* RESIDENCE	NAME AND RANK	DATE OF RECOGNITION

PUERTO RICO

SAN JUAN (HCG) B1 PALMA SOLA BL., GUAYNABO 00966.
(787) 781-6513, FAX (787) 781-6530

MRS. EVA LUZ GARCIA DE PICO, Mar. 23, 2001
HONORARY CONSUL GENERAL

TEXAS

HOUSTON (CG) 8989 WESTHEIMER RD., SUITE 103, 77063.
(713) 789-2762, FAX (713) 789-3164

MR. MICHAEL JOHN CORDUA, Jun. 08, 2005
HONORARY CONSUL

NIGERIA

GEORGIA

ATLANTA (CG) 8060 ROSWELL RD., 30350.
(770) 394-6261

MR. CHUDI OKAFOR, Apr. 06, 2007
CONSUL GENERAL
MR. HAKEEM DOSUNMU, Nov. 26, 2002
CONSUL
MS. JADESOLA ADEJUMOKE ADESUYI, Jun. 24, 2003
CONSUL
MR. RABIU SHEHU, Apr. 16, 2004
CONSUL
MR. MICHAEL OYEDOKUN FAGBOHUN, May. 08, 2007
CONSUL
MR. MARTINS NYONG COBHAM, Jun. 06, 2007
CONSUL
MRS. HELEN INYANG ORU, May. 13, 2002
VICE CONSUL

NEW YORK

NEW YORK (CG) 828 SECOND AV., 10017.
(212) 808-0301

MR. IBRAHIM AUWALU, Apr. 30, 2007
CONSUL GENERAL
MR. EMMANUEL NYEVSUWE AGBEGIR, May. 28, 1997
CONSUL
MR. NURA SULEIMAN ISHAK, Dec. 10, 1999
CONSUL
MR. OBASE BICHENE OKONGOR, May. 09, 2001
CONSUL
MS. VIVIAN N. R. OKEKE, Apr. 08, 2002
CONSUL
MRS. MARY MARGARET HEZEKIAH OKAA, Jun. 11, 2002
CONSUL
MR. OLUSOLA ADEGBITE FAMOYIN, Jul. 12, 2002
CONSUL
MR. NWABUEZE MONK AJANWACHUKU, Jun. 30, 2003
CONSUL
MR. EDWIN ENOSAKHARE EDOBOR, Mar. 03, 2004
CONSUL
MR. SAFIU OLUKAYODE OLANIYAN, Apr. 26, 2007
CONSUL
MR. ABDULLAHI TUKUR, May. 08, 2007
CONSUL
MR. NURA ABBA RIMI, Jun. 12, 2007
CONSUL
MRS. AUGUSTINA OBIAGELI OKONKWO, Jun. 24, 2003
VICE CONSUL

MS. MERCY IJOHO, Feb. 12, 2004
VICE CONSUL

NORWAY

ALABAMA

MOBILE (HC) 6204 BRANDY RUN RD., N, 36608.
(251) 342-2151, FAX (251) 342-2151

MR. LESLIE HAROLD, JR STUART, Aug. 24, 1984
HONORARY CONSUL

ALASKA

ANCHORAGE (HC) 203 W. 15TH AV., SUITE 105C, 99501.
(907) 563-6350

MR. ERLING TRYGVE JOHANSEN, May. 02, 2007
HONORARY CONSUL

ARIZONA

GLENDALE (HC) 4701 W. THUNDERBIRD RD., 85306.
(602) 543-6256

DR. GEORGE ARTHUR OLANDER, Oct. 14, 2005
HONORARY CONSUL

CALIFORNIA

LOS ANGELES (HCG) 468 N. CAMDEN DR., SUITE 200, BEVERLY HILLS 90210.
(310) 788-0858

MR. RICHARD ISAAC FINE, Dec. 14, 1995
HONORARY CONSUL GENERAL
MR. DAGFINN GUNNARSHAUG, Jul. 25, 2001
HONORARY VICE CONSUL

SAN DIEGO (HC) 4491 OSPREY ST., 92107.
(619) 523-5300

MR. GORDON DAVID KOVTUN, Dec. 12, 2003
HONORARY CONSUL

SAN FRANCISCO (CG) 20 CALIFORNIA ST., FLOOR 6TH, 94111.
(415) 986-0766

MR. ARE JOSTEIN NORHEIM, Sep. 29, 2003
CONSUL GENERAL
MRS. HEGE HAALAND, Dec. 15, 2005
CONSUL
MR. SVEIN EGIL NIELSEN, Mar. 19, 2007
CONSUL
MRS. KJELLAUG MYHRE, Apr. 26, 2007
CONSUL
MRS. INGER KRISTINE WIK, Dec. 01, 2006
VICE CONSUL

COLORADO

DENVER (HC) 1775 SHERMAN ST., SUITE 1445, 80203.
(303) 830-1970, FAX (303) 321-8106

MS. RITA I. EHRMAN, Jan. 22, 1990
HONORARY CONSUL

DISTRICT OF COLUMBIA

WASHINGTON (CHN) 2720 34TH ST., NW, 20008.
(202) 333-6000, FAX (202) 337-0870

STATE* RESIDENCE	NAME AND RANK	DATE OF RECOGNITION

MISS MAIJA KRISTINE GRAHAM SMESTAD,   Aug. 17, 2006
    VICE CONSUL

FLORIDA

JACKSONVILLE (HC) 50 N. LAURA ST., SUITE 3900, 32202.
(904) 798-7360, FAX (904) 358-1872
    MR. GEORGE D. GABEL,   Mar. 29, 1989
    HONORARY CONSUL

MIAMI (HCG) 1007 N. AMERICA WA., SUITE 305, 33132--2092.
(305) 358-4386, FAX (305) 374-4359
    MR. TROND SIGURD JENSEN,   Jul. 21, 2003
    HONORARY CONSUL GENERAL
    MR. LEIF ERIC GRIFFIN,   Aug. 13, 2003
    HONORARY CONSUL

PENSACOLA (HC) 4400 BAYOU BL., SUITE 34, 32503.
(850) 494-2194, FAX (850) 494-9175
    MR. RICHARD LESLIE APPLEYARD,   Apr. 09, 1999
    HONORARY CONSUL

TAMPA (HC) 701 HARBOUR POST DR., 33602.
(813) 247-4432, FAX (813) 247-4256
    MR. ARTHUR RENFRO SAVAGE,   Oct. 07, 1998
    HONORARY CONSUL

GEORGIA

ATLANTA (HC) 3715 NORTHSIDE (BUILDING 300) PW., SUITE 650, 30327.
(404) 923-5079, FAX (404) 239-0877
    MR. JOHN R. MCDONALD,   Jan. 15, 1991
    HONORARY CONSUL

HAWAII

HONOLULU (HC) 4215 KILAUEA AV., 96816.
(808) 734-5298, FAX (808) 732-5853
    MS. NINA H. FASI,   Jan. 30, 1998
    HONORARY CONSUL

ILLINOIS

CHICAGO (HCG) 300 S. WACKER DR., SUITE 1220, 60606.
(312) 377-5050, FAX (312) 899-1101
    MR. PAUL S. ANDERSON,   Jan. 06, 2000
    HONORARY CONSUL GENERAL

IOWA

DES MOINES (HC) 2000 FINANCIAL CENTER ., 50309.
(515) 243-7100
    MR. QUENTIN R. BOYKEN,   Dec. 21, 1990
    HONORARY CONSUL

LOUISIANA

NEW ORLEANS (HC) 650 POYDRAS ST., SUITE 1700, 70130.
(504) 522-3526
    MR. JAMES M. , JR BALDWIN,   Sep. 10, 2003
    HONORARY CONSUL

MASSACHUSETTS

BOSTON (HC) 286 CONGRESS ST., FLOOR 6TH, 02210.
(617) 423-2515, FAX (617) 423-2057
    MR. TERJE KORSNES,   Nov. 05, 1990
    HONORARY CONSUL

MICHIGAN

DETROIT (HC) 26017 CONCORD RD., HUNTINGTON WOODS 48070.
(248) 547-6379, FAX (248) 547-7020
    MR. DENNIS M. FLESSLAND,   Jan. 31, 2000
    HONORARY CONSUL

MINNESOTA

MINNEAPOLIS (CG) 901 MARQUETTE AV., SUITE 2750, 55402.
(612) 332-3338, FAX (612) 332-1386
    MR. ROLF WILLY HANSEN,   Dec. 15, 2005
    CONSUL GENERAL
    MR. GEIR TONNESSEN,   Aug. 24, 2006
    CONSUL

MONTANA

BILLINGS (HC) 490 N. 31ST ST., 59103.
(406) 252-3441
    MR. JAMES P. SITES,   Jul. 24, 1987
    HONORARY CONSUL

NEBRASKA

OMAHA (HC) 10330 REGENCY PKWY. DR., 68114.
(402) 397-2200
    MR. VIRGIL K. JOHNSON,   May. 06, 1986
    HONORARY CONSUL

NEW YORK

NEW YORK (CG) 825 THIRD AV., FLOOR 38TH, 10022.
(212) 421-7333
    MS. LIV MOERCH FINBORUD,   Oct. 22, 2003
    CONSUL GENERAL
    MR. JENS PETTER OLSEN,   Nov. 29, 2000
    CONSUL
    MS. INGER BRUSELL,   Sep. 30, 2003
    CONSUL
    MRS. KRISTIN IGLUM,   Oct. 04, 2005
    CONSUL
    MS. KRISTIN DAHLE,   Jul. 30, 2007
    CONSUL
    MRS. KARIN AAROE,   Apr. 11, 2005
    VICE CONSUL
    MR. PER ANDERS NILSEN,   Oct. 06, 2005
    VICE CONSUL
    MS. GRETHE BJORG STRAND,   Dec. 11, 2006
    VICE CONSUL

NORTH DAKOTA

FARGO (HC) 10 ROBERTS ST., 58102.
(701) 232-8957
    MR. RONALD HARVEY MCLEAN,   Dec. 29, 1998
    HONORARY CONSUL

STATE* RESIDENCE	NAME AND RANK	DATE OF RECOGNITION	STATE* RESIDENCE	NAME AND RANK	DATE OF RECOGNITION

OKLAHOMA

TULSA (HC) 2431 E. 61ST ST., SUITE 600, 74136.
(918) 744-5222

   MR. JON ROLF STUART,   Jun. 14, 1987
      HONORARY CONSUL

OREGON

PORTLAND (HC) 4380 S.W. MACADAM AV., SUITE 120, 97238.
(503) 221-0870

   MR. LORENTZ KELLY BRUUN,   Jun. 25, 1991
      HONORARY CONSUL

PENNSYLVANIA

PHILADELPHIA (HC) 1760 MARKET ST., APT 1111, 19103.
(215) 665-8166

   MR. ERIK TORP,   Feb. 20, 2001
      HONORARY CONSUL

PUERTO RICO

PONCE (HC) 3091 SANT.DEL LOS CABALLERO AV., 00716.
(787) 848-9000, FAX (787) 848-0070

   MR. LUIS A. AYALA-PARSI,   Sep. 01, 1977
      HONORARY CONSUL

SAN JUAN (HC) 3091 SAN.DE LOS CABALLERO AV., PLAYA DE
PONCE 00731.
(787) 725-2532

   MR. JOSE O. BUSTO,   Mar. 08, 1977
      HONORARY CONSUL

SOUTH CAROLINA

CHARLESTON (HC) 198 E. BAY ST., SUITE 101, 29401.
(803) 577-5782, FAX (803) 577-3589

   MR. JAMES DOAR LUCAS,   May. 09, 1978
      HONORARY CONSUL

SOUTH DAKOTA

SIOUX FALLS (HC) 509 S. DAKOTA AV., 57102.
(605) 336-1030

   MR. HOWARD W. PAULSON,   May. 11, 1983
      HONORARY CONSUL

TEXAS

DALLAS (HC) 5500 CARUTH HAVEN LA., 75225.
(214) 750-4222, FAX (214) 750-4210

   MR. EDWARD MERLIN FJORDBAK,   Aug. 20, 1996
      HONORARY CONSUL

HOUSTON (CG) 2777 ALLEN PKWY. ., SUITE 1185, 77019.
(713) 521-2900

   MRS. HELLE HAMMER,   Oct. 06, 2005
      CONSUL
   MS. MARY ANN ANDERSEN,   Nov. 07, 2003
      VICE CONSUL

UTAH

SALT LAKE CITY (HC) 2650 DECKER LAKE BL., SUITE 300, 84119.
(801) 364-4800

   MR. LARS ERIK JOHANSEN,   Nov. 08, 2004
      HONORARY CONSUL

VIRGINIA

NORFOLK (HC) 201 E. CITY HALL AV., 23514.
(757) 446-7300, FAX (757) 625-7854

   MR. ROLF A. WILLIAMS,   May. 05, 1994
      HONORARY CONSUL

WASHINGTON

SEATTLE (HC) 7301 5TH AV., NE, SUITE A, 98115.
(206) 284-2323, FAX (206) 448-2033

   MR. KIM NESSELQUIST,   Apr. 16, 2007
      HONORARY CONSUL

OMAN

CALIFORNIA

LOS ANGELES (HC) 10590 WILSHIRE BL., SUITE 1704, 90024.
(310) 446-0249

   DR. JOSEPH ALBERT KECHICHIAN,   May. 23, 2006
      HONORARY CONSUL

PAKISTAN

CALIFORNIA

LOS ANGELES (CG) 10850 WILSHIRE BL., SUITE 1245&1250, 90024.
(310) 441-5114

   MR. SYED IBNE ABBAS,   Aug. 24, 2006
      CONSUL GENERAL
   MR. SHAHID ASHRAF TARAR,   Aug. 16, 2004
      CONSUL
   MR. K K AHSAN WAGAN,   Apr. 06, 2007
      VICE CONSUL
   MR. MUHAMMAD IQBAL,   Jul. 09, 2007
      CONSULAR AGENT

TRADE OFFICE
LOS ANGELES (CONA) 10850 WILSHIRE BL., SUITE 410 & 411, 90024.

SUNNYVALE (CG) 5150 EL CAMINO REAL ., SUITE A32, LOS ALTOS
94022.

ILLINOIS

CHICAGO (CON) 333 N. MICHIGAN AV., SUITE 728, 60601.
(312) 781-1831, FAX (312) 781-1839

   MR. MIAN ASAD HAYAUD DIN,   Feb. 15, 2007
      DEPUTY CONSUL

MAINE

PORTLAND (HC) 30 PLEASANT ST., 04101.
(207) 253-5000, FAX (207) 253-5560

   MR. JACOB DANIEL HOFFMAN,   Apr. 04, 2000
      HONORARY CONSUL

MASSACHUSETTS

BOSTON (HCG) 558 CLAPBOARD ST., WESTWOOD 02090.
(617) 267-9000, FAX (617) 266-6666

STATE* RESIDENCE	NAME AND RANK	DATE OF RECOGNITION	STATE* RESIDENCE	NAME AND RANK	DATE OF RECOGNITION

MR. BARRY D. HOFFMAN,   Dec. 17, 1980
   HONORARY CONSUL GENERAL

NEW YORK

NEW YORK (CG) 12 E. 65TH ST., 10021.
(212) 879-5800

   MR. MOHSIN RAZI,   Feb. 12, 2007
      CONSUL GENERAL
   MR. SHAHID MEHBOOB SIDDIQUI,   Jun. 01, 2004
      CONSUL
   MS. SEEMA NAJEEB,   Oct. 14, 2004
      CONSUL
   MR. SAQIB RAUF,   Aug. 10, 2007
      VICE CONSUL
   MR. ARIF RASHID,   Aug. 08, 2002
      CONSULAR AGENT

TEXAS

HOUSTON (CON) 11850 JONES RD., 77070.
(281) 890-8525, FAX (281) 890-1433

   MR. GHULAM RASOOL BALUCH,   Jul. 23, 2004
      CONSUL
   MR. ZIA AHMED,   Jun. 06, 2007
      VICE CONSUL

PALAU

CALIFORNIA

LA CANADA FLINTRIDGE (HCG) 4368 HAYMAN AV., 91011.
(818) 952-3832

   MR. ANDREW B. LEEKA,   Feb. 07, 2007
      HONORARY CONSUL GENERAL

GUAM

TAMUNING (CON) 590 S. MARINE DR., SUITE 615, 96911.
(671) 646-9281, FAX (671) 646-5322

   MRS. EILEEN NGEDIKES KINTOL,   Dec. 03, 2002
      CONSUL
   MR. JEFF OMSAUBUKL KENTY,   Jul. 02, 2004
      VICE CONSUL

HAWAII

HONOLULU (HCG) 1154 FORT ST., SUITE 300, 96813.
(808) 524-5414

   MR. MICHAEL JOHN MORONEY,   Feb. 11, 2004
      HONORARY CONSUL GENERAL

PANAMA

CALIFORNIA

SAN DIEGO (CG) 402 W. BROADWAY WA., SUITE 670, 92101.
(619) 235-4441, FAX (619) 235-4442

   MR. EDUARDO ARANGO ARIAS,   Mar. 22, 2007
      CONSUL GENERAL
   MR. ADOLFO GONZALEZ RUBIO BECKMANN,   Jan. 09, 1998
      HONORARY VICE CONSUL

SAN FRANCISCO (CG) 870 MARKET ST., SUITE 551-553, 94102.
(415) 391-4268, FAX (415) 391-4269

DISTRICT OF COLUMBIA

WASHINGTON (CHN) 2862 MCGILL TE., NW, 20008.
(202) 483-1407, FAX (202) 483-8416

   MR. ABEY SAID SAIED MALOFF,   May. 29, 2007
      CONSUL GENERAL
   MS. DAMARIS GUARDIA VARELA,   Jun. 06, 2007
      VICE CONSUL

FLORIDA

MIAMI (CG) 5757 BLUE LAGOON DR., SUITE 320, 33126.
(305) 447-3700, FAX (305) 447-4142

   MR. ALBERTO GONZALEZ ABADIA,   Mar. 08, 2005
      CONSUL GENERAL
   MR. FRANKLIN KARDONSKI,   Jun. 10, 1998
      CONSUL
   MS. GLORIELA DE LOS ANGELES SAMUDIO,   Jul. 17, 1996
      VICE CONSUL
   MRS. MONIQUE GILINSKI,   Nov. 26, 1997
      VICE CONSUL
   MRS. ZUNILDA GUEVARA DE MARINA,   Jul. 08, 2002
      VICE CONSUL
   MRS. MARLENE ASHBY CHIAL,   Apr. 07, 2006
      VICE CONSUL

TRADE DEVELOPMENT INSTITUTE
MIAMI (CONA) 1477 S. MIAMI AV., FLOOR 2ND, 33130.
(305) 374-8823, FAX (305) 374-7822

   MS. ROSALINDA PINILLA VALDES,   Feb. 09, 1996
      CONSUL

TAMPA (CG) 2211 3RD AV., 33605.
(813) 283-0063, FAX (813) 283-0064

   MR. FERNANDO NUNEZ FABREGA,   Mar. 22, 2007
      CONSUL GENERAL
   MRS. MARTA HALPHEN DE GONZALEZ,   Sep. 21, 2006
      VICE CONSUL
   MS. ZELITH OSCIRY LEDEZMA CARVAJAL,   Oct. 16, 2006
      VICE CONSUL

GEORGIA

ATLANTA (CG) 225 PEACHTREE ST., NE, SUITE 503, 30303.
(404) 522-4114, FAX (404) 522-4120

HAWAII

HONOLULU (HCG) 1352 S. BERETANIA ST., 96814.
(808) 531-5483

   MR. TRUMAN WILLIAM BROPHY,   Mar. 06, 2000
      HONORARY CONSUL GENERAL

LOUISIANA

NEW ORLEANS (CG) 2 CANAL ST., 70130.
(504) 525-3458, FAX (504) 424-8960

   MR. ERICH ALBERTO RODRIGUEZ TEJEIRA,   Jun. 07, 2006
      CONSUL GENERAL
   MS. MARIA DEL PILAR PITTY CORDOBA,   Sep. 17, 2002
      VICE CONSUL

NEW YORK

NEW YORK (CG) 1212 AVE. OF THE AMERICAS ., FLOOR 6TH, 10036.
(212) 840-2450, FAX (212) 840-2469

STATE* RESIDENCE	NAME AND RANK	DATE OF RECOGNITION	STATE* RESIDENCE	NAME AND RANK	DATE OF RECOGNITION

MS. ARLEEN SUCRE,   Jun. 20, 2006
  CONSUL GENERAL

OFFICE OF MARITIME SAFETY
NEW YORK (CONA) 369 LEXINGTON AV., FLOOR 14TH, 10017.
(212) 869-6440, FAX (212) 575-2285

PENNSYLVANIA

PHILADELPHIA (CG) 124 CHESTNUT ST., 19106.
(215) 574-2994, FAX (215) 625-4876
  MRS. GEORGIA ATHANASOPULOS,   Jun. 04, 1996
    CONSUL GENERAL

PUERTO RICO

SAN JUAN (HC) 1155 PONCE DE LEON ., FLOOR 4TH, 00907.
, FAX (787) 793-0200
  MR. JORGE COLON NEVARES,   Jul. 17, 2006
    HONORARY CONSUL

TEXAS

HOUSTON (CG) 24 GREENWAY PLAZA ., SUITE 1307, 77046.
(713) 622-4451, FAX (713) 622-4468
  MR. ADSINAR RIBSTELL CAJAR,   Oct. 11, 2005
    CONSUL GENERAL
  MS. ANABEL CRISTINA FUENTES BARRIOS,   Feb. 15, 2005
    VICE CONSUL

PAPUA NEW GUINEA

CALIFORNIA

LOS ANGELES (HCG) 1308 BANYAN DR., FALLBROOK 92028.
(760) 731-0436, FAX (760) 731-0472
  MR. CHARLES CHEATHEM,   Sep. 23, 1996
    HONORARY CONSUL GENERAL

TEXAS

HOUSTON (HCG) 4900 WOODWAY DR., SUITE 1200, 77056.
(713) 966-2500
  MR. NATHAN M. AVERY,   Aug. 27, 2002
    HONORARY CONSUL GENERAL

PARAGUAY

CALIFORNIA

LOS ANGELES (CG) 6033 W. CENTURY BL., SUITE 985, 90045.
(310) 417-9500, FAX (310) 417-9520
  MR. SERGIO ADRIAN BESTARD,   Aug. 24, 2006
    CONSUL GENERAL

FLORIDA

MIAMI (CG) 25 S.E. 2ND AV., SUITE 705, 33131.
(305) 374-9090
  MR. CARLOS ALBERTO ORTIZ BAREIRO,   Mar. 09, 2004
    CONSUL GENERAL
  MR. ESTANISLAO LEZCANO,   May. 27, 2003
    CONSUL
  MR. EDUARDO VICTOR FLORENTIN BOLF,   Mar. 09, 2004
    CONSUL

KANSAS

KANSAS CITY (CG) 630 MINNESOTA AV., 66101.
(913) 281-5252

MICHIGAN

DETROIT (HC) 27387 PARKVIEW ., 48092.
(248) 661-5567, FAX (248) 661-3028
  MRS. ALICE ROJAS,   Aug. 18, 1978
    HONORARY CONSUL

NEW YORK

NEW YORK (CG) 211 E. 43RD ST., SUITE 2101, 10017.
  MR. JUAN ALBERTO BAIARDI QUESNEL,   Mar. 09, 3006
    CONSUL GENERAL
  MR. JULIO ALEXIS IGLESIAS SPERANZA,   Feb. 18, 2005
    CONSUL

PUERTO RICO

SAN JUAN (HC) 267 ., APT 5-C, 00903.
  MRS. MARIA ELENA DE HASZARD,   Nov. 05, 1966
    HONORARY CONSUL

TEXAS

BELLAIRE (HC) 4707 WELFORD DR., 77401.
(713) 444-9887
  DR. GUSTAVO ENRIQUE AYALA,   Mar. 24, 2006
    HONORARY CONSUL

FORT WORTH (HC) 3103 N. BEACH ST., 76111.
(817) 222-2223
  MR. RICHARD FRANCIS GONZALEZ,   Mar. 22, 2007
    HONORARY CONSUL

PERU

ARIZONA

MESA (HC) 560 W. BROWN RD., SUITE 4001, 85201.
(480) 834-3907
  DR. RAUL ALBERTO OSORIO,   Jun. 26, 2003
    HONORARY CONSUL

CALIFORNIA

LOS ANGELES (CG) 3450 WILSHIRE BL., SUITE 800, 90010.
(213) 252-5910, FAX (213) 252-8130
  MR. ALBERTO ESTEBAN MASSA MURAZZI,   Mar. 24, 2005
    CONSUL GENERAL
  MS. AELIN SUZANNE PEREZ RAMIREZ,   Jul. 07, 2005
    DEPUTY CONSUL GENERAL
  MR. GABRIEL A. PACHECO,   Jul. 18, 2006
    DEPUTY CONSUL GENERAL
  MS. ANALI MARGARITA AGUILAR LOPEZ,   Apr. 15, 2005
    VICE CONSUL

SACRAMENTO (HC) 8135 ELDER CREEK RD., SUITE 115, 95824.
(916) 919-7605
  MRS. FORTUNA CLARK,   Mar. 16, 2006
    HONORARY CONSUL

STATE* RESIDENCE	NAME AND RANK	DATE OF RECOGNITION	STATE* RESIDENCE	NAME AND RANK	DATE OF RECOGNITION

SAN FRANCISCO (CG) 870 MARKET ST., SUITE 1067, 94102.
(415) 362-7136

MR. NICOLAS A. RONCAGLIOLO HIGUERAS, CONSUL GENERAL	May. 22, 2006	
MR. RUBEN ESPINOZA RAYMONDI, DEPUTY CONSUL GENERAL	Apr. 14, 2005	
MS. MARIA FATIMA TRIGOSO SAKUMA, DEPUTY CONSUL GENERAL	Jun. 13, 2005	
MS. MARIA ISABEL WONG VARGAS, HONORARY CONSUL	Aug. 24, 1998	

COLORADO

DENVER (CG) 1001 S. MONACO PW., SUITE 210, 80224.

MS. MARIA SUSANA LANDAVERI PORTURAS, CONSUL GENERAL	Aug. 07, 2002
MS. MARIA ISABEL SALAZAR SANCHEZ, CONSULAR AGENT	May. 16, 2003
MR. MANUEL BOZA HECK, CONSULAR AGENT	Apr. 06, 2007

CONNECTICUT

HARTFORD (CG) 250D MAIN ST., SUITE D, 06106.

MR. JOSE ARSENIO BENZAQUEN PEREA, CONSUL GENERAL	Nov. 20, 2002

DISTRICT OF COLUMBIA

WASHINGTON (CHN) 1700 MASSACHUSETTS AV., NW, 20036.
(202) 833-9860, FAX (202) 659-8124

CONSULATE GENERAL OFFICE
WASHINGTON (CHA) 1625 MASSACHUSETTS AV., NW, SUITE 605, 20036.
(202) 833-9868

MR. FERNANDO QUIROS CAMPOS, CONSUL GENERAL	Mar. 30, 2007
MR. DAVID ADALBERTO VERGARA PILARES, DEPUTY CONSUL GENERAL	Mar. 24, 2007
MR. RICARDO MALCA ALVARINO, VICE CONSUL	Aug. 04, 2007

FLORIDA

MIAMI (CG) 444 BRICKELL AV., SUITE M-135, 33131.
(305) 374-8935

MR. JORGE ROMAN MOREY, CONSUL GENERAL	Jul. 28, 2004
MR. OSCAR GONZALEZ, DEPUTY CONSUL GENERAL	Jan. 30, 2007
MR. JOSE MARCOS RODRIGUEZ CHACON, DEPUTY CONSUL	Aug. 16, 2002
MS. LORENA GISELLA CAMPOS CAVERO, VICE CONSUL	Jul. 26, 2006
MR. FERNANDO ALBAREDA, CONSULAR AGENT	Feb. 15, 1996
MR. MANUEL ALBERTO ARANA ROTTA, CONSULAR AGENT	Jul. 12, 2007

TAMPA (HC) 6221 WEYMOUTH DR., SARASOTA 34238.
(941) 284-6221, FAX (941) 926-8044

GEORGIA

ATLANTA (CG) 4360 CHAMBLEE DUNWOODY RD., SUITE 580, 30341.
(770) 900-2131

MR. JORGE EDUARDO EMILIO PUENTE LUNA, CONSUL GENERAL	Feb. 06, 2006
MR. JULIO A. ALVAREZ SABOGAL, DEPUTY CONSUL	Feb. 06, 2006
MS. ADRIANA L. VELARDE RIVAS, VICE CONSUL	Dec. 20, 2005

HAWAII

HONOLULU (HC) 1910 ALA MOANA BL., SUITE 40B, 96815.
(808) 554-5858

MR. ALVIN PHILIP , JR ADAMS, HONORARY CONSUL	Jan. 28, 2005

ILLINOIS

CHICAGO (CG) 180 N. MICHIGAN AV., SUITE 1830, 60601.
(312) 853-6173

MR. JOSE EDUARDO CHAVARRI GARCIA, CONSUL GENERAL	Dec. 12, 2006
MS. CANDY G. CHAVEZ DE MARTENS, DEPUTY CONSUL GENERAL	Apr. 16, 2007

LOUISIANA

NEW ORLEANS (HC) 2308 WORLD TRADE CENTER ., 70130.
(504) 523-6496

MS. MARIA ISABEL O'BYRNE STEPHENSON, HONORARY CONSUL	Jul. 19, 2000

MASSACHUSETTS

BOSTON (CG) 20 PARK PZ., SUITE 511, 02116.

MR. ALBERTO VALENCIA CARLO, CONSUL GENERAL	Apr. 25, 2005
MR. FEDERICO ENRIQUE FREUNDT CUEVA, DEPUTY CONSUL GENERAL	Jan. 30, 2007
MS. KARIM MILAGROS DURAND LAZO, DEPUTY CONSUL	Nov. 16, 2005

MISSOURI

SAINT LOUIS (HC) 3 THE PRADO UN., 63124.
(314) 991-1750

MRS. ROSA ANA SCHWARZ, HONORARY CONSUL	Jan. 19, 1978

NEW JERSEY

PATERSON (CG) 100 HAMILTON PZ., SUITE 1220, 07505.
(201) 278-3324

MR. JOSE ANTONIO GARCIA TORRES, CONSUL GENERAL	Jan. 30, 2007
MR. GONZALO E. PAREDES, DEPUTY CONSUL GENERAL	May. 13, 1999
MR. CARLOS ORTEGA GARCIA, DEPUTY CONSUL	Jul. 17, 2003
MR. MARIANO ERNESTO LOPEZ BLACK, VICE CONSUL	Jul. 31, 2003
MS. KATIA ANGELES VARGAS, VICE CONSUL	Jul. 31, 2003

STATE* RESIDENCE	NAME AND RANK	DATE OF RECOGNITION	STATE* RESIDENCE	NAME AND RANK	DATE OF RECOGNITION

NEW YORK

NEW YORK (CG) 241 E. 49TH ST., 10017.
(212) 481-7419, FAX (646) 735-3866

MR. HELI ADELFO PELAEZ CASTRO, CONSUL GENERAL	Jul. 30, 2002	
MR. ALFREDO RAUL CHUQUIHUARA, DEPUTY CONSUL GENERAL	Feb. 08, 2007	
MS. GLADYS MABEL GARCIA PAREDES, DEPUTY CONSUL GENERAL	May. 05, 2007	
MR. JORGE EFRAIN LAZO ESCALANTE, DEPUTY CONSUL GENERAL	Jun. 12, 2007	
MR. ABEL ANTONIO CARDENAS TUPPIA, DEPUTY CONSUL	Jun. 28, 2005	

OKLAHOMA

TULSA (HC) 2430 E. 41ST ST., 74105.
(918) 245-5911

DR. LUIS ALBERTO REINOSO, Nov. 03, 1971
 HONORARY CONSUL

TEXAS

DALLAS (CG) 1500 MARILLA UN., ROOM D, 75201.

HOUSTON (CG) 5177 RICHMOND AV., SUITE 695, 77056.
(713) 355-9571, FAX (713) 355-9377

MR. EDUARDO V. RIVOLDI, CONSUL GENERAL	Jun. 24, 2002	
MRS. SANDRA BELMONT, VICE CONSUL	Jul. 27, 2006	
MRS. HANNIELISE ILLMANN DE MONTERO, CONSULAR AGENT	Apr. 25, 2005	
MR. BERNARDO TREISTMAN, HONORARY CONSUL	May. 03, 1979	

WASHINGTON

SEATTLE (HC) 3717 N.E. 157TH ST., SUITE 100, 98155.
(206) 714-9037

MR. MIGUEL A. VELASQUEZ, Apr. 09, 1998
 HONORARY CONSUL

PHILIPPINES

CALIFORNIA

LOS ANGELES (CG) 3600 WILSHIRE BL., SUITE 500, 90010.
(213) 639-0980, FAX (213) 639-0990

MRS. MARY JO ANTONIA BERNARDO ARAGON, CONSUL GENERAL	Mar. 29, 2007	
MS. MARIA HELLEN MARIANO BARBER, CONSUL	Jun. 24, 2003	
MS. NOEMI TAN DIAZ, CONSUL	Apr. 20, 2006	
MR. EDWARD CO YULO, VICE CONSUL	Nov. 01, 2004	
MR. JIM TITO BALGOS SAN AGUSTIN, VICE CONSUL	Apr. 26, 2007	

TOURISM OFFICE
LOS ANGELES (CONA) 3660 WILSHIRE BL., SUITE 216, 90010.

COMMERCIAL OFFICE
LOS ANGELES (CONA) 3660 WILSHIRE BL., SUITE 216 & 218, 90010.

SAN FRANCISCO

SAN FRANCISCO (CG) 447 SUTTER ST., FLOOR 6TH, 94108.
(415) 433-6666

MRS. MARIA ROWENA M. SANCHEZ, CONSUL GENERAL	Oct. 04, 2004	
MR. WILFREDO CUNANAN SANTOS, CONSUL	Oct. 04, 2005	
MR. ANTHONY A. L. MANDAP, CONSUL	Nov. 06, 2006	
MR. RAPHAEL STA. CRUZ HERMOSO, VICE CONSUL	Oct. 06, 2005	
MR. ARVIC VENTURA AREVALO, VICE CONSUL	Feb. 03, 2006	

DISTRICT OF COLUMBIA

WASHINGTON (CHN) 1600 MASSACHUSETTS AV., NW, 20036.
(202) 467-9300, FAX (202) 328-7614

MR. DOMINGO PRADIEZ NOLASCO, CONSUL GENERAL	Mar. 14, 0006	
MR. CARLOS DEYMEK SORRETA, CONSUL	Mar. 09, 0006	
MS. LOURDES ORTIZ YPARRAGUIRRE, CONSUL	May. 17, 2000	
MISS PATRICIA ANN PAEZ, CONSUL	Jul. 12, 2000	
MS. HJAYCEELYN MANCENIDO QUINTANA, CONSUL	Aug. 02, 2002	
MR. ENRICO TRINIDAD FOS, CONSUL	Nov. 30, 2002	
MR. ANGELITO AYONG NAYAN, CONSUL	Mar. 16, 2007	
MR. EDUARDO JOSE DE VEGA, CONSUL	Jul. 13, 2007	
MR. GINES JAIME RICARDO GALLAGA, VICE CONSUL	Oct. 03, 2006	

FLORIDA

NORTH MIAMI (HCG) 1635 MIAMI RD., SUITE 3, FORT LAUDERDALE
33316.
(954) 524-2610, FAX (954) 768-9996

MR. ANGELO SAN JUAN MACATANGAY, Jun. 24, 2003
 HONORARY CONSUL GENERAL

GEORGIA

ATLANTA (HCG) 3340 PEACH TREE RD., NE, SUITE 2310, 30326.
(404) 239-5740, FAX (404) 233-4041

MR. RAOUL R. DONATO, Sep. 07, 1994
 HONORARY CONSUL GENERAL

GUAM

TAMUNING (CG) XX MARINE DR., SUITE 601 & 602, 96931.
(671) 646-4620, FAX (671) 649-1868

MS. ROSARIO P. LEMQUE, CONSUL	Jan. 23, 2002	
MRS. RAQUEL RAYEL SOLANO, CONSUL	Apr. 27, 2006	
MR. KERWIN ORVILLE CASANO TATE, VICE CONSUL	Feb. 01, 2005	

HAWAII

HONOLULU (CG) 2433 PALI HW., 96817.
(808) 595-6316

STATE* RESIDENCE	NAME AND RANK	DATE OF RECOGNITION	STATE* RESIDENCE	NAME AND RANK	DATE OF RECOGNITION
	MR. ARIEL Y. ABADILLA, CONSUL GENERAL	Dec. 28, 2005	**CALIFORNIA**		
	MRS. IRENE SUSAN BARREIRO NATIVIDAD, CONSUL	Jan. 11, 2006	BELMONT (HC) 1050 RALSTON AV., 94002. (650) 802-1626		
	MR. PAUL RAYMUND PASION CORTES, CONSUL	Mar. 14, 2007		MR. THADDEUS NORMAN TAUBE, HONORARY CONSUL	Apr. 23, 2007
	MRS. ARLENE GONZALES MACAISA, VICE CONSUL	Dec. 04, 2002			
ILLINOIS			LOS ANGELES (CG) 12400 WILSHIRE BL., SUITE 555, 90025. (310) 442-8500, FAX (310) 442-8515		
CHICAGO (CG) 30 N. MICHIGAN AV., SUITE 2100, 60602. (312) 332-6458				MRS. KRYSTYNA TOKARSKA BIERNACIK, CONSUL GENERAL	Oct. 21, 2003
	MRS. BLESILA C. CABRERA, CONSUL GENERAL	Mar. 09, 2004		MR. DARIUSZ DOBROWOLSKI, CONSUL	Nov. 07, 2002
	MR. ORONTES VALDEZ CASTRO, CONSUL	Jun. 29, 2007		MRS. MALGORZATA KOPEC, CONSUL	Aug. 29, 2003
	MR. ROBERTO T. BERNARDO, VICE CONSUL	Apr. 20, 2004		MRS. MARZENA GRONOSTAJSKA, CONSUL	Nov. 03, 2005
				MISS PAULINA KAPUSCINSKA, VICE CONSUL	Oct. 05, 2004
PHILIPPINE TRADE AND INVESTMENT OFFICE CHICAGO (CONA) 30 N. MICHIGAN AV., SUITE 1217, 60602. (312) 332-6458				MR. MICHAL URBANKOWSKI, VICE CONSUL	Feb. 23, 2006
				MRS. JOANNA BARBARA DOBROWOLSKA, CONSULAR AGENT	Dec. 19, 2002
LOUISIANA			SAN FRANCISCO (HC) 785 MARKET ST., SUITE 1120, 94103. (415) 777-4445, FAX (415) 778-8123		
NEW ORLEANS (HCG) 2144 WORLD TRADE CENTER ., 70130. (504) 529-7561				MR. CHRISTOPHER ANTHONY KEROSKY, HONORARY CONSUL	Nov. 10, 2003
	MS. CIELO TOLENTINO MARTINEZ, HONORARY CONSUL GENERAL	Jul. 25, 2001			
			COLORADO		
NEW YORK			LONGMONT (HC) 1916 ANDREW ALDEN ST., 80504. (303) 485-6620		
NEW YORK (CG) 556 5TH AV., 10036. (212) 764-1330				MR. TOMASZ HENRYK SKOTNICKI, HONORARY CONSUL	Jul. 29, 2005
	MRS. CECILIA BALTAZAR REBONG, CONSUL GENERAL	Mar. 09, 2004			
	MRS. MELITA S. STA MARIA THOMECZEK, DEPUTY CONSUL GENERAL	Apr. 20, 2004	**FLORIDA**		
	MRS. MILLICENT CRUZ PAREDES, CONSUL	Aug. 13, 2002	MIAMI (HC) 1440 79TH STREET CAUSEWAY UN., SUITE 117, 33147. (305) 866-0077		
	MS. MARIA LOURDES DAY, CONSUL	Aug. 29, 2003		MRS. BLANKA A. ROSENTIEL, HONORARY CONSUL	May. 14, 1998
	MR. EDGAR BARRAIRO BADAJOS, VICE CONSUL	Dec. 02, 2003		MS. BEATA MAGDALENA PASZYC, HONORARY VICE CONSUL	Sep. 11, 2003
	MS. MARIA ELENA CRISTINA MANINGAT, VICE CONSUL	Jul. 26, 2006			
	MR. LEANDRO BOLESA LACHICA, VICE CONSUL	Nov. 03, 2006	**HAWAII**		
			HONOLULU (HC) 2825 S. KING ST., SUITE 2701, 96826. (808) 955-4567		
TRUST TERRITORIES OF THE PACIFIC ISLANDS				MRS. BOZENA ANNA JARNOT, HONORARY CONSUL	Aug. 13, 1998
MARIANA ISLANDS (CG) BEACH RD., FLOOR 5TH, SAN JOSE, SAIPAN 96950. (670) 234-1848					
			ILLINOIS		
	MR. WILFREDO L. MAXIMO, CONSUL GENERAL	Jul. 28, 2003	CHICAGO (CG) 820 N. ORLEANS ST., SUITE 335, 60610. (312) 337-8166		
				MR. PAWEL PIETRASIENSKI, CONSUL	Jul. 08, 2005
	POLAND			MR. GRZEGORZ MORAWSKI, CONSUL	Jul. 29, 2005
ALASKA				MISS JOANNA KRYSTYNA DOBECKA LEMBERT, VICE CONSUL	Oct. 27, 1998
ANCHORAGE (HC) 7550 OLD SEWARD HW., SUITE 100, 99518. (907) 344-4722				MR. JACEK DOBROWOLSKI, VICE CONSUL	Sep. 30, 2002
	MR. STANISLAW BORUCKI, HONORARY CONSUL	Apr. 05, 2004			

* DEPENDENCIES SUCH AS GUAM, PUERTO RICO, AND THE VIRGIN ISLANDS ARE LISTED HERE.
CG-CONSULATE GENERAL   C-CONSULATE   VC-VICE CONSULATE   CA-CONSULAR AGENCY   H-HONORARY CONSULAR STATUS

STATE* RESIDENCE	NAME AND RANK	DATE OF RECOGNITION	STATE* RESIDENCE	NAME AND RANK	DATE OF RECOGNITION

MR. FELIKS KIERZKOWSKI,　Dec. 19, 2003
　VICE CONSUL
MR. WITOLD MANKOWSKI,　Dec. 17, 2004
　VICE CONSUL
MRS. JOANNA SKUPIEWSKA MORAWSKA,　Nov. 03, 2005
　VICE CONSUL
MR. MARIUSZ GBIORCZYK,　Feb. 13, 2006
　VICE CONSUL
MR. ZDZISLAW WINKIEWICZ,　Nov. 08, 2006
　VICE CONSUL
MS. KATARZYNA ANNA KASPERKIEWICZ,　May. 08, 2007
　VICE CONSUL
MS. ALEKSANDRA KRYSTEK,　May. 31, 2007
　VICE CONSUL

COMMERCIAL DIVISION OF POLAND
CHICAGO (CONA) 333 E. ONTARIO ST., SUITE 3906-B, 60611.
(312) 642-4102
　MRS. LUCYNA JAREMCZUK,　Nov. 03, 2005
　CONSUL

MASSACHUSETTS

BOSTON (HC) 31 MILK ST., 02108.
　MR. MAREK LESNIEWSKI-LAAS,　May. 06, 1994
　HONORARY CONSUL

MISSOURI

SAINT LOUIS (HC) 13421 FEATHERSTONE DR., ST. LOUIS 63131-1206.
(314) 822-6266
　MR. ROBERT V. OGRODNIK,　Apr. 07, 2000
　HONORARY CONSUL

NEW YORK

NEW YORK (CG) 233 MADISON AV., 10016.
(212) 889-8360
　MR. KRZYSZTOF KASPRZYK,　Dec. 01, 2005
　CONSUL GENERAL
MR. JERZY LESZEK KLENIEWSKI,　Sep. 12, 1995
　CONSUL
MR. CEZARY DZIURKOWSKI,　Nov. 06, 1997
　CONSUL
MS. ANNA PELKA,　Nov. 17, 2000
　CONSUL
MR. WOJCIECH LUKASIEWICZ,　Sep. 10, 2003
　CONSUL
MS. MONIKA FABIJANSKA,　Mar. 26, 2004
　CONSUL
MR. JANUSZ MANTYKIEWICZ,　Oct. 06, 2005
　CONSUL
MRS. MALGORZATA KOSINSKA,　Oct. 06, 2005
　CONSUL
MS. ANNA POGORZELEC,　Mar. 02, 2006
　CONSUL
MR. DARIUSZ WOJTASZEK,　Apr. 05, 2007
　CONSUL
MR. BOGDAN MALOTA,　Mar. 15, 1999
　VICE CONSUL
MR. ANDRZEJ STEFANCZYK,　Aug. 29, 2003
　VICE CONSUL
MS. URSZULA SLAZAK,　Aug. 18, 2004
　VICE CONSUL

MR. WOJCIECH BOGUSKI KACZOREK,　Jan. 11, 2005
　VICE CONSUL
MRS. EWA GUMPERT,　Nov. 03, 2005
　VICE CONSUL
MR. JANUSZ ROJEWSKI,　Nov. 04, 2005
　VICE CONSUL

POLISH CULTURAL INSTITUTE OF POLAND
NEW YORK (CONA) 350 FIFTH AV., SUITE 4620-21, 10118.
(212) 889-8360
　MR. PAWEL POTOROCZYN,　Mar. 13, 2001
　CONSUL
MS. AGATA GRENDA,　May. 17, 2006
　VICE CONSUL
MR. PIOTR WALDEMAR ROGULSKI,　May. 05, 2007
　VICE CONSUL

OHIO

OXFORD (HC) XX BONHAM HOUSE, MIAMI UNIVERSITY UN., FLOOR 2ND, 45056.
(513) 529-4041, FAX (513) 529-4040
　MR. MAREK DOLLAR,　Sep. 15, 2004
　HONORARY CONSUL

OREGON

PORTLAND (HC) 11333 S.W. NORTHGATE AV., 97219.
(503) 819-8198, FAX (503) 635-8615
　MR. THADDEUS RICHARD WINNOWSKI,　May. 01, 2003
　HONORARY CONSUL

PENNSYLVANIA

PITTSBURGH (HC) 5853 DOUGLAS ST., 15217.
　DR. JAN NAPOLEON SAYKIEWICZ,　Jul. 23, 2007
　HONORARY CONSUL

PUERTO RICO

SAN JUAN (HC) 2000 MARGINAL KENNEDY AV., SUITE 411, 00920.
(787) 781-3254, FAX (787) 781-3254
　MR. BOHDAN CHESTER HRYNIEWICZ,　Jun. 20, 1994
　HONORARY CONSUL

TEXAS

HOUSTON (HC) 35 HARBOR VIEW DR., SUGAR LAND 77479.
(281) 565-1507
　DR. ZBIGNIEW JACEK WOJCIECHOWSKI,　Jun. 26, 2003
　HONORARY CONSUL

PORTUGAL

CALIFORNIA

LOS ANGELES (HC) 1801 AVENUE OF THE STARS UN., SUITE 400, 90067.
(310) 277-1490
　MR. EDMUNDO DE MACEDO,　Sep. 04, 2003
　HONORARY CONSUL

SAN FRANCISCO (CG) 3298 WASHINGTON ST., 94115.
(415) 346-3400

STATE* RESIDENCE	NAME AND RANK	DATE OF RECOGNITION	STATE* RESIDENCE	NAME AND RANK	DATE OF RECOGNITION

MR. ANTONIO JOSE ALVES DE CARVALHO,   Nov. 17, 2004
  CONSUL GENERAL

COMMERCIAL OFFICE
SAN FRANCISCO (CONA) 88 KEARNEY ST., SUITE 1770, 94108.
, FAX (415) 391-7147
  MR. LUIS MANUEL AVIDES MOREIRA,   Sep. 07, 2004
    CONSUL

TULARE (HC) 520 E. KING ST., 93274.
(559) 688-7511
  MR. HELTER SOUSA MARTINS,   Sep. 17, 2004
    HONORARY CONSUL

CONNECTICUT
WATERBURY (HC) 20 E. MAIN ST., SUITE 220, 06702.
(203) 755-4111
  MR. BILL L. GOUVEIA,   Apr. 05, 2004
    HONORARY CONSUL

FLORIDA
MIAMI (HC) 1901 PONCE DE LEON BL., FLOOR 2ND, CORAL GABLES
33134.
(305) 444-6311, FAX (305) 444-7641
  MR. JOSEPH T. THERIAGA,   Aug. 15, 1983
    HONORARY CONSUL

HAWAII
HONOLULU (HC) 1585 KAPIOLANI BL., SUITE 728, 96814.
(808) 523-4580
  MR. JOHN HENRY FELIX,   Feb. 02, 1987
    HONORARY CONSUL

ILLINOIS
CHICAGO (HC) 71 S. WACKER DR., SUITE 2930, 60606.
(312) 259-9408, FAX (312) 777-3483
  MR. NELSON DE CASTRO,   Jan. 16, 2003
    HONORARY CONSUL

LOUISIANA
NEW ORLEANS (HC) 201 ST. CHARLES AV., 70170-5100.
(504) 582-8272
  MR. WILLIAM HUGH HINES,   Mar. 22, 2000
    HONORARY CONSUL

MASSACHUSETTS
BOSTON (CG) ONE EXETER PL., FLOOR 7TH, 02116.
(617) 536-8740
  MS. MARIA MANUELA FREITAS BAIROS,   Nov. 05, 2004
    CONSUL GENERAL

NEW BEDFORD (CON) 628 PLEASANT ST., SUITE 204/218, 02740.
(508) 997-6151
  MS. FERNANDA COELHO,   Dec. 14, 2005
    CONSUL

NEW JERSEY
NEWARK (CG) ONE RIVERFRONT PZ., 07102.
(973) 643-4200
  MR. FRANCISCO CARLOS AZEVEDO,   Feb. 14, 2005
    CONSUL GENERAL

NEW YORK
NEW YORK (CG) 590 5TH AV., FLOOR 3RD, 10036.
(212) 221-3165, FAX (212) 221-3462
  MR. ALEXANDRE A. FERNANDES,   Jul. 28, 2003
    CONSUL GENERAL
  MR. EDUARDO SOUTO DE MOURA,   May. 02, 2002
    CONSUL
  MR. RUI MATHIAS ABECASSIS,   Jul. 29, 2005
    CONSUL

PUERTO RICO
SAN JUAN (HC) 416 SAN LEANDRO ., RIO PIEDRAS 00926.
(787) 761-4148, FAX (787) 755-8556
  MR. JOSE C. DUARTE DA SILVEIRA,   Jun. 22, 1983
    HONORARY CONSUL

RHODE ISLAND
PROVIDENCE (CON) 56 PINE ST., FLOOR 6TH, 02903.
(401) 272-2003
  MR. RICARDO FERNANDES GARCIA CORTES,   Mar. 08, 2005
    CONSUL

TEXAS
HOUSTON (HC) 4544 POST OAK PLACE DR., SUITE 350, 77027.
(713) 759-1188
  MR. JAMES H. WESTMORELAND,   Nov. 05, 1990
    HONORARY CONSUL

QATAR

TEXAS
HOUSTON (CG) 1990 POST OAK BL., SUITE 810, 77056.
(713) 355-8221, FAX (713) 355-8184
  MR. ABDULLA JASSIM AL MAADADI,   Oct. 02, 2003
    VICE CONSUL

ROMANIA

CALIFORNIA
LOS ANGELES (CG) 11766 WILSHIRE BL., SUITE 560, 90025.
(310) 444-0043
  MR. MIRCEA CATALIN GHENEA,   Feb. 16, 2006
    CONSUL GENERAL
  MR. GABRIEL ION DUTU,   Jan. 23, 2003
    CONSUL
  MR. RAZVAN DUMITRESCU,   Jun. 04, 2007
    CONSUL

SAN FRANCISCO (HCG) 44 MONTGOMERY LAKE LA., SUITE 400,
94104.
(415) 743-2210
  MRS. DANA BELDIMAN KARLSONS,   Jul. 01, 2004
    HONORARY CONSUL GENERAL

STATE* RESIDENCE	NAME AND RANK	DATE OF RECOGNITION	STATE* RESIDENCE	NAME AND RANK	DATE OF RECOGNITION
	MR. GEORGE ROTH, HONORARY CONSUL	Oct. 20, 2006		MRS. AURELIA ARNOLD ROBERTS, HONORARY CONSUL GENERAL	Oct. 06, 2006

DISTRICT OF COLUMBIA

WASHINGTON (CHN) 1607 23RD ST., NW, 20008.
(202) 332-4846, FAX (202) 232-4748

MRS. MIHAELA MARIANA DEACONU, CONSUL	Aug. 23, 2004	

FLORIDA

HOLLYWOOD (HCG) 1507 HOLLYWOOD BL., 33020.
(954) 920-9074

MR. CLAUDE G. MATASA, HONORARY CONSUL GENERAL	Apr. 18, 2005	
MRS. VICTORIA T. BUDISTEANU LONDON, HONORARY CONSUL	Apr. 19, 2005	

ILLINOIS

CHICAGO (CG) 737 N. MICHIGAN AV., SUITE 1170, 60611.

MR. GHEORGHE PREDESCU, CONSUL GENERAL	Nov. 14, 2003	
MS. DOINA BOBLEA, DEPUTY CONSUL GENERAL	Apr. 14, 2005	
MR. GHEORGHE GRUIA, CONSUL	Apr. 18, 2005	
MS. LUCIA FLORENTINA VIANU, VICE CONSUL	Dec. 16, 2004	

LOUISIANA

NEW ORLEANS (HC) 625 ST. CHARLES AV., SUITE 8A, 70130.
(504) 524-6054

DR. E. RALPH LUPIN, HONORARY CONSUL	Oct. 16, 2000	

MASSACHUSETTS

BOSTON (HC) 52 BEDFORD RD., LINCOLN 01773.
(617) 497-1111

MR. DAN DIMANCESCU, HONORARY CONSUL	Apr. 18, 2005	
MR. MIHAI GABRIEL VADUVA, HONORARY VICE CONSUL	Jun. 27, 2006	

MICHIGAN

DETROIT (HCG) 613 ABBOTT ST., 48226.
(313) 442-1200

MR. JOHN, JR RAKOLTA, HONORARY CONSUL GENERAL	Jul. 28, 1999	

MINNESOTA

MINNEAPOLIS (HC) 1250 E. MOORE LAKE DR., SUITE 242, 55432.
(763) 574-9472, FAX (763) 571-0662

MR. PATRICK WILLIAM LEDRAY, HONORARY CONSUL	Jul. 27, 2000	

NEVADA

LAS VEGAS (HCG) 711 RANCHO CI., 89107.
(702) 878-5534

NEW YORK

NEW YORK (CG) 200 E. 38TH ST., FLOOR 3RD, 10016.

MR. PIETRO LUCIAN PAVONI, CONSUL GENERAL	Dec. 01, 2005	
MR. MARIAN PARJOL, DEPUTY CONSUL GENERAL	Feb. 04, 2002	
MS. CORINA IOANA SUTEU, DEPUTY CONSUL GENERAL	May. 19, 2006	
MRS. ANDREEA IOANA BERECHET, DEPUTY CONSUL GENERAL	Oct. 16, 2006	
DR. BOGDAN STEFANESCU, CONSUL	Mar. 25, 2004	
MS. ROXANA NICOLETA STEFAN, CONSUL	May. 17, 2006	
MR. CHIVEL PORUMB, CONSUL	Jul. 06, 2007	
MS. ROXANA ELENA SIMA, VICE CONSUL	Dec. 28, 2005	

OHIO

CLEVELAND (HCG) 5500 S. MARGINAL RD., 44103.
(216) 391-3112

MR. GEORGE DOBREA, HONORARY CONSUL GENERAL	Nov. 21, 2006	

OKLAHOMA

NORMAN (HCG) 1913 BROOKHAVEN BL., 73072.
(405) 447-7500

MRS. NADIA COMANECI, HONORARY CONSUL GENERAL	Mar. 31, 2004	

OREGON

PORTLAND (HC) 888 S.W. 5TH AV., SUITE 1200, 97204.
(503) 382-5165

MR. JAMES H. RUDD, HONORARY CONSUL	Jun. 08, 2005	

PENNSYLVANIA

PHILADELPHIA (HCG) 1907 SPRUCE ST., 19103.
(215) 735-7978, FAX (215) 735-9209

MR. GEORGE SFEDU, HONORARY CONSUL GENERAL	Mar. 22, 2006	

TEXAS

DALLAS (HC) 2200 ROSS AV., SUITE 2200, 75201.
(214) 740-8608

MR. NELU PRODAN, HONORARY CONSUL	Jul. 14, 2000	
MR. HUGH E. HACKNEY, HONORARY VICE CONSUL	Sep. 26, 2000	

HOUSTON (HCG) 4265 SAN FELIPE UN., SUITE 220, 77027.
(713) 629-1551, FAX (713) 629-1553

MR. NICHOLAS ALEXANDER FLORESCU, HONORARY CONSUL GENERAL	Oct. 06, 2006	
MR. ALEXANDER MIHAI POPOVICI, HONORARY VICE CONSUL	Jul. 20, 2004	

STATE* RESIDENCE	NAME AND RANK	DATE OF RECOGNITION	STATE* RESIDENCE	NAME AND RANK	DATE OF RECOGNITION

UTAH

SALT LAKE CITY (HC) 47 E.S. TEMPLE ST., 84150.
(801) 240-6095

MR. ROBERT F. ORTON,
HONORARY CONSUL — Apr. 25, 2006

VIRGINIA

NORFOLK (HCG) 464 S. INDEPENDENCE BL., SUITE C112, VIRGINIA
BEACH 23452.
(757) 456-9463, FAX (757) 456-9465

MR. ANTON SAMOILA,
HONORARY CONSUL GENERAL — Oct. 06, 2006

RUSSIA

ALASKA

ANCHORAGE (HCG) 3581 KACHEMAK CI., 99515.
(907) 349-5481

MR. STEVE R. SMIRNOFF,
HONORARY CONSUL GENERAL — Aug. 26, 1996

CALIFORNIA

SAN FRANCISCO (CG) 2790 GREEN ST., 94123.
(415) 928-6878, FAX (415) 929-0306

MR. VLADIMIR NIKOLAYEVICH VINOKUROV,
CONSUL GENERAL — Jul. 18, 2007

MR. KHALIT AKHMYATOVICH AYSIN,
DEPUTY CONSUL GENERAL — Jul. 19, 2007

MR. MIKHAIL IVANOVICH GORBUNOV,
CONSUL — Oct. 06, 2004

MR. SERGEY IVANOVICH RAKITIN,
CONSUL — Feb. 04, 2005

MR. NIKOLAY GAVRILOVICH BAYGUSHEV,
CONSUL — Nov. 08, 2006

MR. ANDREY ALEKSANDROVICH MILYAEV,
CONSUL — Nov. 22, 2006

MR. NIKOLAY VASILYEVICH ESAULOV,
CONSUL — Jul. 18, 2007

MR. ALEKSEY ANATOLYEVICH GUSEV,
VICE CONSUL — Dec. 22, 2003

MR. ALEXEY IGOREVICH DOBRINSKIY,
VICE CONSUL — Aug. 25, 2004

MR. EVGENY YURYEVICH LUZYANIN,
VICE CONSUL — Dec. 08, 2004

MR. ALEXANDER STEPANOVICH BARANOV,
VICE CONSUL — Feb. 04, 2005

MR. VADIM VYACHESLAVOVICH TATARENKO,
VICE CONSUL — Jul. 11, 2005

MR. DENIS ALEKSANDROVICH POPOV,
VICE CONSUL — Apr. 24, 2007

MR. ALEXEY NIKOLAYEVICH BUDEY,
VICE CONSUL — May. 03, 2007

MR. OLEG VYACHESLAVOVICH SHAPOVALOV,
VICE CONSUL — May. 07, 2007

COLORADO

DENVER (HCG) 1552 PENNSYLVANIA ST., 80203.
(303) 831-0829

DR. DEBORAH ANNE PALMIERI,
HONORARY CONSUL GENERAL — Nov. 29, 2006

DISTRICT OF COLUMBIA

WASHINGTON (CHN) 2650 WISCONSIN AV., NW, 20007.
(202) 298-5700, FAX (202) 298-5735

MR. ROMAN Y. AMBAROV,
CONSUL — May. 28, 2002

MR. ANDREY Y. DANILOV,
CONSUL — Apr. 21, 2005

MR. OLEG BORISOVICH SMOLENKOV,
CONSUL — Oct. 06, 2006

MR. ANDREY YEVGENYEVICH BIRYUKOV,
CONSUL — Jun. 12, 2007

MR. IVAN IGOREVICH GLUSHKO,
VICE CONSUL — Feb. 03, 2005

MR. IVAN ALEKSANDROVICH KISELEV,
VICE CONSUL — Aug. 02, 2006

CONSULAR DIVISION
WASHINGTON (CHA) 2641 TUNLAW RD., NW, 20007.
(202) 939-8907, FAX (202) 939-8917

FLORIDA

PINELLAS PARK (HC) 13805 58TH ST., N, CLEARWATER 33760.
(727) 341-3241, FAX (727) 341-3318

DR. CARL MARTIN , JR KUTTLER,
HONORARY CONSUL — Aug. 05, 2004

HAWAII

HONOLULU (HCG) 4117 KAHALA AV., 96816.
(808) 956-8007

MS. NATASHA B. OWEN,
HONORARY CONSUL GENERAL — Oct. 09, 1998

MINNESOTA

MINNEAPOLIS (HC) 5500 S. STEVENS AV., 55419.
(612) 821-4391

MR. RAYMOND EARL JOHNSON,
HONORARY CONSUL — Sep. 13, 2004

NEW YORK

NEW YORK (CG) 9-11 E. 91ST ST., 10128.
(212) 348-0926, FAX (212) 831-9162

MR. SERGEY VIKTOROVICH GARMONIN,
CONSUL GENERAL — Aug. 12, 2004

MR. KONSTANTIN IVANOVICH MINAKOV,
CONSUL — Mar. 01, 2005

MR. ANDREY YEVGENYEVICH PUGAEV,
CONSUL — Mar. 17, 2005

MR. DMITRY IVANOVICH ZAVORIN,
CONSUL — Aug. 01, 2005

MR. VAGE R. YENGIBARYAN,
VICE CONSUL — Dec. 10, 2001

MR. FILIPP NIKOLAYEVICH RYBIN,
VICE CONSUL — Mar. 08, 2004

MR. VLADIMIR N. KHLEBNIKOV,
VICE CONSUL — Nov. 08, 2004

MR. ANDREY YURYEVICH SAVUSHKIN,
VICE CONSUL — Mar. 01, 2005

MR. ALEXANDER A. KALACHEV,
VICE CONSUL — Dec. 20, 2005

STATE* RESIDENCE	NAME AND RANK	DATE OF RECOGNITION	STATE* RESIDENCE	NAME AND RANK	DATE OF RECOGNITION

MR. VITALY ANDREYEVICH SAGURA,   Nov. 22, 2006
    VICE CONSUL
MR. TIMUR V. SOKOLOV,   Apr. 13, 2007
    VICE CONSUL
MR. ROMAN VICTOROVICH KORNEEV,   May. 07, 2007
    VICE CONSUL

TRADE OFFICE
NEW YORK (CONA) 353 LEXINGTON AV., SUITE 900, 10016.
, FAX (212) 682-8605
    MR. DMITRIY A. BORISOV,   Dec. 03, 2003
        CONSUL
    MR. VALERY DMITRIYEVICH SUROV,   Dec. 22, 2006
        VICE CONSUL

PUERTO RICO

SAN JUAN (HC) 107 SAN JOSE ST., APT 4C, 00901.
(787) 315-0419, FAX (787) 724-8270
    MS. ANASTASIA PAVLOVNA KITSUL,   Sep. 15, 2003
        HONORARY CONSUL

TEXAS

HOUSTON (CG) 1333 W. LOOP SOUTH UN., SUITE 1300, 77027.
(713) 337-3300, FAX (713) 337-3305
    MR. NIKOLAY V. SOFINSKIY,   Dec. 04, 2003
        CONSUL GENERAL
    MR. KIRILL S. MIKHAYLOV,   May. 01, 2006
        DEPUTY CONSUL GENERAL
    MR. VLADIMIR M. MIROSHNICHENKO,   Oct. 22, 2004
        CONSUL
    MR. SERGEY VITALYEVICH MESTON,   May. 01, 2006
        CONSUL
    MR. DENIS LOZINSKIY,   May. 03, 2006
        VICE CONSUL
    MS. TATIANA A. SHUSTROVA,   Nov. 21, 2006
        VICE CONSUL

UTAH

SALT LAKE CITY (HCG) 5244 S. HIGHLAND DR., SUITE 201, 84117.
(801) 764-6021
    DR. ROSS E., JR BUTLER,   Jul. 30, 2001
        HONORARY CONSUL GENERAL

WASHINGTON

SEATTLE (CG) 2001 6TH AV., SUITE 2323, 98121.
(206) 728-1910, FAX (206) 728-1871
    MR. VLADIMIR I. VOLNOV,   Jun. 06, 2003
        CONSUL GENERAL
    MR. DMITRY ANATOLYEVICH REPKOV,   Sep. 30, 2005
        CONSUL
    MR. NIKOLAY N. VINOGRADOV,   Jul. 19, 2007
        CONSUL
    MR. ANDREY NIKOLAYEVICH VLADIMIR,   Nov. 16, 2004
        VICE CONSUL
    MR. MIKHAIL VYACHESLAVOVICH SATUNKIN, Jul. 11, 2005
        VICE CONSUL

RWANDA

CALIFORNIA

SAN FRANCISCO (HC) ONE MARITIME PZ., SUITE 1600, 94111.
(415) 394-5555
    MR. SCOTT R. HELDFOND,   Nov. 01, 1999
        HONORARY CONSUL

ILLINOIS

GENEVA (HCG) 2100 ENTERPRISE AV., 60134.
(630) 406-6408
    DR. JOSEPH JAY RITCHIE,   Jun. 30, 2006
        HONORARY CONSUL GENERAL

MASSACHUSETTS

BOSTON (HCG) 151 TREMONT ST., SUITE 21K, 02111.
(617) 948-9449
    MR. ROBERT C. SAGER,   Jan. 23, 2007
        HONORARY CONSUL GENERAL

SAMOA

AMERICAN SAMOA

PAGO PAGO (CG) O FAGATOGO MAOPUTASI 2 UN., FLOOR 2ND,
96799.

CALIFORNIA

TORRANCE (HC) 833 W. TORRANCE BL., 90502.
(310) 329-4748
    MS. THERESA TUITOGAMAATOE ROTTER,   May. 30, 2006
        HONORARY CONSUL

SAN MARINO

DISTRICT OF COLUMBIA

WASHINGTON (HCG) 3059 Q ST., NW, 20007.
(202) 337-1647
    MRS. SHEILA RABB WEIDENFELD,   May. 05, 1994
        HONORARY CONSUL GENERAL

HAWAII

HONOLULU (HC) 4615 KAHALA AV., 96816.
(808) 734-8926
    MR. YUKIO TAKAHASHI,   Jun. 05, 2002
        HONORARY CONSUL

MICHIGAN

DETROIT (HC) 1685 BIG BEAVER RD., TROY 48084.
(248) 528-1190
    MR. GIUSEPPE PUTTI,   Jul. 07, 1987
        HONORARY CONSUL

NEW YORK

NEW YORK (HCG) 186 LEHRER AV., SUITE 0, ELMONT 11003.
(516) 437-4699, FAX (516) 775-5897
    MR. ROBERTO L. BALSIMELLI,   Jan. 10, 1983
        HONORARY CONSUL GENERAL
    MR. JOSE RIBA,   Nov. 28, 1977
        HONORARY CONSUL

STATE* RESIDENCE	NAME AND RANK	DATE OF RECOGNITION

SAO TOME & PRINCIPE

GEORGIA

ATLANTA (HC) 245 PERIMETER CENTER PW., SUITE 610, 30346.
(678) 259-8146, FAX (770) 454-0032

MR. GARETH N. GENNER, — Oct. 13, 1997
HONORARY CONSUL

MR. ROBERT MOREL, — Apr. 24, 1998
HONORARY VICE CONSUL

ILLINOIS

CHICAGO (HC) 645 W. PARK AV., SUITE B, LIBERTYVILLE 60048.
(847) 362-5615, FAX (847) 362-1637

MR. JAMES KAO, — Jun. 04, 1996
HONORARY CONSUL

SAUDI ARABIA

CALIFORNIA

LOS ANGELES (CG) 2045 SAWTELLE BL., 90025.
(310) 479-6000, FAX (310) 479-2752

MR. ABDULLAH SAEED AHMED AL HARTHI, — May. 28, 2004
CONSUL GENERAL

MR. SAMI A. IBRAHIM, — May. 18, 1998
DEPUTY CONSUL GENERAL

MR. FAISAL A. A. AL SUDAIRY, — Mar. 01, 1999
DEPUTY CONSUL GENERAL

MR. SULTAN BIN SAAD AL SAUD, — Apr. 15, 2005
DEPUTY CONSUL GENERAL

MR. RIAD SOLH, — Mar. 05, 1997
VICE CONSUL

MR. AMER A. AL SHEHRY, — Sep. 29, 2003
VICE CONSUL

MR. SULAIMAN S. AL OTAIBY, — Dec. 24, 2003
VICE CONSUL

MR. BADER AL SHAMMARI, — Nov. 05, 2004
VICE CONSUL

MR. ATALLAH ZAYED AL ZAYED, — Feb. 16, 2006
VICE CONSUL

MR. ALI AHMAD A. ASSERI, — Apr. 04, 2006
VICE CONSUL

MR. TURKI BIN SULTAN AL SAUD, — Oct. 05, 2006
VICE CONSUL

DISTRICT OF COLUMBIA

WASHINGTON (CHN) 601 NEW HAMPSHIRE AV., NW, 20037.
(202) 342-3800, FAX (202) 944-3113

HIS EXCELLENCY ADEL A. M. AL-JUBEIR, — Mar. 08, 2007
CONSUL GENERAL

NEW YORK

NEW YORK (CG) 866 2ND AV., FLOOR 5, 10017.
(212) 752-2740

DR. ABDULRAHMAN M. GDAIA, — Aug. 03, 1999
CONSUL GENERAL

MR. ABDULLAH S. AL SHAHRANI, — Oct. 06, 2005
CONSUL

MR. ESSAM S. ALGETALE, — Oct. 29, 2003
VICE CONSUL

MR. ABDULLAH ABDULKAREEM AL SADOON, — Sep. 20, 2004
VICE CONSUL

MR. FAISAL ABDULAH HAMZA AMODI, — Sep. 20, 2004
VICE CONSUL

MR. ABDULLAH FAHAD B ALSHAMMARI, — May. 25, 2006
VICE CONSUL

MR. BANDER SULAIMAN M. ALMOQBEL, — Feb. 09, 2007
VICE CONSUL

MR. ABDULRAHMAN SALEH AL MAZHOUD, — May. 08, 2007
VICE CONSUL

MR. NADER ALABDULAZIZ, — Jan. 31, 2006
CONSULAR AGENT

MR. MOHAMMAD JALAWI M ALOTAIBI, — May. 07, 2007
CONSULAR AGENT

TEXAS

HOUSTON (CG) 5718 WESTHEIMER UN., SUITE 1500, 77057.
(713) 785-5577

MR. ABDULRAHMAN A. AL SHAYA, — Feb. 28, 2007
CONSUL GENERAL

MR. YAHYA M.S. ALHAMAWI, — May. 30, 2006
DEPUTY CONSUL GENERAL

MR. HAZIM N. AL RASHEED, — Aug. 07, 2002
VICE CONSUL

MR. LAFI FALAH ALMUTARI, — Oct. 29, 2003
VICE CONSUL

MR. MATOOG MOHAMMAD S.M AL THOMALI, — Oct. 06, 2005
VICE CONSUL

MR. MISHAAL MUTLAQ DH AL SHAMMERI, — Feb. 15, 2006
VICE CONSUL

MR. AHMED HODIRY MATHOR AL ANAZI, — Dec. 29, 2006
VICE CONSUL

MR. DHERAR YACOUB AL KESAYER, — Apr. 24, 2007
VICE CONSUL

MR. KHALID ABDULLAH HERSI ALSOMALI, — Sep. 23, 2004
CONSULAR AGENT

MR. AREF HASSAN ABBAS AL AHMED, — Feb. 02, 2005
CONSULAR AGENT

MR. ABDULAZIZ KHALID M. ALDHUWIAN, — Apr. 30, 2007
CONSULAR AGENT

SENEGAL

FLORIDA

MIAMI (HC) 4000 PONCE DE LEON BL., SUITE 700, CORAL GABLES
33146.
(305) 371-4286, FAX (305) 371-4288

MR. MICHAEL STUART HACKER, — Jun. 02, 1983
HONORARY CONSUL

GEORGIA

ATLANTA (HC) 830 WESTVIEW DR., SW, 30314-3773.
(404) 614-6040

MR. JULIUS E. COLES, — Oct. 14, 1997
HONORARY CONSUL

LOUISIANA

NEW ORLEANS (HCG) X INTERNATIONAL TRADE UN., SUITE 1803,
70161.
(504) 529-7561

MR. WILLIAM MANCHESTER AYERS, — Dec. 20, 1994
HONORARY CONSUL GENERAL

MS. DEBORAH ANN ADAMS, — Aug. 21, 1984
HONORARY CONSUL

STATE* RESIDENCE	NAME AND RANK	DATE OF RECOGNITION	STATE* RESIDENCE	NAME AND RANK	DATE OF RECOGNITION

MASSACHUSETTS

BOSTON (HCG) 381 DUDLEY RD., NEWTON 02159.
(617) 244-3605

    DR. MICHEL ROSEN,   Apr. 15, 1995
       HONORARY CONSUL GENERAL

NEW YORK

NEW YORK (CG) 271 W. 125TH ST., SUITE 412/415, 10027.

    MR. CHEIKH NIANG,   Feb. 08, 2007
       CONSUL GENERAL
    MRS. BOUNAMA DIOP SOW,   Aug. 10, 2001
       CONSUL
    MS. AISSATOU MBAYE,   Sep. 29, 2003
       CONSUL
    MR. MOUKHTAR KOUYATE,   Mar. 11, 2004
       CONSUL
    MR. ALLE NDIAYE,   May. 17, 2006
       CONSUL
    MRS. MARIE THERESE NDONG LOPEZ, Aug. 10, 2001
       CONSULAR AGENT
    MRS. MINGUE NDIAYE NGOM,   Nov. 27, 2001
       CONSULAR AGENT
    MR. CHEIKH MBACKE SAMB,   Jul. 28, 2004
       CONSULAR AGENT
    MR. ABABACAR DABO,   Jul. 01, 2005
       CONSULAR AGENT
    MR. BASSIROU LO,   Oct. 11, 2005
       CONSULAR AGENT
    MS. HAWO DIALLO,   Dec. 29, 2005
       CONSULAR AGENT
    MR. MOURTADA KANE,   Feb. 15, 2006
       CONSULAR AGENT
    MR. OUMAR KANE,   Apr. 30, 2007
       CONSULAR AGENT
    MS. CIRE SAVANE SOW,   May. 08, 2007
       CONSULAR AGENT

TEXAS

HOUSTON (CG) 9701 RICHMOND AV., SUITE 212, 77042.
    MRS. FATOU NDIAYE SALL,   Oct. 13, 2005
       CONSUL GENERAL

SERBIA

COLORADO

DENVER (HCG) 535 16TH ST., SUITE 620, 80202.
(303) 825-6100

    MR. STEVEN H. KATICH,   Nov. 21, 2002
       HONORARY CONSUL GENERAL

ILLINOIS

CHICAGO (CG) 201 E. OHIO ST., SUITE 200, 60611.
(312) 670-6707, FAX (312) 670-6787

    MR. DESKO NIKITOVIC,   Apr. 02, 2003
       CONSUL GENERAL
    MS. MELINA KRTINIC,   Feb. 07, 2006
       CONSUL
    MR. NEBOJSA ACIMOVIC,   Mar. 20, 2003
       VICE CONSUL

LOUISIANA

METAIRIE (HCG) 3850 N. CAUSEWAY BL., SUITE 1330, 70002.
(504) 465-1000

    MR. GREGORY RANDOLPH RUSOVICH, Nov. 24, 2003
       HONORARY CONSUL GENERAL

NEW YORK

NEW YORK (CG) 62 W. 45TH ST., FLOOR 7TH, 10036.
(212) 596-4352, FAX (212) 596-4363

    MR. VLADIMIR ZUTIC,   Mar. 09, 2006
       CONSUL
    MR. NEMANJA STEVANOVIC,   Feb. 07, 2006
       VICE CONSUL

OHIO

CLEVELAND (HCG) 127 PUBLIC SQ., 44114.
(216) 344-2010

    MR. ALEX MACHASKEE,   Apr. 19, 2007
       HONORARY CONSUL GENERAL

WYOMING

CHEYENNE (HCG) 1700 LINCOLN WA., 82001.
(307) 635-8931

    MR. JONATHAN LAWRENCE VINNIK, Oct. 07, 2002
       HONORARY CONSUL GENERAL

SEYCHELLES

ALASKA

ANCHORAGE (HC) 1923 SWITZERLAND WA., 99503.
(907) 244-5375, FAX (907) 646-9872

    MR. HAROLD GREEN,   Apr. 03, 1998
       HONORARY CONSUL

WASHINGTON

SEATTLE (HCG) 3620 S.W. 309TH ST., FEDERAL WAY 98063.
(253) 874-4579

    MRS. ANNE LISE M. CHURCH,   Feb. 06, 2002
       HONORARY CONSUL GENERAL

SINGAPORE

CALIFORNIA

SAN FRANCISCO (CG) 595 MARKET ST., SUITE 2450, 94105.
(415) 543-4775, FAX (415) 543-4788

    MR. J. SOHAN SINGH,   Sep. 03, 2003
       CONSUL GENERAL
    MS. HUEY BIN LEONG,   Apr. 17, 2007
       CONSUL

FLORIDA

MIAMI (HCG) 2601 S. BAYSHORE DR., SUITE 800, 33133.
(305) 858-4225, FAX (305) 858-2334

    MR. STEVEN J. GREEN,   Jul. 25, 2003
       HONORARY CONSUL GENERAL

ILLINOIS

CHICAGO (HCG) 1 S. DEARBORN ST., 60603.
(312) 853-7555, FAX (312) 853-7036

STATE* RESIDENCE	NAME AND RANK	DATE OF RECOGNITION	STATE* RESIDENCE	NAME AND RANK	DATE OF RECOGNITION

MR. NEWTON MINOW,
   HONORARY CONSUL GENERAL — Jul. 20, 2004

NEW YORK

NEW YORK (CON) 231 E. 51ST ST., 10022.
(212) 223-3331, FAX (212) 826-5028
   MR. RICHARD T. GROSSE,
   CONSUL — Sep. 14, 2004

TEXAS

HOUSTON (HCG) 600 TRAVIS ST., SUITE 3700, 77002.
(713) 512-4488, FAX (713) 512-4498
   MR. MICHAEL EDWARD DEE,
   HONORARY CONSUL GENERAL — Jan. 27, 2006

SLOVAK REPUBLIC

CALIFORNIA

LOS ANGELES (CG) 10940 WILSHIRE BL., SUITE 2030, 90024.
(310) 209-1253, FAX (310) 209-1261
   MR. FRANTISEK HUDAK,
   CONSUL GENERAL — Mar. 24, 2005
   MRS. MARTINA SIMKOVA,
   VICE CONSUL — Aug. 18, 2004

SAN FRANCISCO (HC) 2220 STOCKBRIDGE AV., REDWOOD CITY 94062.
(925) 457-8380
   MS. BARBARA MILLIKEN PIVNICKA,
   HONORARY CONSUL — May. 14, 2001

COLORADO

DENVER (HC) 300 S. JACKSON ST., SUITE 100, 80209.
(303) 692-8833
   MR. GREGORY JAMES FASING,
   HONORARY CONSUL — Jan. 18, 1995

FLORIDA

FT. LAUDERDALE (HC) 5200 N.W. 67TH AV., LAUDERHILL 33319.
(954) 749-8857
   DR. ROBERT JOSEPH PETRIK,
   HONORARY CONSUL — May. 14, 2001

ILLINOIS

CHICAGO (HC) 34 S. WASHINGTON ST., NAPERVILLE 60540.
(630) 420-7597, FAX (815) 838-9877
   MR. THOMAS KENNETH WARD,
   HONORARY CONSUL — Jan. 18, 1995

INDIANA

INDIANAPOLIS (HC) 111 MONUMENT CI., SUITE 3700, 46204.
(317) 634-3456
   MR. STEVE ZLATOS,
   HONORARY CONSUL — Apr. 04, 2003

MASSACHUSETTS

WESTON (HC) 3 ROUND HILL RD., 02493.

MR. PETER MUZILA,
   HONORARY CONSUL — Nov. 23, 2005

MICHIGAN

DETROIT (HC) 2933 FORT ST., LINCOLN PARK 48146.
(313) 386-6400
   MR. EDWARD MICHAEL ZELENAK,
   HONORARY CONSUL — May. 14, 2001

MINNESOTA

MINNEAPOLIS (HC) 9739 PALMER RD., 55437.
(952) 937-9006
   MR. JOHN J. LUKNIC,
   HONORARY CONSUL — Aug. 05, 1997

MISSOURI

KANSAS CITY (HC) 11729 CENTRAL ST., 64114.
(816) 943-0515
   MR. ROSS PAUL MARINE,
   HONORARY CONSUL — Feb. 22, 2001

NEVADA

LAS VEGAS (HC) 10600 AMBER RIDGE DR., APT 204, 89144.
   DR. GEOFFREY A. VANDERPAL,
   HONORARY CONSUL — Aug. 28, 2006

NEW YORK

NEW YORK (CG) 801 2ND AV., FLOOR 12, 10017.
(212) 286-8434
   MR. IVAN SURKOS,
   CONSUL GENERAL — Dec. 24, 2003
   MR. ONDREJ GAVALEC,
   CONSUL — Sep. 17, 2003

OHIO

CLEVELAND (HC) 1900 E. 9TH ST., 44114.
(216) 861-6772, FAX (216) 687-5375
   DR. EDWARD GEORGE KESHOCK,
   HONORARY CONSUL — Sep. 21, 1998

PENNSYLVANIA

PITTSBURGH (HC) 1910 COCHRAN RD., SUITE 500, 15220.
(412) 531-2990
   MR. JOSEPH T. SENKO,
   HONORARY CONSUL — May. 02, 1997

WASHINGTON

BAINBRIDGE ISLAND (HC) 261 MADISON AV., NE, SUITE 105, 98110.
(206) 842-1932
   MR. RUDOLPH E. ZIGMUND,
   HONORARY CONSUL — Oct. 28, 2004

SLOVENIA

CALIFORNIA

SAN FRANCISCO (HC) 44 MONTGOMERY ST., SUITE 1050, 94104.
(415) 989-1800

---

* DEPENDENCIES SUCH AS GUAM, PUERTO RICO, AND THE VIRGIN ISLANDS ARE LISTED HERE.
CG-CONSULATE GENERAL   C-CONSULATE   VC-VICE CONSULATE   CA-CONSULAR AGENCY   H-HONORARY CONSULAR STATUS

STATE* RESIDENCE	NAME AND RANK	DATE OF RECOGNITION	STATE* RESIDENCE	NAME AND RANK	DATE OF RECOGNITION

MR. THOMAS JOHN BRANDI,
HONORARY CONSUL — Mar. 06, 2007

MR. RICHARD B. III WILKENS,
HONORARY CONSUL — Feb. 12, 1996

COLORADO

DENVER (HC) 1200 17TH ST., SUITE 1600, 80202.
(303) 893-2780

MR. RAYMOND PETER KOGOVSEK,
HONORARY CONSUL — Feb. 09, 1999

FLORIDA

PALM BEACH (HC) 1048 S. OCEAN BL., 33480.
(561) 833-2222, FAX (561) 833-2235

MS. MARIA LOUISE BACINICH,
HONORARY CONSUL — Dec. 19, 2001

GEORGIA

ATLANTA (HC) 400 COLONY SQ., NE, SUITE 200, 30361.
(404) 881-2812, FAX (404) 881-2813

MR. PAUL NEAL STEINFELD,
HONORARY CONSUL — Jan. 20, 1999

HAWAII

HONOLULU (HC) 900 FORT STREET MALL ., SUITE 1450, 96813.
(808) 544-3203

MR. RONALD JOSEPH ZLATOPER,
HONORARY CONSUL — Aug. 28, 2003

KANSAS

MISSION HILLS (HC) 6521 WENONGA TE., 66208.
(913) 236-4661

MRS. BARBARA KOVAL NELSON,
HONORARY CONSUL — Jun. 08, 2005

NEW YORK

NEW YORK (CG) 600 3RD AV., FLOOR 21ST, 10016.
(212) 370-3006, FAX (212) 370-3581

MS. ALENKA SUHADOLNIK,
CONSUL GENERAL — Nov. 19, 2004

MR. TOMAZ SALAMUN,
CONSUL — Oct. 28, 1996

OHIO

CLEVELAND (CG) 55 PUBLIC SQ., SUITE 945, 44113.
(216) 589-9220, FAX (216) 589-9210

MR. ZVONE ZIGON,
CONSUL GENERAL — Oct. 17, 2005

TENNESSEE

KNOXVILLE (HC) 1928 ALCOA HW., SUITE 102, 37920.
(865) 544-9566

MRS. MATEJA DE LEONNI STANONIK,
HONORARY CONSUL — Jul. 20, 2004

TEXAS

HOUSTON (HC) 2925 BRIARPARK ., FLOOR 7, 77042.
(713) 430-7350, FAX (713) 430-7077

SOUTH AFRICA

ALABAMA

MOBILE (HCG) 500 SPANISH FORT BL., DAPHNE 36526.
(251) 626-4452

MR. JOHN H. VAN AKEN,
HONORARY CONSUL GENERAL — May. 13, 1976

CALIFORNIA

LOS ANGELES (CG) 6300 WILSHIRE BL., SUITE 600, 90048.
(323) 651-5902, FAX (323) 651-5969

MS. JEANETTE THOKOZILE NDHLOVU,
CONSUL GENERAL — Feb. 02, 2005

MR. ALAN GRAHAM MOORE,
CONSUL — Mar. 08, 2004

MR. MZINGISI EDWARD MPIYAKHE,
CONSUL — Jul. 08, 2005

ILLINOIS

CHICAGO (CG) 200 S. MICHIGAN AV., FLOOR 6TH, 60604.
(312) 939-7929

MR. YUSUF OMAR,
CONSUL GENERAL — Oct. 12, 2004

MR. MACHIEL RENIER VAN NIEKERK,
CONSUL — Aug. 18, 2004

MR. CHARLES MANUEL,
CONSUL — Feb. 27, 2006

MR. KHUTSO JUSTICE THAMAGA,
CONSUL — Jun. 01, 2006

MS. GILLIAN SAPHIRAH MOTLHAMME,
VICE CONSUL — Jun. 01, 2006

NEW YORK

NEW YORK (CG) 333 E. 38TH ST., FLOOR 9TH, 10016.
(212) 213-4880

MS. FIKILE SYLVIA MAGUBANE,
CONSUL GENERAL — Apr. 15, 2005

MR. IVAN CHARLES VOSLOO,
CONSUL — May. 09, 2002

MR. BENJAMIN FRANCOIS ALEX ROBBERTSE,
CONSUL — Mar. 09, 2004

MS. HEIDI MALESA,
CONSUL — Oct. 13, 2005

MS. NWABISA ELLA NZEYIMANA,
CONSUL — Jun. 09, 2006

MS. MMONADILO A. TSELE MASELOANYANE,
CONSUL — Jun. 21, 2006

MS. SHOLEEN P. MOOLJEE,
VICE CONSUL — Sep. 21, 2001

MRS. NOBATEMBU JOYCE MTIRARA,
VICE CONSUL — Apr. 25, 2006

TEXAS

DALLAS (HC) 400 S. ZANG UN., SUITE 806, 75208.

MRS. HELEN GIDDINGS,
HONORARY CONSUL — Nov. 30, 2006

STATE* RESIDENCE	NAME AND RANK	DATE OF RECOGNITION	STATE* RESIDENCE	NAME AND RANK	DATE OF RECOGNITION

UTAH

SALT LAKE CITY (HC) 2272 RIDGEWOOD WA., S, BOUNTIFUL 84010.
(801) 298-0824

   MR. ROBERT PAUL THORN,   Apr. 29, 1982
   HONORARY CONSUL

SPAIN

ALASKA

ANCHORAGE (HVC) 1200 I ST., APT 407, 99501.
(907) 345-8645

   MR. ROBERTO ALBACETE GONZALEZ,   Sep. 14, 1998
   HONORARY VICE CONSUL

ARIZONA

PHOENIX (HC) 3134 E. CAMELBACK UN., 85016.
(602) 955-2055

   MR. ALFREDO JOSE MOLINA,   Sep. 13, 2002
   HONORARY CONSUL

CALIFORNIA

LOS ANGELES (CG) 5055 WILSHIRE BL., SUITE 860, 90036.
(323) 938-0158

   MR. INOCENCIO FELIX ARIAS LLAMAS,   Jul. 29, 2005
     CONSUL GENERAL
   MR. JOSE MANUEL GIL OSLE,   Apr. 24, 2007
     VICE CONSUL

CONSULAR ANNEX - COMMERCIAL
LOS ANGELES (CONA) 1900 AVENUE OF THE STARS UN., SUITE 2430, 90067.
(301) 277-5125, FAX (213) 627-0883

   MR. JAIME ORMAECHEA LORENZO GARCIA,   Apr. 24, 2007
     CONSUL

CONSULAR ANNEX OF SPAIN
LOS ANGELES (CONA) 8383 WILSHIRE BL., SUITE 960, BEVERLY HILLS 90211.
(213) 658-7188

   MS. ANGELA MARIA CASTANO CABANAS,   Dec. 17, 2004
     CONSUL

EDUCATION OFFICE OF SPAIN
LOS ANGELES (CONA) 6300 WILSHIRE BL., SUITE 830, 90048.
(323) 852-6997, FAX (213) 852-0759

SAN DIEGO (HC) 10922 ANJA WA., LAKESIDE 92040-2717.
(619) 448-7282

   MRS. MARIA ANGELES OLSON,   Nov. 13, 1997
   HONORARY CONSUL

SAN FRANCISCO (CG) 1405 SUTTER ST., 94109.
(415) 922-2995

   MR. MANUEL PRADAS ROMANI,   Nov. 17, 2006
     CONSUL GENERAL

COLORADO

ENGLEWOOD (HC) 9697 E. MINERAL AV., 80112.
(303) 784-8268

   MR. JOSE LUIS PARRADO,   May. 16, 2007
   HONORARY CONSUL

FLORIDA

MIAMI (CG) 2655 LE JEUNE RD., SUITE 203, CORAL GABLES 33134.
(305) 446-5511

   MR. SANTIAGO CABANAS ANSORENA,   Oct. 04, 2005
     CONSUL GENERAL
   MR. JOSE RUIZ ARBELOA,   Feb. 03, 2003
     DEPUTY CONSUL
   MS. MARIA PILAR MENDEZ JIMENEZ,   Apr. 06, 2007
     DEPUTY CONSUL
   MR. FERNANDO JAVIER DIAZ CARVAJAL,   Jul. 09, 2003
     VICE CONSUL

COMMERCIAL OFFICE
MIAMI (CONA) 2655 LE JEUNE RD., SUITE 1111&1114, CORAL GABLES 33134.
(305) 446-4387

   MS. MARIA B. CRISTINO MACHO QUEVEDO, Oct. 04, 2004
     CONSUL

SPANISH TOURIST OFFICE
MIAMI (CONA) 1395 BRICKELL AV., SUITE 1130, 33131.
(305) 358-1992

   MS. BEATRIZ MARCO ARCE,   Aug. 20, 2002
     CONSUL

SPANISH EDUCATION OFFICE
MIAMI (CONA) 2655 LEJEUNE RD., SUITE 1000, CORAL GABLES 33134.
(305) 448-2146, FAX (305) 445-0508

   MR. GONZALO GONZALEZ DE LARA SAENZ, Sep. 06, 2006
     CONSUL

ORLANDO (HVC) 1193 CALANDA AV., 32807.
(407) 273-8912

   MRS. RAQUEL LOPEZ TACON,   Jun. 07, 2006
   HONORARY VICE CONSUL

PENSACOLA (HVC) 100 INGALLS DR., 32506-5259.
(850) 455-5360, FAX (850) 455-9283

   MS. MARIA D. DAVIS,   Aug. 26, 1996
   HONORARY VICE CONSUL

SAINT AUGUSTINE (HVC) ONE KING ST., SUITE 103, 32084.
(904) 827-1177

   MRS. MARICARMEN GUTIERREZ,   Feb. 03, 2005
   HONORARY VICE CONSUL

TAMPA (HVC) 716 W. FLETCHER AV., 33612.
(813) 961-3300

   MR. JOSE VIVERO,   May. 30, 2006
   HONORARY VICE CONSUL

GEORGIA

ATLANTA (HVC) 1010 HUNTCLIFF ., SUITE 2315, 30350.
(770) 518-2406, FAX (770) 518-2410

   MR. IGNACIO LUIS TABOADA,   Apr. 20, 1995
   HONORARY VICE CONSUL

---

* DEPENDENCIES SUCH AS GUAM, PUERTO RICO, AND THE VIRGIN ISLANDS ARE LISTED HERE.
CG-CONSULATE GENERAL   C-CONSULATE   VC-VICE CONSULATE   CA-CONSULAR AGENCY   H-HONORARY CONSULAR STATUS

STATE* RESIDENCE	NAME AND RANK	DATE OF RECOGNITION	STATE* RESIDENCE	NAME AND RANK	DATE OF RECOGNITION

HAWAII

HONOLULU (HVC) 5253 KALANIANAOLE HW., 96821.
(808) 373-9201, FAX (808) 373-2469

MR. JOHN HENRY FELIX,   Oct. 03, 1980
HONORARY VICE CONSUL

IDAHO

BOISE (HC) 999 MAIN ST., FLOOR 13TH, 83702.
(208) 389-7297

MS. ADELIA G. SIMPLOT,   Sep. 17, 2002
HONORARY CONSUL

ILLINOIS

CHICAGO (CG) 180 N. MICHIGAN AV., SUITE 1500, 60601.
(312) 782-4588

MR. JUAN CARLOS VIDAL GARCIA,   Jan. 06, 2006
CONSUL

NATIONAL SPANISH TOURIST OFFICE
CHICAGO (CONA) 845 N. MICHIGAN AV., SUITE 915-E, 60611.
(312) 642-1992

MR. JULIO LOPEZ ASTOR,   Aug. 22, 2002
CONSUL

SPANISH COMMERCIAL OFFICE
CHICAGO (CONA) 500 N. MICHIGAN AV., SUITE 1500, 60611.
(312) 644-1154

MR. MANUEL ENRIQUE ALEJO GONZALEZ,   Feb. 23, 2006
CONSUL

LOUISIANA

NEW ORLEANS (CG) 2 CANAL ST., 70130.
(504) 525-4951

MASSACHUSETTS

BOSTON (CG) 31 ST. JAMES AV., SUITE 905, 02116.
(617) 536-2506

MR. CARLOS ROBLES FRAGA,   Sep. 14, 2006
CONSUL GENERAL

MICHIGAN

ANN ARBOR (HC) 2114 PAULINE BL., FLOOR 2, 48103.
(734) 662-0434

DR. MARIA DEL CORAL LOPEZ GOMEZ,   Apr. 19, 2007
HONORARY CONSUL

MINNESOTA

ST. PAUL (HC) 766 LINWOOD AV., SAINT PAUL 55105.
(651) 227-4439, FAX (651) 227-2906

MRS. CRISTINA F. URDANGARIN,   May. 22, 2006
HONORARY CONSUL

MISSOURI

KANSAS CITY (HC) 316 AVILA CI., 64114.
(816) 942-2649, FAX (816) 942-2649

MR. EUGENE FRANCIS GRAY,   Aug. 31, 1998
HONORARY CONSUL

SAINT LOUIS (HC) 5715 MANCHESTER AV., ST. LOUIS 63110.
(314) 781-1500, FAX (314) 781-1507

MR. JOSE L., JR MOLINA,   Jun. 15, 2007
HONORARY CONSUL

NEW JERSEY

NEWARK (HC) 249 UNIVERSITY AV., 07102.

MR. ARTURO LOPEZ,   Nov. 17, 1992
HONORARY CONSUL

NEW MEXICO

ALBUQUERQUE (HC) 10919 4TH ST., 87114.
(505) 280-1455, FAX (505) 897-1081

MR. ROBERT OLDHAM MOORE,   Jul. 03, 2003
HONORARY CONSUL

SANTA FE (HC) 2211 BRILLIANTE ST., 87505.
(505) 471-6131

MR. ALBERT J. GALLEGOS,   Oct. 02, 2006
HONORARY CONSUL

NEW YORK

NEW YORK (CG) 150 E. 58TH ST., FLOOR 30 AND 31, 10155.
(212) 355-4080

MR. JUAN MANUEL EGEA IBANEZ,   Sep. 03, 2003
CONSUL GENERAL
MR. ROBERTO VARELA FARINA,   Mar. 08, 2005
CONSUL

NATIONAL SPANISH TOURIST OFFICE
NEW YORK (CONA) 666 5TH AV., FLOOR 35TH, 10103.
(212) 265-8822

MR. FRANCISCO JAVIER PINANES LEAL,   Aug. 10, 2004
CONSUL
MR. RAFAEL CHAMORRO,   May. 08, 2007
DEPUTY CONSUL

SPANISH COMMERCIAL OFFICE
NEW YORK (CONA) 405 LEXINGTON AV., FLOOR 44TH-45TH, 10174.
(212) 661-4959

MR. MANUEL GARCIA ARANDA ALVAREZ,   Sep. 29, 2003
CONSUL
MR. FRANCISCO JAVIER SANSA TORRES,   Feb. 23, 2006
CONSUL
MR. RICARDO FERNANDEZ CALVO,   Jan. 16, 2003
DEPUTY CONSUL

SPANISH EDUCATION OFFICE
NEW YORK (CONA) 358 5TH AV., SUITE 1404, 10001.
(212) 629-4435, FAX (212) 629-4438

MR. JESUS FERNANDEZ GONZALEZ,   Jul. 26, 2006
CONSUL

NORTH CAROLINA

DURHAM (HVC) 600 FOSTER ST., 27701.
(919) 667-1988, FAX (919) 667-1888

---

* DEPENDENCIES SUCH AS GUAM, PUERTO RICO, AND THE VIRGIN ISLANDS ARE LISTED HERE.
CG-CONSULATE GENERAL   C-CONSULATE   VC-VICE CONSULATE   CA-CONSULAR AGENCY   H-HONORARY CONSULAR STATUS

STATE* RESIDENCE	NAME AND RANK	DATE OF RECOGNITION

MR. RAFAEL LOPEZ BARRANTES,
   HONORARY VICE CONSUL — Jul. 02, 2002

OHIO

CINCINNATI (HVC) 2605 BURNET AV., 45219.
(513) 961-3737
   MR. SIDNEY L. KAUFMAN,
   HONORARY VICE CONSUL — Jun. 19, 1979

CLEVELAND (HC) 90 E. 197TH ST., 44119.
(216) 531-0761
   MR. MANUEL MALTAS LOPEZ,
   HONORARY CONSUL — Apr. 19, 2007

PENNSYLVANIA

PHILADELPHIA (HVC) 3410 WARDEN DR., 19129.
   MR. HERMINIO MUNIZ,
   HONORARY VICE CONSUL — Nov. 30, 1983

PUERTO RICO

SAN JUAN (CG) EDIFICIO MERCANTIL PZ., SUITE 1101, HATO REY
00918.
(787) 758-6090, FAX (787) 763-0190
   MR. CARLOS VINUESA SALTO,
   CONSUL GENERAL — Jun. 29, 2006
   MR. GABINO IGLESIAS FERNANDEZ,
   CONSULAR AGENT — Feb. 28, 1985

SPANISH COMMERCIAL OFFICE OF SPAIN
SAN JUAN (CONA) 239 ARTERIAL HOSTOS AV., SUITE 705, 00918.
(787) 758-6345, FAX (787) 758-6948
   MR. FRANCISCO JAVIER TENA GARCIA,
   CONSUL — Sep. 29, 2003

TEXAS

CORPUS CHRISTI (HC) 7517 YORKSHIRE BL., 78413.
(512) 994-7517
   MR. FERNANDO MORAL IGLESIAS,
   HONORARY CONSUL — Nov. 13, 1997

DALLAS (HC) 5499 GLEN LAKES DR., SUITE 209, 75231.
(214) 373-1200
   MS. JANET POLLMAN KAFKA,
   HONORARY CONSUL — Aug. 04, 1997

EL PASO (HC) 420 GOLDEN SPRINGS DR., 79912.
(915) 534-0677
   MR. ARTHUR SHELDON HALL,
   HONORARY CONSUL — Feb. 12, 1985

HOUSTON (CG) 1800 BERING DR., SUITE 660, 77057.
(713) 783-6200
   MR. JULIO MONTESINO RAMOS,
   CONSUL GENERAL — Mar. 27, 2003
   MR. LUIS M. CASTANON GUTIERREZ,
   VICE CONSUL — Jul. 18, 2007

SAN ANTONIO (HC) 8350 DELPHIAN ., 78148.

MRS. ISABEL DE PEDRO MARIN,
   HONORARY CONSUL — Oct. 07, 1986

UTAH

SALT LAKE CITY (HC) 5131 S. MORNING SUN DR., TAYLORSVILLE
84123.
(801) 264-8321, FAX (801) 293-8097
   MR. BALDOMERO LAGO,
   HONORARY CONSUL — Mar. 22, 2001

WASHINGTON

SEATTLE (HC) XX PO BOX 3707 MS 65-68 UN., N, 98124.
(425) 237-9373, FAX (425) 228-6239
   MR. LUIS F. ESTEBAN BERNALDEZ,
   HONORARY CONSUL — Jul. 30, 2007

SRI LANKA

ARIZONA

PHOENIX (HC) 329 W. CYPRESS ST., 85003.
(602) 254-1899
   DR. JEREMY ROBERT TORSTVEIT,
   HONORARY CONSUL — Dec. 23, 2002

CALIFORNIA

LOS ANGELES (CG) 3250 WILSHIRE BL., SUITE 1405, 90010.
(213) 387-0213, FAX (213) 387-0216
   MR. JALIYA CHITRAN WICKRAMASURIYA,
   CONSUL GENERAL — Apr. 17, 2007

GEORGIA

ATLANTA (HCG) 1201 W. PEACHTREE ST., 30309-3424.
(404) 881-7164, FAX (404) 263-8643
   MR. KEVIN E. GRADY,
   HONORARY CONSUL GENERAL — Jan. 19, 2000

HAWAII

HONOLULU (HC) 60 N. BERETANIA ST., SUITE 410, 96817-4754.
(808) 524-6738
   MRS. KUSUMA C. COORAY,
   HONORARY CONSUL — Aug. 20, 2001

ILLINOIS

CHICAGO (HC) 200 W. MADISON ST., SUITE 2670, 60606.
(312) 236-6555, FAX (312) 236-6568
   MR. RONALD JAMES SORINI,
   HONORARY CONSUL — Mar. 04, 2004

LOUISIANA

NEW ORLEANS (HC) 401 VETERANS BL., SUITE 102, METAIRIE
70005.
(504) 455-7600, FAX (504) 455-7605
   MR. DAVID R. BURRUS,
   HONORARY CONSUL — Nov. 14, 1991

STATE* RESIDENCE	NAME AND RANK	DATE OF RECOGNITION	STATE* RESIDENCE	NAME AND RANK	DATE OF RECOGNITION

MASSACHUSETTS

BOSTON (HC) 220 BOYLSTON ST., SUITE 1515, 02116.
(617) 426-9543

    MR. MARTIN TRUST,   Dec. 28, 2004
       HONORARY CONSUL

NEW JERSEY

NEWARK (HC) 2 E. GLEN RD., DENVILLE 07834.
(973) 586-3411

    MR. JAYASIRI PARAKRAMA LIYANAGE,   Sep. 04, 2002
       HONORARY CONSUL

NEW MEXICO

SANTA FE (HC) 7610 OLD SANTA FE TRAIL UN., 87505.
(505) 989-7252

    DR. ALTHEA GRAY,   Jul. 31, 2002
       HONORARY CONSUL

NEW YORK

NEW YORK (CON) 630 3RD AV., FLOOR 20TH, 10017.
(212) 986-7040

ST. KITTS AND NEVIS

CALIFORNIA

LOS ANGELES (CG) 1762 WESTWOOD BL., 90024.
(310) 694-5208, FAX (310) 694-8239

    MR. BASSAM ALGHANIM,   Mar. 07, 2006
       CONSUL GENERAL

DISTRICT OF COLUMBIA

WASHINGTON (HC) 2705 ROBINSON PL., SE, 20020.
    MR. U. HUGH M. GUISHARD,   Dec. 03, 1984
       HONORARY CONSUL

FLORIDA

MIAMI (HCG) 6855 RED RD., SUITE 600, 33143--3632.
(305) 273-2333

    MR. BRIAN E. KEELEY,   Jan. 29, 2006
       HONORARY CONSUL GENERAL

GEORGIA

ATLANTA (HC) 644 ANTONE ST., NW, 30318.
    MR. BERNARD M. PORCHE,   Oct. 07, 1985
       HONORARY CONSUL

NEW YORK

NEW YORK (CG) 414 E. 75TH ST., 10021.
    MR. KUTAYBA YUSUF ALGHANIM,   May. 21, 2002
       CONSUL GENERAL

TEXAS

DALLAS (HC) 6336 GREENVILLE AV., 75206.
    MR. WILLIAM R. EWING,   Nov. 21, 1985
       HONORARY CONSUL

VIRGIN ISLANDS

ST. THOMAS (HC) X P.O. BOX 302353 UN., 00803.
(340) 775-6970, FAX (340) 777-1870

    MR. ELRIDGE ST CLAIR TOBIAS,   Jul. 25, 2001
       HONORARY CONSUL

ST. LUCIA

CALIFORNIA

LOS ANGELES (HC) 2250 CENTURY HILL ., 90067.
(310) 557-9000

    MR. DENIS D. ALEXANDER,   Feb. 11, 1999
       HONORARY CONSUL

FLORIDA

MIAMI (CG) 1101 BRICKELL AV., SUITE 1602, 33131.
    MR. KENT MARCEL PRESTON HIPPOLYTE,   May. 24, 2000
       CONSUL GENERAL

NEW YORK

NEW YORK (CG) 800 2ND AV., SUITE 910, 10017.
(212) 697-9360

    MR. HUBERT EMMANUEL,   Mar. 26, 2004
       DEPUTY CONSUL GENERAL
    MR. OLAF FONTENELLE,   Jun. 08, 2005
       DEPUTY CONSUL GENERAL
    MS. ESMA ETHELINE FRICOT,   Aug. 05, 1998
       CONSUL
    MS. EURICE PETULA KHODRA,   Jan. 07, 2003
       VICE CONSUL
    MS. MARTHA CLAUDIE SMITH,   Jan. 09, 2006
       VICE CONSUL

VIRGIN ISLANDS

ST. CROIX (HC) 67 MAHOGANY ., 00850.
    MR. LUTHER F. RENEE,   Nov. 02, 1983
       HONORARY CONSUL

ST. VINCENT AND THE GRENADINES

CALIFORNIA

LOS ANGELES (HCG) 231 W. VERNON AV., SUITE 101, 90037.
(323) 231-5181

    DR. CADRIN EMMANUEL GILL,   Sep. 13, 2002
       HONORARY CONSUL GENERAL

LOUISIANA

NEW ORLEANS (HCG) 650 POYDRAS ST., SUITE 2715, 70130-6111.
(504) 523-1385

    MR. JAMES R. SUTTERFIELD,   Jan. 23, 1997
       HONORARY CONSUL GENERAL

NEW YORK

NEW YORK (CG) 801 2ND AV., FLOOR 21ST, 10017.
(212) 687-4490

    MR. COSMUS E. COZIER,   Dec. 19, 2001
       CONSUL GENERAL

STATE* RESIDENCE	NAME AND RANK	DATE OF RECOGNITION

SURINAME

FLORIDA

MIAMI (CG) 6303 BLUE LAGOON DR., SUITE 325, 33126.
(305) 265-4655, FAX (305) 265-4599

MR. MOHAMED RAKIEB KHUDABUX, CONSUL GENERAL	Jun. 20, 2007
MS. INGE A PIGOT ENSER, CONSUL	Apr. 24, 2007
MS. PATRICIA DENZ, CONSULAR AGENT	Mar. 08, 2002
MR. THEODORUS LEONARD CEDER, CONSULAR AGENT	Mar. 27, 2003

LOUISIANA

NEW ORLEANS (HC) 400 POYDRAS ST., SUITE 2450, 70130.
(504) 527-5450

MR. ROY J., JR RODNEY, HONORARY CONSUL	May. 19, 1998

SWEDEN

ALASKA

ANCHORAGE (HC) 301 W. NORTHERN LIGHTS BL., FLOOR 5TH, 99503.
(907) 265-2930, FAX (907) 265-2068

MR. EDWARD BERNARD RASMUSON, HONORARY CONSUL	Sep. 28, 1978

ARIZONA

PHOENIX (HC) 2 N. CENTRAL AV., SUITE 2200, 85004-4406.
(602) 364-7450, FAX (602) 364-7070

MR. LARS O. LAGERMAN, HONORARY CONSUL	Apr. 13, 1995

CALIFORNIA

LOS ANGELES (CG) 10940 WILSHIRE BL., SUITE 700, 90024.
(310) 445-4008, FAX (310) 473-2229

MR. TOMAS PEDER ROSANDER, CONSUL GENERAL	Sep. 29, 2003
MS. ANNA CAROLINA VAN DER WEYDEN, CONSUL	Oct. 27, 2003
MR. BJORN AXEL PETER FALKENHALL, CONSUL	Apr. 04, 2006
MS. ANNA CARIN THOMER, CONSUL	Apr. 04, 2006
MS. KARIN ULRIKA HOVLIN, CONSUL	Apr. 04, 2006
MS. ANETTE CECILIA JOHANSSON, VICE CONSUL	Apr. 23, 2007
MRS. INGELA SORENSSON, HONORARY VICE CONSUL	Feb. 18, 2000

SWEDISH TRADE COUNCIL
LOS ANGELES (CONA) 10940 WILSHIRE BL., SUITE 700, 90024.
(310) 445-4008, FAX (310) 473-2229

SWEDISH OFFICE OF SCIENCE AND TECHNOLOGY
LOS ANGELES (CONA) 10940 WILSHIRE BL., SUITE 700, 90024.
(310) 445-4008, FAX (310) 473-2229

SAN DIEGO (HC) 750 B ST., SUITE 1020, 92101.
(619) 233-1106

DR. ULF BRYNJESTAD, HONORARY CONSUL	Dec. 23, 2002

SAN FRANCISCO (HCG) 120 MONTGOMERY ST., SUITE 2175, 94104.
(415) 788-2631, FAX (415) 788-6841

MS. BARBRO S. OSHER, HONORARY CONSUL GENERAL	Feb. 11, 1999
MRS. ULLA WIKANDER REILLY, HONORARY VICE CONSUL	Feb. 01, 1997

COLORADO

DENVER (HC) 4242 E. AMHERST AV., 80222.
(303) 758-0999, FAX (303) 758-1091

MR. DONALD GLENN PETERSON, HONORARY CONSUL	Aug. 08, 2001

DISTRICT OF COLUMBIA

WASHINGTON (CHN) 1501 M ST., NW, SUITE 900, 20005.
(202) 467-2600, FAX (202) 467-2699

MR. PONTUS JAERBORG, CONSUL GENERAL	Feb. 17, 2003

FLORIDA

FT. LAUDERDALE (HC) 2550 EISENHOWER BL., SUITE 310, 33316.
(954) 467-3507, FAX (954) 467-1731

MR. PER-OLOF LOOF, HONORARY CONSUL	Jan. 18, 2006
MRS. GUNILLA A. LUNDSTROM NORTH, HONORARY VICE CONSUL	Aug. 09, 1984

TAMPA (HC) 3801 BAY TO BAY BL., 33629.
(813) 839-3800

MR. BO GORAN OLOV HOLMBERG, HONORARY CONSUL	Jul. 29, 2005

GEORGIA

ATLANTA (HC) 600 PEACHTREE ST., NE, SUITE 2400, 30309.
(404) 815-2292, FAX (404) 352-1285

MR. JAN R. MEIJER, HONORARY CONSUL	Feb. 14, 2000
MS. JILL OLANDER, HONORARY CONSUL	Sep. 12, 2005

HAWAII

HONOLULU (HC) 737 BISHOP ST., SUITE 2600, 96813.
(808) 528-4777, FAX (808) 523-1888

MR. JAMES M. CRIBLEY, HONORARY CONSUL	Jan. 11, 1988

ILLINOIS

CHICAGO (HCG) 150 N. MICHIGAN AV., SUITE 1250, 60601.
(312) 781-6262, FAX (312) 781-1816

MRS. KERSTIN B. LANE, HONORARY CONSUL GENERAL	May. 01, 2003
MS. ANNETTE IRENE SEABERG, HONORARY CONSUL	Oct. 28, 2003
MS. KERSTIN BRORSSON, HONORARY VICE CONSUL	Nov. 20, 1996

STATE* RESIDENCE	NAME AND RANK	DATE OF RECOGNITION	STATE* RESIDENCE	NAME AND RANK	DATE OF RECOGNITION

KANSAS

MERRIAM (HC) 6740 ANTIOCH RD., SUITE 100, 66204.
(913) 677-4500, FAX (913) 677-4499

    MR. CRAIG L. ROEDER,   Jun. 15, 2006
      HONORARY CONSUL

LOUISIANA

NEW ORLEANS (HC) 528 GRAVIER ST., 70130.
(504) 586-0084

    MR. THOMAS DUGAN WESTFELDT,   Jan. 14, 2005
      HONORARY CONSUL

MASSACHUSETTS

BOSTON (HC) 286 CONGRESS ST., FLOOR 6TH, 02210.
(617) 451-3456, FAX (617) 423-2057

    DR. SAMUEL ALLEN COUNTER,   Sep. 02, 2004
      HONORARY CONSUL

MICHIGAN

ANN ARBOR (HCG) 7352 PARKER RD., SALINE 48176.
(734) 944-8111, FAX (734) 944-7836

    MR. LENNART NILS JOHANSSON,   Apr. 30, 2004
      HONORARY CONSUL GENERAL

MINNESOTA

MINNEAPOLIS (HCG) 706 2ND AV., S, 55402.
(612) 332-6897, FAX (612) 332-6340

    MR. BRUCE NELSON KARSTADT,   Jun. 05, 2003
      HONORARY CONSUL GENERAL
    MS. KIM MARIE ERICKSON,   Jun. 11, 2003
      HONORARY CONSUL
    MRS. KERSTIN I. JOHNSON,   May. 30, 2006
      HONORARY VICE CONSUL

MISSOURI

SAINT LOUIS (HC) 7701 FORSYTH BL., SUITE 600, 63105.
(314) 540-6532

    MS. LISELOTTE MARIE FOX,   Jun. 15, 2006
      HONORARY CONSUL

NEBRASKA

OMAHA (HC) 1904 FARNAM ST., 68102.
(402) 341-3333, FAX (402) 341-3434

    MR. THOMAS J. LUND,   Oct. 12, 1994
      HONORARY CONSUL

NEVADA

LAS VEGAS (HC) 3097 E. WARM SPRINGS RD., SUITE 100, 89120.
    MS. LENA D. I. WALTHER,   Jul. 12, 2006
      HONORARY CONSUL

NEW YORK

JAMESTOWN (HC) 9-11 E. 4TH ST., 14701.
    MR. STEPHEN E. SELLSTROM,   May. 11, 2006
      HONORARY CONSUL

NEW YORK (CG) 885 2ND AV., FLOOR 45TH, 10017.
(212) 583-2550, FAX (212) 755-2732

    AMBASSADOR KARL HUGO HJERTONSSON,   May. 08, 2006
      CONSUL GENERAL
    MS. EVA LENA STENWALL,   Dec. 11, 2006
      DEPUTY CONSUL GENERAL
    MS. LENA WEDEN,   Dec. 11, 2006
      DEPUTY CONSUL GENERAL
    MS. AMELIE MARIA HEINSJO,   Dec. 11, 2003
      CONSUL
    MR. LARS OLOF OSTLING,   Apr. 04, 2006
      CONSUL
    MR. MAXIMILIAN KARLSEN,   Sep. 21, 2004
      VICE CONSUL

SWEDISH TRADE COUNCIL
NEW YORK (CONA) 599 LEXINGTON AV., SUITE 1204, 10022.
(212) 838-5530

SWEDISH INFORMATION SERVICE
NEW YORK (CONA) 885 SECOND AV., FLOOR 45TH, 10017.

NORTH CAROLINA

RALEIGH (HC) 4900 FALLS OF NEUSE RD., 27609.
(919) 345-1395, FAX (919) 872-0303

    MR. MAGNUS AXEL NATT OCH DAG,   Mar. 29, 2006
      HONORARY CONSUL
    MRS. YLVA ELISABETH WESTIN,   Mar. 31, 2006
      HONORARY VICE CONSUL

OHIO

CLEVELAND (HC) 800 SUPERIOR AV., SUITE 1400, 44114-2688.
(216) 621-4995, FAX (216) 241-0816

    MR. MICHAEL LEE MILLER,   Dec. 03, 1976
      HONORARY CONSUL

OREGON

PORTLAND (HC) 111 S.W. 5TH AV., SUITE 2900, 97204-3690.
(503) 227-0634

    MR. MARK OLIVER JOHNSON,   Jul. 25, 2001
      HONORARY CONSUL
    MR. ROSS ALBIN FOGELQUIST,   Jul. 25, 2001
      HONORARY VICE CONSUL

PENNSYLVANIA

PHILADELPHIA (HC) 1628 J. F. KENNEDY BL., SUITE 2001, 19103.
(215) 496-7200

    MRS. AGNETA HAGGLUND BAILEY,   Nov. 17, 1999
      HONORARY CONSUL

PUERTO RICO

SAN JUAN (HC) 416 PONCE DE LEON AV., SUITE 1111, 00918.
(787) 756-5715

    MS. HEIDIE CALERO,   May. 11, 2006
      HONORARY CONSUL

TEXAS

DALLAS (HC) 6600 LBJ FW., SUITE 183, 75240.
(972) 991-8013

    MR. GARRY GENE JOHNSON,   May. 11, 2006
      HONORARY CONSUL

---

* DEPENDENCIES SUCH AS GUAM, PUERTO RICO, AND THE VIRGIN ISLANDS ARE LISTED HERE.
CG-CONSULATE GENERAL   C-CONSULATE   VC-VICE CONSULATE   CA-CONSULAR AGENCY   H-HONORARY CONSULAR STATUS

STATE* RESIDENCE	NAME AND RANK	DATE OF RECOGNITION

MRS. ANN-KATHRINE KLINTMALM,
HONORARY VICE CONSUL — Jun. 01, 2006

HOUSTON (HC) 2909 HILLCROFT ST., SUITE 515, 77057-5852.
(713) 953-1417, FAX (713) 953-7776
MR. JAN B. DRYSELIUS,
HONORARY CONSUL — Jun. 29, 1993

UTAH

SALT LAKE CITY (HC) 28 S. 400TH EAST ., 84111.
(801) 531-9279
MR. BJORN ERIC ABLAD,
HONORARY CONSUL — Oct. 18, 1999

VIRGIN ISLANDS

ST. THOMAS (HC) 1340 TAARNEBERG ., 00802.
(809) 774-6845, FAX (809) 776-8900
MS. MARIA TANKENSON HODGE,
HONORARY CONSUL — Sep. 07, 1995

VIRGINIA

NORFOLK (HC) 201 E. CITY HALL AV., 23510.
(757) 446-7300, FAX (757) 625-7854
MR. ROLF A. WILLIAMS,
HONORARY CONSUL — Jun. 27, 1989

WASHINGTON

SEATTLE (HC) 520 PIKE ST., SUITE 2200, 98101.
(206) 467-8200
MR. LARS HELGE JONSSON,
HONORARY CONSUL — May. 11, 2006

WISCONSIN

MILWAUKEE (HC) 250 E. WISCONSIN AV., SUITE 800, 53202.
(414) 291-7835, FAX (414) 291-7838
MR. JOHAN CARL RAGNAR SEGERDAHL,
HONORARY CONSUL — Sep. 06, 1994

SWITZERLAND

ARIZONA

PARADISE VALLEY (HC) 7320 E. SHOEMAN LA., SUITE 201,
SCOTTSDALE 85251.
(480) 329-4705, FAX (480) 945-4350
MRS. ALISA CLAIRE JOST,
HONORARY CONSUL — Jun. 04, 2007

CALIFORNIA

LOS ANGELES (CG) 11766 WILSHIRE BL., SUITE 1400, 90025.
(310) 575-1145, FAX (310) 575-1982
MRS. BRIGITTA SCHOCH DETTWEILER,
CONSUL GENERAL — Nov. 21, 2005
MR. NORBERT ARNOLD,
DEPUTY CONSUL GENERAL — Aug. 18, 2004
MR. ALAIN MARC ROH,
CONSUL — Oct. 14, 2004
MS. BRIGITTE LEUTWYLER,
VICE CONSUL — Jul. 28, 2004

SAN FRANCISCO (CG) 456 MONTGOMERY ST., SUITE 1500, 94104.
(415) 788-2272, FAX (415) 788-1402
MR. JEAN-FRANCOIS LICHTENSTERN,
CONSUL GENERAL — Oct. 17, 2005
MR. CHRISTIAN WOLFGANG SIMM,
DEPUTY CONSUL GENERAL — Jan. 09, 1998
MR. MAX ROLAND GROB,
CONSUL — Jul. 07, 2003
MR. HANS ANDREAS BACHMANN,
CONSUL — Nov. 17, 2006

SCIENCE AND TECHNOLOGICAL OFFICE
SAN FRANCISCO (CONA) 730 MONTGOMERY ST., 94111.

COLORADO

BOULDER (HC) 2810 ILIFF ., 80303.
(303) 499-5641, FAX (303) 499-9977
MR. WALTER WYSS,
HONORARY CONSUL — Feb. 02, 1987

DISTRICT OF COLUMBIA

WASHINGTON (CHN) 2900 CATHEDRAL AV., NW, 20008.
(202) 745-7900, FAX (202) 387-2564
MR. ROLF FREI,
CONSUL — Oct. 02, 2002
MR. RAOUL INCERTI,
CONSUL — Mar. 17, 2005
MS. MARGRITH LEDERMANN PRESTOFELIPPO,
CONSUL — May. 24, 2007
MRS. SIMONA ROSANNA REGAZZONI KWENDA,
VICE CONSUL — Aug. 31, 2004

FLORIDA

MIAMI (HC) 825 BRICKELL BAY DR., SUITE 1450, 33131.
(305) 377-6700, FAX (305) 377-9936
MR. URS LINDENMANN,
HONORARY CONSUL — Mar. 24, 1987

ORLANDO (HC) 1011 N. WYMORE RD., WINTER PARK 32789.
(407) 645-3500, FAX (407) 645-3529
MR. LUC SERGE BURKHARDT,
HONORARY CONSUL — Apr. 02, 2001

GEORGIA

ATLANTA (CG) 1349 W. PEACHTREE ST., NW, SUITE 1000, 30309.
(404) 870-2000, FAX (404) 870-2011
MR. ULRICH HUNN,
CONSUL GENERAL — Jan. 06, 2006
MRS. MONICA CAMACHO-BANDLIN,
DEPUTY CONSUL GENERAL — Aug. 07, 2002
MR. DANIEL GRUENENFELDER,
DEPUTY CONSUL GENERAL — Feb. 23, 2004
MS. EDITH RUFER,
VICE CONSUL — Jul. 06, 2007

HAWAII

HONOLULU (HC) 4231 PAPU CI., 96816.
(808) 737-5297, FAX (808) 734-3996

STATE* RESIDENCE	NAME AND RANK	DATE OF RECOGNITION	STATE* RESIDENCE	NAME AND RANK	DATE OF RECOGNITION

MR. NIKLAUS RUDOLF SCHWEIZER,   Feb. 03, 1972
 HONORARY CONSUL

ILLINOIS

CHICAGO (CG) 737 N. MICHIGAN AV., SUITE 2301, 60611.
(312) 915-0061, FAX (312) 915-0388
 MR. MARTIN VON WALTERSKIRCHEN, Oct. 19, 2001
  CONSUL
 MS. RUTH MUEHLESTEIN,   Jul. 29, 2004
  CONSUL

INDIANA

INDIANAPOLIS (HC) 7752 MOLLER RD., 46268.
(317) 217-1645, FAX (309) 405-7023
 MR. ANDREAS FRIEDRICH WEBER, Sep. 02, 2004
  HONORARY CONSUL

LOUISIANA

NEW ORLEANS (HC) 1620 8TH ST., 70115.
(504) 897-6510
 MR. JOHN GEISER,   Aug. 07, 1985
  HONORARY CONSUL

MASSACHUSETTS

BOSTON (CON) 420 BROADWAY ., CAMBRIDGE 02138.
(617) 547-3915, FAX (617) 491-6684
 MR. CHRISTOPH VON ARB,   Mar. 11, 2002
  CONSUL
 MS. MARIANNE GERBER,   Apr. 10, 2002
  DEPUTY CONSUL
 MR. EMIL JOHANN WYSS,   Aug. 24, 2005
  DEPUTY CONSUL
 MR. REMO DANIEL STEINMETZ WINKLER, Apr. 23, 2004
  VICE CONSUL

MICHIGAN

DETROIT (HC) 2175 CROOKS RD., ROCHESTER HILLS 48309.
(248) 852-0040, FAX (248) 853-5665
 MR. KARL A. PFISTER,   May. 15, 1984
  HONORARY CONSUL

MINNESOTA

MINNEAPOLIS (HC) 18250 39TH AV., N, 55446.
(763) 478-3018, FAX (763) 478-3019
 MR. RUDOLF F. GUTMANN,   Feb. 12, 1996
  HONORARY CONSUL

MISSOURI

KANSAS CITY (HC) 5018 MAIN ST., 64112.
(816) 561-3441, FAX (816) 561-2922
 MR. MARCEL BOLLIER,   Jul. 15, 1987
  HONORARY CONSUL

NEW YORK

NEW YORK (CG) 633 3RD AV., FLOOR 30TH, 10017.
(212) 599-5700, FAX (212) 599-4266
 MR. CHRISTOPH HEINRICH BUBB, Mar. 22, 2007
  CONSUL GENERAL

 MR. DANIEL HAENER,   Feb. 16, 2007
  DEPUTY CONSUL GENERAL
 MR. ANDRE GUEDEL,   Mar. 25, 1999
  CONSUL
 MRS. GABRIELA EIGENSATZ, Mar. 26, 2003
  CONSUL
 MR. HERMANN JOSEPH AEBISCHER, Aug. 19, 2004
  CONSUL
 MS. ANNETTE BETTINA MOSER, Dec. 24, 2003
  VICE CONSUL

WILLIAMSVILLE (HC) 199 BRIDLE PATH UN., 14221.
(716) 553-2257
 MR. STEPHEN SLATER,   Apr. 25, 2006
  HONORARY CONSUL

NORTH CAROLINA

CHARLOTTE (HC) 2208 HOUSTON BRANCH RD., 28270.
(704) 292-1237, FAX (704) 292-1137
 MR. HEINZ ROTH,   Feb. 26, 2001
  HONORARY CONSUL

OHIO

CLEVELAND (HC) 6670 W. SNOWVILLE RD., BRECKSVILLE 44141.
(440) 546-1400
 MR. HANS A. KESSLER,   Jun. 01, 1998
  HONORARY CONSUL

PENNSYLVANIA

PHILADELPHIA (HC) INDEPENDENCE SQ. ., 19106.
(215) 922-2215, FAX (302) 652-2316
 MR. FRANZ J. PORTMANN,   Sep. 29, 1994
  HONORARY CONSUL

PITTSBURGH (HC) 4677 BAYARD ST., 15213.
(412) 967-6038, FAX (412) 967-6039
 MR. HEINZ W. KUNZ,   Jun. 15, 1991
  HONORARY CONSUL

PUERTO RICO

SAN JUAN (HC) 816 CALLE DIANA URB. ST., 00923-2334.
(787) 751-3182, FAX (561) 679-6483
 MS. BARBARA HOSTETTLER, May. 08, 2001
  HONORARY CONSUL

SOUTH CAROLINA

SPARTANBURG (HC) I-85 BUSINESS & BRYANT RD., 29303.
(864) 578-7101, FAX (864) 578-7107
 MR. HANS J. BALMER,   Dec. 29, 1994
  HONORARY CONSUL

TEXAS

DALLAS (HC) 2651 N. HARWOOD ., SUITE 455, 75201.
(214) 965-1025, FAX (214) 871-0879
 MR. J. GABRIEL BARBIER MUELLER, Mar. 10, 1995
  HONORARY CONSUL

HOUSTON (HC) 11922 TAYLORCREST UN., 77024.
(713) 467-9889

STATE* RESIDENCE	NAME AND RANK	DATE OF RECOGNITION	STATE* RESIDENCE	NAME AND RANK	DATE OF RECOGNITION

MRS. MARGHERITA YOUNG-ZELLWEGER,
  HONORARY CONSUL — Jun. 11, 2007

TRUST TERRITORIES OF THE PACIFIC ISLANDS

PAGO PAGO (CG) 22 PANAMA ST., WELLINGTON, NZ 00000.
  MR. BEAT WALTER NOBS, — Mar. 09, 2006
    CONSUL GENERAL

UTAH

SALT LAKE CITY (HC) 4641 HUNTERS RIDGE CI., 84124.
(801) 272-7102, FAX (801) 272-1743
  MS. MARION MAZER, — Sep. 02, 1998
    HONORARY CONSUL

WASHINGTON

MERCER ISLAND (HC) 6920 94TH AV., SE, 98040.
(206) 228-8110
  MR. PHILIPPE ANDRE GOETSCHEL, — Nov. 23, 2005
    HONORARY CONSUL

SYRIA

CALIFORNIA

LOS ANGELES (HCG) 660 NEWPORT CENTER DR., SUITE 740,
NEWPORT BEACH 92660.
(949) 640-9888, FAX (949) 640-9292
  DR. HAZEM HIKMAT CHEHABI, — Oct. 04, 1995
    HONORARY CONSUL GENERAL

MICHIGAN

DETROIT (HCG) 900 WILSHIRE ., SUITE 202, TROY 48084.
(248) 519-2496, FAX (248) 519-2399
  MR. NAJI ARWASHAN, — Jan. 02, 2001
    HONORARY CONSUL GENERAL

TEXAS

HOUSTON (HCG) 5433 WESTHEIMER RD., SUITE 1020, 77056.
(713) 622-8860, FAX (713) 965-9632
  MR. AYMAN M. MIDANI, — Jun. 04, 1991
    HONORARY CONSUL GENERAL

TAIWAN

CALIFORNIA

SANTA ANA (CONA) 2901 WEST MACARTHUR BL., SUITE 115&116,
92704.

SANTA CLARA (P) 5201 GREAT AMERICAN PW., SUITE 200, 95054.

MARYLAND

GAITHERSBURG (CHA) 901 WIND RIVER LA., 20878.

NEW YORK

NEW YORK (CON) 1 E. 42ND ST., 10021.

WASHINGTON
TECO-MAIN OFFICE
SEATTLE (CON) 600 UNIVERSITY ST., SUITE 2020, 98101.

TAJIKISTAN

DISTRICT OF COLUMBIA

WASHINGTON (CHN) 1005 NEW HAMPSHIRE AV., NW, 20037.
(202) 223-6090, FAX (202) 223-6091
  MR. BAKHTIER EROV, — Jun. 17, 2003
    CONSUL
  MR. MANUCHEHR MAHMUDOV, — Jun. 07, 2006
    CONSUL

TANZANIA

FLORIDA

BOCA RATON (HC) 1045 E. ATLANTIC AV., SUITE 206, DELRAY
BEACH 33483.
(561) 279-4010, FAX (561) 279-4015
  MR. KJELL BERGH, — Sep. 26, 2000
    HONORARY CONSUL

GEORGIA

ATLANTA (HC) 2245 GODBY RD., SUITE 202, 30349.
(404) 766-8000, FAX (404) 767-5264
  DR. AL H., JR ANDERSON, — Jun. 21, 2000
    HONORARY CONSUL

ILLINOIS

SAINT LOUIS (HC) 937 WHIPPOORWILL WA., EDWARDSVILLE
62025.
(618) 692-6715, FAX (618) 650-3509
  MR. DALLAS LA SALLE BROWNE, — Nov. 07, 2000
    HONORARY CONSUL

THAILAND

ALABAMA

MONTGOMERY (HCG) 919 BELL ST., 36104.
(334) 269-2518, FAX (334) 269-4678
  MR. ROBERT F. HENRY, — Jul. 30, 1987
    HONORARY CONSUL GENERAL

CALIFORNIA

LOS ANGELES (CG) 611 N. LARCHMONT BL., 90004.
(323) 962-9574, FAX (323) 962-2128
  MR. JUKR BOON LONG, — May. 25, 2006
    CONSUL GENERAL
  MR. TAKERNGSAK LEKKLAR, — May. 11, 2007
    DEPUTY CONSUL GENERAL
  MR. SONGSEEN SUSEVI, — May. 11, 1998
    CONSUL
  MR. BOONNA SONCHAI, — Feb. 17, 2004
    CONSUL
  MR. SOMPOP SERMSWATSRI, — Feb. 25, 2005
    CONSUL
  MS. PORNPIMOL THEPRUANGCHAI, — Feb. 25, 2005
    CONSUL
  MR. CHAPPON ROCHANASENA, — Mar. 23, 2006
    CONSUL

STATE* RESIDENCE	NAME AND RANK	DATE OF RECOGNITION	STATE* RESIDENCE	NAME AND RANK	DATE OF RECOGNITION

MR. NARUCHA RUCHUPHAN,   Mar. 23, 2006
   CONSUL
MR. RUTT CHUMDERMPADETSUK,   Mar. 23, 2006
   CONSUL
MR. VUTHIROTH RATANASINGH,   Mar. 23, 2006
   CONSUL
MS. NIPA NIRANNOOT,   Apr. 26, 2007
   CONSUL

THAI TRADE OFFICE
LOS ANGELES (CONA) 611 N. LARCHMONT BL., FLOOR 3RD, 90004.
(323) 664-8535

OFFICE OF THE ECONOMIC COUNSELLOR (INVESTMENT)
LOS ANGELES (CONA) 611 N. LARCHMONT BL., FLOOR 3RD, 90004.
(323) 960-1199, FAX (323) 962-2128

COLORADO

DENVER (HCG) 1123 AURARIA PW., SUITE 200, 80204.
(303) 892-0118
   MR. DONALD WILLIAM RINGSBY,   Dec. 03, 1987
     HONORARY CONSUL GENERAL

FLORIDA

CORAL GABLES (HCG) 2199 PONCE DE LEON BL., SUITE 301, MIAMI
33134.
(305) 444-7577, FAX (305) 444-0487
   MR. GEORGE M. CORRIGAN,   Apr. 05, 2000
     HONORARY CONSUL GENERAL
   MR. LOUIS, JR. STINSON,   Apr. 05, 2000
     HONORARY CONSUL
   MRS. MARIA D. SARIOL,   Aug. 16, 2005
     HONORARY CONSUL

GEORGIA

ATLANTA (HCG) 303 PEACHTREE ST., NE, SUITE 5300, 30306.
(404) 527-4650
   MR. ROY WILLIAM, III IDE,   Mar. 22, 2006
     HONORARY CONSUL GENERAL

HAWAII

HONOLULU (HCG) 1287 KALANI ST., SUITE 103, 96817.
(808) 845-7332
   MR. COLIN T. MIYABARA,   Jul. 01, 1992
     HONORARY CONSUL GENERAL

ILLINOIS

CHICAGO (CG) 700 N. RUSH ST., 60611.
(312) 664-3129, FAX (312) 664-3230
   MR. NARONG SASITORN,   May. 08, 2007
     CONSUL GENERAL
   MR. NAROTE SANGKAMANEE,   Apr. 09, 2004
     DEPUTY CONSUL GENERAL

THAI TRADE CENTER
CHICAGO (CONA) 700 N. RUSH ST., FLOOR 2ND, 60611.
(312) 787-3388, FAX (312) 787-9733
   MRS. KANYA AMORNTHEERAKUL,   Jun. 05, 2006
     CONSUL

MR. NIWAT HANSAWARD,   Dec. 03, 2004
   VICE CONSUL

KANSAS

KANSAS CITY (HC) 3906 W. 103RD ST., OVERLAND PARK 66207.
(913) 385-5555
   MS. MARY FRANCES TAYLOR-KIRKPATRICK,   Nov. 29, 1995
     HONORARY CONSUL

LOUISIANA

NEW ORLEANS (HC) 335 JULIA ST., 70130.
(504) 522-3400
   MR. HENRY M. LAMBERT,   Apr. 02, 2003
     HONORARY CONSUL

MASSACHUSETTS

BOSTON (HCG) 41 UNION ST., 02108.
(617) 227-2750
   MR. JOSEPH A. MILANO,   Sep. 04, 2002
     HONORARY CONSUL GENERAL

NEW YORK

NEW YORK (CG) 351 E. 52ND ST., FLOOR 1-3, 10022.
(212) 754-1770, FAX (212) 754-1907
   MS. VIPAWAN NIPATAKUSOL,   Mar. 24, 2005
     CONSUL GENERAL
   MS. SUCHADA KANECHORN,   Dec. 08, 1993
     DEPUTY CONSUL GENERAL
   MR. MONGKOL PROMPAYUCK,   Feb. 14, 2005
     DEPUTY CONSUL GENERAL
   MS. BOOSARA KANCHANALAI,   Aug. 09, 1994
     CONSUL
   MR. CHETTAPHAN MAKSAMPHAN,   May. 31, 1996
     CONSUL
   MR. ATTHAPONG KOEDKIETPONG,   Mar. 09, 2004
     CONSUL
   MS. PATCHAREE SA NGIEMBHAN,   Mar. 09, 2004
     CONSUL

THAI COMMERCIAL\ECONOMIC \INVESTMENT OFFICES
NEW YORK (CONA) 61 BROADWAY ., SUITE 2810, 10006.
(212) 422-9009, FAX (212) 422-9119
   MR. SURASAK RIANGKRUL,   Mar. 23, 2006
     CONSUL
   MRS. BOOSKORN VUTIVIJARN,   Mar. 23, 2006
     CONSUL
   MS. SUDAKORN SAKIYALAK,   Jan. 12, 2006
     VICE CONSUL
   MR. GARUN CHAVALITDHAMRONG,   Mar. 23, 2006
     VICE CONSUL

OKLAHOMA

BROKEN ARROW (HC) 25900 E.81ST ST., 74014.
(918) 357-2886
   MS. NORA J. GORDON,   Sep. 02, 2004
     HONORARY CONSUL

OREGON

PORTLAND (HCG) 121 S.W. SALMON ., SUITE 1430, 97204.
(503) 221-0440

---

* DEPENDENCIES SUCH AS GUAM, PUERTO RICO, AND THE VIRGIN ISLANDS ARE LISTED HERE.
CG-CONSULATE GENERAL   C-CONSULATE   VC-VICE CONSULATE   CA-CONSULAR AGENCY   H-HONORARY CONSULAR STATUS

STATE* RESIDENCE	NAME AND RANK	DATE OF RECOGNITION	STATE* RESIDENCE	NAME AND RANK	DATE OF RECOGNITION

MR. NICHOLAS JOHN STANLEY,   May. 17, 2004
   HONORARY CONSUL GENERAL

PUERTO RICO

HATO REY (HCG) 159 COSTA RICA ST., SUITE 11-F, HATO REY, SAN
JUAN 00917.
(787) 751-0151, FAX (787) 753-7276
   MR. ROLANDO J. PIERNES ALFONSO,   Jun. 09, 1988
      HONORARY CONSUL GENERAL
   MRS. CARMEN V. MENENDEZ-PIERNES,   Dec. 10, 1998
      HONORARY CONSUL

TEXAS

DALLAS (HCG) 1717 MAIN ST., SUITE 4100, 75201.
   MR. W. FORREST SMITH,   Dec. 29, 1989
      HONORARY CONSUL GENERAL

EL PASO (HCG) 4487 N. MESA ., SUITE 204, 79902.
(915) 533-5757

HOUSTON (HCG) 600 TRAVIS ST., SUITE 2800, 77002-3094.
(713) 229-8733
   MR. CHARLES C. FOSTER,   Jan. 10, 1997
      HONORARY CONSUL GENERAL
   MS. JULIE M. RICHARDSON,   Nov. 06, 2001
      HONORARY VICE CONSUL

TOGO

FLORIDA

MIAMI (HC) 4000 PONCE DE LEON BL., SUITE 700, CORAL GABLES
33146.
(305) 371-4286, FAX (305) 371-4288
   MR. MICHAEL STUART HACKER,   Nov. 16, 1983
      HONORARY CONSUL

TONGA

CALIFORNIA

SAN FRANCISCO (CG) 360 POST ST., 94108.
(415) 781-0365
   MR. JAMES CECIL COCKER,   Dec. 01, 2006
      CONSUL GENERAL
   MRS. LUISA MOALA LEVENI,   Jan. 10, 2005
      CONSUL

HAWAII

HONOLULU (HCA) 738 KAHEKA ST., SUITE 3068, 96814.
(808) 953-2449, FAX (808) 521-5264
   MS. ANNIE MEGUMI KANESHIRO,   Oct. 06, 1994
      HONORARY CONSULAR AGENT

TRINIDAD AND TOBAGO

FLORIDA

MIAMI (CG) 1000 BRICKELL AV., SUITE 800, 33131.
(305) 374-2199
   MR. GERARD PETER GREENE,   May. 25, 2006
      CONSUL GENERAL

MR. KIRK DARREN FRANCOIS,   Oct. 17, 2005
   DEPUTY CONSUL GENERAL
MR. HARVEY ROOSEVELT BORRIS,   Mar. 05, 2004
   CONSUL
MRS. DEBORAH DIANNE HAYNES COLLINS,   Jun. 17, 2004
   CONSUL
MRS. CHARRIE ANN M FORDE GRAHAM,   Nov. 03, 2005
   CONSUL
MR. STIRLING ANTHONY HACKSHAW,   Jan. 31, 2006
   CONSUL
MRS. VERONICA ANN KING,   Aug. 28, 2006
   CONSUL

NEW YORK

NEW YORK (CG) 475 5TH AV., FLOOR 4TH, 10017.
(212) 682-7272
   DR. HAROLD HAMPDEN ROBERTSON,   Dec. 17, 2004
      CONSUL GENERAL
   MS. CHERRY ANN MILLARD WHITE,   Jan. 31, 2006
      DEPUTY CONSUL GENERAL
   MR. GANGARAM BHAGAN,   Feb. 14, 2005
      CONSUL
   MRS. ANDREA R. CHAMBERS,   Feb. 16, 2005
      CONSUL
   MR. HENDERSON LEARIE FERNANDEZ,   Apr. 05, 2006
      CONSUL
   MRS. CHRISTINE ISABEL RAMJIT,   Apr. 14, 1997
      VICE CONSUL
   MS. LORNA BRUCE,   Nov. 18, 1998
      VICE CONSUL
   MISS JANET SMITH,   Sep. 23, 2002
      VICE CONSUL
   MRS. HYACINTH PATRICIA MOKUND,   Nov. 14, 2002
      VICE CONSUL

PUERTO RICO

SAN JUAN (HC) 357 PONCE DE LEON AV., FLOOR 3RD, 00901.
(787) 607-7070, FAX (787) 783-8517
   MR. STEVE JAIPERSAD,   Jun. 15, 2006
      HONORARY CONSUL

TEXAS

HOUSTON (HC) 2400 AUGUSTA UN., SUITE 250, 77057.
(713) 840-1100
   MS. PATRICIA YOUNGER,   Dec. 18, 2000
      HONORARY CONSUL

TUNISIA

CALIFORNIA

SAN FRANCISCO (HCG) 3401 SACRAMENTO ST., 94118.
(415) 922-9222
   MR. PROCTOR PATTERSON JONES,   Jun. 03, 1981
      HONORARY CONSUL GENERAL

FLORIDA

MIAMI (HC) 1236 S.W. 21 TERRACE RD., 33145.
(305) 858-5456, FAX (305) 858-5909
   MS. DEBORAH BALLIETTE JACOBSON,   Jan. 27, 1988
      HONORARY CONSUL

STATE* RESIDENCE	NAME AND RANK	DATE OF RECOGNITION	STATE* RESIDENCE	NAME AND RANK	DATE OF RECOGNITION

NEW YORK

NEW YORK (HCG) 781 FIFTH AV., SUITE 1205, 10022.
(212) 355-2800

MR. ANDRE O. BACKAR,   Dec. 03, 2004
HONORARY CONSUL GENERAL

TEXAS

DALLAS (HC) 4227 N. CAPISTRANO DR., 75287-4002.
(972) 267-4191, FAX (972) 267-4192

MR. FRANK THEODORE KRYZA,   Jun. 27, 2001
HONORARY CONSUL

HOUSTON (HC) 12527 MOSSYCUP UN., 77024.
(713) 935-9427

MR. ALFRED JOHN BOULOS,   Nov. 10, 2003
HONORARY CONSUL

TURKEY

CALIFORNIA

LOS ANGELES (CG) 6300 WILSHIRE BL., SUITE 2010, 90048.
(323) 655-8832, FAX (323) 655-8681

MR. RIZA HAKAN TEKIN,   May. 08, 2007
CONSUL GENERAL
MR. ANIL BORA INAN,   Oct. 14, 2004
VICE CONSUL
MR. CEVDET YILDIRIM,   Sep. 21, 2004
CONSULAR AGENT
MRS. AYNUR UZER,   Oct. 05, 2004
CONSULAR AGENT
MR. EMIR OZBAY,   Dec. 12, 2006
CONSULAR AGENT

CULTURE AND TOURISM OFFICE
LOS ANGELES (CONA) 5055 WILSHIRE BL., SUITE 850, 90036.
(323) 937-8066, FAX (323) 937-1271

TURKISH EDUCATIONAL OFFICE
LOS ANGELES (CONA) 6380 WILSHIRE BL., SUITE 907, 90048.
(323) 782-8636

MR. NAZMI AK,   Jun. 07, 2006
CONSULAR AGENT

COMMERCIAL OFFICE
LOS ANGELES (CONA) 6380 WILSHIRE BL., SUITE 1210, 90048.
(323) 852-1894, FAX (323) 852-1896

MS. SELEN ERYUCE,   May. 11, 2007
CONSULAR AGENT

OAKLAND (HCG) 19229 SONOMA HW., SUITE 345, SONOMA 95476.
(415) 362-0912

MRS. BONNIE JOY KASLAN,   Oct. 26, 1984
HONORARY CONSUL GENERAL

GEORGIA

ATLANTA (HCG) 4287 PARAN WALK UN., NW, 30327.
(404) 262-9524

MRS. MONA TEKIN DIAMOND,   Apr. 27, 2005
HONORARY CONSUL GENERAL

ILLINOIS

CHICAGO (CG) 360 N. MICHIGAN AV., SUITE 1405, 60601.
(312) 263-0644

MR. UGUR KENAN IPEK,   Apr. 27, 2007
CONSUL GENERAL
MR. BAHRI BATU,   Oct. 05, 2004
VICE CONSUL
MS. ESMA DEMIREZEN,   Feb. 22, 2006
CONSULAR AGENT
MR. SULEYMAN SOZERI,   Jul. 06, 2007
CONSULAR AGENT

MARYLAND

BALTIMORE (HCG) 313 WENDOVER RD., 21218.
(301) 889-0697

MR. CENAP REMZI KIRATLI,   Apr. 26, 1976
HONORARY CONSUL GENERAL

MASSACHUSETTS

BOSTON (HCG) 325 HUNTINGTON AV., SUITE 46, 02115.
(617) 821-9660

MR. HIDIR CELEBI ERKUT GOMULU,   Apr. 19, 2005
HONORARY CONSUL GENERAL

MICHIGAN

FARMINGTON (HCG) 25816 ORCHARD LAKE RD., FARMINGTON
HILLS 48336.
(248) 626-3745

MS. NURTEN URAL,   Nov. 08, 2004
HONORARY CONSUL GENERAL

MISSISSIPPI

JACKSON (HCG) 1000 RED FERN PL., FLOWOOD 39232.
(601) 936-3666

MR. EARLE FEURT , JR JONES,   Mar. 18, 2005
HONORARY CONSUL GENERAL

MISSOURI

KANSAS CITY (HCG) 6000 INDUSTRIAL RD., SAINT JOSEPH 64504.
(816) 238-6646

MR. EMRU AHMET ERTEN,   Apr. 27, 2005
HONORARY CONSUL GENERAL

NEW YORK

NEW YORK (CG) 821 UNITED NATIONS PZ., 10017.
(212) 949-0160

MR. MEHMET SAMSAR,   Dec. 12, 2006
CONSUL GENERAL
MRS. GULCAN AKOGUZ KARAGOZ,   Dec. 12, 2000
VICE CONSUL
MR. BARIS CEYHUN ERCIYES,   Nov. 08, 2004
VICE CONSUL
MR. MURAT OMEROGLU,   Mar. 07, 2005
VICE CONSUL
MR. AHMET BASAR SEN,   Jan. 17, 2007
VICE CONSUL
MS. YASEMIN OZTURK,   Nov. 12, 2004
CONSULAR AGENT
MR. SAMIL OCAL,   Jan. 18, 2005
CONSULAR AGENT

STATE* RESIDENCE	NAME AND RANK	DATE OF RECOGNITION
	MRS. TUBA ICEN, CONSULAR AGENT	Apr. 04, 2005
	MR. COSAR OZLER, CONSULAR AGENT	Oct. 04, 2005
	MR. GAZI ERDEM, CONSULAR AGENT	Oct. 06, 2005
	MR. EROL ARI, CONSULAR AGENT	Mar. 27, 2006
	MR. NADIR AYTAN, CONSULAR AGENT	Mar. 27, 2006
	MR. TUNCAY CANANOGLU, CONSULAR AGENT	Mar. 27, 2006
	MS. AYSE TURAN, CONSULAR AGENT	May. 25, 2006
	MR. BABURSAH GUNGOR, CONSULAR AGENT	Dec. 12, 2006
	MR. HASAN ZONGUR, CONSULAR AGENT	Dec. 12, 2006
	MR. MEHMET ALI ERDEM, CONSULAR AGENT	Dec. 12, 2006
	MR. HARUN ARSLAN, CONSULAR AGENT	Apr. 25, 2007
	MR. ORHAN ARSLAN, CONSULAR AGENT	May. 07, 2007

OFFICE OF EDUCATION
NEW YORK (CONA) 821 UNITED NATIONS PLAZA UN., FLOOR 7TH, 10017.

TURKISH CULTURE, TOURIST AND INFORMATION OFFICE
NEW YORK (CONA) 821 UNITED NATIONS PZ., FLOOR 4TH, 10017.

TEXAS

HOUSTON (CG) 1990 POST OAK BL., SUITE 1300, 77056.
(713) 622-5849

	MR. ATILA UZER, CONSUL GENERAL	Oct. 17, 2005
	MR. ALI FINDIK, CONSUL	Dec. 12, 2006
	MRS. SOLMAZ ABILYONDLU, CONSULAR AGENT	Jul. 07, 2005
	MR. HUSEYIN AYDIN TOPCUOGLU, CONSULAR AGENT	Oct. 06, 2005
	MR. YUSUF TOPCAN, CONSULAR AGENT	Jul. 06, 2006
	MR. BULENT ULUTURK, CONSULAR AGENT	Jul. 17, 2006

WASHINGTON

SEATTLE (HCG) 12328 N.E. 97TH ST., KIRKLAND 98033.
(425) 739-6722

	MR. JOHN U. GOKCEN, HONORARY CONSUL GENERAL	May. 06, 2002

UGANDA

CALIFORNIA

LOS ANGELES (HC) 3400 CAHUENGA BL., 90068.

	MR. MATTHEW WENDELL CROUCH, HONORARY CONSUL	May. 18, 2007

FLORIDA

JUPITER (HC) 6710 INLAND CT., 33458.
(561) 676-4808

	MR. PETER SCHOU NIELSEN, HONORARY CONSUL	Jul. 13, 2007

WASHINGTON

GIG HARBOR (HC) 3226 ROSEDALE ST., SUITE 100, 98335.
(206) 571-9798

	MR. ROBERT KENDALL GOFF, HONORARY CONSUL	Jun. 11, 2007

UKRAINE

CALIFORNIA

SAN FRANCISCO (CG) 530 BUSH ST., SUITE 402, 94108.
(415) 999-8612

	MR. MYKOLA TOCHYTSKYI, CONSUL GENERAL	Feb. 13, 2006
	MR. VOLODYMYR P. HORBARENKO, CONSUL	Apr. 12, 2004
	MR. SERHIY NIKOLAICHUK, VICE CONSUL	Dec. 18, 2003
	MR. MYKOLA LUBIV, VICE CONSUL	May. 03, 2007

DISTRICT OF COLUMBIA

WASHINGTON (CHN) 3350 M ST., NW, 20007.
(202) 349-2920, FAX (202) 333-0817

	MR. KOSTIANTYN KUDRYK, CONSUL	Aug. 27, 2002
	MR. YAKIV PYRIH, CONSUL	Mar. 16, 2004
	MISS OLENA BREZHNIEVA, CONSUL	Sep. 19, 2006
	MR. OLEKSIY SVIATUN, VICE CONSUL	Feb. 12, 2003
	MR. ROMAN ANDARAK, VICE CONSUL	Jul. 27, 2004
	MR. VOLODYMYR USHKO, VICE CONSUL	Nov. 17, 2006

ILLINOIS

CHICAGO (CG) 10 E. HURON ST., 60611.
(312) 642-4388

	MR. VASYL KORZACHENKO, CONSUL GENERAL	May. 16, 2006
	MR. OLEH SHEVCHENKO, CONSUL	Nov. 21, 2003
	MR. ANATOLIY OLIYNYK, CONSUL	Jan. 09, 2004
	MRS. OLENA DZHELMACH, VICE CONSUL	May. 15, 2003

MICHIGAN

DETROIT (HC) 26601 RYAN RD., WARREN 48091.
(586) 757-7910, FAX (586) 757-8684

	MR. BOHDAN FEDORAK, HONORARY CONSUL	Dec. 11, 2001

---

* DEPENDENCIES SUCH AS GUAM, PUERTO RICO, AND THE VIRGIN ISLANDS ARE LISTED HERE.
CG-CONSULATE GENERAL   C-CONSULATE   VC-VICE CONSULATE   CA-CONSULAR AGENCY   H-HONORARY CONSULAR STATUS

STATE* RESIDENCE	NAME AND RANK	DATE OF RECOGNITION	STATE* RESIDENCE	NAME AND RANK	DATE OF RECOGNITION

NEW YORK

NEW YORK (CG) 240 E. 49TH ST., 10017.
(212) 371-5690

MR. MYKOLA KYRYCHENKO, CONSUL GENERAL	May. 16, 2006	
MR. OLEXANDER DOLIA, CONSUL	May. 15, 1998	
MR. ANDRII OLEFIROV, CONSUL	Jul. 02, 2004	
MR. MAKSYM VDOVYCHENKO, CONSUL	Sep. 07, 2004	
MR. HEORHII SHEVCHENKO, VICE CONSUL	Dec. 12, 2000	
DR. ANDRII NADZHOS, VICE CONSUL	Jul. 08, 2003	
MR. SERGII KULYKOV, VICE CONSUL	Oct. 06, 2003	
MS. NATALIIA KOSTENKO, VICE CONSUL	Nov. 12, 2004	

TRADE OFFICE
NEW YORK (CONA) 866 UNITED NATIONS PZ., 10017.
, FAX (212) 755-6859

OHIO

CLEVELAND (HC) 5566 PEARL RD., 44129.
(440) 887-9308, FAX (440) 884-5020

MR. ANDREW J. FUTEY,   May. 28, 2002
HONORARY CONSUL

TEXAS

HOUSTON (HC) 2934 FAIRWAY DR., SUGARLAND 77478.
(281) 242-2842

MR. GREGORY BUCHAI,   Feb. 18, 2000
HONORARY CONSUL

UNITED KINGDOM

ALASKA

ANCHORAGE (HC) 3211 PROVIDENCE DR., 99508.

MS. DIDDY R. HITCHINS,   Dec. 11, 1987
HONORARY CONSUL

ARIZONA

PHOENIX (HC) 2425 E. CAMELBACK RD., SUITE 1020, 85016.
(602) 515-1029

MR. DONALD HENRY MARSHALL,   Mar. 16, 2006
HONORARY CONSUL

CALIFORNIA

LOS ANGELES (CG) 11766 WILSHIRE BL., SUITE 1200, 90025.
(310) 477-3322

MR. ROBERT NIGEL PEIRCE, CONSUL GENERAL	Jun. 27, 2005
MR. DAVID WILLIAM WILD, DEPUTY CONSUL GENERAL	Dec. 06, 2006
MR. DAVID JOHN SLATER, CONSUL	Aug. 16, 2002
MR. PAUL ROBINSON, CONSUL	Jan. 26, 2007
MRS. NANCY L. BRIDI, HONORARY VICE CONSUL	Jun. 11, 1996

MR. CHRISTOPHER NICHOLAS BREWER,   Aug. 20, 2001
HONORARY VICE CONSUL

SAN DIEGO (HC) 895 LA JOLLA CORONA CT., LA JOLLA 92037.
(858) 353-3633

MS. ELENA L. SALSITZ,   May. 30, 2006
HONORARY CONSUL

SAN FRANCISCO (CG) 1 SANSOME ST., SUITE 850, 94104.
(415) 617-1300

MR. MARTIN DAVID UDEN, CONSUL GENERAL	Oct. 21, 2003
MR. PETER DAVID BROOM, DEPUTY CONSUL GENERAL	Nov. 21, 2003
MRS. ANNABELLE FRANCES MALINS, CONSUL	Feb. 15, 2006
MRS. KAREN SEYMOUR THOMAS, HONORARY VICE CONSUL	Dec. 15, 1993

SAN JOSE (HC) 1139 KARLSTEAD DR., SUNNYVALE 94089.
(408) 747-7140

DR. WILLIAM WHITE RODEN ELDER,   Dec. 11, 1997
HONORARY CONSUL

COLORADO

DENVER (CON) 1675 BROADWAY UN., SUITE 1030, 80202.
(303) 592-5200

MR. KEVIN J. LYNCH,   May. 08, 2007
CONSUL

DISTRICT OF COLUMBIA

WASHINGTON (CHN) 3100 MASSACHUSETTS AV., NW, 20008.
(202) 588-6500, FAX (202) 588-7870

MR. GRAEME MICHAEL WISE, DEPUTY CONSUL GENERAL	Feb. 10, 2005
MRS. MARIE FORSYTH, CONSUL	Nov. 09, 2005

FLORIDA

MIAMI (CG) 1001 BRICKELL BAY DR., SUITE 2800, 33131.
(305) 374-1522, FAX (305) 374-8196

MR. KEITH RENNIE ALLAN, CONSUL GENERAL	Jul. 05, 2007
MR. BARRY FRANCIS CLARKE, VICE CONSUL	Jan. 21, 2005
MR. DAVID JAMES EDWARDS, VICE CONSUL	Jan. 25, 2007
MRS. SARAH HELEN EDWARDS, VICE CONSUL	Aug. 01, 2007
MR. ROBERT TRAFFORD, VICE CONSUL	Aug. 14, 2007
MS. NICHOLA JANE CROFT, VICE CONSUL	Aug. 14, 2007

ORLANDO (CON) 200 S. ORANGE AV., SUITE 2110, 32801.
(407) 426-7855

MR. DEAN GRAHAM CHURM,   Feb. 01, 2006
CONSUL

TALLAHASSEE (HC) 2073 CRESTDALE DR., 32308.

* DEPENDENCIES SUCH AS GUAM, PUERTO RICO, AND THE VIRGIN ISLANDS ARE LISTED HERE.
CG-CONSULATE GENERAL   C-CONSULATE   VC-VICE CONSULATE   CA-CONSULAR AGENCY   H-HONORARY CONSULAR STATUS

STATE* RESIDENCE	NAME AND RANK	DATE OF RECOGNITION	STATE* RESIDENCE	NAME AND RANK	DATE OF RECOGNITION

MR. JOHN B. PHELPS,   Jun. 11, 2007
    HONORARY CONSUL

GEORGIA

ATLANTA (CG) 133 PEACHTREE ST., NE, SUITE 3400, 30303-1818.
(404) 954-7700, FAX (404) 954-7702

MR. MARTIN JOHN KILBURN RICKERD,   Feb. 13, 2006
    CONSUL GENERAL

MRS. HELEN MARIE ARBON,   May. 24, 2004
    CONSUL

MR. J. GLEN WHITLEY,   Dec. 07, 1999
    HONORARY VICE CONSUL

MR. MARK ANDREW BORST,   Aug. 14, 2002
    HONORARY VICE CONSUL

MRS. CLAIRE LOUISE NEWMAN,   Dec. 02, 2005
    HONORARY VICE CONSUL

MS. NATALIE CHRISTINA PAWELSKI,   Dec. 05, 2005
    HONORARY VICE CONSUL

ILLINOIS

CHICAGO (CG) 400 N. MICHIGAN AV., FLOOR 13TH, 60611.
(312) 346-1810

MR. ANDREW JAMES SEATON,   Sep. 03, 2003
    CONSUL GENERAL

MR. GEOFFREY IAN BRAMMER,   Jul. 27, 2006
    DEPUTY CONSUL GENERAL

MR. BRENDAN GERARD DOYLE,   Feb. 22, 2006
    CONSUL

INDIANA

INDIANAPOLIS (HC) 10 W. MARKET ST., SUITE 200, 46204.
(317) 237-8338

MR. PHILLIP EUGENE BAINBRIDGE,   Jun. 03, 2002
    HONORARY CONSUL

KANSAS

KANSAS CITY (HC) 12109 ABERDEEN RD., LEAWOOD 66209.
(913) 469-9786

MR. J. SCOTT BROWN,   May. 29, 1996
    HONORARY CONSUL

LOUISIANA

NEW ORLEANS (HC) 321 ST. CHARLES AV., FLOOR 10TH, 70130.
(504) 586-1979

MR. JAMES JULIAN COLEMAN,   Aug. 28, 1975
    HONORARY CONSUL

MASSACHUSETTS

BOSTON (CG) 1 MEMORIAL DR., SUITE 1500, CAMBRIDGE 02142.
(617) 245-4500, FAX (617) 621-0220

MR. JOHN RANKIN,   Oct. 31, 2003
    CONSUL GENERAL

MR. DAVID JOHN CHUN,   Nov. 05, 2004
    DEPUTY CONSUL GENERAL

MICHIGAN

DETROIT (HC) 150 W. JEFFERSON AV., SUITE 900, 48226.
(313) 225-7000

MR. NICHOLAS J. STASEVICH,   Oct. 30, 2002
    HONORARY CONSUL

MINNESOTA

MINNEAPOLIS (HC) 800 NICOLLET MALL UN., SUITE 2600, 55402.
(612) 338-2525

MR. WILLIAM R. MCGRANN,   Mar. 15, 1995
    HONORARY CONSUL

NEVADA

LAS VEGAS (HC) 8628 SCARSDALE DR., 89117.
(702) 341-7789

MR. JEROME FREDERICK SNYDER,   May. 15, 2006
    HONORARY CONSUL

NEW YORK

NEW YORK (CG) 845 3RD AV., FLOOR 9 & 10TH, 10022.
(212) 745-0200

SIR ALAN STANLEY COLLINS,   Mar. 19, 2007
    CONSUL GENERAL

MR. JONATHAN STANLEY PAYNE,   Oct. 04, 2005
    DEPUTY CONSUL GENERAL

MR. JONATHAN BENJAMIN,   Oct. 17, 2005
    DEPUTY CONSUL GENERAL

MR. GORDON DAVID INNES,   Dec. 20, 2005
    DEPUTY CONSUL GENERAL

MR. ANDREW KERRY PIKE,   Mar. 09, 2004
    CONSUL

MS. SARA FRANCES MOONEY,   May. 24, 2004
    CONSUL

MS. CHRISTINE ANNE CARR ALLOWAY,   Nov. 12, 2004
    CONSUL

MS. SHEILA MARY O'CONNOR,   May. 31, 2006
    CONSUL

MR. JOHN RICHARD LINDFIELD,   Jun. 13, 2006
    CONSUL

MR. STEPHEN C. THOMPSON,   Nov. 29, 2000
    VICE CONSUL

MRS. JACQUELINE H. CERDAN,   Jul. 05, 1995
    HONORARY VICE CONSUL

MRS. LESLIE SLOCUM,   Jul. 14, 2000
    HONORARY VICE CONSUL

BRITISH INFORMATION SERVICES OF UNITED KINGDOM
NEW YORK (CONA) 845 3RD AV., 10022.

NORTH CAROLINA

CHARLOTTE (HC) 301 S. TYRON ST., FLOOR 7TH, 28205.
, FAX (704) 383-6545

MR. MICHAEL DAVID TEDEN,   Jan. 09, 2002
    HONORARY CONSUL

OHIO

CLEVELAND (HC) 1268 W. 112TH ST., 44102.
(216) 228-2515

MS. SANDRA MORGAN,   May. 28, 2002
    HONORARY CONSUL

---

* DEPENDENCIES SUCH AS GUAM, PUERTO RICO, AND THE VIRGIN ISLANDS ARE LISTED HERE.
CG-CONSULATE GENERAL   C-CONSULATE   VC-VICE CONSULATE   CA-CONSULAR AGENCY   H-HONORARY CONSULAR STATUS

STATE* RESIDENCE	NAME AND RANK	DATE OF RECOGNITION	STATE* RESIDENCE	NAME AND RANK	DATE OF RECOGNITION

OKLAHOMA

TULSA (HC) 4502 E. 41ST ST., 74135.
(918) 660-3495

    PROFESSOR RODGER ALLEN RANDLE,   Oct. 14, 2005
       HONORARY CONSUL

OREGON

PORTLAND (HC) 825 N.E. MULTNOMAH ST., SUITE 2000, 97232.
(503) 227-5669

    MR. ANDREW NORMAN MACRITCHIE,   Aug. 14, 2003
       HONORARY CONSUL

PENNSYLVANIA

PHILADELPHIA (HC) 1818 MARKET ST., FLOOR 33RD, 19103.
(215) 557-8500

    MR. OLIVER ST. CLAIR FRANKLIN,   Sep. 23, 1998
       HONORARY CONSUL

PITTSBURGH (HC) 107 CATHEDRAL OF LEARNING UN., 15260.
(412) 624-4200

    MR. MARK ALAN NORDENBERG,   Oct. 25, 2004
       HONORARY CONSUL

PUERTO RICO

SAN JUAN (HVC) 243 MONACO ST., HUMACAO 00791.
(787) 758-9828, FAX (787) 758-9809

    MRS. PATRICIA TULLY MARTINEZ,   Jun. 28, 2005
       HONORARY CONSUL

TENNESSEE

NASHVILLE (HC) 211 COMMERCE ST., SUITE 100, 37201.
(615) 743-3061, FAX (615) 256-6982

    MR. JOHN STANLEY BUTLER,   Jul. 05, 1996
       HONORARY CONSUL

TEXAS

DALLAS (CON) 2911 TURTLE CREEK BL., SUITE 940, 75219.
(214) 637-3600

HOUSTON (CG) 1000 LOUISIANA ST., SUITE 1900, 77002.
(713) 659-6270

    MR. MICHAEL DONALD MORLEY,   Feb. 24, 2006
       DEPUTY CONSUL GENERAL
    MRS. PAULETTE DENISE HARRIS,   Aug. 19, 2005
       CONSULAR AGENT
    MS. LINDA KELLY,   Feb. 26, 2001
       HONORARY VICE CONSUL

SAN ANTONIO (HC) 254 SPENCER LA., 78201.
(210) 735-9393

    MR. ANDREW M. VISCOUNT DUNROSSIL,   Jul. 29, 2005
       HONORARY CONSUL

TRUST TERRITORIES OF THE PACIFIC ISLANDS

NUKU'ALOFA, TONGA (CON) HIGH COMMISSION ., 00000.
    MR. WILLIAM L. CORDINER,   Feb. 19, 1992
       CONSUL

UTAH

SALT LAKE CITY (HC) 60 E. SOUTH TEMPLE UN., SUITE 2100, 84111.
(801) 237-1717

    MR. G. FRANZ JOKLIK,   Oct. 19, 1994
       HONORARY CONSUL

WASHINGTON

BELLEVUE (HC) 500 108TH AV., NE, SUITE 1500, 98004.
(425) 453-9400

    MR. ROBERT WILLIAM CREMIN,   Apr. 25, 2006
       HONORARY CONSUL

WISCONSIN

MADISON (HC) 123 E. DOTY ST., SUITE 205-207, 53703.
(608) 257-6544

    MR. MICHAEL BRIGHT,   Nov. 08, 2002
       HONORARY CONSUL

URUGUAY

CALIFORNIA

LOS ANGELES (CG) 429 SANTA MONICA BL., SUITE 400, SANTA MONICA 90401.
(310) 394-5777

    MR. CARLOS GITTO SPINGOLA,   Apr. 06, 2004
       CONSUL GENERAL

SAN FRANCISCO (HC) 351 CALIFORNIA ST., SUITE 150, 94104.
(415) 986-5222

    MR. MARK RITCHIE,   Sep. 29, 1994
       HONORARY CONSUL
    MR. FERNANDO SASCO CASELLI,   May. 25, 2004
       HONORARY VICE CONSUL

DISTRICT OF COLUMBIA

WASHINGTON (CHN) 1913 I ST., NW, 20006.
(202) 331-1313, FAX (202) 331-8142

    MS. MARIELLA CROSTA RODRIGUEZ,   Mar. 18, 2005
       CONSUL

FLORIDA

MIAMI (CG) 1077 PONCE DE LEON BL., SUITE B, CORAL GABLES 33134.
(305) 443-9764, FAX (305) 443-7802

    MR. MANUEL GONZALO VIEIRA MEROLA,   Feb. 13, 2006
       CONSUL GENERAL
    MR. CESAR ENEAS RODRIGUEZ ZAVALLA,   Jul. 30, 2003
       DEPUTY CONSUL GENERAL
    MS. VERONICA PAULA ROLANDO,   Jan. 21, 2005
       CONSUL

ILLINOIS

CHICAGO (CG) 875 N. MICHIGAN AV., SUITE 1422, 60611.
(312) 642-3430, FAX (312) 642-3470

    MR. BORIS EDUARDO SVETOGORSKY MARINO,   Jul. 21, 2004
       CONSUL GENERAL
    MR. CARLOS GUILLERMO RIZOWY,   Jul. 27, 1994
       HONORARY CONSUL

STATE* RESIDENCE	NAME AND RANK	DATE OF RECOGNITION

LOUISIANA

NEW ORLEANS (HC) 2 CANAL ST., SUITE 2002, 70130.
(504) 525-8354

MR. JULIO E. RIOS PENA, HONORARY CONSUL	Aug. 18, 1995

NEVADA

RENO (HC) 562 N. MAINE ST., FALLON 89406.
(775) 423-6041

DR. DAVID CLEMENT HENLEY, HONORARY CONSUL	Aug. 20, 1999

NEW YORK

NEW YORK (CG) 420 MADISON AV., FLOOR 6TH, 10017.
(212) 753-8581, FAX (212) 753-1603

MRS. ADRIANA LISSIDINI DOTTI, CONSUL GENERAL	Feb. 15, 2006
MR. JUAN PABLO WALLACE COLINA, CONSUL	May. 24, 2007

PUERTO RICO

SAN JUAN (CON) 254 HIMALAYA AV., 00926.
(787) 764-7941

MS. JOSEFINA DE HILLYER, HONORARY CONSUL	Jan. 22, 1988

TEXAS

HOUSTON (HCG) 1220 S. RIPPLE CREEK DR., 77057.
(713) 974-7855

MR. CHRISTOPHER COX ASHBY, HONORARY CONSUL GENERAL	Apr. 25, 2006

UTAH

SALT LAKE CITY (HC) 8191 S. 700TH UN., E, SANDY 84070.
(801) 256-0182, FAX (801) 256-0183

MR. CIRO AROLDO DARELLI, HONORARY CONSUL	Sep. 12, 2000

UZBEKISTAN

COLORADO

DENVER (HCG) 948 HAMILTON CREEK RD., SILVERTHORNE 80498.
(970) 513-8000

DISTRICT OF COLUMBIA

WASHINGTON (CHN) 1746 MASSACHUSETTS AV., NW, 20036.
(202) 887-5300, FAX (202) 293-6804

MR. NODIRJON KIRGIZBAEV, CONSUL	Aug. 01, 2007

GEORGIA

GREENSBORO (HCG) 1110 NEILSFORT ST., 30642.
(706) 467-3447

MR. LAWRENCE T. KURLANDER, HONORARY CONSUL GENERAL	Jun. 20, 2007

NEW YORK

NEW YORK (CG) 801 SECOND AV., FLOOR 20TH, 10017.
(212) 754-6178, FAX (212) 486-7998

MR. KHASAN IKRAMOV, CONSUL GENERAL	Dec. 12, 2003
MR. SALOKHITDIN SIDIKOV, VICE CONSUL	Oct. 30, 2003

WASHINGTON

SEATTLE (HCG) 800 FIFTH AV., SUITE 4000, 98104.
(206) 625-1199, FAX (206) 292-9736

MR. GARY C. FURLONG, HONORARY CONSUL GENERAL	Jun. 07, 2002

VANUATU

NORTHERN MARIANA ISLANDS

SAIPAN (HC) X JOETEN CENTER UN., 96950.
(670) 234-6547

MR. MICHAEL ALAN WHITE, HONORARY CONSUL	Jun. 07, 2002

VENEZUELA

CALIFORNIA

SAN FRANCISCO (CG) 311 CALIFORNIA ST., SUITE 620, 94104.
(415) 955-1982

MR. JOSE EGIDIO RODRIGUEZ , DEPUTY CONSUL GENERAL	Nov. 10, 2003
MRS. ISIS C. CEDENO GARCIA, CONSUL	Jun. 04, 2004

FLORIDA

MIAMI (CG) 1101 BRICKELL AV., SUITE 300, 33131.
(305) 577-4301

MR. ANTONIO J. HERNANDEZ BORGO, CONSUL GENERAL	Sep. 28, 1999
MS. SILVIA PADRON, CONSUL	Apr. 24, 2007
MR. JHON ELLERY PENA UZCATEGUI, CONSULAR AGENT	Nov. 19, 2004

ILLINOIS

CHICAGO (CG) 20 N. WACKER DR., SUITE 1925, 60606.
(312) 236-9658

MR. MARTIN ERNESTO SANCHEZ, CONSUL GENERAL	Dec. 06, 2004
MR. OMAR FERNANDO SIERRA, CONSUL	Mar. 01, 2006
MR. JESUS ALBERTO RODRIGUEZ ESPINOZA, CONSUL	Mar. 07, 2006
MR. ALFREDO JOSE MARTINEZ YANEZ, CONSULAR AGENT	Aug. 28, 2006

LOUISIANA

NEW ORLEANS (CG) WORLD TRADE CENTER ., SUITE 2300, 70130.
(504) 522-3284

MRS. MARIA DE L. MADRIZ BUSTAMANTE, CONSUL GENERAL	Aug. 16, 2002
MRS. MARIA VICTORIA LINARES, CONSUL	Jan. 02, 2002

STATE* RESIDENCE	NAME AND RANK	DATE OF RECOGNITION	STATE* RESIDENCE	NAME AND RANK	DATE OF RECOGNITION

MASSACHUSETTS

BOSTON (CG) 545 BOYLSTON ST., FLOOR 3RD, 02116.
(617) 266-9355

MR. CARLOS G. OSORIO ESCOBAR, DEPUTY CONSUL GENERAL	Jan. 23, 2007	
MRS. MARIA CAROLINA MENDOZA OMANA, CONSUL	Apr. 06, 2006	

NEW YORK

NEW YORK (CG) 7 E. 51ST ST., 10022.
(212) 826-1660

MRS. LEONOR CECILIA OSORIO GRANADO, DEPUTY CONSUL GENERAL — May. 14, 2002

MR. JESUS JAVIER ARIAS FUENMAYOR, CONSUL — Aug. 03, 2007

MISS LISETH TERESA ANCIDEY RODRIGUEZ, VICE CONSUL — Feb. 12, 2004

PUERTO RICO

SAN JUAN (CG) PISO 6 PONCE DE LEON AV., SUITE 601, HATO REY 00936.
(787) 766-4250

MR. ORLANDO JOSE PEREZ JIMENEZ, CONSUL GENERAL — Apr. 26, 2007

MRS. NELLY VARGAS, CONSUL — Mar. 10, 2004

TEXAS

HOUSTON (CG) 2925 BRIARPARK DR., SUITE 900, 77042.
(713) 961-5141

MR. ANTONIO RAMON PADRINO QUINTERO, CONSUL GENERAL — Dec. 01, 2006

MRS. JAIDYS JULIETA BRICENO, CONSUL — Jul. 07, 2005

MR. RAFAEL DAVID BARRETO, CONSUL — May. 08, 2006

MS. DAMELYS ROJAS, CONSUL — Jun. 09, 2006

MRS. AYSKEL CAROLINA TORRES RODRIGUEZ, VICE CONSUL — Mar. 08, 2004

VIETNAM

CALIFORNIA

SAN FRANCISCO (CG) 1700 CALIFORNIA ST., SUITE 370, 430, 94109.
(415) 922-1707, FAX (415) 922-1848

MR. ANH TUAN TRAN, CONSUL GENERAL — Nov. 04, 2004

MR. GIANG TRUONG PHAM, DEPUTY CONSUL GENERAL — Apr. 19, 2006

MRS. SON THU LE, CONSUL — Jun. 01, 2004

MR. LAM KIM LE, CONSUL — Jun. 18, 2004

MR. MAI KHAC NGUYEN, CONSUL — Jul. 28, 2004

MRS. DUONG THUY NGUYEN, CONSUL — Nov. 04, 2004

MR. CHAU LE DO, CONSUL — Feb. 24, 2005

MR. TUAN QUOC TRAN, CONSUL — Jul. 07, 2005

MRS. HUONG THI BAO NGUYEN, CONSUL — Jul. 07, 2005

MR. DUNG TIEN NGO, CONSUL — May. 31, 2006

MR. TUAN NGOC NGUYEN, CONSUL — Mar. 19, 2007

MS. PHUONG THI HA TRAN, CONSUL — May. 03, 2007

MR. HA MINH LE, CONSUL — Jul. 18, 2007

MS. NGA XUAN NGUYEN, VICE CONSUL — Nov. 19, 2004

MR. DUNG CONG LE, VICE CONSUL — Apr. 19, 2007

MR. HIEP XUAN TRINH, VICE CONSUL — May. 08, 2007

TRADE OFFICE
SAN FRANCISCO (CONA) 100 PINE ST., SUITE 605, 94111.
(415) 989-1194, FAX (415) 989-1197

YEMEN

CALIFORNIA

SAN FRANCISCO (HC) 1255 POST ST., SUITE 1030, 94109.
(415) 567-3036

MR. ISMAEL A. MANSOOR, HONORARY CONSUL — Feb. 05, 1992

DISTRICT OF COLUMBIA

WASHINGTON (CHN) 2319 WYOMING AV., 20008.
(202) 965-4760, FAX (202) 337-2017

MR. MOHSIN RAJEH ABU LOHOM, CONSUL — Dec. 30, 2004

MICHIGAN

DETROIT (HCG) 10415 DIX AV., DEARBORN 48120.
(313) 842-7032

MR. ABDULHAKEM AHMED ALSADAH, HONORARY CONSUL GENERAL — Apr. 24, 1995